The Rebel and the Imām in Early Islam

Engaging with contemporary debates about the sources that shape our understanding of the early Muslim world, Najam Haider proposes a new model for Muslim historical writing that draws on late antique historiography to challenge the imposition of modern notions of history on a premodern society.

Haider discusses three key case studies – the revolt of Mukhtār b. Abī ʿUbayd (d. 67/687), the life of the Twelver Shīʿī Imām Mūsā al-Kāẓim (d. 183/799), and the rebellion and subsequent death of the Zaydī Shīʿī Imām Yaḥyā b. ʿAbd Allāh (d. 187/803) – in calling for a new line of inquiry which focuses on larger historiographical questions. What were the rules that governed historical writing in the early Muslim world? What were the intended audiences for these works? In the process, he rejects artificial divisions between Sunnī and Shīʿī historical writing.

NAJAM HAIDER is a professor in the Department of Religion at Barnard College, Columbia University. He is the author of *The Origins of the Shīʿa* (2011), focusing on the role of ritual and sacred space in the formation of Shīʿī identity, and *Shīʿī Islam* (2014), which examines three branches of Shīʿī Islam – Zaydī, Twelver, and Ismāʿīlī – through a framework of memory. He has travelled extensively in the Middle East, including Syria, where he was a Fulbright scholar, and Yemen, where he studied with traditional Zaydī scholars.

The Rebel and the Imām in Early Islam

Explorations in Muslim Historiography

NAJAM HAIDER
Barnard College, Columbia University

CAMBRIDGE
UNIVERSITY PRESS

CAMBRIDGE
UNIVERSITY PRESS

University Printing House, Cambridge CB2 8BS, United Kingdom

One Liberty Plaza, 20th Floor, New York, NY 10006, USA

477 Williamstown Road, Port Melbourne, VIC 3207, Australia

314–321, 3rd Floor, Plot 3, Splendor Forum, Jasola District Centre, New Delhi – 110025, India

79 Anson Road, #06–04/06, Singapore 079906

Cambridge University Press is part of the University of Cambridge.

It furthers the University's mission by disseminating knowledge in the pursuit of education, learning, and research at the highest international levels of excellence.

www.cambridge.org
Information on this title: www.cambridge.org/9781107026056
DOI: 10.1017/9781139199223

First published 2019

Printed in the United Kingdom by TJ International Ltd, Padstow Cornwall

A catalogue record for this publication is available from the British Library.

ISBN 978-1-107-02605-6 Hardback

For Hamza and Fizza

Contents

Figures and Tables

Acknowledgments

This book is the culmination of nearly twenty years of obsessing over early Muslim historical writing. This subject was the focal point of my MA and the basis for my application for doctoral programs. I have benefited from hundreds of conversations on the topic. My initial guide in exploring the topic was Chase Robinson, and I have continued to profit from conversation with him on the subject over the years. I presented individual chapters of this book at a number of scholarly venues: NYU Abu Dhabi (2014), the Shīʿī Studies Symposium at the University of Chicago (2015), the Arabic Pasts Conference at SOAS and the Aga Khan University (2015), and the School of Abbasid Studies at New Haven (2018). I was also invited to present the larger argument of the book at the University of Colorado at Boulder in 2016 and as a part of the Trehan Lecture Series in Islamic Studies at the University of Pennsylvania in 2018. On these – and other – occasions, I received valuable feedback from a number of colleagues including Aun Hasan Ali, Teresa Bernheimer, Antoine Borrut, Paul Cobb, Alireza Doostdar, Matthew Gordon, Ed Hayes, Konrad Hirschler, Nancy Khalek, Joe Lowry, James Montgomery, John Nawas, Andrew Newman, Letizia Osti, Maurice Pomerantz, Maxim Romanov, Sarah Savant, Justin Stearns, Devin Stewart, Shawkat Toorawa, Isabel Torhal-Niehoff, Peter Webb, and Travis Zadeh. Much of Chapters 1 and 2 was written with the support of the Institute for Advanced Study at Princeton where I was a Whitehead Fellow in the spring of 2016. Many other colleagues and students have contributed to this book through informal conversations. These include Beth Berkowitz, Grace Bickers, Elizabeth Castelli, Mahmood Gharavi, Jack Hawley, Gale Kenny, Abdul Rahman Latif, Brinkley Messick, Verena Meyer, Aseel Najib, John Nawas, Intisar Rabb, Hussein Rashid, and Asma Sayeed. A special thanks to Michael Cook for reading and commenting on early iterations of the book proposal as well as a complete draft of Chapter 1. I am also deeply indebted to Hossein Modarressi for his consistent and impeccable guidance and insight. Many of the ideas at the heart of this project were refined in long conversations with Andrew McLaren, who also read drafts of Chapters 1 and 5, over the last five years. I would be remiss if I did not thank Nazia Malik for her patience and understanding. Although this book would not be possible without the help and support of my teachers, colleagues, and friends, I bear full responsibility for any errors of fact or interpretation.

Note on Transliteration and Dates

The system of transliteration employed for rendering Arabic names, technical terms, and other phrases in Latin characters is essentially the same as that employed in most contemporaneous academic journals (e.g. the *International Journal of Middle Eastern Studies* and *Islamic Law and Society*). The primary exceptions to this strict transliteration are certain well-established locations which are referred to by their common names. Most prominent among these are the cities of Mecca and Medina and the geographical regions of Syria, Yemen, Iraq, and Iran. The final *tāʾ marbūṭa* is indicated in transliteration only when in a conjunctive form and audibly pronounced.

Dates are given according to the Hijrī and Gregorian calendars (e.g. 122/740). Death dates are provided at the first mention of a historical figure in the main text. The death dates of authors mentioned exclusively in footnotes are included in the bibliography.

Note on Front Cover Image

An illustration depicting the storming of the fortress in the region of Kish held by the mysterious al-Muqanna' (d. 166/783), who rebelled in Transoxiana against the 'Abbāsid caliph al-Mahdī (r. 158–69/775–84), taken from the earliest extant illustrated manuscript of al-Bīrūnī's (d. 440/1048) *Athār al-bāqiya 'an al-qurūn al-khāliya* (commonly known as *The Chronology of Ancient Nations*). The manuscript (Or. Ms. 161, illustration on folio 93v), located in the Special Collections Department of Edinburgh University Library, was produced by the calligrapher Ibn Kutbī in the year 1307. The image depicts troops on horseback aiming arrows at the archers on the wall of the building, who are also preparing to fire. According to al-Bīrūnī, al-Muqanna' was killed during this siege, with considerable controversy surrounding the details of his death.

Explanation of Citation

The footnotes in each chapter are in an abbreviated form. The full citation for each work is provided in the bibliography. Important historical figures and geographical locations are identified at their first mention in each chapter.

1 *Modeling Islamic Historical Writing*

To what extent do contemporary approaches to the study of Islamic historiography reflect the presuppositions that informed the writing of early Muslim historians? A proper answer to this question requires a consideration of the classical and late antique periods. Numerous studies over the last fifty years have shown that Muslim political, social, and intellectual structures appropriated (and further elaborated) preexisting models.[1] This claim is not universally applicable, but it seems to hold in areas ranging from coinage and court culture to legal codes and literature.[2] A similar dynamic likely governed the relationship between late antique and early Muslim historical writing. At the very least, an approach that highlights such continuity promises a better understanding of the source material than does the current propensity to utilize categories drawn from a modern European context.[3]

In order to properly understand early Muslim historical works, it is useful to first examine the contours of historical writing in late antiquity. Contemporary scholars document the prevalence of two types of historiography in this period.[4] The first valued dry readings of the past that minimized personal commentary and were informed by "research."[5] Historians of this variety, such as Thucydides (d. 395

[1] For a good overview of this topic, see *The New Cambridge History of Islam*, parts 1 and 4. For some representative examples, see Brown, *Late Antiquity*, and Crone, *Roman, Provincial, and Islamic Law*.

[2] To be clear, this argument is not predicated on Arabs and/or Muslims borrowing foreign concepts. It also rejects the nativist position that Arabs developed their own historical categories internally and in isolation. The reality likely lies between these extremes. This book emphasizes cultural connection rather than arguments predicated on derivativeness.

[3] Meisami argues this point in "Mas'ūdī," esp. 152.

[4] There is a large corpus of scholarship that focuses on the development of classical and late antique historiography. See, for example, Fornara, *The Nature of History* and Croke, "Historiography."

[5] Fornara, *The Nature of History*, 134–5.

BCE), sought verifiable information through eyewitness accounts and drew on documentary evidence such as letters or official decrees. The second (and dominant) form of late antique historiography relied on highly stylized elements and often included wondrous and fantastical details.[6] This type of material is often referred to as "rhetorical historiography" because it developed under the influence of the classical schools of rhetoric.[7] Historical works of this type placed primacy on narrative logic, credibility devices, and emotive persuasion.[8]

It was this second category of historical writing that may have exerted a particular influence on early Muslim historical writing. Before turning to the historiographical tradition, however, the narrative materials preserved in the Qur'ān merit some discussion. Bear in mind that the Qur'ān, despite its status as one of the few extant sources on early Islam datable to the seventh century CE, is not a book of history. Its relationship to and influence on historical writing lies outside the scope of the present study.[9] Even so, it is worth noting that the Qur'ān's engagement with biblical stories (e.g. Abraham's interactions with God prior to the destruction of

[6] For the prevalence of these typologies of historical writing in the classical and late antique world, see Gabba, "True History," 338–44.

[7] The term "rhetorical historiography" is not without controversy. The most widespread criticism asserts the rhetorical nature of all writing, historical or otherwise. This truism misreads the technical sense of the term "rhetoric" as explained by Cicero (who was himself drawing on Aristotle). For a discussion of rhetoric and medieval historiography, see Partner, "The New Cornificius." For a critique of a different nature, see Brunt, "Cicero and Historiography," who argues that the blurring of rhetoric and historiography stems from a partial misreading of Cicero. For rhetoric in late antique historical writing, see Van Nuffelen, *Orosius*. Other scholars whose work on rhetoric and historical narrative inform the discussion that follows include M. J. Wheeldon ("True Stories") and Patricia Cox (*Biography*). For a similar approach in Judaic studies, see Rubenstein, *Talmudic Stories*.

[8] This characterization draws on Cicero's use of the Aristotelian terms *logos*, *ethos*, and *pathos*. For the connection between rhetorical historiography and Cicero, see T. P. Wiseman, "Lying Historians." For the influence of Aristotle and Cicero on historical writing, see Fornara, *The Nature of History*, 135–41. For the application of a "rhetorical" model in the Muslim sources, see Meisami, *Persian Historiography*, 287–92.

[9] For the connection between the Qur'ān and historical writing, see Khalidi, *Arabic Historical Thought*, 1–16. The seminal study of the Qur'ān in its historical context is Wansbrough's *Quranic Studies*, which generated considerable (and justified) criticism, but still provides much of the conceptual framework for contemporary scholars. There is voluminous scholarship on the larger topic of the origins of the Qur'ān. See, for example, Neuwirth, *Scripture*.

Sodom)[10] presupposes an audience's knowledge of the larger narrative and utilizes subtle changes to make theological points (e.g. a different conception of God). In other words, the Qur'ān engages biblical narratives in a manner reminiscent of the rhetorical historiography of late antiquity.

The example of the Qur'ān, though not decisive, is suggestive of the larger thesis of this book: namely, that authors of the early Muslim world held presuppositions about historical writing that resembled those of late antiquity. The identification of these presuppositions, which are never explicitly mentioned, requires a close examination of the source material. This is, in fact, the only means for reconstructing the parameters that governed the scholarly output of early Muslim historians. It is noteworthy, then, that these historians employed literary devices and stylistic elaborations that both made a story more edifying and conveyed some type of moral lesson.[11] At the same time, they wove stories into interpretive frameworks that inscribed meaning onto an event or biography. This suggests that the literary characteristics of the material – often the sole focus of modern historical studies – were only one component of a larger historical project mainly centered on interpretation.[12]

[10] Compare, for example, Q11:69–83 with Genesis 18. In Genesis 18, divine messengers visit Abraham, who offers them food (bread, curds, milk, and meat), which they consume in his presence. Abraham later negotiates for the lives of the people of Sodom, securing God's agreement to spare them if the city is home to even ten innocent people. In the Qur'ān, by contrast, the messengers decline the offered food (variation 1), and God later reprimands Abraham for even contemplating intercession on behalf of the city's population (variation 2). The first variation clearly highlights the divide between the divine and the human through the messengers' refusal to consume earthly food. This is especially striking given the biblical story's emphasis on Abraham's hospitality as exemplified by his elaborate preparation of food. The second variation reiterates one of the overarching themes in Qur'ānic renderings of biblical stories, namely, humanity's unconditional submission to God. There is no space for negotiation in this relationship, even for a figure as revered as Abraham.

[11] These literary devices are discussed by many contemporary scholars (e.g. Albrecht Noth, Stefan Leder), who characterize Muslim historiography as "fictional." In their view, Muslim historians were fiction writers only loosely constrained by fact and prone to filling informational lacunae with stock literary devices. This idea is further developed in the sections pertaining to rhetorical approaches and terminology. See Noth and Conrad, *Historical Tradition* and Leder, "Conventions."

[12] The lack of attention devoted to the larger historical frame has contributed to the mischaracterization of some early historical works and the marginalization of others. I return to this point in the conclusion.

Early Muslim historians were influenced by classical and late antique "rhetoricized"[13] historiography in a number of ways.[14] First, they composed narratives with the assumption that audiences[15] knew the broad contours of a given event or episode. This mirrors the approach of many late antique historians, who, for example, assumed their audience's familiarity (in broad strokes) with certain historical narratives, such as the biography of Julius Caesar or the outline of the Punic Wars. This familiarity then allowed them to construct accounts with subtle differences that the audience could discern without difficulty. Second, historians felt *authorized* to endow narratives with significance and present them in an edifying form. In other words, they produced not merely dry timelines but embellished accounts that highlighted the importance of an event through the use of literary devices such as anecdotes, poetry, letters, or speeches. The result was a meaningful rendering of the past that was deemed more truthful than a documentary recitation of figures or events.[16]

The key dynamic here centers on the relationship between the author's text and the audience's expectations. This, of course, first requires us to identify the audience for a particular text. There is scant material available on this topic for the early period but, at the very least, it is reasonable to assume an elite, educated audience from a privileged socioeconomic background potentially familiar with a shared set of source materials. Building on this assumption, Michael Cooperson argues that audiences (presumably of biographical material in the early period) authorized the embellishment of historical narratives as long as this process (i) did not disguise the narrative as a Prophetic tradition (*ḥadīth*) and (ii) remained within the bounds of

[13] I prefer to speak of "rhetoricized" rather than "rhetorical" historiography for two reasons. First, the former descriptor better reflects the idea of historical writing composed under the influence of the classical rhetorical tradition. Second, it addresses criticism rooted in the claim that all writing is rhetorical which misinterprets an argument about the presuppositions of historical writing as one concerned with literary composition.

[14] For a treatment of Muslim historical writing that covers authorial intent, epistemology, and audience expectations, see Waldman, *Historical Narrative*, 3–25.

[15] Few sources address audience in the early period. See Robinson, *Islamic Historiography*, 105–14.

[16] Although one could argue that the term "documentary" in this context is synonymous with "truthful." See Van Nuffelen, *Orosius*, 113, and Meisami, "Mas'ūdī," esp. 152.

plausibility.[17] The historian remained faithfully within the epistemological borders of the discipline when he altered details, elaborated speeches, and related encounters that *could have* occurred in order to make a larger point. This was an integral and accepted component in the vocation of historical writing.

The description of rhetoricized historical writing presented here is not a revelation to scholars of other periods and regions. A number of studies have documented, for example, the prevalence of rhetorical elements and moralizing in premodern European historical writing.[18] The most interesting parallel, however, is found in South Asian historiography, where Rao, Shulman, and Subrahmanyam have proposed an analytic model that highlights a reader's ability to sense the "texture" of a source and thereby differentiate factual elements from interpretive embellishment based on internal markers.[19] Such embellishment does not constitute an attempt at willful distortion, as the audience is perfectly capable of decoding the author's intentions. In other words, the audience recognizes the text not as an exact reproduction of the past, but rather as a historical narrative that plays with time, form, and content in a readily decipherable manner. Rao and his collaborators note that such historical texts are best referred to as myths "in the sense of being more deeply saturated with meaningfulness and also more creative of the reality that they purpose to describe than are other expressive modes."[20] In their discussion of the early eighteenth-century conflict between Desingu Raja and the Nawab of Arcot, for example, they note the fluidity of a historical narrative that "may realign itself with a template of patterned mythic recurrence" which requires a "creative movement within the awareness of the observer."[21] The account retains a strong notion of "fact," which is central to the endeavor, while remaining open to transformation.[22]

[17] See Cooperson, "Probability." There is, of course, an inherent ambiguity in the concept of "plausibility," which is relative to time and place. To offer one example, reports of conversations with animals may seem "plausible" in some historical and geographical settings but would be dismissed as "implausible" in many modern American contexts.

[18] See, for example, the essays compiled in Breisach (ed.), *Classical Rhetoric*, particularly Partner's "The New Cornificius" (5–59) and Wilcox's "Sense of Time." For a discussion of issues of historicity from an anthropological perspective, see Sahlins's *Islands*.

[19] Rao, Schulman, and Subrahmanyam, *Textures of Time*, 5–18.

[20] Ibid., 15 and 225. [21] Ibid., 17–18. [22] Ibid., 17.

Many contemporary scholars of early Islam, by contrast, continue to employ literary approaches that, while revealing important structural insights, largely ignore governing presuppositions (see section II on rhetorical approaches to historical writing).[23]

I Method

This book illuminates the value and potential benefits of applying a rhetoricized framework to early Muslim historical writing. It does so by proposing an analytic model consisting of three steps, which are outlined in Figure 1.1 and described further in this section. These steps do not, in and of themselves, constitute a radical departure from previous studies of early Muslim historiography (see sections II and III). A number of past scholars have discussed narrative emplotment, literary embellishment, and frameworks of meaning. The difference here lies in the integration of these elements into a single approach that is applicable to the early Muslim historical tradition as a whole. Put differently, this book attempts to detect the outline of large-scale structures that unite these historical sources.

The first step involves the identification of a *core structure* that is presumed to be known to the audience. This is done through the comparison of multiple sources (across genre, period, and communal affiliation[24])

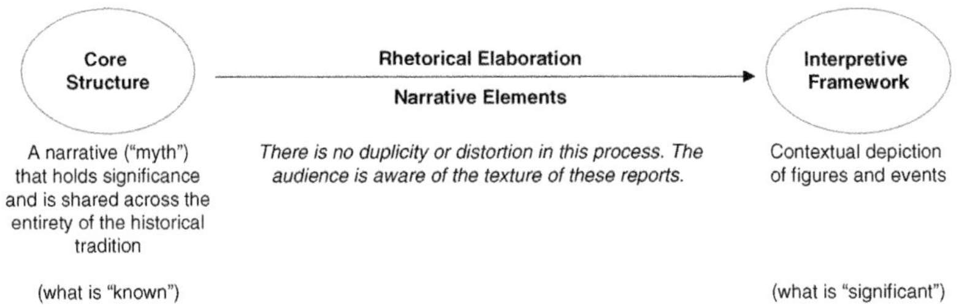

Figure 1.1 The Model

[23] Meisami expresses some frustration on this point, which contributes to her harsh (perhaps overly harsh) assessment of the field. She writes, "[the] concept of 'ethical-rhetorical' historiography, which is widely accepted in Western scholarship, has not yet penetrated our field, and I seem to be the only person to have made use of it." See Meisami, "History as Literature," 19.

[24] I use the terms "communal affiliation" and "communal group" in the place of "sectarian" or "sect." The latter are imprecise categories with a Christian genealogy that do not map well onto the early Muslim context.

that discuss the event/subject in question. The shared components in these sources represent the core structure and provide the backbone for the larger historical account. Historians populate this structure with rhetorical elaborations (step 2) to produce a cohesive text that addresses contemporaneous circumstances in a manner that is both persuasive and edifying (step 3). The core structure also represents the so-called factual element in historical writing. In some cases it is strikingly bare, whereas in others it includes considerable detail.

The identification of the core structure is made difficult by the absence of information pertaining to audience. It is always a tenuous endeavor to make assumptions about audience or scholars in the distant past. That being said, relatively similar core structures are often found across a wide range of sources. While it is untenable to argue that the simple presence of a story in myriad sources establishes its historicity, the presence of that story (in varied forms) across the historical tradition suggests, even if it does not prove, its ubiquity among the educated elite. Although the term "core structure" is unwieldy and difficult to use, it has a number of advantages over possible alternatives, including, most prominently, "myth." These terms are discussed in greater detail in section III on terminology.

The second step of the model involves categorizing and comparing *narrative elements*, smaller units of text that populate the core structure. These are crafted by historians in a process of rhetorical elaboration and embellishment. They are the individual stories or vignettes that, taken together, constitute the flesh of a historical work. Historians might forward narratives that differ from previous versions in minor but significant ways or present variants with radical changes in context and content involving, for example, the expansion of a speech or the insertion of dialogue. They might even create (or "discover") episodes designed to inscribe new meanings onto an established core structure.[25] In many cases, the elaborations of one writer will contradict those of another. The audience, however, is able to navigate such contradictions through its ability to recognize the texture of the source material and thereby separate the historical from the polemical/rhetorical.[26]

[25] Boaz Shoshan's work (*Poetics of Islamic Historiography*) operates at this level, as he analyzes the rhetorical methods that al-Ṭabarī used to develop multiple registers of meaning. This point is further elaborated in section III on terminology.

[26] Rao, Schulman, and Subrahmanyam, *Textures of Time*, 5–18.

Overall, this step is concerned with the identification of rhetorical embellishments.

The broader purpose or intent of a historical text is the subject of the third step, which attempts to ascertain the *interpretive frameworks* that inform an author's description of an event or person. These frameworks provide the superstructure for the stitching together of the narrative elements. There is still room for rhetorical elaboration at this point. An author might alter an account in subtle or substantial ways to fit a larger purpose. It is at this level of organization that the audience grasps the full intent of an author's composition. By way of example, a historian writing an imperial history may shape individual accounts around an interpretive framework of 'Abbāsid decline. A historian composing a genealogical work may offer similar accounts but craft them in a manner that highlights the rise or fall of tribalism. It is worth mentioning that this step conveys a truism in historical studies, namely, that a given text reflects the sociopolitical circumstances surrounding its composition. A number of contemporary scholars have addressed this topic in isolated historical case studies.[27] This book, by contrast, incorporates interpretive frameworks into a broader model that also includes historical context (step 1) and composition (step 2).

A detailed example may help to communicate the idea behind the proposed model and decipher its terminology. Take the following three narrative reports:

1. A dog ventured into the woods and, passing a stream, came across a squirrel, which it killed. The town then passed a leash ordinance to protect wildlife.
2. A pitbull bit his owner's hand and was expelled from the house. It ran into the woods, where it saw a squirrel with a bushy tail drinking from a spring. The pitbull leaped at the squirrel and chased it for hours. The terrified squirrel hid behind a tree. Eventually, the pitbull came upon the squirrel from behind and killed it. It left the poor squirrel's body next to the stream.
3. A poodle was mistakenly locked out of the house and drifted into the woods, looking for water. It found a stream and paused to take

[27] For representative examples of this type of scholarship, see Cooperson, *Classical Arabic Biography* and Pierce, *Twelve Infallible Men*. See also Haider, "Contested Life," "Community Divided," and "Lunatics and Loving Sons."

> a drink when a malevolent squirrel began throwing acorns at it from a nearby tree. The poodle moved to a different part of the stream, but the barrage continued. The poodle ran away, but two hours later it came upon the same squirrel, laughing about the incident with his bushy-tailed friends. The poodle attacked and, after a prolonged struggle, killed the squirrel.

The core structure (step 1) of these reports is quite straightforward: A dog went into the woods and killed a squirrel near a stream. This skeletal series of events conveys the information that the audience expects from each report. The narrative elements (step 2) are quite numerous and include the breed of the dog (unspecified; pitbull; poodle), the reasons for his entry into the woods (unspecified; expulsion after misbehavior; mistaken exile), the description of the squirrel (unspecified; bushy-tailed and thirsty; malicious), the nature of the encounter (random; dog aggression; squirrel aggression), the timing of the fight (immediate; hours later; two hours later), and the particulars of the fatal encounter (unstated; surprise attack; prolonged struggle). In examples taken from early Muslim historical writing, each of these details would entail vignettes or longer anecdotes with considerable rhetorical elaboration. Turning to the final, third step, the three reports are embedded in larger interpretive frameworks. The first example places the incident in the context of town politics and policy. The second example emphasizes the mercurial nature and destructive behavior of dogs. The possibility of a cat-loving author cannot be ruled out (with apologies to Abū Hurayra). The third example highlights the aggression and danger of squirrels who victimize other animals out of sheer maliciousness. The dog's killing of the squirrel here constitutes a general good. Overall, then, authors work off a known template to produce variant reports that convey competing meanings. This is a process that is both familiar to and authorized by the audience.[28]

[28] It is worth repeating that the model central to this study is indebted to scholarship on late antique historiography. This influence is apparent in three areas. First, it shapes the priorities of each chapter, as an author's production of meaning is given primacy over his preservation of information. Second, it underlies differences between narrative elements that result from rhetorical tinkering (step 2). And finally, it informs the discussion of the interpretive frameworks through which authors endow larger narratives with significance (step 3).

II Rhetorical Approaches to Islamic Historiography

Before proceeding further, it is helpful, and perhaps necessary, to place the proposed model within the context of contemporary scholarship in early Islamic historiography. The primary debate in this field over the last half-century has concerned the nature of the source material.[29] In recent years, scholars have increasingly favored literary approaches in their analyses of this material. Stefan Leder has gone furthest in this regard, characterizing early Islamic history as largely fictitious and describing extended historical accounts as novels.[30] Tayeb El-Hibri has also embraced this approach, discovering a complicated set of biblical allusions and symbolic references in early Muslim historical works.[31] Such studies offer intriguing conclusions, but they assume that the proper standard for the evaluation of historical materials posits truth against fiction/distortion.

This book proposes an analytic reorientation that pivots away from debates over veracity and toward a new understanding of early Muslim historical writing. In so doing, it builds on developments in the field over the last two decades. Previous scholars have considered emplotment and thematic approaches to early source material. They have offered close literary readings of particular historical accounts. They have even extrapolated interpretive frameworks informed by the sociopolitical context of a given author or by the constraints of a genre. The model presented in this chapter draws on all of these approaches while also accounting for factors such as the internal structure of a text or the communal identities of authors. In the process, it engages the question of what it meant to write history during the early Islamic period.

In his seminal study of Muslim historiography, Chase Robinson describes early Muslim historians as "creating as much as preserving" the past.[32] He notes that "imposing narrative form upon disparate

[29] There is extensive literature on this controversy. For a good summary of the debates, see Donner, "Modern Approaches," and *Narratives of Islamic Origins*, 1–31.

[30] See Leder, "Features of the Novel." In a later article ("Conventions"), Leder expresses some discomfort at the use of the term "fiction." See also Noth's useful discussion of the role of fiction in historical writing in "Fiktion."

[31] See El-Hibri, *Parable and Politics*.

[32] Robinson, *Islamic Historiography*, 154–5. I am deeply indebted to Robinson's book, particularly his consideration of audience (105–14) and of the context of early Muslim historical writing (143–55).

materials ... is a creative act" with techniques resembling those of fiction writing.[33] He hesitates, however, at classifying Muslim historians as authors of fictional literature, preferring instead to leave the issue open to further debate.[34] Robinson argues that historical reconstruction becomes increasingly possible (though still problematic) in later periods, when the source material begins to adhere more closely to modern notions of history.[35] Early works, by contrast, are best understood as collections of narratives creatively constructed by writers to convey a specific set of meanings to a given audience.

Julie Meisami agrees with Robinson's characterization of the early source material but goes further by proposing an analytic framework informed by late antique historiography. In Meisami's view, Muslim historians did not subscribe to the standards of early modern European historians. Instead, they held a view of historical writing that valued "meaning" over "fact."[36] Events that "were a matter of historical record" and whose "outcome was already known to their audiences" were endowed with significances "geared both to contemporary and to general concerns."[37] The audience's familiarity allowed the writer to conjure new meanings through slight changes and elaborations. The value of a story rested on these small alterations through which authors worked "to convey, and to persuade audiences of, the event's political and ethical significance."[38]

The present study draws considerably on Meisami's conception of historiography, but it differs in two important ways. First, Meisami is mainly interested in Persian historical works, whereas the current study centers on the early Muslim historical tradition, which was primarily composed in Arabic. Second, Meisami structures her analysis around the ethical dimensions of the historical sources, while the current study assumes a wider perspective in interrogating the motivations of individual historians.

In terms of analysis, the scholar whose approach most closely resembles that of this book is Boaz Shoshan, who concentrates on the rhetorical devices and stylistic choices of al-Ṭabarī (d. 310/

[33] Ibid., 154. [34] Ibid. [35] Ibid.

[36] A similar point is made by Marshall Hodgson in "Pre-Modern Muslim Historians."

[37] Meisami, "History as Literature," 29. For a more detailed discussion of her views, see her *Persian Historiography*, esp. 1–14 and 281–302.

[38] Meisami, "History as Literature," 30.

923).[39] Shoshan conditionally embraces Meisami's view that early Muslim historical writing was not grounded in a desire to record historical "fact."[40] Although he is reluctant to accept her description of these texts as "rhetorical historiography," he concedes that early historians utilized rhetoric to persuade their audiences of a particular reading of the past.[41] In Shoshan's view these early sources exhibit literary characteristics and conflict with modern notions of history. Specifically, he argues that "there is no such thing as pure fiction and no such thing as history so rigorous that it abjures the techniques of fiction."[42] In arguing for such hybridity as the nature of historical material, Shoshan is critical of scholars who interpret sources purely through a literary lens.[43] His own approach sees historical writing, and particularly that of al-Ṭabarī, as a vehicle for the creation of meaning and for argumentation.[44] His interest in the poetics of writing produces an analysis that foregrounds the structural features of an account, such as the invocation of eyewitnesses,[45] the insertion of poetry,[46] the creation of dialogue,[47] and the usage of multiple, contradictory versions.[48]

39 Although I largely agree with Robinson's depiction of the early historical tradition in *Islamic Historiography*, he does not offer any kind of analytic framework, perhaps because of the limited scope of his project. Shoshan, by contrast, methodically engages the source material through his notion of "poetics"; see his *Poetics of Islamic Historiography*.

40 Shoshan, *Poetics of Islamic Historiography*, x. 41 Ibid. 42 Ibid., xxi.

43 Shoshan's critique of El-Hibri's recent work is pointed and insightful. See ibid., 5–6.

44 The influence of Hayden White is apparent in Shoshan's discussion of method. White insists on an analysis of historical works centered on narrative form, i.e. the organization of information into sequential frames. These frames place limits on the ability of authors to convey meaning. White's argument is grounded in his reading of nineteenth-century European historiography, which makes its application to other traditions and periods problematic. For example, White focuses primarily (though not exclusively) on historians concerned with a factual rendering of the past and exposes the fallacy of "objective" historical writing. In the early Muslim world, by contrast, historians seemed to operate under a different set of assumptions regarding the purpose of their writing. They might exhibit some of the characteristics identified by White, but the degree to which his method is pertinent to their work is questionable. There are other problems with applying White's method to early Islamic historiography (e.g. his ideological categories, his frames/emplotment), but these fall outside the scope of the current study. See White, *Metahistory*.

45 Shoshan, *Poetics of Islamic Historiography*, 41–9. 46 Ibid., 82.

47 Ibid., 50. 48 Ibid., 124–40.

Shoshan is not invested in the "historical past" but in the "narrative that the particular facts sustain."[49]

Shoshan breaks significant new ground in his study of early Muslim historiography. First, he carves out a space for scholarship that rejects the fact/fiction dichotomy. Historical reports are not reduced to literary constructions with minimal connection to the past. They are, rather, representations of the past informed by rhetorical concerns and intended to convince the audience of an event's significance and meaning. Second, he provides an explanation for contradictions that bypasses charges of unreliability. Shoshan thus dismisses critiques of Muslim historical writing that are grounded in an anachronistic view of the source material. He correctly argues that these authors had their own perspectives regarding the nature and purpose of their scholarly project.

This book is an attempt to implement in concrete terms the conceptual claims of both Robinson and Meisami. It also draws considerably on Shoshan's work, but adopts a more expansive perspective in two areas. First, Shoshan is principally interested in the literary tools utilized in rhetorical elaboration (step 2 in my model). This study, by comparison, has a broader focus that includes the identification of a core structure (step 1) as well as interpretive frameworks (step 3) that contextualize the meaning of an episode. Second, Shoshan concentrates almost exclusively on al-Ṭabarī, whose work, though of critical importance, is not typical of the early Muslim historical corpus.[50] As a universal historical chronicle, it represents an imperial historiography bound by the constraints of chronography (see my discussion of the genre in section IV). The case studies in this book, by contrast, cover a range of historical works that span genres (chronicles, biographies, prosopographies), periods (from the second/eighth through the fifth/eleventh centuries), and communal affiliations (Twelver Shī'ī, Zaydī Shī'ī, and Sunnī).[51] This breadth allows for the development of a model with broad potential applicability.

49 Ibid., xxv.

50 An overreliance on al-Ṭabarī's chronicle is pervasive in many modern studies. See, for example, El-Hibri, *Reinterpreting Islamic Historiography* and Borrut, *Entre mémoire et pouvoir*.

51 I use the word "Sunnī" with considerable reservation. Given the complexities associated with identity in the early period, "non-Shī'ī" would be a more accurate (though unwieldy) description of this group.

III Terminology

The rhetoricized model proposed in this book raises a number of questions concerning terminology. The most obvious relates to the use of the word "rhetorical." It is certainly true that all writing is rhetorical. Any composition of words or phrases in the form of a narrative employs rhetorical elements. My use of the phrase "rhetoricized historiography," however, denotes more than just the rhetorical nature of narrative; it points to a larger set of presuppositions about historical writing. How did early Muslim historians conceive of their own work? How would they define its purpose? What were the parameters of the discipline of history? As noted previously, historical writing was not seen as an exact reconstruction of the past but rather as an attempt to render the past in a meaningful manner. It rested on a relationship between historian and audience in which embellishment and elaboration (and even composition) were permitted within the constraints of a core structure channeling the classical and late antique rhetorical tradition. The term "rhetoricized historiography," though not wholly satisfactory, approximates an approach to history writing that best fits the expectations and assumptions of early Muslim society.

On a more general level, I have considered and rejected a number of terms to describe aspects of early Muslim historiography, including "fiction," "poetics," and "myth." As previously mentioned, many contemporary scholars view Muslim historical works through the prism of fiction; the most notable is Leder, who describes authorial corpora as novels.[52] Although there are certainly fictional elements in early Muslim historical writing, fiction is a modern construct whose projection into earlier periods risks anachronism. The binary of fact versus fiction or distortion was not a prime consideration for many premodern historians, and it seems quite problematic to evaluate them based on this standard. In Figure 1.1, approaches that view the sources through the lens of fiction operate exclusively on the right side of the arrow, asking questions of significance.

Another possible term for the analysis of Muslim historical works is "poetics," which Shoshan utilizes to considerable effect in his study of al-Ṭabarī's universal history.[53] As discussed previously, Shoshan is chiefly interested in the literary devices and tools that contribute to

[52] For Leder, see n. 30 in this chapter.
[53] For Shoshan, see *Poetics of Islamic Historiography*.

the creation of meaningful accounts. He also explicitly rejects, perhaps due to constraints of space, the utility of comparing variant accounts from disparate sources. Such a comparison, however, is critical to a proper understanding of the interpretive frameworks embedded in al-Ṭabarī's (and other authors') works. Poetics are certainly important in my analysis, but they are a subset of a historical approach with a wider conceptual focus. In Figure 1.1, Shoshan's poetics-based approach is situated above the arrow that connects the core structure to interpretive frameworks.[54]

The term that perhaps best fits the "core structure" in my proposed model of historical writing is "myth." Scholars of classical and late antique historiography have demonstrated the utility of this word, documenting the tendency toward the "historicizing of myth" and the "mythologizing of history."[55] Many classical works, for example, make no distinction between the legend of the founding of Rome or the biography of Hercules and their later imperial history. The mythological past is thus given a historical rendering while historical accounts acquire mythical elements, thereby producing the false impression of continuity. The same tendency informs early Muslim genealogical works that posit an imagined ancestor or universal histories that stretch back to the lives of pre-Islamic prophets. In other words, myths, like core structures, provide a backbone for the telling and retelling of important historical events. They accommodate embellishment as long as it respects the integrity of known elements of the narrative. In the case of the ʿAbbāsid revolution (132/750), for example, certain events are so widely known that they must appear in historical narratives. These might include Abū Muslim's (d. 137/755) defeat of the Umayyad forces of Naṣr b. Sayyār (d. 131/748), the pursuit and killing of Marwān II (r. 127–32/744–50), and the elevation of al-Saffāḥ (r. 132–6/750–4) to the caliphate. This foundation, however, is supplemented by narrative elements – stories – that feature rhetorical embellishments such as dramatic battlefield confrontations, conversations, poetic insertions, and explanations.

[54] White's approach falls between those of Leder and Shoshan. His emphasis on literary devices embedded in historical sources is reminiscent of Leder, whereas his interest in the inscription of meaning through emplotment or under the influence of ideology resembles the work of Shoshan.

[55] This point is made quite cogently by Hans-Joachim Gehrke in "Myth, History, and Politics."

The central problem with the term "myth" lies in its popular usage in reference to a distant, legendary past with little connection to actual historical events. In the premodern period it was also routinely applied to explain natural phenomena in the absence of scientific knowledge or to legitimize the political status quo. Some Muslim historical writing certainly serves these purposes, but there is also considerable material that provides didactic guidance, exemplifies proper ethical behavior, sheds light on the human condition, or forwards a polemical argument. These uses align with the technical definition of myth as an expressive mode that depicts the past in a meaningful manner and creatively imbues it with significance. There remains, however, the possibility of ambiguity or misunderstanding due to the common assumption that "myths" are in some ways falsehoods rooted in the supernatural. For these reasons, I favor the more unwieldy "core structure" over the perhaps more accurate but potentially misconstrued "myth."

IV Complications: Compilation and Genre

The model proposed here is meant to provide a starting point for broader discussions about the nature of early Muslim historical writing. The analytic framework does not claim universal applicability; rather, it offers a potential path forward for future studies. As a first step, it is marked by a degree of reductionism and simplification. This section lays out two potential objections to the model I have outlined, centering on the issues of compilation and genre.

The historical sources at the core of each of the book's case studies are compilatory in nature. This produces several potential complications pertaining to authorship and purpose. With respect to the former, it is important to note that the roots of Muslim historical writing remain somewhat obscure. The fact that most of the extant early historical works are composed of even earlier (and now lost) sources raises serious questions. If al-Ṭabarī is weaving together accounts taken from other sources (e.g. Abū Mikhnaf [d. 157/774]), then to what extent is his presentation original? Does he appropriate the interpretive frameworks of his sources or does he create wholly unique frameworks? There is little evidence of the structure of early texts, as they were only partially preserved in later sources.[56] In addition, recorded titles provide only minimal insight into a book's thematic focus. A number of scholars have worked toward the excavation of earlier layers of authorship through studies that, for example, emphasize the importance of chronography, focus on connections with previous historical traditions, or attempt to identify the earliest strata of historical material.[57] The results of these studies remain inconclusive.

As for complications of purpose, it is worth considering the motives of early compilers of now lost historical works. How did their conception of history differ from the conceptions of those who subsequently cannibalized their works? Did they present a coherent picture that overtly imbued the past with meaning? Was this meaning nested in their criteria for inclusion or in the structure or organization of their works? If they, too, utilized interpretive frameworks, is it possible to recover those frameworks through the surviving fragments of their works? These questions are difficult to answer, and lie outside the scope of the present study. The earliest text considered here is ascribed to Ibn Saʿd (d. 230/845), who lived in a period associated with "large-scale and synthetic collection" of historical narratives.[58] The remaining sources date from between the third/ninth and fifth/eleventh centuries.

Although source criticism is certainly important, this book does not scrutinize chains of transmission or attempt to reconstruct the stemmata of historical reports.[59] Instead, it focuses on the postformative historical tradition characterized by broad works preserved in later manuscripts and informed by a specific authorial voice. Bearing this in mind, issues of compilation do not undercut the model presented here. It is just as easy to create meaning through the selection and placement of relatively stable narrative elements as it is through the

[56] There are a few exceptions to this general rule. Al-Ṭabarī, for example, explicitly cites al-Wāqidī (d. 207/822), whose *Kitāb al-maghāzī* is extant.

[57] For a discussion of the origins of Muslim historiography, see Robinson, *Islamic Historiography*, 3–30. Other pertinent works include Humphreys, *Islamic History*, 69–103; Khalidi, *Arabic Historical Thought*; and Donner, *Narratives of Islamic Origins*, esp. part 2, 126–296.

[58] Robinson, *Islamic Historiography*, 34–6.

[59] Numerous scholars have demonstrated the potential power of this type of analysis. For the state of the field, see Motzki, "Whither *Ḥadīth* Studies." For examples of scholarship focusing on chains of transmission, see Schoeler, *The Biography of Muḥammad*; Motzki, *The Origins of Islamic Jurisprudence*; Görke, "Historical Tradition"; Sadeghi, "Traveling Tradition Test"; Haider, *The Origins of the Shīʿa* and "Geography of the *Isnād*."

conjuring of a new encounter or speech. Regardless of the origins of individual historical reports, the present study is interested in the interpretive frameworks crafted by identifiable authors located in a specific historical context.

A second potential objection to this study stems from its engagement with genre. The earliest layer of Muslim historical writing includes a range of topical genres that either focused on historical events such as conquests (*futūḥ*, *maghāzī*) or adhered to a specific logic or organization, such as that of genealogy or astrology.[60] The present study, however, covers a later period characterized by the prevalence of three main genre categories: chronography, biography, and prosopography. The proposed method engages differently with each of these genres. This unevenness requires further discussion.

Chronographical works are primarily organized around units of time, such as individual years or caliphal reigns.[61] Certain elements of the rhetoricized model outlined in section I are less evident in chronographies than they are in either biographies or prosopographies because of the structural constraints of the genre. Whereas biographical works, for example, utilize anecdotes and vignettes to paint a distinctive portrait of a subject's life, chronographies must fit their arguments within the limits of an annalistic organization. This often requires the division of a cohesive narrative into smaller units spread over multiple years. Still, as Shoshan and others have shown, even al-Ṭabarī's annalistic history is littered with poetry, speeches, and other literary devices that conform to a larger interpretive framework. The outlines of that framework are not as apparent as they are in other genres, but they are certainly discernible upon careful examination.

Biographical and prosopographical works are interrelated genres that share an interest in the lives of individuals. Robinson, who notes the overlap between these forms and documents their evolution, characterizes their essential difference in the following manner:

60 For a basic discussion of these historical forms, see Khalidi, *Arabic Historical Thought*, 1–82. For *maghāzī* works, see Zaman, "*Maghāzī*"; Görke, "Relationship"; Anthony, "Crime and Punishment." For an examination of the importance of astrology in early historical writing, see Borrut, "Court Astrologers."

61 Robinson makes the point that "Islamic historiography exaggerates chronography's significance within the tradition" as a result of the modern preference for this form of historical writing. See Robinson, *Islamic Historiography*, 74–5.

"Biographies accentuate the individual; prosopographies make individuals members."[62] Biographies stand alone, and generally present the life of a historical figure in isolation. This is done in a piecemeal fashion through a series of encounters that reveal the figure's character and often rely on societal archetypes, such as the scholar, the Ṣūfī shaykh, or the Shīʿī Imām.[63] These archetypes are not wholly determinative, but they exert a strong influence on the depiction of individual subjects. The writer enjoys great latitude in the selection and rendering of events and episodes, enabling substantial rhetorical and literary elaboration. In his seminal study of the genre, Cooperson notes that biographical works "assume a knowledge of context ... identical to the content of annalistic history," provide a venue for the expression of authorial opinions, and assume the "air of veracity" in offering historical insights.[64] Biographies thus embody a number of rhetorical characteristics.

Prosopographical works are primarily defined by their interest in specific social groupings or categories of individuals. They often consist of compilations of (usually) condensed biographies that are shaped by a broader perspective. It is this latter element that differentiates prosopographies from biographies. In more concrete terms, the information in prosopographical entries is not comprehensive but rather "conforms to the designs of the compiler."[65] In biographical dictionaries of traditionists, for example, the compiler will focus on elements conducive to an evaluation of reliability. This might include the names of teachers and students, travel history, and anecdotes about trustworthiness. Another variety of prosopographical works centers on notables associated with a specific geographical location. Such texts cover famous scholars or other elites who spent time (even on brief visits) in cities such as Baghdad or Damascus. Genealogical works constitute a third type of prosopography in that they utilize tribal categories, emphasizing the connection between important personalities and their forebears and descendants. Other prosopographical sources are organized around generations (*ṭabaqāt*). These texts focus on clearly demarcated periods or construct sequential generations stemming from an important figure or event. In many cases, generational works are exercises in

[62] For the general discussion, see ibid., 61–74. For the quotation, see ibid., 66.
[63] Ibid., 61–6; Cooperson, *Classical Arabic Biography*, 1–23.
[64] Cooperson, *Classical Arabic Biography*, 22–3.
[65] Robinson, *Islamic Historiography*, 68.

identity formation that trace the history of, for example, a given social class (e.g. historical notables) or scholarly community (e.g. jurists or Ṣūfīs).[66] A fifth type of prosopographical work is the *maqātil* text, structured around the murders of a particular social group (e.g. the Ṭālibids). In the current study, al-Iṣbahānī's (d. 356/967) *Maqātil al-Ṭālibiyyīn*, which documents the deaths of descendants of Abū Ṭālib (d. ca. 619 CE) at the hands of political authorities, falls under this heading.[67] Like biographical works, prosopographies are ideally suited for analysis through the rhetoricized model at the center of this study.

One source utilized in the case studies that defies classification within the three genre categories is al-Kulaynī's (d. 329/940–1) *al-Kāfī*.[68] This work is a topical collection of traditions in the manner of the earliest variety of historical writing, organized along the lines of Imāmī Shīʿī theology and jurisprudence. Biographical accounts of the Imāms are scattered throughout the text, but they are primarily found in sections pertaining to the Imāmate. This material is not woven into a clear and coherent narrative. Although al-Kulaynī's work is prosopographical in that each Imām is considered part of a special cohort (the infallible Imāms), the lack of cohesive biographical entries makes the work's classification as prosopography untenable. The text is particularly pertinent to the second case study, and will be discussed as a theological–historical collection rather than as a chronography, biography, or prosopography.

V Structure and Rationales

This book applies the proposed method for analyzing early Muslim historical works to three case studies. Each begins with the identification of a core structure (step 1) that was presumably familiar to the audience and that is ascertained through a comprehensive survey of the source material. Recall that the presence of a known structure is one of the prerequisites for rhetoricized historiography. This is followed by

66 For an examination of generational works focusing on jurists, see Jaques, *Authority*.

67 For both al-Iṣbahānī and the *maqātil* subgenre, see Günther, "*Maqātil* Literature," and *Quellenuntersuchungen*.

68 EI^2, s.v. "Al-Kulaynī" (W. Madelung); Ansari, *L'imamat et l'Occultation*, 13–17 and 27–36.

a survey of the narrative elements (step 2), which are the products of rhetorical elaboration and depict specific events or encounters. These historical reports sometimes diverge dramatically between sources. In simple terms, this step involves identifying the various embellishments in a given text. Because of differences in the source material, the strategy employed in communicating narrative elements varies from case study to case study. Each chapter concludes with a discussion of the interpretive frameworks (step 3) employed by individual authors or groups of authors, accompanied by potential explanations for their prevalence.

The structure of each case study is entirely dependent on the nature of the source material. This fact produces considerable variance among the three chapters. In the first case study (Chapter 2), the accounts are examined in a single comprehensive group in chronological order by author. In an effort to avoid repeating the same anecdote or account in multiple places, narrative elements are not listed in the main body of the chapter. They are instead compiled in the appendix for easy reference.[69] The second (Chapter 3) and third (Chapter 4) case studies organize accounts based on the communal affiliations of authors. Twelver Shīʿī sources are foregrounded in the second case study, whereas Zaydī Shīʿī sources are the focal point of the third case study.

The first case study centers on the rebellion of Mukhtār b. Abī ʿUbayd al-Thaqafī (d. 67/687) in Kūfa as depicted mainly in historical works compiled in the third/ninth and fourth/tenth centuries. Two aspects of this case are particularly significant. First, the source material mostly consists of chronographies supplemented by a few prosopographical and biographical works. Chronography's preoccupation with linear narrative poses a significant challenge to my historiographical model. Instead of a single cohesive account of a rebellion and its aftermath, for example, a chronicle might discuss the organization of the revolt in one year, detail its outbreak in another year, and then document its consequences over two or three years. This scattering of relevant information throughout a text complicates the identification of interpretive frameworks. Second, the historians utilized in this case study tackle the source material in similar ways despite their differing communal affiliations. The rebellion of Mukhtār is, in fact, one of the

[69] For reasons that will become clear in the course of the analysis, an appendix is not necessary for the second and third case studies.

few historical episodes that do not directly involve an Imām but are nonetheless covered by Shīʿī sources. This reduces the theological stakes, which permits a more direct textual comparison across communal traditions. It also lends credence to one of the central arguments of this book: namely, that categories such as "Shīʿī" or "Sunnī" had little bearing on the project of history writing in the early period.

These points notwithstanding, Mukhtār's rebellion is a textbook example of the broad utility and power of the proposed model of rhetoricized historiography. Chapter 2 opens with a summary of the core structure (step 1) and a listing of the narrative elements (step 2). It then documents authorial portrayals of Mukhtār's revolt, beginning with the earliest extant source and proceeding chronologically. The material reveals three primary interpretive frameworks (step 3): (i) conflict between Arabs and non-Arabs, (ii) tensions among varying strains of Shīʿism, and (iii) competition between local and imperial interests. It also gestures to a fourth interpretive framework, in which Mukhtār serves as a minor or secondary character in a larger narrative. Genre or communal affiliations do not sufficiently explain a given author's adherence to a specific framework. The case does, however, suggest an overarching uniformity in approach, within which historians exercised considerable flexibility.

The second and third case studies involve subjects with notable Shīʿī connections. At this point, it is worth repeating that this book expressly rejects the idea of a distinctive Shīʿī historiography, arguing instead that Shīʿī and non-Shīʿī authors shared a common approach to historical writing. The perception of an inherent difference stems from the fact that the Shīʿa portray a smaller set of subjects through theologically inflected interpretive frameworks. Most early Twelver and Zaydī historical works are either biographies or prosopographies of the Imāms, who are considered the sole legitimate sources of religious and political authority. Every depiction of these figures carries obvious theological implications. Any modern study that hopes to utilize Shīʿī historical sources must, by sheer necessity, focus on the lives of the Imāms, which, in turn, requires direct engagement with key aspects of Shīʿī theology. There is, however, a difference between interpretation and historical approach.[70] Shīʿī authors certainly constructed their biographies around

[70] As mentioned previously, the current study focuses on the latter while attempting to bypass the obvious communal baggage of the former.

distinctive interpretive frameworks, but they did so through an approach that transcended communal boundaries.

The second case study (Chapter 3) focuses on the biography of Mūsā al-Kāẓim (d. 183/799), the seventh Twelver Shīʿī Imām. In a number of ways, this subject is an ideal illustration of the proposed model in that the relevant sources consist mainly of biographical works whose rhetorical tendencies are fairly self-evident. The chapter first outlines the shared core structure (step 1) of al-Kāẓim's life. It then divides the source texts into two groups. The first includes non-Twelver (Sunnī and Zaydī Shīʿī) accounts, whereas the second consists of the more copious Twelver Shīʿī material. Such a separation is not the result of any innate differences in the two corpora, but rather reflects the greater complexity and detail in the Twelver Shīʿī sources. The analysis of non-Twelver accounts begins with a general survey of the narrative elements (step 2), organized into five main categories. It then identifies three major interpretive frameworks (step 3). Sunnī authors either highlight al-Kāẓim's exemplary qualities (framework 1) or place his life in the broader context of ʿAlid–ʿAbbāsid animosity (framework 2). Zaydī sources, by contrast, emphasize court politics (framework 3) while drawing unfavorable comparisons between al-Kāẓim and Yaḥyā b. ʿAbd Allāh (who is discussed in Chapter 4). The second part of this chapter examines the Twelver Shīʿī sources chronologically by author. These primarily biographical works reflect changes in the community's political standing. Overall, writers populate the core structure with altered or even new narrative elements to produce unique interpretive frameworks that oscillate between an emphasis on the supernatural attributes of the Imām and an insistence on his eagerness to confront the ʿAbbāsids. The analysis reveals that Twelver Shīʿī depictions of al-Kāẓim embody the community's relations with political power.

The third and final case study (Chapter 4) centers on the last twelve years in the life of the Zaydī Shīʿī Imām Yaḥyā b. ʿAbd Allāh (d. 187/803). The most distinctive feature of the chapter is the incorporation of Zaydī Shīʿī historical sources, which are rarely, if ever, utilized by contemporary scholars. In terms of genre, the relevant sources are a balanced mix of chronographies and biographies/prosopographies. Although this diversity increases the complexity of the analysis, the power of the proposed model remains quite apparent. The chapter, like the preceding chapters, begins by identifying the core structure (step 1) and then proceeds to a two-part analysis. The first is organized around the five narrative elements (step 2) most prevalent in the Sunnī sources. These reports largely adhere to an interpretive framework (step 3) that treats Yaḥyā as a marginal figure manipulated by more powerful political actors. The second part turns to the Zaydī sources, whose complicated structure necessitates a different approach. Each Zaydī work is examined individually, with narrative elements placed in one of three chronological segments (rebellion, conflict with the caliph, and prison and death). The main interpretive frameworks in the Zaydī sources use Yaḥyā to debate the requirements of the Imāmate, particularly with respect to activism, lineage, and personal qualities. As in the previous case study, the division between Zaydī and non-Zaydī sources is due to discrepancies in length and complexity. The larger analysis, however, reveals the analytic similarity of early historical texts irrespective of the communal loyalties of their authors.

The selection of these three case studies requires some explanation. I chose to examine the rebellion of Mukhtār for two reasons. First, a majority of the pertinent sources are chronicles, which permits testing the applicability of my model in a genre restricted by linear organization. Second, this revolt is one of the rare subjects that is discussed by both Sunnī and Shīʿī authors but that has few theological implications. For this reason, it is possible to examine the sources as a whole without artificial divisions based on their authors' communal affiliations. Turning to the second and third case studies, al-Kāẓim is one of the few Twelver Imāms beyond ʿAlī, Ḥasan, and Ḥusayn who is widely mentioned in non-Twelver historical works, whereas Yaḥyā b. ʿAbd Allāh appears in numerous non-Zaydī sources because of his involvement in two rebellions and his contentious relationship with the Ḥusaynids. The unusual ubiquity of these ʿAlids across the historical tradition allows a comparative application of the proposed model. In addition, these final two cases diversify the present study in important ways. First, they largely involve biographical and prosopographical works as opposed to historical chronicles. And second, they incorporate sources often ignored because of their Shīʿī provenance. In the case of the Zaydī Shīʿa, these historical works are unknown to many scholars.

VI Final Notes

This book proposes an approach to early Muslim historical writing that integrates disparate strands of analysis within a single comprehensive method. The method is designed to provide new insights into the presuppositions that informed early Muslim historiography. As mentioned earlier in this chapter, my study directly contests widespread assumptions about the categorical unreliability and thoroughly hagiographic nature of Shīʿī (and other non-Sunnī) historical writing. It does so by demonstrating that Shīʿī historians adhered to the same general rules of historical writing that governed non-Shīʿī sources. It also speaks to the connections among multiple genres of historical writing. There are certainly structural differences between chronographies, biographies, and prosopographies as defined by modern-day scholars. Moreover, it is likely that the early tradition includes other genre categories that remain obscure to modern literary sensibilities. Despite these differences, however, the method proposed in this book sheds light on fundamental similarities that tie together early threads of Muslim historical writing. To put this point in more concrete terms, let us consider chronographical and biographical works. Although they differ in organization, they both craft information around a framework that imbues the past with meaning. This is self-evident for biographies, but it is a striking assertion for chronographies, which are often – mistakenly – viewed through a modern lens. In the most basic formulation, this book is an attempt to answer the question of what it meant to write history in the early Islamic period.

2 *The Rise and Fall of Mukhtār b. Abī ʿUbayd (d. 67/687)*

Chapter 1 detailed a model according to which historians worked within the constraints of an established core structure to endow a past event or series of events with meaning. This activity involved the use of rhetorical tools such as selection, embellishment, and elaboration in a process that lent texture to a historical report and offered a truthful rendering of an event's importance. Authors did not intend to deceive their audiences; rather, audiences anticipated curated accounts, and seamlessly separated factual elements from rhetorical elaborations. This model encapsulates the central tenets of rhetoricized historiography, whose influence on Muslim historical writing varies according to genre. It is most apparent in biographies and prosopographies (see, in particular, Chapter 3), in which anecdotes serve as building blocks for the portrait of a given figure. In chronographies, by contrast, anecdotes are embedded within a larger temporal structure that constrains authorial choices. Despite such a limitation, the broad parameters of the proposed model remain clearly discernible.

This initial case study focuses on nine historical sources (see Table 2.1) composed in the third/ninth and fourth/tenth centuries that document the rise and fall of Mukhtār b. Abī ʿUbayd al-Thaqafī between 61/680 and 67/687.[1] The majority of these works are chronographic in their organization (Ibn Aʿtham, Pseudo-Ibn Qutayba, al-Yaʿqūbī, al-Dīnawarī, al-Ṭabarī, and al-Masʿūdī). The remainder includes two texts with a generational or genealogical focus (Ibn Saʿd and al-Balādhurī) and one overtly polemical work organized around biographical entries (*Akhbār al-dawla al-ʿAbbāsiyya*). The analysis that follows considers these sources in chronological order based on the death dates (or presumed death dates) of their authors. As will become clear, the communal affiliations of

[1] The only possible exception is Ibn Aʿtham al-Kūfī's *Futūḥ*, whose composition (ascribed to the late second/eighth century) remains contested. See Conrad, "Ibn Aʿtham." This case study does not include sources from later periods.

Table 2.1 – ***The Sources for Mukhtār b. Abī ʿUbayd***

Ibn Aʿtham al-Kūfī (third/ninth century?) Shīʿī	*al-Futūḥ* Chronography
Ibn Saʿd (d. 230/845) Sunnī	*al-Ṭabaqāt al-kubrā'* Prosopography
Anonymous (third/ninth century) Shīʿī	*Akhbār al-dawla al-ʿAbbāsiyya* Prosopography/biography
al-Balādhurī (d. 279/892) Sunnī	*Ansāb al-ashrāf* Prosopography
Pseudo-Ibn Qutayba (third/ninth century) Shīʿī	*al-Imāma wa-l-siyāsa* Chronography
al-Yaʿqūbī (d. 284/897) Shīʿī	*Tārīkh* Chronography
al-Dīnawarī (d. by 290/903) Sunnī	*al-Akhbār al-ṭiwāl* Chronography
al-Ṭabarī (d. 310/923) Sunnī	*Tārīkh* Chronography
al-Masʿūdī (d. 346/957) Sunnī	*Murūj al-dhahab* Chronography

individual historians do not appear to affect their presentation of information. This may result from the marginal and ambiguous status of Mukhtār in the later Sunnī and Shīʿī traditions.

The structure of this chapter is shaped by the intertextuality of the source material: all of the accounts appear to be in conversation with one another despite differences in their authors' communal affiliations and genres of writing. This intertextuality allows for a direct application of the proposed model of rhetoricized historiography. In practical terms, the core structure of the case is easily discernible, the narrative elements are largely shared across texts, and interpretive frameworks fall into clear categories. The first section summarizes the core structure embedded in most depictions of Mukhtār's rebellion. The second section briefly lists the dominant narrative elements that populate the core structure, reflecting the influence of rhetorical embellishment or elaboration. In order to minimize repetition, the basic forms of the narrative elements and their variants are catalogued in the appendix. The third section analyzes individual authorial treatments of Mukhtār's rebellion in an effort to isolate their interpretive frameworks. Readers primarily interested in analysis (the forest) as opposed to the narrative elements (the trees) may choose to skip to the subheadings entitled "interpretive framework" for each author in this section.

I The Core Structure: Mukhtār's Rebellion, Rule, and Defeat (61–7/680–7)

Mukhtār b. Abī ʿUbayd first appears in the historical record in the period preceding Ḥusayn b. ʿAlī's (d. 61/680) revolt against the Umayyads. He works with Muslim b. ʿAqīl[2] (d. 60/680), who is sent by Ḥusayn b. ʿAlī to investigate the political situation in Kūfa amidst reports of unrest and potential revolution. Muslim discovers some support for Ḥusayn among the Kūfans, but is eventually betrayed and executed by ʿUbayd Allāh b. Ziyād[3] (d. 67/686) acting on the orders of the Umayyad caliph Yazīd I b. Muʿāwiya (r. 60–4/680–3). According to most reports, Mukhtār is away during this period and returns to find Ibn Ziyād in firm control of the city. He is then imprisoned for supporting the uprising and only freed through the intercession of his brother-in-law ʿAbd Allāh b. ʿUmar[4] (d. 73/693) after Ḥusayn's death at Karbalāʾ in 61/680.

Mukhtār's release from prison marks the start of the core structure of the present case study. He immediately flees to Mecca, where (according to most sources) he seeks out ʿAbd Allāh b. al-Zubayr (d. 72/692).[5] During this period, he meets with ʿAbd Allāh b. ʿAbbās[6] (d. 68/687) and a number

2 Muslim b. ʿAqīl was Ḥusayn's first cousin. For Muslim, see *EI*[2], s.v. "Muslim b. ʿAḳīl b. Abī Ṭālib" (E. Kohlberg); al-Ziriklī, 7:222.

3 For ʿUbayd Allāh b. Ziyād and his contentious relations with the ʿAlids, see *EI*[2], s.v. "ʿUbayd Allāh b. Ziyād" (C. F. Robinson); Ziriklī, 4:193.

4 For ʿAbd Allāh b. ʿUmar b. al-Khaṭṭāb, see Ibn Saʿd, 4:105–42. See also *EI*[2], s.v. "ʿAbd Allāh b. ʿUmar" (L. Veccia Vaglieri); al-Ziriklī, 4:108.

5 For ʿAbd Allāh b. al-Zubayr, see *EI*[3], s.v. "ʿAbdallāh b. al-Zubayr" (S. Campbell); al-Ziriklī, 4:87.

6 ʿAbd Allāh b. ʿAbbās b. ʿAbd al-Muṭṭalib, a paternal cousin and Companion of the Prophet, was the forebear of the ʿAbbāsid caliphs and a well-regarded transmitter of traditions. See *EI*[3], s.v. "ʿAbdallāh b. ʿAbbās" (C. Gilliot).

of prominent 'Alids, including Muḥammad b. al-Ḥanafiyya[7] (d. 81/700–1) and Zayn al-'Ābidīn 'Alī b. Ḥusayn[8] (d. 94–5/712–13). Mukhtār eventually swears allegiance to Ibn al-Zubayr and helps defend Mecca against an advancing Umayyad army led by Ḥuṣayn b. Numayr[9] (d. 67/686). Months later, Mukhtār, angered by Ibn al-Zubayr's unwillingness to appoint him to an important post, returns to Kūfa amid reports of civil unrest.

The second segment of the core structure begins with Mukhtār's arrival, around 64/684, in Kūfa, where he tries to muster support among the Shī'a. These efforts are bolstered by the massacre of Sulaymān b. Ṣurad's[10] (d. 65/685) Tawwābūn[11] movement at 'Ayn al-Warda by an Umayyad army led by Ibn Ziyād. Mukhtār is arrested a second time prior to Ibn Ṣurad's death but is again released through the intervention of Ibn 'Umar. In 65/685, Ibn al-Zubayr appoints 'Abd Allāh b. Muṭī'[12] (d. 73/692) as governor of Kūfa. Mukhtār organizes against the new governor, rallying the remnants of the Tawwābūn and with the backing of Ibrāhīm b. Mālik al-Ashtar al-Nakha'ī[13] (d. 72/691). In 66/685, he seizes control of the city, purportedly on behalf of Muḥammad b. al-Ḥanafiyya.

7 Muḥammad b. al-Ḥanafiyya was a son of 'Alī and a woman (Khawla) from the Banū Ḥanīfa. This is notable since it meant that he was not a direct blood descendant of Muḥammad. For Ibn al-Ḥanafiyya, see *EI*², s.v. "Muḥammad Ibn al-Ḥanafiyya" (F. Buhl); al-Ziriklī, 6:270.

8 Zayn al-'Ābidīn 'Alī b. Ḥusayn was the grandson of 'Alī b. Abī Ṭālib and the fourth Imām of the Twelver Shī'a. He was present in Karbalā' but did not take part in the fighting due to an illness. See Ibn Sa'd, 5:162–72; al-Mufīd, *Irshād*, 253–61; al-Ziriklī, 4:277; *EI*², s.v. "Zayn al-'Ābidīn" (E. Kohlberg).

9 Ḥuṣayn b. Numayr was an important military commander for the early Umayyads. See *EI*², s.v. "Al-Ḥuṣayn b. Numayr" (H. Lammens and V. Cremonesi); al-Ziriklī, 2:262.

10 Sulaymān b. Ṣurad was an early settler in Kūfa who regretted his complicity in Ḥusayn's death at Karbalā' and later headed the Tawwābūn movement. See Ibn Sa'd, 4:219–20 and 6:102; *EI*², s.v. "Sulaymān b. Ṣurad" (E. Kohlberg); al-Ziriklī, 3:127.

11 For the Tawwābūn, see *EI*², s.v. "Tawwābūn" (F. M. Denny). For a discussion of their impact on ritual practice, see Hawting, "Tawwabun."

12 'Abd Allāh b. Muṭī' was a leading opponent of the Umayyads in Medina who later swore fealty to the Zubayrids. For his life, see Ibn Sa'd, 5:109–13; *EI*³, s.v. "'Abdallāh b. Muṭī'" (I. Hasson); al-Ziriklī, 4:139.

13 Ibn al-Ashtar initially backed Mukhtār, but his support was always tepid. He died fighting with Muṣ'ab b. al-Zubayr against the Umayyads in 72/691. His father, Mālik al-Ashtar, was one of the leaders of the party that killed the third caliph, 'Uthmān, in 35/656, and he later became a staunch supporter of 'Alī. For Ibrāhīm, see *EI*², s.v. "Ibrāhīm b. al-Ashtar" (editors); al-Ziriklī, 1:58. For Mālik, see n. 49 in this chapter.

The third segment centers on Mukhtār's actions during his brief rule. These include his consolidation of power through the killing of figures tied to the death of Ḥusayn and his undermining of tribal elites (*ashrāf*). Most sources also mention his material support for Ibn al-Ḥanafiyya during a showdown with Ibn al-Zubayr in Mecca. This period features two major military engagements. The first is a rebellion organized by Kūfan tribal leaders that Ibn al-Ashtar crushes at Jabbānat al-Sabī' in 66/686. The second is a victory over Ibn Ziyād at the Battle of the Khāzir River in 67/686. The latter part of this segment documents the pursuit and execution of tribal leaders implicated in the events at Karbalā', most prominently Shamir b. Dhī al-Jawshan[14] (d. 66/686) and 'Umar b. Sa'd b. Abī Waqqāṣ[15] (d. 66/686).

The fourth and final segment in the core structure focuses on Mukhtār's defeat and death. The primary antagonist in these reports is Muṣ'ab b. al-Zubayr[16] (d. 72/691), the newly appointed Zubayrid governor of Baṣra. Mukhtār's forces are decisively routed in battle and he is forced to retreat to the fort complex (*qaṣr*) in Kūfa, where he remains besieged for a number of months. He is finally killed in the course of a desperate raid in 67/687. His few remaining followers then surrender to Muṣ'ab, who orders their execution.

II The Narrative Elements

The four segments described in the previous section constitute the core structure of Mukhtār's revolt. Each of the segments consists of narrative elements that depict an incident or an event. Table 2.2 summarizes these narrative elements and their textual variants. There are, for example,

14 Shamir b. Dhī al-Jawshan was initially a supporter of 'Alī but later shifted his loyalties to the Umayyads. Most sources ascribe to him a prominent role in the killing of Ḥusayn, which explains his largely negative portrayal. For his life, see *EI*^{2}, s.v. "Shamir (also al-Shamir, commonly Shimr) b. Dhi'l-Djawshan" (E. Kohlberg); al-Ziriklī, 3:175–6. For his actions at Karbalā', see Haider, *Shī'ī Islam*, 66–8.

15 'Umar b. Sa'd b. Abī Waqqāṣ was the son of a prominent Companion of the Prophet who founded the garrison city of Kūfa. 'Umar served as a military commander for the Umayyads under 'Abd Allāh b. Ziyād and is widely known for leading the Kūfan forces against Ḥusayn b. 'Alī at Karbalā'. See Ibn Sa'd, 5:128; al-Ziriklī, 5:47.

16 For Muṣ'ab b. al-Zubayr and his role as a deputy for and supporter of his brother 'Abd Allāh b. al-Zubayr in the civil strife that followed the death of Yazīd b. Mu'āwiya, see *EI*^{2}, s.v. "Muṣ'ab b. al-Zubayr" (C. Pellat and H. Lammens).

Table 2.2 – *The Narrative Elements of Mukhtār's Rise and Fall*

		Variant a	Variant b	Variant c
The Ḥijāz (61–4/680–4)				
1.1	Ibn al-Zubayr oath	Implicit. Brief.	Two encounters with extensive negotiation. Detailed.	
1.2	Return to Kūfa	Authorized by Ibn al-Zubayr.	Break with Ibn al-Zubayr.	
Sedition (64–6/684–5)				
2.1	Entry and recruitment	Smooth recruitment of Shīʿī supporters without rivalry.	Gradual recruitment opposed by rival figures.	
2.2	Kūfan arrest	On the urging of Kūfan elites. Released after oaths.		
2.3	Feigned sickness	Summarized. Brief.	Strategy after being informed of possible arrest.	
2.4	Kūfan delegation	Kūfans travel to Mecca and confront Ibn al-Ḥanafiyya.		
2.5	Ibrāhīm b. al-Ashtar letter	One meeting with no skepticism from Ibn al-Ashtar about authenticity.	Two meetings with extreme skepticism and subsequent oaths.	
2.6	Rebellion	Swift organization based on mourning for Prophet's family.	One battle. Few participant details. Ibn Muṭīʿ surrenders.	Multiple battles. Kūfan elite involvement. Ibn Muṭīʿ escapes.

Table 2.2 (*cont.*)

		Variant a	Variant b	Variant c
Rule (66–7/685–6)				
3.1	Ibn al-Ḥanafiyya siege	Mukhtār sends cavalry to help Ibn al-Ḥanafiyya against Ibn al-Zubayr.		
3.2	Ibn Ziyād battle/elite uprising	Isolated battle with Ibn Ziyād. Includes one or two battles.	Hybrid account. Two battles with Ibn Ziyād separated by elite uprising. Ibn al-Ashtar's key role.	Isolated elite uprising. No role for Ibn al-Ashtar.
3.3	Ḥijāzī expansion	Attempt to seize Ḥijāz through Shuraḥbīl b. Wars.		
3.4	Baṣran expansion	Attempt to seize Baṣra through al-Muthannā b. al-Mukharriba.		
3.5	'Alī's chair	Worship of 'Alī's chair. Ṭufayl b. Ja'da makes it for profit or deception.	Worship of 'Alī's chair. Ṭufayl b. Ja'da forced to make it by Mukhtār.	
3.6	Surāqa's angels	Surāqa is captured and claims to see angels fighting with Mukhtār.		
3.7	Shamir revenge	Killed with companions in surprise cavalry attack.	Killed because of intercepted letter. Companions escape.	Killed by advancing Kūfan army.
3.8	'Umar b. Sa'd revenge	Ibn al-Ḥanafiyya as direct cause.	No role for Ibn al-Ḥanafiyya.	
Fall (67/687)				
4.1	Final defeat	One prolonged battle at Ḥarūrā'.	Muṣ'ab plans campaign. Two battles. Kūfan elite involvement.	One battle, with Mukhtār retreating to Kūfa out of cowardice.
4.2	Mukhtār's death	Long siege. Death in a skirmish.		
4.3	Surrender and execution	Promise of safe-conduct.	No safe-conduct.	

multiple versions of Ibn Ziyād's death that agree on the general context (he died in battle) but differ regarding specific details. The same is true for other important events, such as Mukhtār's rebellion and his final defeat. These variations are in line with the expectations of the model outlined in Chapter 1. Readers interested in these differences are encouraged to consult the appendix, which summarizes the narrative elements in greater detail. The next section assumes familiarity with these variants and focuses instead on how historians employed the narrative elements in constructing interpretive frameworks (see Table 2.3).

III The Sources

This section surveys the nine historical works that depict Mukhtār's rebellion and downfall. The analysis is organized around the four segments of the core structure identified in the first section of the chapter: (1) the Ḥijāz, (2) sedition, (3) rule, and (4) fall. The discussion that follows foregrounds the authorial creation of meaning as embodied by interpretive frameworks. As discussed in Chapter 1, these frameworks were produced by populating a common core structure with embellished narrative elements.

A Ibn A'tham al-Kūfī (d. third/ninth century?)[17]

The first source under consideration is Ibn A'tham al-Kūfī's *Kitāb al-futūḥ*, a chronographical work covering the early history of the Muslim state from a supposedly Shī'ī perspective.[18] Ibn A'tham's long and detailed account of Mukhtār includes most of the narrative elements listed in Table 2.2.[19]

The Ḥijāz	Sedition	Rule	Fall
1.1b, 1.2b	2.1b, 2.2a, 2.3b, 2.4a, 2.5b, 2.6a	3.8b, 3.1a, 3.2b, 3.6a, 3.7a	4.1b, 4.2b, 4.3a

The elements are listed in the order of their appearance in the text.

[17] For Ibn A'tham's death date, see Conrad, "Ibn A'tham," 87–96 and Lindstedt, "al-Madā'inī's *Kitāb al-Dawla*," 103–130. In his forthcoming doctoral dissertation, Andrew McLaren convincingly argues that Ibn A'tham lived into the fourth/tenth century. This issue of dating, however, has little bearing on my larger argument.
[18] Ibid., 96–103.
[19] For the larger account, see Ibn A'tham, 1:196–207, 1:249–80, and 2:281–354.

Table 2.3 – *The Narrative Elements for Mukhtār by Author*

		Ibn A'tham al-Kūfī	Ibn Sa'd	*Akhbār al-dawla*	al-Balādhurī	Ps.-Ibn Qutayba	al-Ya'qūbī	al-Dīnawarī	al-Ṭabarī	al-Mas'ūdī
The Ḥijāz (61–4/680–4)										
1.1	Ibn al-Zubayr oath	b	a		b		a		b	a
1.2	Return to Kūfa	b	a		b	a	b		b	a
Sedition (64–6/684–5)										
2.1	Entry and recruitment	b	a		a		a	a	b	b
2.2	Kūfan arrest	a			a				a	
2.3	Feigned sickness	b			a			a	b	
2.4	Kūfan delegation	a	a		a		a		a	
2.5	Ibrāhīm b. al-Ashtar letter	b	a		b			a	b	
2.6	Rebellion	c			c		b		c	a

		Ibn Aʿtham al-Kūfī	Ibn Saʿd	*Akhbār al-dawla*	al-Balādhurī	Ps.-Ibn Qutayba	al-Yaʿqūbī	al-Dīnawarī	al-Ṭabarī	al-Masʿūdī
Rule (66–7/685–6)										
3.1	Ibn al-Ḥanafiyya siege	a	a	a	a		a		a	a
3.2	Ibn Ziyād battle/elite uprising	b	a		b	a	a	a / c	b	a
3.3	Ḥijāzī expansion				a				a	
3.4	Baṣran expansion				a				a	
3.5	ʿAlī's chair				b				a / b	
3.6	Surāqa's angels	a			a			a	a	
3.7	Shamir revenge	a			b			c	b	
3.8	ʿUmar b. Saʿd revenge	b			a	a		b	a	
Fall (67/687)										
4.1	Final defeat	b			b	a	a	b	b	a
4.2	Mukhtār's death	b		a	a		a	a	a	a
4.3	Surrender and execution	a		b	b	b	a		b	a

The Ḥijāz (61–4/680–4)[20]

Ibn Aʿtham's account of Mukhtār in the Ḥijāz begins with the longer variant (1.1b) of the "Ibn al-Zubayr oath" narrative.[21] In his first meeting with Mukhtār, Ibn al-Zubayr equates the duplicity of the Kūfans to that of slaves who display love to their owners' faces while cursing them behind their backs. He also rejects Mukhtār's offer to take the oath of allegiance, which compels the latter to leave Mecca and settle in Ṭā'if. Some time later, Ibn al-Zubayr characterizes Mukhtār's boastful prediction that he will overthrow tyrants as the words of a soothsayer and a hypocrite. Mukhtār returns to Mecca three days later. Here the narrative adheres to the standard form: ʿAbbās b. Sahl[22] (d. before 96/715) questions Mukhtār about his hostility toward Ibn al-Zubayr while attributing the latter's previous dismissive attitude to political caution. Mukhtār agrees to meet Ibn al-Zubayr again, but this time he demands influence and an official position in exchange for his oath. According to Ibn Aʿtham, he also asks for financial compensation for his family. Although Ibn al-Zubayr is averse to these terms, Ibn Sahl convinces him to accept them for the time being.[23]

Ibn Aʿtham explains Mukhtār's break with Ibn al-Zubayr through the "return to Kūfa" narrative (1.2b).[24] In this version, Mukhtār is angered by Ibn al-Zubayr's refusal to appoint him to political office. He meets Hānī b. Abī Ḥayya al-Wādiʿī[25] (d. after 67/687), who describes Kūfa as a city of restlessness and discontent. Ibn Aʿtham also relates a distinctive exchange in which Mukhtār questions Hānī concerning the movements and status of Sulaymān b. Ṣurad. He then departs from Mecca without Ibn al-Zubayr's permission, and encounters another traveler (Salama b. Marthad [d. unknown]),[26] who confirms Hānī's report and depicts the Kūfans as sheep without a shepherd. Ignoring Salama's advice to avoid these notoriously fickle people, Mukhtār vows to become their missing shepherd.

[20] For this section, see ibid., 1:200–7 and 1:252–3.
[21] Ibid., 1:200–2.
[22] For ʿAbbās b. Sahl, see Ibn Saʿd, 5:207–8.
[23] Ibn Aʿtham, 1:202–3. Mukhtār upholds his obligations during the subsequent conflict with the Umayyads. He is often characterized as emotional and hot-headed, with Ibn al-Zubayr tolerating his occasional outbursts.
[24] Ibid., 1:252–3.
[25] Al-Ṭabarī (3:292–3 and 3:404) depicts Hānī b. Abī Ḥayya as complicit with the Umayyads and strongly opposed to Mukhtār.
[26] According to al-Ṭabarī (3:404), he was a Hamdānī Bedouin famed for his courage. His death date is unknown.

Sedition (64–6/684–5)

Ibn Aʿtham includes six narrative elements that pertain to Mukhtār's rebellion. The first, a variant of the "entry and recruitment" narrative (2.1b), focuses on Mukhtār's rivalry with Sulaymān b. Ṣurad.[27] He enters the city in an ostentatious fashion, announcing himself as the people's salvation. After he reaches the Friday mosque (having generated great excitement), Mukhtār performs his prayers, changes clothes, and heads to a secret location where later that evening he confers with the Shīʿa. As in most reports, he claims that he was sent by the "Mahdī"[28] Muḥammad b. al-Ḥanafiyya to avenge the blood of the Prophet's family. The Shīʿa, however, note that they have already chosen a leader, Ibn Ṣurad, and so Mukhtār backs down and decides to bide his time.

Ibn Aʿtham next provides a comprehensive account of the Tawwābūn campaign against the Umayyads.[29] At one point, Ibn Ṣurad blames Mukhtār for his loss of support, but this accusation appears largely baseless.[30] Just prior to the defeat of the Tawwābūn, Ibn al-Zubayr appoints ʿAbd Allāh b. Yazīd al-Khaṭmī[31] (d. before 72/692) and Ibrāhīm b. Muḥammad b. Ṭalḥa b ʿUbayd Allāh[32] (d. 110/728) to govern Kūfa on his behalf. The text here mentions Ibn al-Zubayr's fear that Mukhtār will turn the region against him.[33] This is followed by Ibn Aʿtham's fairly typical version of the "Kūfan arrest" narrative (2.2a).[34] In this report, ʿUmar b. Saʿd convinces the new governor, ʿAbd Allāh b. Yazīd, to arrest Mukhtār and denigrates his supporters as *turābīs*, a derogatory term discussed later in this chapter. A group of Kūfan tribal leaders lobby for Mukhtār's release, but he remains in prison and spends his time composing rhymed prose about killing tyrants. He eventually writes to Ibn ʿUmar (disingenuously

[27] Ibn Aʿtham, 1:253–4.

[28] This term has considerable resonance among the Shīʿa, referring to the rightly guided successor of the Prophet. For a general discussion of the concept, see EI^2, s.v. "Al-Mahdī" (W. Madelung).

[29] Ibn Aʿtham, 1:254–65.

[30] For Ibn Ṣurad's claim that the decline in his support was due to Mukhtār, see ibid., 1:256. For Mukhtār's anticipation of the Tawwābūn movement's failure, see ibid., 1:264–6.

[31] ʿAbd Allāh b. Yazīd b. Zayd al-Khaṭmī al-Anṣārī was a companion of ʿAlī b. Abī Ṭālib. Before he was sent to Kūfa, he briefly served as the governor of Mecca for Ibn al-Zubayr. See Ibn Saʿd, 6:96; al-Ziriklī, 4:146.

[32] For Ibrāhīm b. Muḥammad, a half-brother of Ḥasan b. Ḥasan b. ʿAlī b. Abī Ṭālib through his mother, see Ibn Saʿd, 5:321–4; al-Mizzī, 2:172–3.

[33] Ibn Aʿtham, 1:254. [34] Ibid., 1:264–6.

swearing innocence), who again intercedes on his behalf with ʿAbd Allāh b. Yazīd and Ibrāhīm b. Muḥammad.[35] They free Mukhtār after ten prominent Shīʿa vouch for his future conduct.

Ibn Aʿtham's version of the "feigned sickness" narrative (2.3b) recounts the arrival of a new governor, ʿAbd Allāh b. Muṭīʿ, in Kūfa in Ramaḍān 65/685.[36] Ibn Muṭīʿ delivers a speech (quoted in full) revealing his ignorance of the economic demands and pro-ʿAlid sentiments of the city's population. This prompts a public outcry, during which, at the urging of Mukhtār, al-Sāʾib b. Mālik al-Ashʿarī[37] (d. 67/687) makes two demands: that public funds remain in Kūfa and that the governor adhere to the precedents of ʿAlī as opposed to those of ʿUmar or ʿUthmān. Ibn Muṭīʿ acquiesces to these conditions. Iyās b. Muḍārib al-ʿIjlī[38] (d. 66/685) later identifies Mukhtār as the cause of the unrest and advises Ibn Muṭīʿ to dispatch two deputies, Zāʾida b. Qudāma al-Thaqafī[39] (d. 76/690) and Ḥusayn b. ʿAbd Allāh al-Bursumī[40] (d. after 65/685), to summon him to court. As in the standard account, Zāʾida discreetly reveals the governor's intentions to Mukhtār, who then feigns sickness. He also asks *both* messengers to affirm the validity of his excuse to the governor. Specifically, he warns Ḥusayn b. ʿAbd Allāh, one of the messengers, that this would best serve his (Ḥusayn's) long-term interests.

After eluding imprisonment, Mukhtār is faced with a new crisis, as his Shīʿī supporters express doubts about his ties to Ibn al-Ḥanafiyya. Ibn Aʿtham's version of the "Kūfan delegation" narrative (2.4a) opens with the arrival of a party of unnamed Kūfan Shīʿa in Mecca.[41] Ibn al-Ḥanafiyya is surprised to see the Kūfans outside the Ḥajj season. He takes them aside, and they ask whether Mukhtār was sent to avenge the blood of Ḥusayn. They also disclose their intention to support Mukhtār's rebellion so long as this accords with Ibn al-Ḥanafiyya's

35 Ibn Aʿtham includes brief versions of both Mukhtār's letter to Ibn ʿUmar and Ibn ʿUmar's letter to ʿAbd Allāh and Ibrāhīm.

36 Ibn Aʿtham, 1:273–5.

37 For al-Sāʾib b. Mālik, see al-Ṭabarī, 3:491 and index.

38 For Iyās b. Muḍārib, see ibid., 3:435 and index.

39 Zāʾida was Mukhtār's paternal cousin. He later died in battle against the Khārijite leader Shabīb b. Yazīd (d. 78/697–8). See al-Ziriklī, 3:40; al-Ṭabarī, index.

40 Little is known about him beyond his association with the Banū Hamdān. See al-Ṭabarī, 3:435.

41 Ibn Aʿtham, 1:275–6.

wishes. At the end of the report, the delegation interprets an ambiguous remark from Ibn al-Ḥanafiyya as an endorsement. They then return home and inform Mukhtār that "we were commanded to follow you and rebel with you."[42] He has them attest to this in a public setting.

The delegation episode is followed by a two-meeting version of the "Ibrāhīm b. al-Ashtar letter" narrative (2.5b).[43] In this report, Mukhtār questions his companions about Ibn al-Ashtar.[44] After they praise him and characterize his support as critical to victory over their enemies, Mukhtār dispatches a small recruiting party that includes Aḥmar b. Shumayṭ al-Bajalī[45] (d. 67/686), Yazīd b. Anas[46] (d. 66/686), Abū ʿUthmān ʿAbd al-Raḥmān b. Mall al-Nahdī[47] (d. between 95/714–5 and 100/719), and ʿĀmir b. Sharāḥīl al-Shaʿbī[48] (d. between 103/721 and 110/728). As in the standard version, Ibn al-Ashtar encourages them to present their proposal without fear of reprisal. Aḥmar b. Shumayṭ, however, remains vague, drawing parallels between Ibrāhīm and his father, Mālik al-Ashtar[49] (d. 38/658), a famous supporter of ʿAlī. Ibn al-Ashtar understands what is being requested and agrees to join them as their leader. Yazīd b. Anas, however, responds that Ibn al-Ḥanafiyya has already delegated leadership to Mukhtār. Ibn al-Ashtar remains silent and the group departs.

42 Ibid., 2:276.

43 Ibn Aʿtham places the recruitment of Ibn al-Ashtar immediately after the testimony of the delegation. See ibid., 1:276–9.

44 For Ibrāhīm b. Mālik al-Ashtar, see n. 13 in this chapter.

45 Aḥmar b. Shumayṭ, one of Mukhtār's chief military commanders, took part in campaigns against the Umayyads and the Zubayrids. He died in the battle at Madhār against the forces of Muṣʿab b. al-Zubayr. For his life, see al-Ziriklī, 1:276.

46 Yazīd b. Anas al-Mālikī al-Asadī was known primarily for his staunch support of Mukhtār. See al-Ziriklī, 8:179–80; al-Tustarī, 11:93–4.

47 ʿAbd al-Raḥmān b. Mall b. ʿAmr was a transmitter of good reputation who converted to Islam during the lifetime of the Prophet. He refused to live in Kūfa after Ḥusayn was killed and spent the rest of his life in Baṣra. He is not associated with Mukhtār (or Kūfa) in other sources. See Ibn Saʿd, 7:68–9; al-Mizzī, 17:424–30; al-Tustarī, 6:145.

48 ʿĀmir b. Sharāḥīl al-Shaʿbī was a well-known transmitter and legal authority in Kūfa. In addition to his early involvement with Mukhtār, he later took part in the rebellion led by Ibn al-Ashʿath (see below). For his scholarly importance, see al-Mizzī, 14:28–40; *EI*², s.v. "Al-Shaʿbī" (G. H. A. Juynboll).

49 Mālik al-Ashtar b. al-Ḥārith al-Nakhaʿī was renowned for his support of ʿAlī b. Abī Ṭālib during the first *fitna*. He was poisoned by Muʿāwiya en route to his governorship of Egypt in 38/658–9. See *EI*³, s.v. "Al-Ashtar, Mālik b. al-Ḥārith al-Nakhaʿī" (H. Munt).

When the group relates the incident to Mukhtār, he sequesters himself in his home for three days. He then leads a second delegation, which presents Ibn al-Ashtar with a letter in which the "Mahdī" Ibn al-Ḥanafiyya asks for his support. In the text of the letter (which Ibn Aʿtham quotes at length), Ibn al-Ḥanafiyya names Mukhtār his representative and promises Ibn al-Ashtar a high rank and control over all conquered territory west of Kūfa through Syria and Egypt. Ibn al-Ashtar doubts the letter's authenticity because of the use of the title "Mahdī." He notes that Ibn al-Ḥanafiyya expressly avoided this term in their previous correspondence. The extent to which Ibn al-Ashtar accepts Mukhtār's explanation ("That was then and this is now"[50]) is unclear, but he nonetheless takes the oath of allegiance. Ibn al-Ashtar then has al-Shaʿbī record the names of those who testified to the validity of the letter. The next day he privately questions al-Shaʿbī about his absence from the group that affirmed the letter. Al-Shaʿbī confesses uncertainty but then praises the other witnesses as trustworthy men. The report ends with al-Shaʿbī's suspicion "that Mukhtār had written that letter himself."[51]

The final account in this section is Ibn Aʿtham's complicated multiple-battle version of the "rebellion" narrative (2.6c).[52] Rather than presenting the entirety of this episode, the following discussion highlights events of particular importance. Few writers provide such a comprehensive rendering of the rebellion.

The proximate cause of the rebellion is a skirmish between Ibrāhīm b. al-Ashtar and Iyās b. Muḍārib. According to Ibn Aʿtham, Iyās (correctly) interprets Ibn al-Ashtar's regular visits to Mukhtār as evidence of a plot to take over the city. He informs the governor, Ibn Muṭīʿ, who orders his supporters – mostly tribal elites – to prevent the rebels from gathering in public areas. Many of these loyalists (most notably Shamir b. Dhī al-Jawshan and Shabath b. Ribʿī al-Tamīmī[53] [d. 70/690]) dismiss the severity of the threat, describing Mukhtār's men as a small group of fanatics (*turābī*s). The tension culminates when Iyās intercepts Ibn al-Ashtar on his way to visit Mukhtār. Ibn al-Ashtar approaches a fellow tribesman among Iyās' men, grabs his spear, and kills Iyās. This signals the start of the rebellion.

50 Ibn Aʿtham, 2:278. 51 Ibid., 1:279. 52 Ibid., 1:279–91.

53 For Shabath b. Ribʿī's complicated relationship with Islam, his role in the killing of Ḥusayn, and his interactions with Mukhtār, see Ibn Saʿd, 6:241; al-Ṭabarī, index; al-Ziriklī, 3:153.

In the next part of the narrative, Mukhtār and Ibn al-Ashtar must contend with the positional advantages and intimidation tactics of their opponents. At one critical point, Shabath b. Ribʿī, a supporter of the governor, scolds his men for complaining about the brevity of Qur'ānic recitations in their communal prayer. He also describes Mukhtār's men as "Turks and Daylamites."[54] At another juncture, Shabath rallies his soldiers from the edge of defeat by accusing them of fleeing from their "slaves" and "riff-raff."[55] His forces recover and push back Mukhtār's men, taking many prisoners in the process. Shabath then orders the execution of all non-Arab captives.[56] The decisive battle takes place in the streets and alleyways. The Shīʿa (identified by this term) rally around al-Sā'ib b. Mālik al-Ashʿarī, who recounts their history of persecution and urges them to avenge the blood of the Prophet's family. They force the governor's men into a full retreat. Meanwhile, in another part of Kūfa, Ibn al-Ashtar urges his men to disregard the noble tribal lineages of their opponents as he leads them to victory. Ibn Muṭīʿ eventually retreats to the fort complex with a small group of supporters.

In the final section of the rebellion narrative, Shabath b. Ribʿī counsels Ibn Muṭīʿ to surrender in exchange for a guarantee of safe-conduct. The governor, however, deems this a betrayal of Ibn al-Zubayr's trust. Shabath then suggests that he sneak out at night alone. Ibn Muṭīʿ agrees to this plan, but before leaving he praises the tribal leaders (*ashrāf*) for their loyalty and again characterizes his enemies as lowly slaves. The rest of the account follows a typical pattern. The deposed governor hides in the compound (*dār*) of Abū Mūsā al-Ashʿarī[57] (d. ca. 48/668) while his remaining loyalists obtain a safe-conduct in return for the oath of allegiance. Mukhtār then delivers two speeches in rhymed prose, warning the people against treachery, encouraging them to support the Prophet's family, and urging unity between Arabs and non-Arabs.[58]

54 Ibn Aʿtham, 1:284–5. 55 Ibid., 1:285. 56 Ibid., 1:286.

57 Abū Mūsā ʿAbd Allāh b. Qays al-Ashʿarī was a Companion of the Prophet and a significant political player during the early caliphate and the first *fitna*. He is famous for his role as ʿAlī's representative in the arbitration that followed the Battle of Ṣiffīn (37/657). According to Michael Lecker, Abū Mūsā was granted a significant portion of the stable of Kūfa located near the main mosque and therefore close to the palace and fort. The use of the term *dār Abū Mūsā* likely refers to this area. See Ibn Saʿd, 4:78–87; al-Ziriklī, 4:114; *EI*[3], s.v. "Al-Ashʿarī, Abū Mūsā" (M. Lecker). For a map of early Kūfa, see Djait, *al-Kūfa*, 301–2.

58 Ibn Aʿtham, 1:290–1.

He later discovers Ibn Muṭī''s location and secretly sends him money (10,000 *dirhams*) to facilitate his departure from the city.

Rule (66–7/685–6)

Ibn A'tham's depiction of Mukhtār's rule features five narrative elements woven together with a few additional, sometimes quite elaborate, episodes. Mukhtār first appoints his own governors to the cities and districts administered from Kūfa.[59] He then raises the anxiety level of Kūfan tribal elites[60] by vowing to punish those who participated in the campaign against Ḥusayn.[61] Specifically, he solicits information about these individuals, takes them into custody, and executes them in a manner that evokes the injuries they inflicted on Ḥusayn ("those who split open his stomach," "those who gouged out his eyes," etc.).[62] Ibn A'tham includes a particularly gruesome account of the execution of Khawalī b. Yazīd al-Aṣbaḥī[63] (d. 66/686), who reportedly cut off and carried away Ḥusayn's head.

Ibn al-A'tham is unique in placing his version of the "'Umar b. Sa'd revenge" narrative (3.8b) in the early part of Mukhtār's reign.[64] He describes Mukhtār dispatching a messenger, Abū 'Amra Kaysān[65] (d. 67/686), to 'Umar's home with two orders. The first instructs Kaysān to summon 'Umar to appear in court. The second is an authorization to kill 'Umar on the spot should he request his shawl (*ṭaylasān*), as this word is, according to Mukhtār, a code for sword. The truth of this latter claim is left uncertain. When Kaysān delivers the summons, 'Umar b. Sa'd initially refuses to comply, citing a safe-conduct (reproduced in full in Ibn A'tham's text) that he secured through the intercession of 'Abd Allāh b. Ja'da b. Hubayra b. Abī Wahb al-Makhzūmī[66] (d. after 67/687).

59 Ibid., 2:191. 60 For a typical account of this type, see ibid., 1:291–4.
61 Ibid., 1:294. 62 Ibid., 1:295.
63 For his death, see al-Ṭabarī, 3:464. For his actions in Karbalā', see ibid., 3:333–5.
64 Ibn A'tham, 2:295–8.
65 Abū 'Amra Kaysān is a nebulous historical figure, identified as a non-Arab client of the Banū Bajīla and sometimes cited as the eponym of the Kaysānī Shī'a. He served as the leader of Mukhtār's personal guard, often carrying out executions on his behalf. See *EI*[2], s.v. "Kaysān" (A. A. Dixon) and references therein.
66 The text here refers to his father Ja'da, who is mentioned as a Companion of the Prophet, but this is likely a mistake as other sources clearly name 'Abd Allāh b. Ja'da as the intermediary for the safe-conduct (al-Ṭabarī, 3:464–5). 'Abd Allāh remained with Mukhtār until the siege in Kūfa, when, recognizing Mukhtār's intention to lead a final suicidal raid, he slipped out of the fort and

The document grants him and his family immunity for past actions, orders him to stay in his home, and requires that he refrain from indecent acts.[67] Kaysān replies that the provision of "committing indecent acts" is ambiguous, and might literally be interpreted as a reference to defecation. He also disparages 'Umar b. Sa'd for killing the son of the Prophet's daughter but concedes that perhaps Mukhtār only means to consult him on a different matter. 'Umar then calls for his shawl, at which point Kaysān kills and beheads him. It is unclear whether Kaysān genuinely believes that 'Umar b. Sa'd is requesting his sword.

The remainder of the narrative is fairly straightforward. Mukhtār presents 'Umar's head to his son, Ḥafṣ b. 'Umar b. Sa'd[68] (d. 66/686), who is understandably despondent. Ḥafṣ is then killed and his head placed alongside that of his father. Mukhtār observes that these executions are not adequate compensation for the killing of Ḥusayn and his son 'Alī b. Ḥusayn.[69] Both heads are sent to Ibn al-Ḥanafiyya along with 30,000 *dīnār*s and a long letter, quoted in its entirety, promising to pursue Ḥusayn's remaining killers (i.e. 'Ubayd Allāh b. Ziyād). They arrive in Mecca just as Ibn al-Ḥanafiyya is criticizing Mukhtār for espousing love of the Prophet's family while fraternizing with its enemies (i.e. 'Umar b. Sa'd). Shocked by this turn of events, Ibn al-Ḥanafiyya vows to never again speak ill of Mukhtār.[70]

Ibn A'tham's version of the "Ibn al-Ḥanafiyya siege" narrative (3.1a) begins by noting the tension between Ibn al-Zubayr and Ibn al-Ḥanafiyya after Mukhtār's seizure of Kūfa.[71] When Ibn al-Zubayr questions some of Ibn al-Ḥanafiyya's Kūfan supporters about their loyalties, he receives replies that range from dismissive to hostile. One of the Kūfans reaffirms

hid with relatives (ibid., 3:491). 'Abd Allāh then disappears from the historical record (ibid., index). For his father, see al-Mizzī, 4:563–6.

67 The safe-conduct is witnessed by al-Sā'ib b. Mālik al-Ash'arī, Aḥmar b. Shumayṭ al-Bajalī, and Yazīd b. Anas al-Asadī, among others.

68 Interestingly, Ḥafṣ b. 'Umar was Mukhtār's nephew through his sister. See also al-Ṭabarī, 3:465.

69 Ḥusayn had two sons with the name 'Alī. The reference here is to the 'Alī b. Ḥusayn who died at Karbalā'. The other 'Alī b. Ḥusayn was the fourth Imām of the Twelver Shī'a (see n. 8 in this chapter). The relative ages of the two brothers are unclear. See Haider, *Shī'ī Islam*, 66–70; EI^2, s.v. "Zayn al-'Ābidīn" (E. Kohlberg).

70 In other accounts, Ibn al-Ḥanafiyya's complaints are the proximate cause of 'Umar b. Sa'd's execution.

71 Ibn A'tham, 1:299–307.

Ibn al-Ḥanafiyya's avowed neutrality. Another observes that Ibn al-Ḥanafiyya only counsels people about their conduct whereas Ibn al-Zubayr confiscates his enemies' possessions and kills them. A third expressly accuses Ibn al-Zubayr of tyranny. The Kūfans then take refuge with Ibn al-Ḥanafiyya (although he is initially hesitant to associate with them) in the Kaʿba and expressly declare themselves his "Shīʿa."[72]

Convinced that Ibn al-Zubayr will violate the sanctity of the Kaʿba, Ibn al-Ḥanafiyya writes Mukhtār a letter (quoted in full), in which he details the desperation of his situation – the lack of food and water, the constant threats – and reminds the Kūfans of their previous failures to support the family of the Prophet. Mukhtār dispatches small groups of cavalry under the command of Abū ʿAbd Allāh al-Jadalī[73] (d. after 67/687) to Mecca. He also sends money (400,000 *dirhams*) and a letter that refers to Ibn al-Ḥanafiyya as the "Mahdī" and promises further support. When the Kūfans arrive, they greet Ibn al-Ḥanafiyya in the traditional Shīʿī manner ("Make our fathers and mothers your sacrifice") and ask for permission to fight; he refuses. Ibn al-Zubayr is astonished by their claim that they are avenging the family of the Prophet. He notes that he was not involved in Ḥusayn's murder and that the Kūfans (whom he labels "*turābīs*") themselves bear primary responsibility for Ḥusayn's death. The standoff escalates when Ibn al-Zubayr denigrates Ibn al-Ḥanafiyya as a "hired hand" (*ʿasīf*) to his brothers Ḥasan and Ḥusayn. Ibn al-Ḥanafiyya responds by mentioning his closeness to his brothers and the superiority of ʿAlid claims to the caliphate. Visiting pilgrims eventually mediate between the two sides, and Ibn al-Ḥanafiyya is permitted to settle in a district (*shiʿb*) outside Mecca with his family and followers.

At this point, Ibn Aʿtham provides a set of revenge accounts. The first involves Asmāʾ b. Khārija al-Fazārī[74] (d. after 68/688), who is sought for his role in the killing of Muslim b. ʿAqīl but flees before arrest.[75]

72 Ibid., 1:302.

73 Abū ʿAbd Allāh ʿAbda b. ʿAbd al-Jadalī was known for his ardent Shīʿism. He remained with Ibn al-Ḥanafiyya in Mecca for the duration of Mukhtār's rule. See Ibn Saʿd, 6:248 (for the origins of his *nisba*); and al-Ṭabarī, 3:489 (for his location in 67/687).

74 ʿAsmāʾ b. Khārija b. Ḥuṣn b. Ḥudhayfa took refuge in Syria, where he was welcomed by ʿAbd al-Malik b. Marwān (r. 65–86/685–705). According to al-Ṭabarī (3:501), he was still alive in 68/688. See also al-Ziriklī, 1:305; Ibn al-Jawzī, 6:235–6.

75 Ibn Aʿtham, 2:308.

A second accuses Muḥammad b. al-Ash'ath al-Kindī[76] (d. 67/686) of insulting Ḥusayn at Karbalā'.[77] Ibn al-Ash'ath escapes to Baṣra, where he urges Muṣ'ab b. al-Zubayr to fight the "Turks and Daylamites" led by "this Mukhtār" who kill people for mere suspicion of complicity in the murder of Ḥusayn.[78]

The remaining sequence of this segment of Ibn A'tham's text is distinctive. It first reproduces a substantial portion of the hybrid "Ibn Ziyād battle/elite uprising" narrative (3.2b). This is interrupted, before the final confrontation between Ibn al-Ashtar and Ibn Ziyād, by the "Surāqa's angels" (3.6a) and "Shamir revenge" (3.7a) narratives. The analysis that follows adheres to this unconventional ordering of events.

The composite account begins with the first part of the "Ibn Ziyād battle" narrative (3.2b).[79] Ibn Ziyād leads a large Umayyad army into Jazīra, forcing 'Abd al-Raḥmān b. Sa'īd b. Qays al-Hamdānī[80] (d. 66/686), Mukhtār's governor, to flee from Mawṣil to Tikrīt. Mukhtār then asks Yazīd b. Anas in rhymed prose to take charge of a military expedition against Ibn Ziyād. Yazīd meticulously selects a small force of 3,000 cavalry. Mukhtār instructs him to fight without delay, to provide daily updates, and to ask for reinforcements and supplies as needed. The Kūfans are met by two contingents of 3,000 cavalry on the outskirts of Mawṣil. The night before the battle, Yazīd falls gravely ill and establishes a line of succession beginning with Waraqa b. 'Āzib al-Asadī al-Nakha'ī[81] (d. 67/687?). The next day he sits on a chair in the battlefield and rallies his men to avenge the blood of Ḥusayn. They are victorious and take 3,000 prisoners, all of whom are executed on Yazīd's orders. By this point, he is so sick that he can only communicate through gestures, and he dies later that night. Waraqa, now in charge, praises the Kūfans but notes the overwhelming numerical advantage of

76 Muḥammad b. al-Ash'ath b. Qays al-Kindī was a leader of the Banū Kinda who died in the final battle against Mukhtār. See Ibn Sa'd, 5:48; al-Mizzī: 24:494–8; al-Ziriklī, 6:39; *EI*², s.v. "Muḥammad b. al-Ash'ath" (G. R. Hawting).

77 Ibn A'tham, 2:308–9. 78 Ibid.

79 For this section of the narrative, see ibid., 2:310–14.

80 'Abd al-Raḥmān b. Sa'īd later took part in the elite uprising against Mukhtār and was killed at Jabbānat al-Sabī'. For his death, see al-Ṭabarī, 3:462; Ibn al-Athīr, 4:239.

81 Waraqa b. 'Āzib fought with Ibn al-Ashtar against Ibn Ziyād (al-Ṭabarī, 3:482) and with Mukhtār against Muṣ'ab b. al-Zubayr (ibid., 3:489). His disappearance from the historical record at this point suggests his death in the battle.

the Syrians, reinforced by the population of Jazīra. He concludes that further fighting might diminish the glory of their victory. The men agree to slip away in the middle of night. When news of this reaches Mukhtār, he orders Ibn al-Ashtar to muster a new army, gather the remnants of Yazīd b. Anas's cavalry, and reengage the enemy.

The second part of the hybrid "Ibn Ziyād battle/elite uprising" narrative (3.2b) opens with a catalogue of grievances against Mukhtār.[82] The elites, referred to as "the people of Kūfa," select Shabath b. Rib'ī as their spokesman. On their behalf, he accuses Mukhtār of coercion in securing the oath of allegiance and criticizes policies that allow slaves and non-Arabs (mentioned separately) to secure mounts, stipends, and a share of the *fay'* (communal property) reserved for the benefit of orphans and widows. These actions, Shabath contends, conflict with Mukhtār's religion (*dīn*) and his tribal standing (*sharaf*). Mukhtār agrees to disavow these positions if tribal leaders promise to fight loyally on his behalf. The elites, however, refuse and instead decide to launch their own rebellion. Ibn A'tham quotes one tribesman, 'Abd al-Raḥmān b. Mikhnaf al-Azdī[83] (d. 75/690), who counsels against this course of action for two reasons: first, it violates their previous oaths; and second, it is destined to fail given the stark contrast between their disunity and bickering, on the one hand, and the loyalty and strength of Mukhtār's supporters, on the other. He suggests waiting for a third party – the Zubayrids or the Umayyads – to depose Mukhtār. At the very least, he urges them to hold off until Ibn al-Ashtar is outside the city.

The uprising is led by men of high tribal standing (e.g. Shamir b. Dhī al-Jawshan, Shabath b. Rib'ī), many of whom are in hiding because of their complicity in Ḥusayn's killing. Aware of the impending danger, Mukhtār sends a messenger to retrieve Ibn al-Ashtar while he stalls his enemies in negotiations. Ibn al-Ashtar races back, arriving on the second day of the conflict. His arrival is followed by a complicated two-front battle in which Ibn al-Ashtar defeats a coalition of the Rabī'a and Muḍar while Mukhtār leads his men against the Yaman. The decisive encounter occurs in Jabbānat al-Sabī', after which many of the surviving rebels flee to the countryside or to Baṣra.

82 For this section of the narrative, see Ibn A'tham, 2:315–18.

83 'Abd al-Raḥmān b. Mikhnaf b. Sulaym al-Azdī was a leader of the Banū Azd who survived into the Marwānid period and died fighting with al-Muhallab b. Abī Ṣufra against the Azāriqa. See al-Ziriklī, 3:336–7; al-Ṭabarī, index.

Following Mukhtār's victory, Ibn A'tham offers a second set of revenge accounts that reflect a dramatic shift in policy.[84] There is no longer any pretense of appeasing the tribal elites. Mukhtār instructs his men to search out anyone who had a part in Ḥusayn's death. If a witness comes forward to corroborate the charges, Mukhtār orders the immediate execution of the accused. If there are no witnesses, he subjects the accused to brutal punishments. In some cases, it is clear that Mukhtār is using these executions as a pretext to eliminate political enemies.

Ibn A'tham's version of the "Surāqa's angels" narrative (3.6a) occurs in the aftermath of the elite revolt.[85] It begins with Surāqa b. Mirdās al-Bāriqī[86] (d. 79/698) disavowing involvement in the campaign against Ḥusayn's death and reciting a lengthy poem in praise of Mukhtār. He then swears that he saw angels fighting alongside Mukhtār in the battle. The next part of the narrative is unique in two ways. First, Mukhtār does not compel Surāqa to testify in public; instead, he accuses him of swearing falsely and banishes him from Kūfa. Second, Surāqa immediately confesses that he lied to save his life. In other accounts, he admits this only after he is safely outside Kūfa. Surāqa then flees to Baṣra, where he composes verses that openly mock Mukhtār.

Ibn A'tham now relates one of the longest versions of the "Shamir revenge" narrative (3.7a).[87] Mukhtār sends a slave, Razīn,[88] in pursuit of Shamir, who is referred to as the killer of Ḥusayn with the most intense hatred of the Prophet's family. Shamir defeats the slave in single combat. Mukhtār then dispatches Abū Kanūd 'Abd al-Raḥmān b. 'Ubayd[89] (d. after 70/689) with ten of his best men to complete the task. At this point, Shamir is in Kunāsa,[90] a village just outside Kūfa on the bank of the Euphrates. His companions advise him to continue his journey with haste, as Mukhtār is likely to send more men after him.

84 Ibn A'tham, 2:319. 85 Ibid., 2:319–21.

86 Surāqa b. Mirdās b. Asmā' al-Bāriqī was an Azdī poet of Yemeni origins. Following this episode, he traveled first to Baṣra and then to Damascus. He eventually returned to Kūfa but was forced to flee a second time after he lampooned al-Ḥajjāj b. Yūsuf (d. 95/714) in verse. Surāqa later died in Syria. See al-Ziriklī, 3:80–1.

87 Ibn A'tham, 2:321–2.

88 Al-Ṭabarī records the name of the slave as Zarbī (3:433).

89 Abū Kanūd 'Abd al-Raḥmān b. 'Ubayd al-Azdī transmitted traditions on the authority of 'Alī and later held an official position under Ziyād b. Abīhī (d. 53/673). See Fishbein, *The Victory of the Marwanids*, 26, n. 25.

90 Yāqūt, 4:546; Djait, *al-Kūfa*, 230.

Shamir, however, vows to remain in the same location for three days even if Mukhtār, "the liar," were to approach with all of his supporters. Just as he finishes these words, the Kūfans arrive at the camp. The text describes Shamir, whom it calls the "enemy of God," as pockmarked by leprosy. He grabs a spear and, following an exchange of derogatory poems with ʿAbd al-Raḥmān, is killed along with all his companions. Mukhtār displays their heads on the walls of the Friday mosque.

Ibn Aʿtham now returns to the "Ibn Ziyād battle/elite uprising" narrative (3.2b) with his account of the Battle of the Khāzir River.[91] After the conclusion of the elite uprising, Ibn al-Ashtar is again ordered to lead a large army (10,000 cavalry and 7,000 foot soldiers) against Ibn Ziyād.[92] As he departs, he utters a prayer asking God for support, loyalty, and closeness to Ḥasan and Ḥusayn. Mukhtār accompanies him on the first day and offers his own prayer in his signature rhymed prose. He also advises Ibn al-Ashtar to remember God in public and private, to march quickly, and to fight the enemy without delay.

Ibn al-Ashtar collects taxes along the way, and establishes his camp near Mawṣil. He then offers ʿUmayr b. al-Ḥubāb al-Sulamī[93] (d. after 67/687, fighting on the side of Ibn Ziyād) a considerable bribe to defect on the eve of battle.[94] There are two critical differences between this account and those of most other sources. First, Ibn Aʿtham does not attribute ʿUmayr's defection to tribal tensions within the Umayyad army between the Qays and the Kalb stemming from the Battle of Marj Rāhiṭ. Second, Ibn Aʿtham places ʿUmayr's betrayal prior to the battle, whereas most writers claim that he retreated in the course of the actual fighting, if he did so at all. The report ends with Ibn al-Ashtar testing ʿUmayr's sincerity by asking whether he should attack immediately or first reinforce his position; ʿUmayr passes the test by advising the former.

The next part of the narrative touches on some minor incidents that precede the main battle. In a distinctive report, Ibn Ziyād recalls Ibn

91 For this narrative, see Ibn Aʿtham, 2:323–5 and 2:334–43.

92 A central strand in the narrative, concerning ʿUbayd Allāh b. Ḥurr's questionable loyalties, lies outside the scope of this study.

93 ʿUmayr b. al-Ḥubāb's death date is unclear. His importance in this episode stems from his tribal affiliation with the Qays, who still harbored resentments over their defeat at Marj Rāhiṭ. See al-Ṭabarī, 3:479–81.

94 Ibn Aʿtham, 2:335.

al-Ashtar playing with pigeons as a child. He marvels at the latter's growth into a man who now leads an army against him. Another report emphasizes that Ibn al-Ashtar and his outnumbered men viewed the battle as an opportunity to avenge the blood of the Prophet's family. There are also exchanges that help contextualize the conflict and in which the Kūfans are invariably vindicated.

On the day of the battle, Ibn al-Ashtar makes a rousing speech, detailing Ibn Ziyād's crimes against Ḥusayn and his household (the refusal of a safe-conduct, the deprivation of water, the imprisonment of the surviving family, etc.). The Syrians are thoroughly defeated and Ibn Ziyād's body is identified on the basis of dress and smell (musk). Ibn al-Ashtar sends his head along with those of other prominent Syrians to Mukhtār, who forwards them to Ibn al-Ḥanafiyya along with 30,000 *dīnār*s and a letter (quoted at length). It is worth noting that the letter, composed in rhymed prose, repeatedly refers to Ibn al-Ḥanafiyya as the "Mahdī."[95]

Fall (67/686)

Ibn A'tham presents the detailed, two-battle variant of the "final defeat" narrative (4.1b).[96] He identifies Ibn al-Ashtar's deployment in the Jazīra as the primary impetus for Muṣ'ab b. al-Zubayr's decision to march on Kūfa. This differs from other reports that emphasize the mobilizing efforts of Kūfan refugees. Muṣ'ab writes to al-Muhallab b. Abī Ṣufra[97] (d. 83/703), out on campaign against the Azāriqa, summoning him back to Baṣra. The letter is delivered by Muḥammad b. al-Ash'ath, who personally complains to al-Muhallab about Mukhtār's persecution of tribal elites (without explicitly mentioning non-Arabs or slaves). After al-Muhallab returns to Baṣra, Muṣ'ab sets out for Kūfa with an army organized along tribal lines. At this point, Mukhtār is aware that Ibn al-Ashtar has abandoned him to his fate. He tries to rally the people by (correctly) noting that the Kūfans in the Baṣran army are the same men who killed Ḥusayn. Before the fighting

95 The narrative claims that the Kūfans gathered 70,000 of their opponents' heads. See ibid., 2:341.

96 Ibid., 2:344–9.

97 Abū Sa'īd al-Muhallab b. Abī Ṣufra al-Azdī al-'Atakī was an important military commander for Ibn al-Zubayr and was later appointed to the governorship of Khurāsān by 'Abd al-Malik b. Marwān. He is particularly well known for his campaigns against the Azāriqa in the East. See al-Ziriklī, 7:315; *EI*², s.v. "Al-Muhallab b. Abī Ṣufra" (P. Crone).

begins, the Baṣrans reiterate their support for the Zubayrids while the Kūfans propose submitting the conflict to arbitration by the family of the Prophet. In the subsequent battle at Madā'in, the Kūfan army, led by Aḥmar b. Shumayṭ, is almost completely destroyed.

This compels Mukhtār to write a series of desperate letters to Ibn al-Ashtar that receive no response. Ibn Aʿtham then relates the tactical maneuvers of each side (e.g. Muṣʿab's use of boats, Mukhtār's blocking of the canals), which culminate in a second battle near Ḥarūrā'. After a series of indecisive skirmishes, the tide turns decisively against Mukhtār's smaller force as Muṣʿab rallies his men by appealing to their Arab lineage. The text places a great emphasis on the merciless ferocity of the exiled Kūfan tribal elites. Mukhtār and his remaining men are forced to fall back to the fort in Kūfa. When questioned about the defeat, Mukhtār invokes the Shīʿī doctrine of *badā'*.[98]

Ibn Aʿtham's version of the "Mukhtār's death" narrative (4.2b) is fairly standard.[99] Mukhtār's men are besieged in the fort and denied access to food or water. They are forced to buy waterskins from passing sellers for exorbitant prices. Initially, they are also brought supplies by their female relatives, but Muṣʿab soon cracks down on this practice. The men eventually resort to drinking brackish water made slightly more palatable with the addition of honey or cooked grapes. As the siege drags on, the two sides trade taunts and insults that sometimes result in minor encounters outside the walls. Eventually, Mukhtār urges his supporters to join him in a final attempt to break the siege, leaving open the possibility that God will come to their aid and grant them victory. His men respond positively to this call. This contrasts with other reports in which the men adamantly refuse to leave the fort. Before leading this last desperate charge, Mukhtār explains his motivations. He confesses that he saw Ibn al-Zubayr and the Umayyads seizing territory and felt he was on a par with them, but notes that he was also avenging the family of the Prophet.[100] He is killed in the subsequent scuffle.

98 Specifically, he quotes Q13:39, which reads: "God effaces what He wills, and establishes (what He wills), and with Him is the source of ordinance." *Badā'* is commonly understood as the belief that God may change a given decree or outcome. Another interpretation views it as an unexpected occurrence that nevertheless reflects God's will. See Haider, *Shīʿī Islam*, 47 and 93; *EI*², s.v. "Badā'" (I. Goldziher and A. S. Tritton).

99 Ibn Aʿtham, 2:349–52.

100 He paraphrases the last part of Q33:33, which reads: "God wishes to remove uncleanliness from you, O People of the Household, and to purify you."

Ibn A'tham's text ends with the "surrender and execution" narrative (4.3a).[101] After Mukhtār's death, Muṣ'ab convinces the remaining men in the fort to open the gates in exchange for a guarantee of safe-conduct (*amān*).[102] This detail contradicts other accounts, which claim that the surrender was unconditional. The prisoners are brought before Muṣ'ab, who calls them "the Shī'a of the Dajjāl." Bujayr b. 'Abd Allāh al-Muslī[103] (d. 67/687) responds that they are actually the Shī'a of the family of the Prophet, and then delivers an oft-cited speech in which he counsels forgiveness as the path preferable to God, mentioning their shared religion and alluding to previous conflicts in the city and the region that ended in reconciliation. Muṣ'ab is inclined to free the prisoners, but he backs down when Kūfan tribal leaders demand revenge and threaten rebellion. Instead, he orders their execution.

Interpretive Framework

Ibn A'tham's dominant interpretive framework is religious in that it highlights the Shī'ī character of Mukhtār's rebellion.[104] On a very basic level, Mukhtār and his supporters are repeatedly described by their opponents (e.g. Ibn Ziyād, 'Umar b. Sa'd, Shabath b. Rib'ī, and Ibn al-Zubayr) as "*turābī*s," a pejorative term applied to the followers of 'Alī b. Abī Ṭālib. More substantive evidence is found in Mukhtār's unflinching claim that he represents Ibn al-Ḥanafiyya and his repeated promises to punish the killers of Ḥusayn and the enemies of the family of the Prophet. After his arrival in Kūfa, Mukhtār remains mostly passive until the massacre of the Tawwābūn movement. There is no ambiguity here regarding his unwavering support for the existing leadership of the Kūfan Shī'a who then facilitate his first release from prison. The Shī'a are further convinced of his credibility after a visit to Ibn al-Ḥanafiyya, and help Mukhtār, perhaps dishonestly, in his

101 Ibn A'tham, 2:352–3.

102 Recall that in the previous narrative element, Mukhtār rallied his men to join him in one final attack. In this case, however, it appears that many refused his summons and remained in the fort.

103 Bujayr b. 'Abd Allāh al-Muslī is primarily known through his son Salama, who led the Kaysānī Shī'a during the transfer of authority from the 'Alids to the 'Abbāsids. See also *Akhbār al-dawla*, 180–1; al-Balādhurī, 6:441–3; al-Ṭabarī, 3:492.

104 Note that the various interpretive frameworks applied to Mukhtār's rebellion are summarized in Table 2.4.

recruitment of Ibn al-Ashtar. They also constitute a distinct contingent within Mukhtār's army led by al-Sa'ib b. Mālik al-Ashʿarī.

Once in power, Mukhtār immediately targets those involved in the massacre at Karbalā'. Ibn Aʿtham differs from other writers, who frame his pursuit of these figures as a purely political act. In these latter accounts, Mukhtār initially ignores influential tribal figures with ties to Ḥusayn's killing in hopes of winning their support. Ibn Aʿtham's version of Mukhtār makes no such concessions. Some of these individuals (e.g. ʿUmar b. Saʿd) are killed relatively quickly despite agreements of safe-conduct, while others (e.g. Shamir b. Dhī al-Jawshan) only survive by hiding. The Shīʿī nature of Mukhtār's movement also permeates the conflict with Ibn Ziyād. Prior to the first battle, Yazīd b. Anas inspires his men by invoking religion and revenge for Ḥusayn. Ibn al-Ashtar articulates a similar sentiment before the Battle of the Khāzir River, uttering a prayer for closeness to Ḥasan and Ḥusayn. He later rallies his supporters against a numerically superior Umayyad army by framing their fight as an attempt to exact retribution for Ḥusayn and his family.

In his final conflict with Muṣʿab, Mukhtār repeatedly expresses strong Shīʿī sentiments. He associates the approaching Baṣran army with the Kūfan elites who took part in the campaign against Ḥusayn. After his defeat, Mukhtār explains the negative outcome by invoking the Shīʿī doctrine of *badā'* through Q13:39. In his final speech to his besieged followers, Mukhtār characterizes his actions as a mixture of personal ambition and sincere love for the Prophet's family. When Muṣʿab disparages Mukhtār's supporters as the "Shīʿa of the Dajjāl," Bujayr b. ʿAbd Allāh reiterates their devotion to the family of the Prophet.

Alongside the narrative emphasis on Shīʿism, Ibn Aʿtham forwards a second, less pronounced, interpretive framework, one focused on tribal and ethnic distinctions, which places slaves and non-Arabs (Mukhtār's supporters) in opposition to tribal elites (Mukhtār's opponents). During the initial rebellion, for example, Shabath b. Ribʿī labels Mukhtār's followers as foreigners ("Turks and Daylamites") and criticizes his men for failing to stand up to their slaves. After a skirmish leaves him with a large number of prisoners, Shabath questions each man and executes those who are non-Arabs. A similar ethos informs Ibn al-Ashtar's advice to his soldiers on the cusp of battle, as he urges them to ignore the names of their opponents. Before fleeing Kūfa, ʿAbd Allāh b. Muṭīʿ praises his tribal elite supporters for their loyalty but describes the rebels as slaves. In his first speech as ruler of Kūfa, Mukhtār makes an explicit call for unity between Arabs and non-Arabs. On the eve of the elite uprising at Jabbānat al-Sabī', Shabath, acting on behalf of tribal notables, demands that Mukhtār revoke policies that favor slaves and non-Arabs. Interestingly, Shabath considers this a violation of both religious principles and the established tribal order. Finally, the Kūfan elites appeal to Muṣ'ab for military aid against Mukhtār in tribal terms, again characterizing their opponents as foreigners.

Ibn A'tham's text thus presents two interpretive frameworks in conversation with each other. The descriptions of Mukhtār and his followers suggest a sincere religious movement grounded in a Shī'ī desire to avenge the family of the Prophet. There are a few instances in which Mukhtār exhibits dubious morals (the initial claim to represent Ibn al-Ḥanafiyya, the letter to Ibrāhīm b. al-Ashtar, the killing of 'Umar b. Sa'd), but his sincerity shines through in much of the text. He always frames his argument in Shī'ī terms, and repeatedly demonstrates his allegiance to Ibn al-Ḥanafiyya. Similarly, most of his followers express a clear belief in the religious virtue of their cause. By contrast, Mukhtār's opponents are defined by their opposition to policies that favor non-Arabs. There is little in the way of dialogue between tribal leaders and non-Arabs despite Mukhtār's attempts at facilitating reconciliation. Ibn A'tham weaves these two interpretive frameworks into a larger narrative that manages to preserve the individuality of both.

B Ibn Sa'd (d. 230/856)

Ibn Sa'd's *al-Ṭabaqāt al-kubrā* is a prosopographical source featuring biographies of prominent figures from the first three Islamic centuries, organized by generation. Although there is not a separate entry on Mukhtār, he is mentioned in the biographies of other important figures. Specifically, Ibn Sa'd relates seven narrative elements spanning three segments of the core structure of Mukhtār's life (i.e. The Ḥijāz, Sedition, and Rule).

The Ḥijāz	Sedition	Rule	Fall
1.1a, 1.2a	2.1a, 2.4a, 2.5a	3.2a, 3.1a	None

The elements are listed in the order of their appearance in the text.

The Ḥijāz (61–4/680–4)

Most of Ibn Sa'd's material on Mukhtār is found in the biography of Ibn al-Ḥanafiyya. This includes a composite account of his actions in the Ḥijāz that combines the "Ibn al-Zubayr oath" (1.1a) and "return to Kūfa" narratives (1.2a).[105] The report begins by describing Mukhtār as an important supporter of Ibn al-Zubayr during the Umayyad siege of Mecca. This suggests that Mukhtār had previously taken the oath of allegiance. After detailing Ibn al-Zubayr's consolidation of power, Ibn Sa'd relates his version of the "return to Kūfa" narrative. Mukhtār approaches Ibn al-Ḥanafiyya and informs him of his desire to leave for Iraq. The 'Alid outwardly supports this course of action and asks him to take along 'Abd Allāh b. Kāmil al-Shakirī[106] (d. 67/686), to whom he reveals his doubts regarding Mukhtār's true intentions. Ibn al-Zubayr eventually grants Mukhtār permission to travel, conceding to the argument that he is more useful in Kūfa than in the Ḥijāz. This narrative differs from other accounts, in which Mukhtār departs without permission, motivated by a sense of personal betrayal. In the course of his journey, Mukhtār gathers additional information about the popular discontent in Kūfa.

Sedition (64–6/684–5)

Ibn Sa'd's description of Mukhtār's rebellion features a brief version of the "entry and recruitment" narrative (2.1a) that does not mention Ibn Ṣurad or any of the other Shī'ī leaders in Kūfa.[107] Instead, Mukhtār feigns support for the Zubayrid governor, Ibn Muṭī', while secretly mobilizing the Shī'a to seize control of the city. Ibn Sa'd briefly notes Ibn Muṭī''s departure to Baṣra prior to the revolt before circling back to the organization of the rebellion.[108] In this report, Mukhtār claims that Ibn al-Zubayr seized Mecca in the name of Ibn al-Ḥanafiyya but then turned on the 'Alid and began persecuting him. The betrayal prompted Ibn al-Ḥanafiyya to dispatch Mukhtār to Kūfa to procure the oath of allegiance on his behalf. Mukhtār then produces a document that purportedly confirms this story,

105 Ibn Sa'd, 5:72–3.

106 'Abd Allāh b. Kāmil al-Shakirī al-Hamdānī was one of Mukhtār's chief supporters, embodying his tribe's strong backing of the movement. He died with Aḥmar b. Shumayṭ in the first battle between Mukhtār and Muṣ'ab b. al-Zubayr. See al-Ṭabarī, 3:486 (for his death) and index (for his involvement with Mukhtār).

107 Ibn Sa'd, 5:73. 108 Ibid.

but instead of showing it to anyone, he only reads it aloud to close associates.

The next part of Ibn Sa'd's account features two narrative elements. The first is a standard version of the "Kūfan delegation" narrative (2.4a).[109] There is little that is distinctive in Ibn Sa'd's rendering of this episode. It culminates with Ibn al-Ḥanafiyya praising anyone who comes to the aid of the Prophet's family, a sentiment the Kūfans interpret as an endorsement of Mukhtār. The delegation's return to Kūfa is not described in detail. The second element is a one-meeting variant of the "Ibrāhīm b. al-Ashtar letter" narrative (2.5a).[110] In this report, Mukhtār produces a fabricated letter bearing the name of Ibn al-Ḥanafiyya which praises Ibn al-Ashtar's family as stalwart supporters of the Prophet's family. Its authenticity is then verified by a series of false witnesses.[111] Ibn al-Ashtar agrees to help with no hint of doubt or suspicion.

Rule (66–7/685–6)

Ibn Sa'd's portrayal of Mukhtār's rule is strongly influenced by its location within the biography of Ibn al-Ḥanafiyya. The text first documents the growing tension between Ibn al-Ḥanafiyya and Ibn al-Zubayr in the aftermath of Mukhtār's rebellion. It then notes Mukhtār's pursuit of those complicit in the murder of Ḥusayn without providing specific names. This is followed by a brief, one-battle version of the "Ibn Ziyād battle" narrative (3.2a), featuring Ibn al-Ashtar's departure at the head of a large army of 20,000 and his victory over Ibn Ziyād.[112] In this report, Ibn Sa'd focuses primarily on the reception of Ibn Ziyād's head in Mecca. 'Alī b. Ḥusayn and 'Abd Allāh b. 'Abbās are effusive in their praise of Mukhtār, whereas Ibn al-Ḥanafiyya maintains a cautious distance.

The second element within this segment is the "Ibn al-Ḥanafiyya siege" narrative (3.1a).[113] It begins in the typical manner with Ibn al-Ḥanafiyya's refusal to pledge allegiance to Ibn al-Zubayr absent the consensus of the larger Muslim community. This prompts Ibn al-Zubayr to blockade Ibn al-Ḥanafiyya, along with his family and companions, and to threaten them with fire. Ibn al-Ḥanafiyya dispatches

[109] Ibid. [110] Ibid., 5:73–4.

[111] These include Yazīd b. Anas, Aḥmar b. Shumayṭ, 'Abd Allāh b. Kāmil, and Abū 'Amra Kaysān.

[112] Ibn Sa'd, 5:74. [113] Ibid., 5:74–6.

Abū al-Ṭufayl 'Āmir b. Wāthila[114] (d. ca. 100/718) to Kūfa to appeal for help, and Mukhtār responds by sending a rescue party of 4,000 led by Abū 'Abd Allāh al-Jadalī.[115] The remainder of the account is an elaborate description of al-Jadalī's arrival in Mecca and the lifting of the siege. Ibn Sa'd's version of this episode is quite distinctive. He relates unique conversations that convey points also found in other sources.[116] Ibn al-Ḥanafiyya and Ibn 'Abbās are eventually allowed to leave Mecca. Ibn al-Zubayr only renews his demand for allegiance after Mukhtār's death.[117]

Interpretive Framework

Ibn Sa'd depicts Mukhtār through a propagandist interpretive framework, in which Mukhtār plays a secondary role in the rivalry between Ibn al-Zubayr and Ibn al-Ḥanafiyya. This emphasis likely results from Ibn Sa'd's placement of these narratives within Ibn al-Ḥanafiyya's biographical entry. Mukhtār's actions are one of the primary causes for tension between the 'Alids and the Zubayrids in Mecca. His early attempts at gaining Ibn al-Ḥanafiyya's approval for his planned revolt are met with only tepid support. Mukhtār seizes control of Kūfa by exploiting the Shī'a and fabricating a letter to Ibn al-Ashtar, backed by false testimony. There is little here to suggest a religious motivation. Mukhtār later kills Ibn Ziyād and rescues the family of the Prophet from a siege, earning him the appreciation of many important 'Alids including 'Alī b. Ḥusayn. Ibn al-Ḥanafiyya, however, continues to doubt his sincerity. Ibn Sa'd's interpretive framework is informed less by religious or tribal concerns than by familial rivalries over the caliphate. Mukhtār is a manipulative and opportunistic figure who exploits these tensions toward his own ends.

C *Akhbār al-dawla al-'Abbāsiyya (third/ninth century)*

The *Akhbār al-dawla al-'Abbāsiyya* focuses on Mukhtār's connections to Ibn al-Ḥanafiyya and other figures associated with the 'Abbāsid

[114] Abū al-Ṭufayl 'Āmir b. Wāthila b. 'Abd Allāh b. 'Amr was a staunch opponent of the Umayyads throughout his life and reportedly the last of the Prophet's Companions to die. See al-Ziriklī, 3:255–6; al-Mizzī, 14:79–82.

[115] Ibn al-Ḥanafiyya considers traveling to Kūfa himself, but Mukhtār (out of clear self-interest) rejects this idea as too dangerous.

[116] This is the case, for example, in Ibn al-Ḥanafiyya's command to not shed blood in the sanctuary at Mecca. Ibn Sa'd, 5:74–6.

[117] Ibid., 5:79.

revolution.[118] Specifically, it confirms the link between the early ʿAbbāsids and the Kaysānī Shīʿa, who considered Ibn al-Ḥanafiyya the rightful Imām after Ḥusayn.[119] The text includes only three narrative elements; the first (the "Ibn al-Ḥanafiyya siege" narrative) takes place in the period of Mukhtār's rule, while the second and third (a combination of the "Mukhtār's death" and "surrender and execution" narratives) focus on his fall.

The Ḥijāz	Sedition	Rule	Fall
None	None	3.1a	4.2a, 4.3b

The elements are listed in the order of their appearance in the text.

Rule (66–7/685–6)

The *Akhbār* offers a detailed version of the "Ibn al-Ḥanafiyya siege" narrative (3.1a) in a section that opens with the history of the conflict between Ibn al-Zubayr and the Prophet's family in Mecca.[120] As in other sources, Ibn al-Ḥanafiyya and (in this case) Ibn ʿAbbās refuse the oath of allegiance until the rest of the Muslim community has reached a consensus. Ibn al-Zubayr confines them to an area around Zamzam and threatens to burn them alive. In the face of this threat, Ibn al-Ḥanafiyya and Ibn ʿAbbās send four messengers to Kūfa to ask for help. The messengers are first instructed to approach Mukhtār. If he proves unresponsive, they are told to appeal directly to the Kūfan population. The messengers slip past the sleeping guards and deliver a letter to Mukhtār, which he reads aloud in public. The letter (which the *Akhbār* quotes at length) recalls previous instances when the Kūfans abandoned the family of the Prophet and later expressed regret.[121] Mukhtār adds that the "Mahdī" is in the position of a sheep awaiting slaughter, and swears an oath to remedy the situation. He immediately dispatches a series of small cavalry detachments and names Abū ʿAbd Allāh al-Jadalī the leader of the main rescue operation. Mukhtār also sends a large sum of money – 400,000 *dirhams* – together with a reply

[118] For background on the text itself, see Daniel, "Anonymous History."

[119] For an uncritical use of this source in the reconstruction of the ʿAbbāsid revolution, see Sharon's *Black Banners*. The best study of the Kaysānī movement remains al-Qāḍī's *al-Kaysāniyya*.

[120] For the first part of the text, see *Akhbār al-dawla*, 99–101.

[121] For this part of the text, see ibid., 101–4.

(likewise quoted at length) that promises continued support ("Shīʿī helpers to fight your enemies"[122]) and requests regular correspondence.[123]

The remainder of the narrative is a typical, albeit detailed, description of the confrontation between Ibn al-Ḥanafiyya and Ibn al-Zubayr.[124] The Kūfans enter Mecca, having replaced their weapons with pieces of wood, and find Ibn al-Ḥanafiyya and Ibn ʿAbbās in the sanctuary surrounded by kindling. The author admits that the threat of fire may have been intended only to intimidate the Prophet's family into submission. He notes, however, that the threat was backed by an oath to God, which speaks to its sincerity. The Kūfans greet Ibn al-Ḥanafiyya in the traditional Shīʿī manner ("Make our mothers, fathers, family, and children a sacrifice for you"). Despite the gravity of the situation, he prohibits bloodshed in the sanctuary. In the subsequent standoff, Ibn al-Zubayr reiterates his innocence in Ḥusayn's death and labels his opponents *al-khashabiyya al-saba'iyya.*[125] He also notes his side's numerical advantage and again demands capitulation under threat of violence. After three days, waves of Kūfan reinforcements begin to arrive in the city, shouting "Revenge for Ḥusayn." This clearly unsettles Ibn al-Zubayr, who then allows Ibn al-Ḥanafiyya to leave the sanctuary. The ʿAlid releases the Kūfans from any further orders,[126] and they remain at his side until Mukhtār's death.

A unique detail in the *Akhbār*'s "Ibn al-Ḥanafiyya siege" narrative centers on the Kūfan use of wooden weapons. The text offers two contradictory explanations for this measure. According to the first, Mukhtār ordered al-Jadalī to carry wooden weapons upon his entry into the city.[127] In a subsequent passage, however, Ibn al-Ḥanafiyya writes to al-Jadalī, expressing his aversion to the presence of metal weapons in the sanctuary.[128] This prompts al-Jadalī to replace them with wooden ones. Both reports are meant to explain Ibn al-Zubayr's reference to the Kūfans as the *khashabiyya.*[129]

122 Ibid., 103.

123 Ibn al-Zubayr is here addressed as Ibn al-Kāhiliyya on account of his Kāhilī maternal grandmother. See ibid.

124 For this part of the narrative, see ibid., 104–7.

125 The first term (*khashabiyya*) refers to their use of wooden weapons. For a more detailed explanation than the one offered in the next paragraph, see the relevant discussion in section D on al-Balādhurī. The second term (*saba'iyya*) is yet another derogatory label applied to the supporters of ʿAlī b. Abī Ṭālib. See Anthony, *The Caliph*, 280–4 (for the *khashabiyya*) and 241–311 (for a detailed examination of the *saba'iyya* in this period).

126 The text notes that Mukhtār had ordered them to kill Ibn al-Zubayr.

127 *Akhbār al-dawla*, 104. 128 Ibid., 106. 129 Ibid., 105.

Fall (67/687)

The second and third narrative elements preserved in the *Akhbār* are a composite version of the "Mukhtār's death" (4.2a) and "surrender and execution" (4.3b) narratives.[130] The author includes these accounts in a section that details the lineage of the important 'Abbāsid client Salama b. Bujayr[131] (d. ca. 98/716–17). The report notes that Bujayr b. 'Abd Allāh, Salama's father, was a close companion of Ibn al-Ḥanafiyya and a leading figure in Mukhtār's revolt. He was strongly committed to the pursuit of Ḥusayn's killers and remained with Mukhtār through the final siege in Kūfa. At this point, the author provides a familiar version of Mukhtār's final speech, in which he urges his companions to leave the fort and embrace death. After they refuse to do so, he predicts their eventual killing at the hands of their enemies.

The *Akhbār*'s version of the "surrender and execution" narrative (4.2b) quotes Bujayr echoing Mukhtār's advice that the men in the fort should charge the enemy and die in the field lest they face execution as captives. He then tries to grab his sword and fight alone, but his companions restrain him and offer their unconditional surrender. The fettered prisoners are brought before Muṣ'ab, and Bujayr makes the same passionate speech found in other sources, appealing to the unity of the Muslim community and mentioning previous examples of reconciliation. Muṣ'ab is moved by the appeal but still orders their execution under pressure from a number of Kūfan tribal leaders led by 'Abd al-Raḥmān b. Muḥammad b. al-Ash'ath[132] (d. 85/704).

Interpretive Framework

Mukhtār's importance in the *Akhbār* stems primarily from his link with figures associated with the 'Abbāsid revolution. Isolated narrative elements adhere to a propagandist interpretive framework designed to legitimize the 'Abbāsids. This is apparent in the "Ibn al-Ḥanafiyya siege" narrative, in which Ibn 'Abbās, the forebear of the 'Abbāsid caliphs, plays a leading role. He is not merely an advisor to Ibn al-Ḥanafiyya but one of the main targets

130 For the combined account, see ibid., 180–2.

131 Salama b. Bujayr was a member of the Banū Musliyya and a leading figure among the Kūfan Kaysānīs. He played a critical role in the purported transfer of leadership from Abū Hāshim b. Muḥammad b. al-Ḥanafiyya (d. 96/716–17) to the 'Abbāsids. For Salama, see Sharon, *Black Banners*, 133–8 and 146.

132 'Abd al-Raḥmān b. Muḥammad b. al-Ash'ath al-Kindī later led a rebellion of his own against al-Ḥajjāj and the Umayyads in 81/700–1. See al-Ziriklī, 3:323–4; *EI*², s.v. "Ibn al-Ash'ath" (L. Veccia Vaglieri).

of Ibn al-Zubayr's threats and persecution. The same dynamic informs the "Mukhtār's death" and "surrender and execution" narratives, which showcase Bujayr b. ʿAbd Allāh's revolutionary credentials and eloquence. They provide no explanation for Bujayr's curious absence from the skirmish that resulted in Mukhtār's death. Instead, they contend that he was later prevented from fighting by the cowardice of his companions.

The *Akhbār* is conspicuously devoid of other interpretive frameworks. Although the text utilizes religious language, repeatedly identifying the Shīʿa as a distinctive group, this is a secondary concern, decisively overshadowed by politics. Tribal dynamics are prominent only once near the end of the "surrender and execution" account. Finally, the scattering of these narratives throughout the text undermines any geographic or regional interpretive framework. The author is content with embellishing well-known narrative elements for the express purpose of buttressing ʿAbbāsid legitimacy.

D al-Balādhurī (d. 279/892): The Primary Narrative

In his prosopographical–genealogical work *Ansāb al-ashrāf*, al-Balādhurī offers a single cohesive narrative of Mukhtār's rebellion[133] followed by thirty-nine individual reports that either reinforce previously established details or introduce new ones.[134] The present analysis focuses exclusively on the main account.

The Ḥijāz	Sedition	Rule	Fall
1.1b, 1.2b	2.1a, 2.2a, 2.3a, 2.4a, 2.5b, 2.6c	3.2b, 3.6a, 3.8a. 3.7b. 3.5b, 3.3a, 3.4a, 3.1a	4.1b, 4.2a, 4.3b

The elements are listed in the order of their appearance in the text.

[133] The only exception is the "Ibn al-Ḥanafiyya siege" narrative, which al-Balādhurī places in a section on civil strife.

[134] Al-Balādhurī presents these reports, which come mostly from al-Madāʾinī, with full chains of transmission immediately after his primary narrative. It is possible that al-Balādhurī simply deemed these reports (which are largely sympathetic to Mukhtār) unreliable or untrustworthy. They are referenced in the footnotes in cases where they complicate al-Balādhurī's dominant narrative. See al-Balādhurī, 6:445–57.

The Ḥijāz (61–4/680–4)

Al-Balādhurī includes two narrative elements pertaining to Mukhtār's time in the Ḥijāz. The first is a detailed version of the "Ibn al-Zubayr oath" narrative (1.1b) that recounts two meetings separated by a few years.[135] In their initial encounter, Mukhtār notes the Kūfans' secret opposition to the Umayyads and proposes seizing Kūfa on Ibn al-Zubayr's behalf. Ibn al-Zubayr refuses the offer, condemning Kūfan duplicity as the behavior of "wicked slaves."[136] Note that this offer is not mentioned in any other source. Mukhtār eventually leaves for Ṭā'if, where he makes grandiose predictions about his future victory over the tyrants, predictions which Ibn al-Zubayr dismisses as soothsaying and hypocrisy. As in a number of other sources, Mukhtār returns to Mecca one year later and is met by 'Abbās b. Sahl, who attributes Ibn al-Zubayr's prior aloofness to political caution. In their second meeting, Mukhtār again pledges his support in exchange for the usual set of demands (i.e. influence and an appointment). When Ibn al-Zubayr responds by swearing to govern in accordance with the Qur'ān and the Sunna, Mukhtār rejects such an oath as fitting for only slaves and commoners. Ibn al-Zubayr eventually acquiesces to Mukhtār's conditions.

The second narrative element in this segment is a version of the "return to Kūfa" narrative (1.2b) that opens by acknowledging that Mukhtār fought bravely with Ibn al-Zubayr against the Umayyads, going so far as to quote a speech he made in rhymed prose at the height of the conflict.[137] As in other sources, Mukhtār gradually realizes that Ibn al-Zubayr will not appoint him to a meaningful post. He then questions unnamed visitors about the political climate in Kūfa, learns of the general turmoil, and resolves, in another rhymed prose passage, to leave for the city without informing Ibn al-Zubayr.[138]

[135] Ibid., 6:378–9. [136] Ibid., 6:378. [137] Ibid., 6:379.

[138] Al-Balādhurī preserves a different version of the "return to Kūfa" narrative in his supplementary reports, where Ibn al-Zubayr tasks Mukhtār with organizing the Kūfan Shī'a into an army to fight the Umayyads. Mukhtār then ingratiates himself with the Shī'a by feigning sadness for Ḥusayn and rallies them into a mob that ousts Ibn Muṭī' from power. This report is also mentioned by al-Mas'ūdī (discussed in section I), who claims that Mukhtār remained loyal to Ibn al-Zubayr through much of his rule. It differs dramatically from al-Balādhurī's featured version, which depicts a clear break between Mukhtār and Ibn al-Zubayr. See ibid., 6:453.

Sedition (64–6/684–5)

Al-Balādhurī's main account includes all six of the narrative elements from the segment pertaining to Mukhtār's rebellion. In the "entry and recruitment" narrative (2.1a), Mukhtār enters Kūfa in his typical lavish manner, reaches out to Kinda and Hamdān tribesmen with Shīʿī proclivities, and claims to represent Ibn al-Ḥanafiyya.[139] Specifically, he tries to recruit 'Abīda b. 'Amr al-Baddī[140] (d. after 67/687), who is identified as an ardent partisan (*shīʿa*) of 'Alī. This account is followed by three variants of a report in which Mukhtār seeks Ibn al-Ḥanafiyya's approval for his subversive activity in Kūfa. The 'Alid remains silent in the first version but endorses the uprising in the second and third versions.[141] The text then highlights Mukhtār's attempts to undermine the Tawwābūn movement through his disparagement of Ibn Ṣurad as an inexperienced leader intent on martyrdom.

The "Kūfan arrest" narrative (2.2a) starts with Ibn al-Zubayr's appointment of Ibrāhīm b. Muḥammad and 'Abd Allāh b. Yazīd as his agents in Kūfa.[142] They are approached by a group of tribal elites led by 'Umar b. Sa'd and Shabath b. Ribʿī, who characterize Mukhtār as a troublemaker.[143] He is then imprisoned and, as in other comparable versions of this narrative, issues a series of statements in rhymed prose that predict his future success. At the same time, he secretly writes a letter (quoted in full) to Ibn 'Umar, asking for his intercession. Ibrāhīm and 'Abd Allāh agree to release him on two conditions: (i) that he produce witnesses[144] to vouch for his conduct; and (ii) that he take a strong oath backed by onerous penalties. Mukhtār later reveals his intention to break the oath for the greater good and quickly resumes his machinations.

[139] Ibid., 6:379–80.

[140] Abū 'Amr 'Abīda (or 'Ubayda) b. 'Amr al-Baddī al-Kindī is mentioned only in a handful of sources. In addition to al-Balādhurī, al-Ṭabarī describes him as sympathetic to Ḥujr b. 'Adī (d. 52/672) (3:223) and as an early partisan of Mukhtār (3:405).

[141] The third report suggests that Ibn al-Ḥanafiyya initially favored the plan but that Mukhtār did not follow through on his promises. See al-Balādhurī, 6:380.

[142] Ibid., 6:380–2.

[143] The tribal leaders note that "Sulaymān b. Ṣurad wants to fight your enemies while Mukhtār wishes to rise up against you in your city and sabotage you" (ibid., 6:481).

[144] The text lists the names of thirteen witnesses from the Kūfan Shīʿa, most of whom later backed Mukhtār's rebellion. Ibid., 6:381–2.

At the start of al-Balādhurī's "feigned sickness" narrative (2.3a), 'Abd Allāh b. Muṭī' arrives in Kūfa as the new Zubayrid governor. In his initial address, he foolishly promises to govern in accordance with the precedents of 'Umar and 'Uthmān. This immediately stirs discontent among the Kūfans. In the face of this opposition, Ibn Muṭī' walks back his initial statement and instead agrees to adhere to the example of 'Alī. The report then documents the new governor's attempts at arresting Mukhtār. There is no explicit mention of elite involvement, but their influence is strongly implied. Mukhtār avoids capture by feigning sickness.

The fourth element in this segment is a condensed version of the "Kūfan delegation" narrative (2.4a) in which a group of the Shī'a travel to Mecca to verify Mukhtār's association with Ibn al-Ḥanafiyya. The report explicitly names the members of the delegation, including 'Abd al-Raḥmān b. Shurayḥ al-Shibāmī[145] (d. 67/687) and Si'r b. Abī Si'r al-Ḥanafī[146] (d. after 66/686). As in most sources, Ibn al-Ḥanafiyya vaguely praises those who act in God's name, which the Kūfans interpret as an endorsement of Mukhtār. When the men return to Kūfa, a relieved Mukhtār has them publicly testify to the truth of his claims. It is notable that the Kūfan Shī'a here refer to Ibn al-Ḥanafiyya as the "Mahdī."

The text now transitions into a two-meeting variant of the "Ibrāhīm b. al-Ashtar letter" narrative (2.5b).[147] This report is typical. The Shī'a attempt to recruit Ibn al-Ashtar, who is receptive to their message but demands leadership of the movement (the first visit). Some days later, Mukhtār visits Ibn al-Ashtar (the second visit) with a letter allegedly written by Ibn al-Ḥanafiyya, which asks for his support and promises him control of the areas that he conquers. As in most other sources, Ibn al-Ashtar suspects the provenance of the letter because of Ibn al-Ḥanafiyya's use of the term "Mahdī." In order to allay these doubts, a number of Shī'ī leaders, including Yazīd b. Anas, Aḥmar b. Shumayṭ, and 'Abd Allāh b. Kāmil, attest to its authenticity.[148]

145 'Abd al-Raḥmān b. Shurayḥ al-Shibāmī was in charge of Mukhtār's treasury and was likely killed in battle against Mu'ṣab b. al-Zubayr. See al-Ṭabarī, 3:487.

146 Si'r b. Abī Si'r appears in the sources as one of Mukhtār's closest supporters. In addition to his participation in the delegation, he is placed third in the line of succession by Yazīd b. Anas (al-Ṭabarī, 3:452), helps quell the uprising at Jabbānat al-Sabī' (ibid., 3:462), and provides information about Ḥusayn's killers (ibid., 3:463). The sources do not specify his death date.

147 Al-Balādhurī, 6:385–6.

148 Note that this account is narrated from the perspective of al-Sha'bī (for whom see n. 48).

At this point, al-Balādhurī provides multiple reports to explain Mukhtār's popular appeal.[149] In one representative example, al-Mughīra b. Shuʿba[150] (d. 50/670) observes that non-Arabs are easily swayed by calls in the name of the Prophet's family.[151] The point here is clear: Mukhtār's power is predicated on his ability to manipulate the sympathies of non-Arabs.

These accounts build to a long, multiple-battle variant of the "rebellion" narrative (2.6c).[152] The details of the revolt are by now familiar. Iyās b. Muḍārib receives reports of the unrest and informs Ibn Muṭīʿ, who instructs his supporters to prevent the rebels from mustering their forces. The governor's support consists mainly of tribal elites, including, most prominently, Shamir b. Dhī al-Jawshan and Shabath b. Ribʿī. The catalyst for the rebellion is a street skirmish in which Ibn al-Ashtar grabs a long spear from a fellow tribesman and impales Iyās. The rebels gradually converge in the center of town. Ahead of the decisive battle, Ibn al-Ashtar urges his men to ignore the names and lineages of their opponents.[153] Ibn Muṭīʿ is defeated and retreats to the fort with his few remaining, mostly tribal elite, supporters. As in most sources, he is unwilling to surrender for fear of disappointing Ibn al-Zubayr. Shabath then suggests that he flee under the cover of night. Ibn Muṭīʿ gives a final speech in which he praises his loyalists and then slips away to the complex of Abū Mūsā al-Ashʿarī. His men secure a safe-conduct from Ibn al-Ashtar in exchange for taking the oath of allegiance for Mukhtār. At the end of the episode, Mukhtār allows Ibn Muṭīʿ to depart the city unharmed.[154]

[149] Al-Balādhurī, 6:386–7.

[150] Al-Mughīra b. Shuʿba b. Abī ʿĀmir al-Thaqafī was a Companion of the Prophet known for his shrewd political skills. He served multiple caliphs, including Muʿāwiya (r. 41–60/661–80), who appointed him to the governorship of Kūfa in 41/661. See Ibn Saʿd, 6:97–8; al-Ziriklī, 7:276–7; *EI*[2], s.v. "Mughīra b. Shuʿba" (H. Lammens).

[151] Al-Balādhurī, 6:387. [152] Ibid., 6:389–95.

[153] Al-Balādhurī does not mention Shabath b. Ribʿī's execution of non-Arab prisoners or his anger at complaints over the Qurʾānic recitation in the communal prayer.

[154] Al-Balādhurī's supplementary reports provide an alternate account of Mukhtār's rebellion. In one pertinent account (4:454), Mukhtār writes to Ibn al-Zubayr and claims that he expelled Ibn Muṭīʿ only because of his incompetence. When Ibn al-Zubayr rejects this explanation, Mukhtār offers his support to Zayn al-ʿĀbidīn (who publicly refuses it) and to Ibn al-Ḥanafiyya (who stays silent). Incidentally, this is al-Masʿūdī's primary account (further discussed in section I).

Rule (66–7/685–6)

Al-Balādhurī's portrayal of Mukhtār's rule includes variants of all eight narrative elements. The early part of this period is generally cast in a positive light.[155] The section begins with Mukhtār's initial speech to the Kūfans, followed by several reports of revenge killings carried out in the name of Ḥusayn.[156] In these accounts, al-Balādhurī refers to Mukhtār's supporters as the "Shī'a"[157] and identifies Abū 'Amra Kaysān as the head of his personal guard (*ḥars*) and the leader of the *kaysāniyya*.[158]

The first narrative element in this segment is a hybrid version of the "Ibn Ziyād battle/elite uprising" narrative (3.2b).[159] It opens with Mukhtār sending Yazīd b. Anas against an Umayyad army led by Ibn Ziyād. In contrast to other sources, al-Balādhurī does not mention Yazīd's selection of his men. The initial battle takes place near Mawṣil and follows the standard chronology as Yazīd's men (referred to as the *mukhtāriyya*) defeat two detachments of Ibn Ziyād's larger force. This is followed by a brief notice of Yazīd's death and a description of his army's reluctance to continue fighting. In Kūfa, meanwhile, Mukhtār appoints Ibn al-Ashtar to take Yazīd's place at the head of the military campaign.

Prior to the "elite uprising" narrative, al-Balādhurī offers a number of seemingly unrelated reports. The first of these posits three possible explanations for the term *khashabiyya*, which is applied to Mukhtār and his men:[160] (i) their general preference for wooden weapons; (ii) their seizure of wood from the pile gathered by Ibn al-Zubayr to burn Ibn al-Ḥanafiyya; and (iii) their aversion to entering the sanctuary in Mecca with metal weapons. A second report describes Yazīd b. Anas's decision to execute all his Syrian prisoners. At one point, close to death, he loses the capacity to speak and relates his orders by movements of his finger.[161]

Al-Balādhurī then cites a long version of the "elite uprising" narrative from the perspective of tribal elites (i.e. Shabath b. Rib'ī and Shamir b. Dhī al-Jawshan), who accuse Mukhtār of soothsaying.[162] The account includes complicated details of strategic movements but

155 Ibid., 6:395. 156 Ibid., 6:394–5. 157 Ibid., 6:394. 158 Ibid., 6:395.
159 Ibid., 6:396–7.
160 Ibid., 6:397. For this term, see also n. 125 and the related discussion in the main text.
161 Ibid. 162 Ibid., 6:398–401.

makes no mention of negotiations between the two sides. The tribal leaders claim that Mukhtār intends to kill all his opponents and deride his men as outsiders ("the Banū Yamān"). Meanwhile, Ibn al-Ashtar rushes back to Kūfa and easily defeats a small force led by Shabath b. Rib'ī. The decisive battle takes place at Jabbānat al-Sabī', where Mukhtār directs a contingent of tribesmen from the Banū Shibām to a path that allows them to surprise the enemy from behind. The descriptions of the battle chiefly center on tribal dynamics.

Al-Balādhurī now quotes a series of reports that cast Mukhtār as a liar who systematically deceived his followers (the *mukhtāriyya*). In one account, he claims that the cushions to his left and right are occupied by angels (Jibrā'īl and Mīkā'īl).[163] In another, Nu'mān b. Ṣuhbān al-Rāsibī[164] (d. 66/686) travels to Kūfa to join Mukhtār but is so disturbed by his lies that he participates in the elite uprising instead.[165] This is followed by a brief variant of the "Surāqa's angels" narrative (3.6a) in which the poet falsely testifies that angels fought alongside Mukhtār at Jabbānat al-Sabī' before he flees to Baṣra.[166] Mukhtār is also condemned for his killing of anyone even loosely associated with the murder of Ḥusayn.[167] The section ends with poems that lampoon Mukhtār and examples of his rhymed prose that are meant to substantiate the accusations of soothsaying.[168]

In the aftermath of the rebellion at Jabbānat al-Sabī', al-Balādhurī offers a series of revenge accounts. It is noteworthy that he includes more of these reports than any other writer.[169] They are also concentrated at this point in the text, whereas other sources scatter such reports throughout their depiction of Mukhtār's rule. For comparative purposes, the two accounts that are of primary interest here involve 'Umar b. Sa'd and Shamir b. Dhī al-Jawshan.

Al-Balādhurī's version of the "'Umar b. Sa'd revenge" narrative (3.8a) opens with Ibn al-Ḥanafiyya in Medina criticizing Mukhtār for his refusal to act against the leader of the army that massacred Ḥusayn and his family – that is, 'Umar b. Sa'd.[170] It then shifts to Kūfa, where

[163] Ibid., 6:400.
[164] For al-Nu'mān b. Ṣuhbān, see Fishbein, *Victory of the Marwanids*, 22, n. 85; al-Tustarī, 10:388.
[165] Al-Balādhurī, 6:400–1. [166] Ibid., 6:401. [167] Ibid.
[168] For the poems, see ibid., 6:401–2. For the rhymed prose, see ibid., 6:402–5.
[169] Ibid., 6:405–11. [170] Ibid., 6:405–6.

Mukhtār publicly vows to kill a figure of great importance the next day. Al-Haytham b. al-Aswad al-Nakhaʿī[171] (d. ca. 100/718) ascertains that ʿUmar is the target of this threat and sends his son al-ʿUryān to warn him of the impending danger. ʿUmar is unconcerned, noting that Mukhtār has given him a safe-conduct (*amān*) that protects him so long as he refrains from "indecent acts." The next day Mukhtār orders Kaysān to bring him ʿUmar's head. As in most reports, ʿUmar's death is followed by that of his son. Both heads are then sent to Ibn al-Ḥanafiyya in Mecca. Mukhtar justifies his violation of the safe-conduct by equating the "indecent acts" clause with going to the bathroom.[172]

In al-Balādhurī's rendering of the "Shamir revenge" narrative (3.7b), Mukhtār tasks a slave named Zirbiyya to pursue Shamir, who has fled the city after the failure of the elite uprising.[173] Shamir kills the slave and then dispatches a messenger to Muṣʿab b. al-Zubayr, presumably to request asylum in Baṣra. In contrast to most other sources, al-Balādhurī's account does not specify the messenger's ethnic or tribal background.[174] The messenger is captured before he reaches the city and forced to reveal Shamir's location. Mukhtār now sends a full detachment of cavalry, who kill Shamir and feed his body to the dogs. This report lacks the colorful exchanges and depth of detail found in many other reports.

The next element in this section is the coerced version of the "ʿAlī's chair" narrative (3.5b), in which Mukhtār forces the family of Jaʿda b. Hubayra to surrender a chair that is (falsely) associated with ʿAlī.[175] The account documents the chair's decoration and names the figures designated as its guardians. It also compares the chair with the Ark of the Covenant, noting that Mukhtār's followers would circumambulate it and seek God's aid through it. The skeptical tenor of this report casts these men as misguided at best and delusional at worst.

171 Abū al-ʿUryān al-Haytham b. al-Aswad al-Nakhaʿī al-Madhḥijī was a poet and a reputable transmitter who is described in the sources as a partisan of the Umayyads. See Ibn Saʿd, 6:240; al-Mizzī, 30:362–4; al-Ziriklī, 8:103.

172 As in other versions of this narrative, he observes that the deaths of ʿUmar and his son do not make up for the killing of Ḥusayn and his son.

173 Al-Balādhurī, 6:407.

174 The term used for messenger here is *fayj*, which Edward Lane traces back to Persian, suggesting the messenger's likely non-Arab origins. See Lane, *Arabic–English Lexicon*, 5:2469.

175 Al-Balādhurī, 6:413–14.

At this point, al-Balādhurī presents a composite version of the "Ḥijāzī expansion" (3.3a) and "Baṣran expansion" (3.4a) narratives. In the first part, Ibn al-Zubayr responds to Mukhtār's overtures at reconciliation by appointing 'Umar b. 'Abd al-Raḥmān b. al-Ḥārith[176] (d. after 66/685) as the new governor of Kūfa.[177] On his way to the city, however, 'Umar is intercepted by a squad of Kūfan cavalry led by Zā'ida b. Qudāma al-Thaqafī, who offers him a bribe while simultaneously threatening him. At this point, al-Balādhurī presents the entirety of the "Baṣran expansion" narrative, in which Mukhtār sends al-Muthannā b. al-Mukharriba al-'Abdī[178] (d. after 67/686) to organize the "Shī'a" in Baṣra.[179] The mission fails due to a series of tribal miscalculations. This is followed by the second part of the "Ḥijāzī expansion" narrative, which culminates in the massacre of a small Kūfan army.[180] The account displays a few notable anomalies. First, there is no mention of 'Abbās b. Sahl distracting the hungry troops of Shuraḥbīl b. Wars[181] (d. 66/686) with food. 'Abbās simply waits until they are unprepared before launching a full-scale attack. Second, the fate of many of Shuraḥbīl's men who surrender under an offer of safe-conduct is left unclear. The report concludes with Ibn al-Ḥanafiyya's professing his neutrality to an enraged Mukhtār.

It is only after this long digression that al-Balādhurī finally returns to the second part of the "Ibn Ziyād battle/elite uprising" narrative.[182] In the wake of the victory at Jabbānat al-Sabī', Ibn al-Ashtar is again tapped to lead a military campaign against Ibn Ziyād. On his march toward Syria, Ibn al-Ashtar observes "Mukhtār's Shī'a" congregating around the chair and condemns them through a comparison with the Banū Isrā'īl.[183] The

176 'Umar b. 'Abd al-Raḥmān b. al-Ḥārith al-Makhzūmī was a highly reputable Medinan transmitter who, after this incident, joined Ibn Muṭī' in Baṣra. See al-Mizzī, 21:424–5; al-Ṭabarī, 3:468 and 3:470.

177 Ibid., 6:415–16.

178 Al-Muthannā b. al-Mukharriba was a partisan of 'Alī who took part in the Tawwābūn movement. Specifically, he led a group of Baṣrans who reached the Battle of 'Ayn Warda (65/685) after Ibn Ṣurad had already been killed. He then returned to Baṣra when the Tawwābūn began to bicker over leadership, and later took the oath of allegiance to Mukhtār in Kūfa. He is absent from reports of Mukhtār's final battle and subsequent death. See al-Ziriklī, 5:286.

179 Al-Balādhurī, 6:416–18.

180 Ibid., 6:419–21.

181 Shuraḥbīl b. Wars is primarily mentioned in connection with this episode. See al-Ziriklī, 3:159–60; al-Ṭabarī, 3:471–2.

182 Al-Balādhurī, 6:423–7.

183 Specifically, he draws a parallel between Shī'ī reverence for the chair and the Banū Isrā'īl's treatment of the Ark of the Covenant.

remainder of the narrative follows a familiar pattern. The two armies camp near the Khāzir River. ʿUmayr b. al-Ḥubāb al-Sulamī offers to defect, citing tribal animosities in the wake of Marj Rāhiṭ, and Ibn al-Ashtar tests his sincerity by asking for tactical advice. Before the battle, the two sides engage in a series of exchanges, during which the Shīʿa in Ibn al-Ashtar's army reference Karbalāʾ and the denial of water to Ḥusayn b. ʿAlī and his supporters.[184] In the course of the fighting, Ibn al-Ashtar leads the decisive charge that breaks the enemy lines. He also kills Ibn Ziyād, whose body is later identified by its distinctive scent (musk).[185]

Al-Balādhurī's "Ibn al-Ḥanafiyya siege" narrative (3.1a) is not included in his biographical entry on Mukhtār. Instead, it is preserved in a later section that documents the complicated relationship between Ibn al-Ḥanafiyya, Ibn al-Zubayr, and ʿAbd al-Malik b. Marwān[186] (r. 65–86/685–705).[187] As in other sources, Ibn al-Ḥanafiyya refuses to take the oath of allegiance, which prompts Ibn al-Zubayr to blockade and threaten him. Ibn al-Ḥanafiyya then sends four messengers to Kūfa with letters (quoted in full) asking for help. Mukhtār reads the letters in public, summons the people to support the "Mahdī," and sends detachments of cavalry led by Abū ʿAbd Allāh al-Jadalī. The Kūfans, who number 150, enter Mecca chanting "Revenge for Ḥusayn," but Ibn al-Ḥanafiyya forbids them to fight. In the resulting standoff, Ibn al-Zubayr reiterates his innocence in Ḥusayn's death and labels the Kūfans the *khashabiyya* (again) due to their wooden weapons.[188] The arrival of a larger Kūfan force three days later forces Ibn al-Zubayr to back down. He allows Ibn al-Ḥanafiyya to withdraw to a more secure location. The report ends by noting that many of these Kūfan cavalrymen fought *against* Mukhtār at Jabbānat al-Sabīʿ.

Fall (67/687)

Al-Balādhurī depicts Mukhtār's fall from power through a two-battle variant of the "final defeat" narrative (4.1b) in which Kūfan tribal elites

184 Al-Balādhurī, 6:425.

185 There is an anecdote at the end of the account on the authority of al-Shaʿbī in which Mukhtār allegedly predicts the Kūfan victory in vague terms. This seems to convince many people of his special knowledge, but al-Shaʿbī notes its lack of specificity. Ibid., 6:426.

186 *EI*[2], s.v. "ʿAbd al-Malik b. Marwān" (H. A. R. Gibb); Robinson, *ʿAbd al-Malik*.

187 Al-Balādhurī, 3:474–9.

188 See n. 125 and n. 160 and the related discussion in the main text.

play a pivotal role.[189] The account opens with a disheveled Shabath b. Ribʿī riding a mule through Baṣra and beseeching the people for help. As in other, similar reports, Muṣʿab sends Muḥammad b. al-Ashʿath to recall al-Muhallab b. Abī Ṣufra from the East, where he is leading a campaign against the Khawārij. Ibn al-Ashʿath explains the urgency of the situation, noting the plight of "our women and children" and highlighting Mukhtār's persecution of tribal leaders.[190] When al-Muhallab arrives in Baṣra, Muṣʿab mobilizes his forces and marches against Mukhtār. He also sends ʿAbd al-Raḥmān b. Mikhnaf ahead to covertly organize the Kūfan opposition.

In Kūfa, meanwhile, Mukhtār gives a speech, praising his supporters as "the Shīʿa of the messenger of God" and attributing the impending conflict to renegade Kūfan tribal leaders. The remainder of the narrative follows a standard form. Mukhtār delegates command of the army (including a contingent of non-Arabs led by Kaysān) to Aḥmar b. Shumayṭ.[191] In the ensuing battle, the Baṣrans are victorious, and both Ibn Shumayṭ and Ibn Kāmil are killed. Al-Balādhurī notes the particular brutality of the Kūfan cavalry fighting alongside Muṣʿab.[192] The Baṣrans then try to reach Kūfa by boat, but Mukhtār cuts off the flow of water, setting up a final confrontation at Ḥarūrā'. The Kūfans are decisively defeated in this second battle, forcing Mukhtār and his men to fall back to the central fort in Kūfa.

Al-Balādhurī intersperses the battle narrative with small vignettes that attack Mukhtār's credibility.[193] These include a quotation from a non-Arab (translated from the Persian) who accuses Mukhtār of lying and a report in which Mukhtār gives Ibn Shumayṭ a relic that he falsely claims will guarantee victory. Mukhtār later attributes the Baṣran triumph to the doctrine of *badā'*.[194] These examples unequivocally depict Mukhtār as a manipulative fraud.

189 Al-Balādhurī, 6:427–32 and 6:436–9. 190 Ibid., 6:428.

191 Al-Balādhurī later cites an alternative narrative of this first battle in which Mukhtār instigates the conflict by sending a large army of 40,000 under the command of Ibn Shumayṭ to conquer Baṣra. The two sides meet at Madhār, but the battle is not described in any detail. See ibid., 4:454–5.

192 The Baṣrans are equally brutal toward Mukhtār's men. Muʿāwiya b. Qurra b. Iyās al-Muzanī (d. 113/731), for example, deems the killing of Mukhtār's men more permissible than that of Turks and Daylamites. For this incident, see al-Balādhurī, 6:431; al-Ṭabarī, 3:485. For Muʿāwiya b. Qurra, see Ibn Saʿd, 7:165; al-Mizzī, 28:210–17.

193 Al-Balādhurī, 6:31–2.

194 For the concept of *badā'*, see n. 98 in this chapter.

Al-Balādhurī begins his "Mukhtār's death" narrative (4.2a) with a detailed description of the siege of the fort.[195] As material conditions deteriorate, Mukhtār urges his companions to join him in a final desperate charge. This compels some of his followers (most prominently 'Abd Allāh b. Ja'da) to abandon him, while others ask for an explanation for the apparently hopeless situation. When al-Sā'ib b. Mālik al-Ash'arī, for example, expresses his confusion about the turn of events, Mukhtār mocks him for his stupidity and confesses his political and material motivations. He also predicts that those who surrender will be slaughtered like sheep by their opponents as a means of exacting blood revenge. Mukhtār then leads a small group of his men – twenty-nine in total – into battle, where he is killed.

The final narrative element in this segment is a variant of the "surrender and execution" narrative (4.3b).[196] In al-Balādhurī's version, the remaining men in the fort surrender with no guarantee of safe-conduct. When they are brought before Muṣ'ab, the text quotes the standard arguments about mercy and reconciliation.[197] As in other sources, Muṣ'ab is inclined to forgive them, but the Kūfan tribal leaders demand retribution. At one point, he considers killing only the non-Arabs, but this is rejected as patently unjust. He eventually orders the execution of all 6,000 prisoners. Al-Balādhurī condemns this decision in numerous reports that counsel forgiveness.

Interpretive Framework

The main interpretive framework in al-Balādhurī's primary account deftly combines a focus on tribe and ethnicity with condemnation of the movement's religious, Shī'ī, character. Mukhtār is depicted as a shrewd opportunist who garners support through Shī'ī religious discourse while remaining invested in tribal hierarchy.

Al-Balādhurī's emphasis on a broad tribal/ethnic framework permeates virtually every narrative element. The main actors are tribal units motivated by parochial concerns and self-interest. A tribal awareness is projected directly onto Mukhtār, who regularly composes rhymed prose – an echo of pre-Islamic soothsaying – to predict his grand future. He is also keenly attuned to the importance of tribal dynamics in his

[195] Al-Balādhurī, 6:439–41. [196] Ibid., 6:441–3.

[197] These are usually ascribed to Bujayr b. 'Abd Allāh (see section C on the *Akhbār al-dawla al-'Abbāsiyya*), but al-Balādhurī does not name a specific speaker.

recruitment of influential groups (the Kinda) and individuals (Ibn al-Ashtar). Al-Balādhurī repeatedly frames Mukhtār's sense of self-importance in a tribal context. Thus, Mukhtār rejects the simple oath of allegiance to Ibn al-Zubayr as appropriate only for slaves and the masses. Tribalism also informs Mukhtār's conflicts with elites angered by his attempts to undercut their power and influence. These efforts precipitate both the uprising at Jabbānat al-Sabīʿ and Mukhtār's conflict with Muṣʿab b. al-Zubayr. The tension culminates in the final battle where Kūfan tribal leaders justify their brutality against Mukhtār's men by characterizing them as "worse than Turks and Daylamites."[198]

A second interpretive framework embedded in al-Balādhurī's account centers on Mukhtār's pragmatic manipulation of religion. Initially, he recites large chunks of rhymed prose that convey his desire for political power and revenge but are devoid of any religious imagery. He later violates his oath of allegiance to Ibn al-Zubayr and flees to Kūfa in search of power. In Kūfa, Mukhtār works relentlessly to undermine Ibn Ṣurad and the Tawwābūn. According to al-Balādhurī, he repeatedly manipulates gullible non-Arabs through calls to avenge the Prophet's family. He even unabashedly forges a letter from Ibn al-Ḥanafiyya to win the support of Ibn al-Ashtar. Once in control, Mukhtār routinely utilizes religious rhetoric to maintain his hold on the city. He goes so far as to claim knowledge of the future and the ability to communicate with angels. These exaggerations result in the defection of many of his early Shīʿī supporters, such as Rifāʿa b. al-Shaddād[199] (d. 65/685). Al-Balādhurī also highlights the discrepancy between Mukhtār's rhetoric of revenge against Ḥusayn's murderers and his actions as ruler. Shamir b. Dhī Jawshan is not pursued until after the battle at Jabbānat al-Sabīʿ, and ʿUmar b. Saʿd is killed only at the prodding of Ibn al-Ḥanafiyya. In order to placate his Shīʿī followers, Mukhtār demands that the family of Jaʿda b. Hubayra surrender ʿAlī's chair. He also forces Surāqa to testify in public about the presence of angels among his troops. Ahead of the initial battle with the Baṣrans, Mukhtār even produces an object that he

[198] Al-Balādhurī, 6:429–31.

[199] Rifāʿa b. Shaddād al-Bajalī was a Shīʿī partisan who first participated in the Tawwābūn movement and then backed Mukhtār. He eventually grew suspicious of Mukhtār and fought against him at Jabbānat al-Sabīʿ before changing sides in the course of the battle after hearing a slogan sympathetic to ʿUthmān. See al-Tustarī, 4:378–9; al-Ziriklī, 3:29.

promises will protect Ibn Shumayṭ from death. These are all manipulative uses of religion, a fact that he explicitly admits to al-Sā'ib during the final siege, when he equates his political ambitions with those of his rivals.

Finally, it is worth noting that al-Balādhurī distinguishes between Mukhtār's core supporters and the larger Kūfan Shī'ī community. As mentioned in the previous paragraph, al-Balādhurī identifies a number of Shī'a who condemned Mukhtār and even fought him on the battlefield. The terms most often associated with Mukhtār's Shī'ī supporters are *khashabiyya*, *mukhtāriyya* and *kaysāniyya*. The first of these is explicitly linked to the use of wooden weapons, while the second applies to a contingent of Mukhtār's army that held particularly eccentric beliefs. The final term, *kaysāniyya*, is associated with the leader of Mukhtār's personal guard, Abū 'Amra Kaysān, and seems to specify non-Arabs. These words are not synonyms for "Shī'a," which al-Balādhurī reserves for partisans of the family of the Prophet. As a result, the religious connotations of Mukhtār's movement are eclipsed by the tensions between Arab tribal elites and the non-Arab population. Mukhtār is thus presented as an ambitious man with an astute understanding of both demographic changes and the utility of religion in exploiting those changes.

E Pseudo-Ibn Qutayba (third/ninth century)

Al-Imāma wa-l-siyāsa is a chronographical text dubiously ascribed to Ibn Qutayba; I will refer to the author as Pseudo-Ibn Qutayba. The work includes a distinctive set of reports covering some parts of Mukhtār's rebellion. Specifically, it preserves five narrative elements spread over three core segments. They do not occur in the proper sequence.

The Ḥijāz	Sedition	Rule	Fall
1.2a	None	3.8a, 3.2a	4.1a, 4.3b

The elements are listed in the order of their appearance in the text.

The Ḥijāz (61–4/680–4)

Pseudo-Ibn Qutayba offers a very brief version of the "return to Kūfa" narrative (1.2a) in the course of a section covering political changes in the city.[200] Following the death of Yazīd I b. Muʿāwiya in Damascus, Ibn al-Zubayr claims the caliphate and names Yazīd b. Ziyād[201] (d. ?) as his governor over Iraq. He then replaces Yazīd with Ibn Muṭīʿ before formally appointing Mukhtār to govern the region. Subsequent reports affirm Mukhtār's loyalty to Ibn al-Zubayr, with no indication of any tension between the two men.

Rule (66–7/685–6)

Pseudo-Ibn Qutayba's main discussion of Mukhtār takes the form of a distinctive version of the "ʿUmar b. Saʿd revenge" narrative (3.8a).[202] In this account, Mukhtār sends two messages to Mecca, the first addressed to Ibn al-Zubayr and the second intended for Ibn al-Ḥanafiyya. In the latter, Mukhtār greets Ibn al-Ḥanafiyya as the "Mahdī" and expresses his love for the family of the Prophet. Ibn al-Ḥanafiyya, however, criticizes him for his continued association with ʿUmar b. Saʿd, the man he holds responsible for Ḥusayn's murder.[203] Mukhtār then commands Kaysān, the head of his personal guard (*ḥars*), to hire mourners to lament loudly for Ḥusayn outside ʿUmar's home. Disturbed by the clamor, ʿUmar sends his son Ḥafṣ to request their removal. Mukhtār now discreetly orders Kaysān to kill ʿUmar. Ḥafṣ, meanwhile, remains at court, unaware of these developments, until he is presented with his father's head and then summarily executed.

Pseudo-Ibn Qutayba's version of the "Ibn Ziyād battle/elite uprising" narrative (3.2a) begins suddenly with ʿAbd al-Malik b. Marwān dispatching an army led by Ibn Ziyād toward Iraq.[204] In his role as the Zubayrid governor of Kūfa, Mukhtār gathers his own forces and meets Ibn Ziyād near the Khāzir River.[205] The report does not mention either Yazīd b. Anas or Ibn al-Ashtar, suggesting instead that Mukhtār personally commanded his men. The battle ends in a Kūfan victory with reports of heavy Umayyad casualties, including, most prominently, Ibn Ziyād. The text takes a special interest in the deaths of those who pillaged Medina after the Battle of Ḥarra (5/627).

200 Pseudo-Ibn Qutayba, 2:31. This narrative element is placed between the "ʿUmar b. Saʿd revenge" narrative and the "Ibn Ziyād battle/elite uprising" narrative.

201 The name Yazīd b. Ziyād is certainly a mistake. In every other source, ʿAbd Allāh b. Yazīd and Ibrāhīm b. Muḥammad are the initial Zubayrid governors of Kūfa, followed by Ibn Muṭīʿ.

202 Pseudo-Ibn Qutayba, 2:30–1. 203 Ibid., 2:30. 204 Ibid., 2:31.

205 The published edition incorrectly refers to the location as the "Jāzir" river.

Fall (67/687)

According to Pseudo-Ibn Qutayba, Muṣʿab b. al-Zubayr is appointed the new Zubayrid governor of Baṣra and Kūfa after Ibn Ziyād's death. It is only at this point that Mukhtār renounces his allegiance to Ibn al-Zubayr, summons people to the family of the Prophet, and claims to represent Ibn al-Ḥanafiyya. The text then offers a composite version of two narrative elements: the "final defeat" narrative (4.1a) and the "surrender and execution" narrative (4.3b).[206] When Ibn al-Zubayr learns of Mukhtār's betrayal, he orders Muṣʿab to march on Kūfa immediately. The subsequent battle lasts for three days and culminates in Mukhtār's death and Muṣʿab's execution of 8,000 prisoners. Muṣʿab then travels to Mecca and asks his brother to reward those tribal leaders who fought with him against Mukhtār.[207] Ibn al-Zubayr refuses, disparaging them as "slaves" and comparing them unfavorably to the Syrians.[208] This slight later prompts the Kūfans to back ʿAbd al-Malik and the Umayyads against the Zubayrids.

Interpretive Framework

Pseudo-Ibn Qutayba's interpretive framework is shaped by regional caliphal politics and is devoid of religious sentiments. Mukhtār is a typical provincial governor appointed by the caliph (Ibn al-Zubayr), who carries out his duties until his dismissal from power forces him to seek another source of authority, namely, the charisma vested in Ibn al-Ḥanafiyya and the Prophet's family. This political interpretation does not preclude Mukhtār's potential Shīʿī sympathies. Prior to his disavowal of Ibn al-Zubayr, Mukhtār expresses his love of the family of the Prophet to Ibn al-Ḥanafiyya, to whom he refers as the "Mahdī." He also executes ʿUmar b. Saʿd at the instigation of Ibn al-Ḥanafiyya for his complicity in the killing of Ḥusayn. These actions suggest a sincerity of religious conviction that is nonetheless subordinate to political concerns. Overall, Mukhtār is a minor character in a narrative about the conflict between the Zubayrids and the Umayyads. This explains the elision and simplification of multiple narrative elements that are marginal to the larger struggle for control of the caliphate.

[206] Pseudo-Ibn Qutayba, 2:31–2. The author does not mention the siege. Instead, Mukhtār dies in battle and his men are taken prisoner.

[207] Ibid., 2:32–3. [208] Ibid., 2:32.

F al-Yaʿqūbī (d. 284/897)

Al-Yaʿqūbī's historical chronicle presents a thorough account of Mukhtār's rebellion that features ten narrative elements, often condensed into hybrid accounts. The longest of these narratives detail Mukhtār's actions as a ruler and related political developments in the Ḥijāz.

The Ḥijāz	Sedition	Rule	Fall
1.1a, 1.2b	2.1a, 2.4a, 2.6b	3.2a, 3.1a	4.1a, 4.2a, 4.3a

The elements are listed in the order of their appearance in the text.

The Ḥijāz (61–4/680–4)

Al-Yaʿqūbī's depiction of Mukhtār's time in the Ḥijāz combines the "Ibn al-Zubayr oath" (1.1a) and "return to Kūfa" narratives (1.2b).[209] Although al-Yaʿqūbī does not directly refer to the oath of allegiance, he clearly describes Mukhtār as a staunch partisan of Ibn al-Zubayr. He also alludes to their contentious relationship, portraying Mukhtār as a political opportunist. After he realizes that he will not be appointed to an influential post, Mukhtār leaves for Iraq on his own initiative.

Sedition (64–6/684–5)

In al-Yaʿqūbī's "entry and recruitment" narrative (2.1a), Mukhtār's arrival in Kūfa coincides with Ibn Ṣurad's departure from the city at the head of the Tawwābūn.[210] The two men are not described as rivals. The text then documents Mukhtār's recruitment efforts, which focus on two points: a claim to represent Ibn al-Ḥanafiyya and a promise to exact revenge from those who spilled the blood of the Prophet's family – i.e. Ibn Ziyād. This account is followed by an abbreviated version of the "Kūfan delegation" narrative (2.4a).[211] As in other sources, Ibn al-Ḥanafiyya does not directly speak to the situation in Kūfa, but rather praises anyone who supports the Prophet's family and fights its enemies. The Kūfan Shīʿa interpret this statement as a validation of Mukhtār.

[209] Al-Yaʿqūbī, 2:174. [210] Ibid., 2:174–5. [211] Ibid., 2:175.

In his "rebellion" narrative (2.6b), al-Yaʿqūbī identifies Ibn Muṭīʿ's harassment of the Kūfan Shīʿa as the proximate cause of the unrest.[212] Although Ibn al-Ashtar plays an important role in the revolt, al-Yaʿqūbī does not relay Mukhtār's attempts to win his support (i.e. the "Ibrāhīm b. al-Ashtar letter" narrative). The Shīʿī motivations of the insurgents are evident in their calls for revenge for Ḥusayn b. ʿAlī. At the end of the battle, Ibn Muṭīʿ retreats to the fort and Mukhtār secures the oath of allegiance for the family of the Prophet. Recall that in other sources Ibn Muṭīʿ secretly flees the fort and hides in the complex of Abū Mūsā al-Ashʿarī. This is not the case in al-Yaʿqūbī's account, where Mukhtār grants Ibn Muṭīʿ (presumably still in the fort) 100,000 *dirhams*[213] and openly allows him to leave for a destination of his choosing.

Rule (66–7/685–6)

Al-Ya'qūbī includes two narrative elements that pertain to Mukhtār's rule. The first is a brief and isolated two-battle variant of the "Ibn Ziyād battle/elite uprising" narrative (3.2a) that opens with Mukhtār's appointment of ʿAbd al-Raḥmān b. Saʿīd al-Hamdānī as the new governor of Mawṣil.[214] The surrounding area, however, remains under the control of an Umayyad army led by Ibn Ziyād. In order to remedy the situation, Mukhtār first sends a small cavalry force led by Yazīd b. Anas and then dispatches a larger army under the command of Ibn al-Ashtar. Al-Yaʿqūbī provides no details of the subsequent battles, which culminate in the deaths of Ibn Ziyād and other figures complicit in the killing of Ḥusayn. After the victory, Ibn al-Ashtar names his own men to local administrative posts. Ibn Ziyād's head eventually reaches Medina, and al-Yaʿqūbī records, in a particularly detailed passage, the joyous reaction of the family of the Prophet: ʿAlī b. Ḥusayn laughs for the first time since his father's death and distributes fruit in celebration, and the women of the Prophet's family begin to comb and dye their hair again. The report ends by noting Mukhtār's pursuit of others linked to Ḥusayn's death, most prominently ʿUmar b. Saʿd.

Al-Yaʿqūbī includes in his "Ibn al-Ḥanafiyya siege" narrative (3.1a) an affirmation of Ibn al-Zubayr's hatred of the Prophet's family.[215] He notes

212 Ibid.
213 Ibid. The text does not specify a currency denomination, but this is certainly a reference to *dirhams* as opposed to *dīnārs*.
214 Ibid., 2:175–6. 215 Ibid., 2:176–80.

that Ibn al-Zubayr refused to pray for the Prophet, citing the excessive arrogance of his descendants. The narrative then turns to Ibn al-Zubayr's efforts at pressuring the Banū Hāshim, led by Ibn al-Ḥanafiyya and Ibn 'Abbās, into taking the oath of allegiance. When they refuse, he blockades them in an enclave near Zamzam and threatens in an oath to burn them alive. As in most sources, Ibn al-Ḥanafiyya writes a letter (quoted at length) to the people of Kūfa, asking for their help. Mukhtār sends a single contingent of 4,000 cavalry under the command of Abū 'Abd Allāh al-Jadalī. Note that this force is considerably greater than those mentioned in other sources. Ibn al-Ḥanafiyya prohibits the Kūfans from fighting, which leads to a prolonged standoff.[216] In recognition of his inability to compel the Banū Hāshim, Ibn al-Zubayr instead banishes Ibn al-Ḥanafiyya and Ibn 'Abbās from Mecca.[217]

Fall (67/687)

Al-Ya'qūbī's account of Mukhtār's fall from power begins with the "final defeat" narrative (4.1a).[218] In this version, Ibn al-Zubayr appoints his brother Muṣ'ab to the governorship of Iraq and orders him to march against Mukhtār in Kūfa. The resulting conflict is tersely described as "well known." According to al-Ya'qūbī, Mukhtār develops a stomach sickness during the battle, which apparently lasts four months. His army gradually melts away and he is left with a small group of supporters, who fall back to the fort in Kūfa. The report does not include any of the figures (e.g. al-Muhallab and Ibn Shumayṭ) featured in other variants of this narrative.

The segment ends with a combination of the "Mukhtār's death" (4.2a) and "surrender and execution" (4.3a) narratives.[219] Mukhtār and his men venture out each day to fight in the streets before returning to the fort. Meanwhile, Muṣ'ab contests Mukhtār's claim to represent the family of the Prophet by putting forward another of 'Alī's sons, 'Ubayd Allāh, as Ḥusayn's rightful blood heir. Mukhtār is killed during

[216] Ibid., 2:179. In the course of the standoff, Ibn al-Zubayr disparages Ibn al-Ḥanafiyya's maternal lineage in an attempt to distinguish him from his half-brothers Ḥasan and Ḥusayn. Ibn al-Ḥanafiyya responds by emphasizing his lineal connections to the Prophet's family through a number of women named Fāṭima.

[217] Ibid., 2:180. Al-Ya'qūbī preserves numerous reports about Ibn 'Abbās's activities in Ṭā'if leading up to his death in 68/687.

[218] Ibid., 2:180–1. [219] Ibid., 2:181–2.

one of his daytime raids. His remaining 7,000 supporters surrender after Muṣʿab grants them a safe-conduct backed by very stringent oaths and promises. He then breaks this agreement, marches them out of the fort individually, and beheads them. Al-Yaʿqūbī describes this as "one of the most infamous betrayals in Islam."[220]

Interpretive Framework

In the early part of al-Yaʿqūbī's text, an interpretive framework emphasizing regional politics is evident: Mukhtār is a mild opportunist seeking political power and influence. There is a notable absence, however, of the narrative elements most critical of Mukhtār. He does not, for example, make political demands before taking the oath of allegiance to Ibn al-Zubayr. In Kūfa, he recruits supporters only after Ibn Ṣurad's departure from the city, thereby defusing accusations that he sabotaged the Tawwābūn. Even Ibn al-Ḥanafiyya's statement in the "Kūfan delegation" narrative is largely positive in its assessment of Mukhtār. Finally, al-Yaʿqūbī omits the episode in which Mukhtār forges a letter to win Ibn al-Ashtar's allegiance. These authorial choices explicitly undercut accusations of perfidy and opportunism.

Another striking feature of al-Yaʿqūbī's account is its minimizing of tribal factors. This is evidenced by the absence of the Kūfan elites who play a prominent role in other comparable sources. Recall that, in these other sources, tribal leaders advocate for Mukhtār's arrest on multiple occasions, and subsequently bristle under his policies, which favor non-Arabs. They later rebel against him at Jabbānat al-Sabīʿ and then vigorously lobby Muṣʿab b. al-Zubayr to attack Kūfa. None of these events appears in al-Yaʿqūbī's text. The tribal dimension is not even present in the "surrender and execution" narrative, where most writers note elite demands for blood revenge for the deaths of their kin. The lack of a tribal element is further reflected in al-Yaʿqūbī's complete omission of non-Arabs. Whereas other historians (such as al-Balādhurī and al-Ṭabarī) identify a contingent of Mukhtār's supporters led by Kaysān as non-Arabs, al-Yaʿqūbī simply describes them as "Shīʿī."

Al-Yaʿqūbī's depiction of Mukhtār, like Ibn Aʿtham's, is primarily shaped by a religious interpretive framework. Mukhtār's initial organizational efforts are directed at a Kūfan Shīʿī community persecuted by Ibn Muṭīʿ. He later seizes control of the city with the help of Ibn

[220] Ibid.

al-Ashtar and pursues Ḥusayn's killers with a particular fervor. Al-Ya'qūbī devotes considerable space to the joyous reception of Ibn Ziyād's head in Medina.[221] At a later point, Mukhtār kills 'Umar b. Sa'd on his own initiative. He then sends a large contingent of cavalry to aid the Prophet's besieged family without the spectacle of a public announcement. Mukhtār's sincerity is strongly intimated in all of these reports, with no hint of political manipulation. Al-Ya'qūbī also omits elements that suggest deceit, such as the "Surāqa's angels" and "'Alī's chair" narratives.

G al-Dīnawarī (d. by 290/903)

In his historical chronicle, entitled *Akhbār al-ṭiwāl*, al-Dīnawarī presents ten narrative elements that begin with Mukhtār's rebellion and culminate in his death. These accounts are distinguished by two characteristics: a unique chronology and a strong emphasis on tribal politics.

The Ḥijāz	Sedition	Rule	Fall
None	2.1a, 2.3a, 2.5a	3.2a, 3.2c, 3.8b, 3.7c, 3.6a	4.1b, 4.2a

The elements are listed in the order of their appearance in the text.

Sedition (64–6/684–5)

Al-Dīnawarī opens his discussion of Mukhtār's rebellion with two brief reports. The first is the "entry and recruitment" narrative (2.1a), in which Mukhtār urges the Shī'a to avenge the killing of Ḥusayn and wins the support of nearly 20,000 Hamdānī tribesmen and non-Arabs (whom al-Dīnawarī calls *al-ḥamrā'*).[222] The second, a truncated version of the "feigned sickness" narrative (2.3a), depicts the attempt by Ibn Muṭī', the Zubayrid governor, to summon Mukhtār to court in order to question him about rumors of his subversive activities.[223] Mukhtār, however, pretends to be ill and remains in his home. This account is notably devoid of any context.

[221] The 'Alid featured in this episode is Zayn al-'Ābidīn 'Alī b. Ḥusayn, as opposed to Ibn al-Ḥanafiyya.

[222] Al-Dīnawarī, 288. [223] Ibid.

The next part of al-Dīnawarī's text is a one-meeting variant of the "Ibrāhīm b. al-Ashtar letter" narrative (2.5a),[224] in which Mukhtār personally delivers the letter to Ibn al-Ashtar. Based on the freshness of the seal, al-Sha'bī, the narrator of the account, deduces that it was written the previous night. Mukhtār is accompanied by his four closest associates.[225] The text here follows a familiar form. Ibn al-Ashtar listens to Mukhtār's appeal, which invokes the close ties between Ibn al-Ashtar's father and the Prophet's family, and then receives the letter, whose authenticity is attested to by Mukhtār's companions. In the letter, Ibn al-Ḥanafiyya asks for Ibn al-Ashtar's help, but – importantly – he does not refer to himself as the "Mahdī." Ibn al-Ashtar expresses no doubts about the letter's veracity and immediately agrees to support Mukhtār. Al-Sha'bī, however, remains skeptical.[226] He first questions the three Arab witnesses, Ibn Anas, Ibn Shumayṭ, and Ibn Kāmil, who confirm the letter's authenticity. Al-Sha'bī then asks the sole non-Arab witness, Kaysān, whether he actually saw Ibn al-Ḥanafiyya write the letter. Kaysān admits that his testimony is based only on his trust in Mukhtār, who possesses tokens or signs from Ibn al-Ḥanafiyya. Al-Sha'bī concludes that Mukhtār is a liar and immediately departs for the Ḥijāz.

Al-Dīnawarī's version of the "rebellion" narrative (2.6c) is unique.[227] The report begins when Iyās b. Muḍārib[228] learns of the impending revolt and orders Ibn al-Ashtar to remain in his home. Mukhtār then authorizes Ibn al-Ashtar to kill Iyās. In the other sources, by contrast, this fatal encounter occurs by chance and without Mukhtār's approval. In the subsequent fighting, Ibn al-Ashtar, backed by a small detachment of cavalry, defeats the government forces and pushes Ibn Muṭī' back to the fort. The rebels are reinforced by 7,000 horsemen and up to 13,000 foot soldiers responding to calls to avenge Ḥusayn. At this point al-Dīnawarī quotes a poem, praising tribes known for their loyalty to the Prophet's family. Ibn Muṭī' leads one final charge but is again forced to retreat to the fort, where he negotiates a safe-conduct for himself and his men. Mukhtār then gives

224 Ibid., 288–90.
225 Ibid., 289. These men are identified as Yazīd b. Anas, Aḥmar b. Shumayṭ (the text incorrectly reads "Sulayṭ"), 'Abd Allāh b. Kāmil, and Abū 'Amra Kaysān.
226 Ibid., 289–90. 227 Ibid., 290–2.
228 The text here incorrectly reads "Iyās b. Niḍār al-'Ijlī."

Ibn Muṭīʿ 1,000,000 *dirhams*, partly on account of his kinship with ʿUmar b. al-Khaṭṭāb (r. 13–23/634–44).[229]

Rule (66–7/685–6)

Al-Dīnawarī's discussion of Mukhtār's rule starts with a list of officials appointed over areas administered from Kūfa.[230] Abū ʿAmra Kaysān is placed in charge of a security force (*shurṭa*) comprising 1,000 local workers armed with pickaxes, and is ordered to pursue those complicit in the murder of Ḥusayn.[231] Here the text highlights Kaysān's abuse of power as he destroys homes, kills many people, and confiscates property from Arabs which he then distributes to non-Arabs.[232]

Al-Dīnawarī divides the "Ibn Ziyād battle/elite uprising" narrative into two distinct parts. The first covers the conflict with Ibn Ziyād (3.2a) and features Mukhtār sending a well-equipped force of 20,000 men toward Syria under the command of Yazīd b. Anas.[233] They are met and decisively defeated near Naṣībīn by a Syrian army personally led by the caliph, ʿAbd al-Malik b. Marwān.[234] Yazīd b. Anas is killed in the course of the battle. Mukhtār then asks Ibn al-Ashtar to lead a new campaign. He selects another 20,000 men, most of whom are non-Arabs previously identified as the *ḥamrāʾ*. As he marches toward Syria, Ibn al-Ashtar rallies the remnants of Yazīd b. Anas's forces, raising the total number of soldiers in his army to 30,000.

Al-Dīnawarī places an emphasis on the lingering discontent of Qaysī elements of the Syrian army still angered by their defeat at Marj Rāhiṭ. The repercussions of this resentment are embodied by the figure of ʿUmayr b. al-Ḥubāb, who secretly visits Ibn al-Ashtar before the battle. ʿUmayr laments the fact that he does not hear any Arabic from the Kūfan soldiers, and predicts that they will falter in battle against the 40,000 Arabs on the Syrian side. In response, Ibn al-Ashtar defends the competence and ferocity of his non-Arab troops. ʿUmayr then reveals that the Qaysī tribesmen on the Umayyad left flank will withdraw from the field because of their grievances against the Marwānids. According to most sources, the Qays later change their minds and remain at their posts. In al-Dīnawarī's account, however, the Qays carry through on their threat and leave the battlefield, chanting

229 *EI*², s.v. "ʿUmar b. al-Khaṭṭāb" (G. Levi Della Vida and M. Bonner); al-Ziriklī, 5:45–6. Note that most versions of this narrative element claim that Ibn Muṭīʿ fled the fort before its surrender.

230 Al-Dīnawarī, 292. 231 Ibid. 232 Ibid. 233 Ibid., 292–6. 234 Ibid.

"Revenge for Marj Rāhiṭ."[235] Many figures associated with Ḥusayn's murder are killed in the fighting, including Ibn Ziyād, whose corpse is identified by scent and whose head eventually reaches Ibn al-Ḥanafiyya in Mecca.[236]

The second part of al-Dīnawarī's "Ibn Ziyād battle/elite uprising" narrative (3.2c) returns to developments in Kūfa after the Battle of the Khāzir River.[237] The report mentions Mukhtār's reliance on non-Arabs and his alienation of Arabs. His policy of distributing tax revenues among non-Arabs is particularly unpopular with the larger Arab population. Mukhtār defends his actions by citing the strong and unyielding support of the non-Arabs both during and after the rebellion. The Arabs are also skeptical of Mukhtār's claim to represent the Banū Hāshim and publicly accuse him of worldly motivations. They eventually decide to rebel, bolstered by the return of tribal elites who had previously fled the city, including, most prominently, Shamir b. Dhī al-Jawshan, 'Umar b. Sa'd, and Muḥammad b. al-Ash'ath. Mukhtār's followers consist chiefly of Hamdānī tribesmen and a large contingent of non-Arabs who believe (with Mukhtār's encouragement) that the tribal leaders intend to return them to subordinate positions. The final battle takes place at Jabbānat al-Ḥashshāshīn and ends in a decisive victory for Mukhtār. This outcome precipitates an exodus of Kūfan tribal leaders to Baṣra.

After the battle, Mukhtār accelerates his pursuit of those complicit in the campaign against Ḥusayn. Many of al-Dīnawarī's reports differ markedly from those found in other sources. His version of the "'Umar b. Sa'd revenge" narrative (3.8b), for example, is placed immediately after the elite uprising, as Kūfan tribal leaders flee, fearing retribution.[238] They are pursued by a detachment of cavalry, and in the subsequent

235 Ibid., 295.

236 After his account of the battle with Ibn Ziyād, al-Dīnawarī describes Mukhtār's chilly relations with Kūfa's tribal leaders. The most detailed report centers on Mukhtār's break with one of his key early supporters, 'Ubayd Allāh b. al-Ḥurr (ibid., 297–8). This conflict is often ascribed to a financial dispute that erupted during Ibn al-Ashtar's campaign against the Syrians (Ibn A'tham, 2:324–34). Other Kūfan tribal leaders (notably 'Umar b. Sa'd and Muḥammad b. al-Ash'ath) flee the city when Mukhtār intensifies his search for those responsible for Ḥusayn's death.

237 Al-Dīnawarī, 299–301.

238 Ibid., 301. The tribal leaders are identified as Shabath b. Rib'ī, Shamir b. Dhī al-Jawshan, Muḥammad b. al-Ash'ath, and 'Umar b. Sa'd.

skirmish, 'Umar b. Sa'd is captured and brought back to the city, where Mukhtār orders his execution. This account does not include two distinctive elements mentioned by every other source: the agreement of safe-conduct and the execution of 'Umar's son Ḥafṣ.

A number of idiosyncrasies also characterize al-Dīnawarī's "Shamir revenge" narrative (3.7c).[239] In this version, Shamir refuses to enter Baṣra because of his unwillingness to bear the scorn of its inhabitants. Instead, he takes refuge in a small town north of the city, Dastumīsān,[240] where he is attacked by a Kūfan cavalry force sent by Mukhtār under the command of Zirbiyya (a client of the Bajīla). Shamir kills Zirbiyya and sets up camp in a small village on the outskirts of Baṣra, where he remains for some time. In most other sources, Mukhtār discovers this new location and sends a second party that kills Shamir and his companions. Al-Dīnawarī, by contrast, mentions no further pursuit and attributes Shamir's death to the advance of the Kūfan army prior to the battle with Muṣ'ab b. al-Zubayr.[241]

The final element[242] in this part of al-Dīnawarī's text is the "Surāqa's angels" narrative (3.6a).[243] The account first relates Mukhtār's decision to execute all of his prisoners after the elite uprising, regardless of whether they had taken up arms against Ḥusayn. At this point, Surāqa claims to have seen white figures fighting alongside Mukhtār during the battle. Mukhtār identifies them as angels and then orders Surāqa's release. It is noteworthy that, unlike in other sources, here Mukhtār expresses no skepticism regarding Surāqa's testimony.

Fall (67/687)

Al-Dīnawarī discusses Mukhtār's fall from power in a two-battle version of the "final defeat" narrative (4.1b).[244] The report begins after the failure of the tribal revolt, as 10,000 Kūfans flee to Baṣra. The refugees are led by Muḥammad b. al-Ash'ath, who complains to Muṣ'ab of Mukhtār's persecution of tribal leaders and of his favoritism toward non-Arabs. As in other sources, Muṣ'ab recalls al-Muhallab

[239] Ibid., 301–2.
[240] According to Yāqūt (2:518), this is likely a village located near Ahwāz in the direction of Baṣra.
[241] Al-Dīnawarī, 305.
[242] This narrative is preceded by a report about the execution of Qays b. al-Ash'ath that lies outside the scope of this study but highlights Mukhtār's willingness to violate moral norms in pursuit of his enemies. See ibid., 302.
[243] Ibid., 303. [244] Ibid., 304–7.

b. Abī Ṣufra from Kirmān and begins military preparations. In Kūfa, Mukhtār places his army of 60,000 under the command of Aḥmar b. Shumayṭ.[245] The remainder of the account follows a familiar course, as the Baṣrans win a series of battles and force Mukhtār to retreat to the fort in Kūfa.

According to al-Dīnawarī's death narrative (4.2a), Mukhtār is besieged for forty days.[246] When the situation becomes critical, he urges his men, led by al-Sā'ib b. Mālik al-Ash'arī, to rush out of the fort and make a final stand, not for their religion but for their honor. Al-Sā'ib is distressed by this speech and questions Mukhtār about the motives for his rebellion. Mukhtār responds by drawing clear parallels between himself and his contemporaries, Ibn al-Zubayr and 'Abd al-Malik b. Marwān, and admitting that his calls to avenge Ḥusayn were simply a ploy for power. He then leads three men in a final sortie that culminates in his death.

Interpretive Framework

Al-Dīnawarī's text, like al-Balādhurī's, adheres closely to a tribal/ethnic interpretive framework. This framework is embodied by the figure of Kaysān, a non-Arab who initially serves as one of Mukhtār's closest aides and later heads an independent internal security force (*shurṭa*). Al-Dīnawarī explicitly states that Mukhtār's strongest support in the rebellion came from the Banū Hamdān and the descendants of non-Arabs (*al-ḥamrā'*). In preparing his campaign against Ibn Ziyād, Ibn al-Ashtar chooses an army of 20,000 men, consisting chiefly of non-Arabs. This fact is mentioned by 'Umayr b. al-Ḥubāb, who is disturbed that Ibn al-Ashtar's soldiers do not speak Arabic. He predicts that such an army will flounder against the Syrians, but Ibn al-Ashtar lauds their tenacity and competence. 'Umayr later abandons the battlefield along with the rest of the Qays as a result of tribal tensions within the Umayyad army. During the elite uprising, the rebels harshly criticize Mukhtār's elevation of non-Arabs to positions of influence and their inclusion in the distribution of stipends. Mukhtār motivates his non-Arab troops by openly suggesting that the Arabs intend to return them to a subordinate position. In his description of the conflict, al-Dīnawarī repeatedly refers to tribal units, noting the loyalty of the Hamdān and the strategic withdrawal of the Rabī'a. After their defeat, the Kūfan tribal leaders appeal to Muṣ'ab, again

[245] Ibid., 305. The text reads, incorrectly, "Aḥmar b. Salīṭ." [246] Ibid., 307–8.

citing Mukhtār's favoritism toward non-Arabs. This conflict between Arabs and non-Arabs is the defining feature of al-Dīnawarī's overarching narrative.

Al-Dīnawarī's account is also partially shaped by a regional–political interpretive framework bereft of religious sentiment. Mukhtār's pursuit of individuals complicit in the death of Ḥusayn is thus framed as a purely political act. Along these lines, Mukhtār kills 'Umar b. Sa'd to consolidate his hold on power through the elimination of a rival with considerable tribal standing. His political pragmatism is also on display in his decision to execute prisoners following the elite uprising. Most sources limit the executions to those who participated in the campaign against Ḥusayn, but al-Dīnawarī makes no such distinction: the prisoners are killed solely for political reasons. Surāqa only escapes by supplying an important piece of supernatural propaganda. In his final exchange with al-Sā'ib b. Malik, Mukhtār reduces religion to a tool used for garnering popular support.

Al-Dīnawarī further dampens the religious dimension of his account by excluding several narrative elements. Although he mentions Mukhtār's appeal to the Kūfan Shī'a, most of his reports minimize religious terminology and instead emphasize the non-Arab nature of the movement. The role of Ibn al-Ḥanafiyya is notably diminished in al-Dīnawarī's account. In the forged letter to Ibn al-Ashtar, for example, Mukhtār does not describe Ibn al-Ḥanafiyya as the "Mahdī." Al-Dīnawarī also omits the "Ibn al-Ḥanafiyya siege" narrative altogether. In addition, the text offers little insight into the religious commitments of Mukhtār's supporters. Many of them seem motivated by calls to avenge Ḥusayn, but is this enough to characterize them as members of the Kūfan Shī'a? Al-Dīnawarī is silent on this question. Furthermore, there is no mention of the "'Alī's chair" narrative and no coherent set of revenge accounts highlighting the importance of the Prophet's family. Overall, Mukhtār is depicted as the head of a primarily non-Arab movement built on the political manipulation of religious sentiments. For al-Dīnawarī, Mukhtār represents the struggle between an emerging social group (non-Arabs) and an entrenched power structure (Arabs).

H al-Ṭabarī (d. 310/923)

Al-Ṭabarī's historical chronicle preserves the longest and most detailed version of Mukhtār's rebellion. The discussion that follows focuses mainly on the unique structure and distinctive features of al-Ṭabarī's account.

The Ḥijāz	Sedition	Rule	Fall
1.1b, 1.2b	2.1b, 2.2a, 2.3b, 2.4a, 2.5b, 2.6c	3.2b, 3.7b, 3.6a, 3.8a, 3.4a, 3.3a, 3.1a, 3.5a, 3.5b	4.1b, 4.2a, 4.3b

The elements are listed in the order of their appearance in the text.

The Ḥijāz (61–4/680–4)

Al-Ṭabarī's depiction of Mukhtār in the Ḥijāz includes two narrative elements. The first is a two-encounter variant of the "Ibn al-Zubayr oath" narrative (1.1b).[247] In his initial meeting with Mukhtār, Ibn al-Zubayr disparages the Kūfans for their disloyalty, comparing them to bad slaves. Mukhtār offers his oath of allegiance but then suddenly departs the city in frustration. Al-Ṭabarī attributes this to impatience rather than any actual disagreement with Ibn al-Zubayr. As in other sources, Ibn al-Zubayr is later informed that Mukhtār has settled in Ṭā'if, where he continues to predict that he will bring down tyrants. This prompts Ibn al-Zubayr to label him a liar and a soothsayer.[248] At that very moment, Mukhtār reappears in Mecca and performs the rites of the lesser pilgrimage while conspicuously ignoring Ibn al-Zubayr. 'Abbās b. Sahl is sent to investigate the situation. He explains that Ibn al-Zubayr's prior aloofness was motivated by political caution and asks Mukhtār to meet with his patron after the night prayers. In this second encounter, Mukhtār demands influence and a political appointment in exchange for his oath of allegiance. When Ibn al-Zubayr responds with an oath in which he promises to adhere to the Qur'ān and the Sunna, Mukhtār dismisses it as appropriate only for slaves.[249] Ibn Sahl then convinces Ibn al-Zubayr to accept the conditions as the price for Mukhtār's religion.

The next part of al-Ṭabarī's account details the conflict between Ibn al-Zubayr and an Umayyad army led by al-Ḥuṣayn b. Numayr al-Sakūnī, in the course of which Mukhtār fulfills the obligations of his oath.[250] Two

[247] Al-Ṭabarī, 3:402–3. [248] Ibid., 3:402. [249] Ibid., 3:403.
[250] Ibid., 3:403–4.

reports in this portion of al-Ṭabarī's text merit mention. In the first, Mukhtār, fearful of being killed by slaves (referred to as "dogs") in battle, vows to fight only those of known lineage in the future.[251] This attitude toward non-Arabs is consistent with his refusal to accept Ibn al-Zubayr's version of the oath of allegiance. In the second report, Ibn al-Zubayr expresses a distrust of Mukhtār and fails to treat him as an equal.[252] Five months later, a disgruntled Mukhtār begins questioning pilgrims about the political situation in Kūfa.

In al-Ṭabarī's "return to Kūfa" narrative (1.2b), Hānī b. Abī Ḥayya describes the Kūfans as receptive to Ibn al-Zubayr with the exception of one disenchanted group.[253] Although he does not explicitly identify the latter as Shī'a, he notes that the right figure could organize them into a powerful, almost invincible army. Mukhtār claims this role for himself, declares his intention to fight tyranny, and departs for Kūfa despite Hānī's warnings about the dangers of civil strife. On the road, he meets a second figure, Salama b. Marthad al-Qābiḍī,[254] who refers to the Kūfans as sheep in search of a shepherd. Mukhtār again expresses his determination to take charge of the city, ignoring Salama's advice to the contrary.

Sedition (64–6/684–5)

Al-Ṭabarī opens his "entry and recruitment" narrative (2.1b) by describing Mukhtār's arrival in Kūfa and his outreach to important tribes and individuals.[255] In particular, Mukhtār praises the Kinda for honoring their covenant with God and their willingness to avenge the blood of the Prophet's family.[256] A substantial crowd follows him to the city's main mosque, where he remains until the end of the afternoon prayer. After a discreet change of clothes, Mukhtār passes through the neighborhood of the Banū Hamdān and arrives at his house, where he addresses the Shī'a in the name of Ibn al-Ḥanafiyya (here referred to as the "Mahdī").[257] He discovers that most of the Shī'a[258] have already pledged themselves to Ibn Ṣurad, a figure Mukhtār disparages as naïve

[251] Ibid., 3:404. [252] Ibid. [253] Ibid., 3:404–5.

[254] This is al-Ṭabarī's only reference to Salama. His tribal affiliation with the Banū Hamdān is given in al-Ṭabarī's index.

[255] In one case, he promises 'Abīda b. 'Amr al-Baddī that God will forgive him for his consumption of alcohol.

[256] Al-Ṭabarī, 3:405. [257] Ibid., 3:405–6.

[258] The exceptions include 'Abīda b. 'Amr and Ismā'īl b. Kathīr.

and inexperienced. He decides, however, to wait for the resolution of Ibn Ṣurad's military campaign before pursuing any further action.

At the start of al-Ṭabarī's "Kūfan arrest" narrative (2.2a), a number of tribal leaders, including 'Umar b. Sa'd and Shabath b. Rib'ī, strongly advise 'Abd Allāh b. Yazīd and Ibrāhīm b. Muḥammad, Ibn al-Zubayr's deputies in Kūfa, to act against Mukhtār.[259] As in other sources, they deem him as a greater threat than Ibn Ṣurad given the latter's single-minded focus on the Umayyads. Ibrāhīm wants to parade Mukhtār through the streets barefoot and in chains, but he is overruled by 'Abd Allāh, who notes that Mukhtār has not yet committed a crime. When the deputies confront him, Mukhtār pleads his innocence and then slanders Ibrāhīm's father and grandfather (Ṭalḥa b. 'Ubayd Allāh[260] [d. 36/656]). He is taken to prison, where he composes rhymed prose predicting his future role in deposing tyrants. He also continues to network with the Kūfan Shī'a. At this point, al-Ṭabarī covers the defeat of the Tawwābūn, which lies outside the scope of this study. Mukhtār later writes to the survivors, praising their efforts and nominating himself as their new leader.[261]

The next part of al-Ṭabarī's account documents the success of Mukhtār's recruitment efforts.[262] His new supporters (i.e. Rifā'a b. Shaddād, Yazīd b. Anas, Aḥmar b. Shumayṭ, and 'Abd Allāh b. Kāmil) offer to break him out of prison, but he refuses and instead predicts his imminent release. According to al-Ṭabarī, Mukhtār's confidence stems from the fact that he had previously written to 'Abd Allāh b. 'Umar, asking him to intercede with Ibrāhīm and 'Abd Allāh. They free him on the condition that (i) ten of his companions of high tribal standing act as guarantors for his behavior and (ii) he take a burdensome oath disavowing rebellion. The narrative concludes with a well-known report in which Mukhtār brazenly asserts his intention to violate the oath for the greater good of the Muslim community.[263]

After a summary of Mukhtār's subversive activities,[264] al-Ṭabarī turns to the "feigned sickness" narrative (2.3b). As in other sources, Ibn Muṭī', the new governor of Kūfa, appoints Iyās b. Muḍārib al-'Ijlī as his head of

259 Al-Ṭabarī, 3:406, 420–1, and 433–4.
260 For Ṭalḥa, see *EI*[3], s.v. "Ṭalḥa b. 'Ubaydallāh" (W. Madelung).
261 Al-Ṭabarī, 3:420–1. There is some confusion in the text here, as one report ascribes Mukhtār's arrest to this letter even though the larger narrative places his arrest prior to the defeat of the Tawwābūn.
262 Ibid., 3:433–4. 263 Ibid., 3:434. 264 Ibid.

security (*shurṭa*) and then delivers an ill-conceived speech praising 'Umar and 'Uthmān.[265] He is forced to reverse course in the face of public criticism led by al-Sā'ib b. Mālik and instead agrees to follow the example of 'Alī. Iyās traces the disorder to partisans of Mukhtār and advises his immediate arrest. The subsequent report is more detailed than those found in most other sources. Ibn Muṭī' sends two messengers to summon Mukhtār to court. However, one of them, Zā'ida b. Qudāma, warns Mukhtār of his impending arrest by quoting Q8:30.[266] Mukhtār then feigns illness and recites a line of poetry that clearly conveys his grasp of the Qur'ānic reference. The other messenger, Ḥusayn b. 'Abd Allāh al-Bursumī, plays along with the ruse for fear of future reprisals.

Al-Ṭabarī's "Kūfan delegation" narrative (2.4a) follows the standard form.[267] The Kūfans travel to Mecca, where they privately question Ibn al-Ḥanafiyya about Mukhtār. They then interpret a number of his ambiguous statements as an implicit confirmation of Mukhtār's claims. During their absence, Mukhtār first tries to launch the revolt preemptively and then criticizes the delegation members for their lack of faith. After the Kūfans return to the city, he has them publicly attest to Ibn al-Ḥanafiyya's support.

Al-Ṭabarī preserves a two-meeting version of the "Ibrāhīm b. al-Ashtar letter" narrative (2.5b). In the first meeting, a small group of Mukhtār's supporters[268] cautiously approach Ibn al-Ashtar, describing themselves as the "Shī'a" and recalling his father Mālik al-Ashtar's support of 'Alī.[269] Ibn al-Ashtar asks for command of the rebellion but is told that the "Mahdī" has placed Mukhtār in charge. Three days later, Mukhtār personally delivers a letter in which Ibn al-Ḥanafiyya requests Ibn al-Ashtar's help and refers to himself both as the *mahdī* and the *waṣī*.[270] Ibn al-Ashtar is suspicious of these titles, observing that in previous correspondence Ibn al-Ḥanafiyya had used only his name and patronym.

265 Ibid., 3:434–6. Earlier, Ibn Muṭī' ignores the advice of an astrologer, which perhaps precipitates his fall from power.
266 Q8:30 reads: "And when those who disbelieved plotted against you to restrain you or kill you or evict you. But they plot, and God plots. And God is the best of plotters."
267 Al-Ṭabarī, 3:436–7.
268 The group includes Aḥmar b. Shumayṭ, Yazīd b. Anas, and Ibn Kāmil.
269 Al-Ṭabarī, 3:437–8.
270 The Shī'a commonly reserve these titles for the legitimate Imām. The first, *mahdī*, denotes the rightly guided successor of the Prophet (see n. 28), while the second, *waṣī*, designates the Prophet's legatee.

At this point, most of Mukhtār's companions testify to the authenticity of the letter, with the notable exceptions of the narrator (al-Sha'bī) and his father. Ibn al-Ashtar is seemingly convinced and takes the oath of allegiance, but he later questions al-Sha'bī about the letter's authenticity in private. Instead of expressing his personal doubts, al-Sha'bī praises the integrity of his companions. The report ends with al-Sha'bī recording the names and testimony of the witnesses at Ibn al-Ashtar's request.

Al-Ṭabarī's "rebellion" narrative (2.6c) starts with Ibn Muṭī' learning of Mukhtār's machinations and deploying his supporters to tribal neighborhoods to quell the unrest.[271] The catalyst for the violence is the familiar street skirmish between Ibn al-Ashtar and Iyās b. Muḍārib. Mukhtār then tasks Ibn al-Ashtar and a small force to clear out the loyalists positioned in public spaces while he musters the bulk of his army.[272]

Al-Ṭabarī's account features a number of incidents mentioned by other sources. In one episode, Mukhtār sends a spy to investigate a disturbance among Ibn Muṭī''s men.[273] He discovers that it was prompted by complaints regarding Shabath b. Rib'ī's recitation of two very short Qur'ānic chapters (Q99 and Q100) during the communal prayer. Shabath is incredulous at this criticism: at a time when the city is occupied by "Daylamites," his men are more interested in matters such as the recitation of Q2 or Q3! Another noteworthy incident occurs during a minor skirmish between Shabath and Nu'aym b. Hubayra[274] (d. late first/seventh century). When his men begin to lose ground, Shabath berates then for fleeing from their "slaves."[275] This turns the tide of the battle. Nu'aym is killed and a large number of prisoners are captured. Shabath orders the release of Arab captives and executes all the non-Arabs, whom he disparagingly labels the *saba'iyya*. In a third report, Ibn Muṭī' characterizes his opponents as a small band of freed slaves with wicked (*khabīth*)

[271] Al-Ṭabarī, 3:439. [272] Ibid., 3:440–2. [273] Ibid., 3:442–3.

[274] Nu'aym b. Hubayra b. Shibl al-Tha'labī is described by al-Ṭabarī as a close supporter of and advisor to 'Alī. His brother Maṣqala (d. ca. 50/670) abandoned 'Alī for Mu'āwiya and later died leading an Umayyad military campaign in Ṭabaristān. For Nu'aym, see al-Ṭabarī, 3:147. For Maṣqala, see al-Ziriklī, 7:249; al-Tustarī, 10:90; al-Ṭabarī, index.

[275] Al-Ṭabarī, 3:443.

religious beliefs, intent on illegally seizing communal property (*fay'*).[276]

The rebels eventually push into the heart of the city under the leadership of both Ibn al-Ashtar and Mukhtār.[277] At this point, al-Ṭabarī offers a curious account in which Ibn Kāmil describes Mukhtār, who is fasting during the conflict, as inerrant (*ma'ṣūm*).[278] Before the decisive encounter, Ibn al-Ashtar delivers a speech in which he counsels his men to ignore the tribal lineages of their foes, as they will certainly flee in the heat of battle. He also utilizes a Shī'ī expression of deference usually reserved for interactions with the Imām, namely, "Make my paternal and maternal uncles a sacrifice for you."[279] Ibn al-Ashtar then leads the final charge that forces Ibn Muṭī' to fall back to the fort.

The rebellion narrative concludes with the siege of the fort.[280] As in other sources, Ibn Muṭī' refuses to request a safe-conduct because he sees this as a betrayal of Ibn al-Zubayr. Shabath then advises him to sneak out of the fort and hide until it is safe to leave the city. Before slipping away, Ibn Muṭī' praises his supporters and condemns his opponents as low and base, reinforcing the tribal and class undercurrents of the overall account. The safety of his remaining supporters is guaranteed by Ibn al-Ashtar. When Mukhtār later discovers Ibn Muṭī''s location, he sends him money and orders his immediate departure from the city.[281]

Rule (66–7/685–6)

Al-Ṭabarī's description of Mukhtār's rule includes several reports that, despite lying outside the scope of this study, provide insight into his interpretive framework. In the first, Mukhtār adds a provision for seeking revenge for the blood of the Prophet's family to his oath of allegiance.[282] The second depicts Mukhtār's anger at his Shī'ī supporters for undermining his efforts at reconciliation by killing two prominent Arab tribesmen.[283] In a third report, he is speaking with some Arab tribal leaders when he overhears a group of non-Arabs whispering to Kaysān, the chief of security.[284] He later learns that his non-Arab

276 Ibid., 3:445. 277 Ibid., 3:445–6. 278 Ibid., 3:445. 279 Ibid., 3:446.
280 Ibid., 3:446–7. 281 Ibid., 3:448. 282 Ibid., 3:447.
283 Ibid. The men are identified as Mundhir b. Ḥassān b. Ḍirār al-Ḍabbī (d. 66/685) and his son Ḥayyān. They had just taken the oath of allegiance to Mukhtār.
284 Ibid., 3:448.

followers are concerned about his overtures to the Arabs. Mukhtār remains silent for a long time. He then recites Q32:22[285] and instructs Kaysān to reassure the non-Arabs that he intends to punish their enemies.[286] These reports illustrate the tenuous nature of the relationship between Mukhtār and his predominantly non-Arab supporters.

Al-Ṭabarī's version of the "Ibn Ziyād battle/elite uprising" narrative (3.2b) is presented in two parts. The first is placed at this point in the text, whereas the second follows narrative elements pertaining to revenge, expansion, and the religious inclinations of Mukhtār's followers. The report begins with Marwān's consolidation of his control of Syria and his dispatch of two armies, one in the direction of the Ḥijāz and the other in the direction of Kūfa.[287] The latter, led by Ibn Ziyād, encounters strong opposition from Qaysī tribesmen loyal to Mukhtār and eventually sets up camp in Mawṣil. The remainder of al-Ṭabarī's report is fairly typical.[288] Yazīd b. Anas arrives at the head of 3,000 cavalry and is met by a numerically superior Umayyad force consisting of two cavalry detachments. The Syrian troops show open disdain for the Kūfans, with Rabī'a b. al-Mukhāriq[289] (d. 66/686), the head of a group of Syrian cavalry, referring to them as "fugitive slaves" who had "left Islam" and "did not speak Arabic."[290] In the subsequent battle, Yazīd b. Anas, who is gravely ill, guides his men to victory from a litter positioned on the frontlines. He dies soon after and his men withdraw in the face of the more numerous enemy. Mukhtār then orders Ibn al-Ashtar to gather a new army of 7,000 men, to rally the remnants of Yazīd's cavalry, and to reengage the Syrians.

At this point, al-Ṭabarī transitions to the "elite uprising" narrative, as Kūfan tribal leaders assemble in the home of Shabath b. Rib'ī to voice their discontent with Mukhtār.[291] They are particularly upset at

[285] The portion of Q32:22 that is cited in the text reads: "Indeed We, from the criminals, will take retribution."

[286] For another account highlighting tribal and/or religious factions among Mukhtār's supporters, see al-Ṭabarī, 3:449–51.

[287] Ibid., 3:451. [288] Ibid., 3:451–4.

[289] Ibid., 3:416–18. Rabī'a b. al-Mukhāriq al-Ghanawī was a Qaysī military commander for the Umayyads who took part in the campaign against the Tawwābūn. For his death in battle, see ibid., 3:452–3.

[290] Ibid., 3:453. In the course of the fight, some of Yazīd's men admit that they were once Khawārij but subsequently repented of their betrayal of 'Alī.

[291] Ibid., 3:454–9.

his decision to allocate to non-Arabs (*mawālī*) a portion of the *fay'* and at his tolerance of their growing audacity. Shabath transmits these complaints to Mukhtār, who seems genuinely interested in negotiation but balks at stripping the non-Arabs of their stipends.[292] He offers to do so only if the tribal leaders pledge to fight with him against the Umayyads and Ibn al-Zubayr. They reject this condition outright.

Al-Ṭabarī devotes considerable space to the preliminaries of the subsequent revolt. In one report, Shabath disputes Mukhtār's claim to represent Ibn al-Ḥanafiyya and characterizes his followers (whom he calls *saba'iyya*) as slaves and non-Arabs who break with the "righteous predecessors."[293] ʿAbd al-Raḥmān b. Mikhnaf al-Azdī is more cautious, noting that Mukhtār has the support of many skilled Arab fighters.[294] His army therefore combines the courage of the Arabs with the ferocity of the non-Arabs. ʿAbd al-Raḥmān recommends waiting for an outside party (i.e. the Umayyads or Ibn al-Zubayr) to overthrow Mukhtār.

The uprising erupts soon after Ibn al-Ashtar's departure for Mawṣil. As in other sources, Mukhtār dispatches a messenger to recall Ibn al-Ashtar while simultaneously promising to meet the rebels' demands.[295] He also proposes sending a joint delegation to Mecca to verify his connection to Ibn al-Ḥanafiyya. Al-Ṭabarī makes clear that these are only ploys meant to delay hostilities until Ibn al-Ashtar's return. The uprising is beset by reports of disunity and mistrust among the rebels. The fighting culminates in two battles; Ibn al-Ashtar decisively defeats the Muḍar[296] in Kunāsa, while Mukhtār overcomes most of the Yaman[297] in Jabbānat al-Sabīʿ. The remainder of the "Ibn Ziyād battle/elite uprising" narrative is found much later in al-Ṭabarī's text.

292 In contrast to Ibn Aʿtham, al-Ṭabarī does not depict Mukhtār's conciliatory attitude as a delaying tactic.

293 Al-Ṭabarī, 3:454–5. 294 Ibid., 3:455. 295 Ibid.

296 Ibid., 3:456. Mukhtār's decision to send Ibn al-Ashtar against the Muḍar is rooted in the fear that he might hold back in fighting his own Yamanī tribesmen. Ibn al-Ashtar belongs to the Madhḥij clan of the Yamanī tribal confederation.

297 Ibid., 3:457–8. The battle turns decisively in Mukhtār's favor after a multipronged attack by the Shibām (a subdivision of the Hamdān from among the Yaman), who rally around a cry to avenge Ḥusayn. In a particularly powerful report, their leader, Abū al-Qalūṣ, dispels his men's doubts about fighting fellow tribesmen by quoting Q9:123 (the quoted part reads: "Fight those adjacent to you of the disbelievers and let them find in you harshness"),

The elite uprising is depicted as having a deeply unsettling effect in Kūfa. According to one account, Rifāʿa b. Shaddād, on the side of the elites, struggles with reconciling his Shīʿī inclinations with his mistrust of Mukhtār.[298] He changes his mind in the course of the battle and dies fighting alongside Mukhtār. In another report, one of Mukhtār's supporters, ʿAbd Allāh b. Sharīk[299] (d. mid-second/eighth century), orders the execution of non-Arab prisoners and the freeing of Arab prisoners.[300] Mukhtār tries to intervene by restricting executions to those who participated in the campaign against Ḥusayn.[301] When this fails to curtail the killings, which are actually motivated by personal feuds, he issues a general amnesty for the rebels.

After the revolt, Mukhtār changes his governance strategy, targeting the elites and for the first time vigorously pursuing anyone complicit in Ḥusayn's death. It is unclear whether these measures are genuinely motivated by religious concerns or an attempt to appease his core supporters.[302] The discussion that follows does not examine all twenty-one of the revenge accounts presented by al-Ṭabarī.[303] Instead, it focuses on three narrative elements pertinent to this study: those involving Shamir b. Dhī Jawshan, Surāqa b. Mirdās, and ʿUmar b. Saʿd.

Al-Ṭabarī's version of the "Shamir revenge" narrative (3.7b) follows a familiar course.[304] Mukhtār sends a slave – here called Zirbī – in pursuit of Shamir, who has fled Kūfa after the failure of the rebellion. Shamir kills the slave, after which, for unclear reasons, Mukhtār disavows knowledge of the mission. The narrative then adopts the perspective of a member of

and he clears their heads by repeatedly forcing them to sit down and then rise up.

298 Ibid., 3:458.

299 ʿAbd Allāh b. Sharīk al-ʿĀmirī al-Nahdī was a prominent Shīʿa who survived into the middle of the second/eighth century. For his role as a transmitter of Shīʿī traditions, see al-Tustarī, 6:402–4. For his problematic reputation in Sunnī circles, see al-Mizzī, 15:87–9. For his later questioning of Mukhtār's religious claims, see al-Ṭabarī, 3:489.

300 Al-Ṭabarī, 3:458–9. This episode mirrors a similar incident ascribed to Shabath in the "rebellion" narrative (see the previous section on sedition).

301 This policy results in the summary execution of 248 prisoners.

302 Al-Ṭabarī, 3:461–2. Mukhtār claims that the pursuit of Ḥusayn's killers is an integral part of his religion.

303 Ibid. Many revenge narratives are folded into a broad discussion of the consequences of the elite failure at Jabbānat al-Sabīʿ. These include a number that highlight the complexities of tribal dynamics.

304 Ibid., 3:459–60.

Shamir's party as they camp in a small village called Kalthāniyya.[305] He notes Shamir's ill treatment of a non-Arab whom he sends to deliver a letter to Muṣ'ab b. al-Zubayr. One of Mukhtār's men overhears the non-Arab complaining about the abuse on the road to Baṣra. This leads to the confiscation of the letter which reveals Shamir's location. Meanwhile, Shamir stubbornly vows to remain in the village for three days despite the objections of his companions. He is killed when Mukhtār's men attack the camp later that night.

Al-Ṭabarī begins the "Surāqa's angels" narrative (3.6a) with the poet in custody, composing panegyric verses in the hope of securing amnesty after the uprising.[306] Specifically, he recites a long, pandering poem in which he swears to have witnessed angels on piebald horses fighting behind Mukhtār. He is forced to repeat this claim from the pulpit, and admits to its falseness only much later. Mukhtār frees Surāqa and expels him from the city lest he spread corruption among the people. He makes his way to Baṣra, where he joins other Kūfan elites in advocating for a military campaign against Mukhtār.[307]

The "'Umar b. Sa'd revenge" narrative (3.8a) opens with Mukhtār's announcement that he will kill a prominent man the next day.[308] He provides a physical description of his intended target and claims that the death will be welcomed by angels and believers. As in other sources, al-Haytham b. al-Aswad sends his son to warn 'Umar b. Sa'd about the impending danger. Al-Ṭabarī then quotes the text of the safe-conduct that 'Umar had secured through the intercession of 'Abd Allāh b. Ja'da b. Hubayra, one of Mukhtār's principal supporters. Al-Ṭabarī places particular emphasis on the vagueness of the stipulation that 'Umar cause no offense. As a precaution, 'Umar flees the city in the middle of the night, but one of his clients convinces him to return. The next day, Mukhtār summons him to court. 'Umar stumbles as he leaves his house, and is immediately killed by Kaysān.[309] Soon thereafter, 'Umar's son Ḥafṣ is also executed. Mukhtār deems these deaths inadequate compensation for the murders of Ḥusayn and his son 'Alī. At the end of the report, al-Ṭabarī

305 For the village's location between Ṣaymara and Sūs, see Yāqūt, 4:540.

306 Al-Ṭabarī, 3:460–1.

307 Ibid., 3:461. Al-Ṭabarī includes a second version of this narrative in which Surāqa testifies only to having seen men on piebald horses; Mukhtār then identifies them as angels.

308 Ibid., 3:464–5.

309 Note that unlike Ibn A'tham, al-Ṭabarī does not suggest that Mukhtār secretly ordered this killing.

attributes the incident to Ibn al-Ḥanafiyya's complaint that Mukhtār had maintained relations with Ḥusayn's killers.[310]

Al-Ṭabarī's "Baṣran expansion" narrative (3.4a) resembles the versions found in other sources, albeit with considerably more detail.[311] Mukhtār sends an agent, al-Muthannā b. al-Mukharriba, to secure the oath of allegiance from sympathetic tribesmen in Baṣra. He manages to gain control of a provisions depot, prompting the Zubayrid governor, al-Qubā' al-Ḥārith b. 'Abd Allāh[312] (d. ca. 80/700), to send two officials, 'Abbād b. al-Ḥuṣayn[313] (d. after 80/700) and Qays b. Haytham al-Sulamī[314] (d. after 71/690), to deal with the disturbance. Al-Ṭabarī here conveys the hierarchical and coercive nature of the relationship between Arabs and non-Arabs in Baṣra, as the latter are forced to take part in the military operation. Al-Muthannā retreats to the tribal district of the 'Abd al-Qays, where the head of the Azd, Ziyād b. 'Amr al-'Atakī[315] (d. after 77/696–7), grants him protection, intercedes with al-Qubā' on his behalf, and negotiates a settlement through which al-Muthannā and his men are permitted to leave the city.[316] The episode ends with a few reports critical of Mukhtār in particular and the Kūfans in general.[317]

The "Ḥijāzī expansion" narrative (3.3a) opens with the text of a letter in which Mukhtār professes his loyalty to Ibn al-Zubayr despite the latter's failure to live up to his promises (i.e. to appoint Mukhtār to

310 Mukhtār sends Ibn al-Ḥanafiyya the two heads along with a letter detailing his executions of those individuals in his jurisdiction who had fought Ḥusayn.

311 Al-Ṭabarī, 3:467–9.

312 Al-Ḥārith b. 'Abd Allāh b. Abī Rabī'a al-Makhzūmī was one of the first men to take the oath of allegiance to Ibn al-Zubayr and served as his governor in Baṣra for one year. See Ibn Sa'd, 5:20–1; al-Mizzī, 5:239–44; al-Ziriklī, 2:156.

313 'Abbād b. al-Ḥuṣayn b. Yazīd b. 'Amr al-Ḥabaṭī al-Tamīmī was in charge of the police (*shurṭa*) in Baṣra. He took part in the battle against Mukhtār, survived the fall of the Zubayrids, and was later involved in military campaigns in the East. He was still alive at the time of 'Abd al-Raḥmān b. Muḥammad b. al-Ash'ath's rebellion. See al-Ṭabarī, 3:617 and index; al-Ziriklī, 3:257.

314 Qays b. Haytham al-Sulamī remained loyal to the Zubayrids but disappears from the historical record after 71/690, when he cautions the Baṣrans that their deceit will facilitate Umayyad rule. See al-Ṭabarī, 4:518 and index.

315 Abū al-Mughīra Ziyād b. 'Amr al-'Atakī was the leader of the Azd at a time of tribal conflict with the Rabī'a in Baṣra. He later sided with 'Abd al-Malik b. Marwān against Muṣ'ab b. al-Zubayr and took part in a campaign against the Khawārij. See Fishbein, *Victory of the Marwanids*, 47, n. 190; al-Ṭabarī, 3:569–71, 590, and index.

316 This outcome reflects the close kinship between the Banū 'Abd al-Qays and the Banū Azd.

317 For these accounts, see al-Ṭabarī, 3:469–70.

an important post).[318] He does this out of fear that Kūfa will be attacked simultaneously on two fronts, by the Umayyads and the Zubayrids.[319] As in other sources, Ibn al-Zubayr tests Mukhtār's sincerity by sending ʿUmar b. ʿAbd al-Raḥmān to Kūfa as his new governor. ʿUmar is intercepted by a contingent of Kūfan cavalry led by Zāʾida b. Qudāma, who first offers him a bribe of 70,000 *dirham*s and then openly threatens his life.[320]

Soon thereafter, the Umayyads send a large army toward the Ḥijāz. Mukhtār again writes to Ibn al-Zubayr, this time with an offer of military assistance. Ibn al-Zubayr accepts on the condition that Mukhtār renew his oath of allegiance. Mukhtār pretends to acquiesce, and dispatches a force of 3,000 men (including only 700 Arabs) led by Shuraḥbīl b. Wars al-Hamdānī. The rest of the narrative is fairly standard. The commander of the Zubayrid army, ʿAbbās b. Sahl, asks the Kūfans to march with him to Wādī al-Qurā.[321] When Shuraḥbīl insists on entering Medina, Ibn Sahl is convinced of his ulterior motives. He distracts the Kūfans with food and attacks them when they are unprepared. Shuraḥbīl is killed early in the fighting. Another 300 Kūfans surrender under the promise of a safe-conduct, but Ibn Sahl nonetheless orders their execution. Some of the captors are unwilling to kill the prisoners, so 200 are set free, only to die in the desert. The report ends with Ibn al-Ḥanafiyya politely declining Mukhtār's offer of further support.

Al-Ṭabarī's "Ibn al-Ḥanafiyya siege" narrative (3.1a) starts with the appearance of the *khashabiyya* in Mecca during the pilgrimage of 66/685.[322] Their arrival is tied to Ibn al-Ḥanafiyya's prior refusal to take the oath of allegiance to anyone until the community has reached a consensus on the matter. Ibn al-Zubayr then threatens Ibn al-Ḥanafiyya and his family with burning unless they acquiesce by a certain deadline. In line with most sources, Ibn al-Ḥanafiyya sends three messengers to Kūfa for help, referencing the city's previous betrayal of Ḥusayn. Mukhtār reads the letter in public, referring to Ibn al-Ḥanafiyya as the "Mahdī," and dispatches multiple cavalry detachments under the general

318 Ibid., 3:470–2.
319 Mukhtār conceals the existence of this letter from even his closest advisors.
320 Al-Ṭabarī places the encounter before the events of the "Baṣran expansion" narrative.
321 Yāqūt, 5:397. 322 Al-Ṭabarī, 3:472–3.

command of Abū ʿAbd Allāh al-Jadalī. The first group, consisting of 150 men, enters Mecca with wooden clubs, proclaiming "Revenge for Ḥusayn." Ibn al-Ḥanafiyya, however, forbids them to shed blood in the sanctuary, leading to a stalemate between the two sides. The siege is finally broken by the arrival of Kūfan reinforcements.

Al-Ṭabarī next offers two variants of the "ʿAlī's chair" narrative.[323] In the first version (3.5a), Ṭufayl b. Jaʿda b. Hubayra al-Makhzūmī[324] (d. after 67/686) purchases the chair and brings it to Mukhtār, claiming that it had belonged to his father, Jaʿda, and that it contains a vestige of ʿAlī's knowledge.[325] Mukhtār presents the chair to his companions, comparing it to the Ark of the Covenant.[326] This causes a public fervor, especially among the *saba'iyya*, that reaches a fevered pitch after news of Ibn al-Ashtar's victory. Al-Ṭabarī notes the efforts of some tribal leaders (e.g. Shabath b. Ribʿī) to caution people about venerating a material object. The chair later disappears from the historical record. In the second version of the chair narrative, Mukhtār compels Ṭufayl's family to produce the relic as part of a calculated campaign to manipulate the Shīʿa.[327] He later disavows it.

At this point, al-Ṭabarī finally returns to the second part of the "Ibn Ziyād battle/elite uprising" narrative (3.2b). The report begins two days after the suppression of the elite revolt, when Mukhtār again orders Ibn al-Ashtar to march against Ibn Ziyād.[328] As he departs the city, Ibn al-Ashtar notices people circling the chair and asks God to protect him from such foolish acts that recall the Israelite worship of the golden calf.[329] Al-Ṭabarī is here differentiating Ibn al-Ashtar from the most ardent of Mukhtār's supporters. The rest of the report follows a familiar pattern.[330] There is tribal unrest among the Syrian forces, exemplified by the alleged defection of ʿUmayr b. al-Ḥubāb al-Sulamī.[331] Before describing the hostilities, al-Ṭabarī relates a long exchange between an unidentified Syrian and an unidentified Kūfan that summarizes their

323 Ibid., 3:475–6.
324 There is little information about Ṭufayl. For his brother ʿAbd Allāh, see n. 66 in this chapter.
325 Al-Ṭabarī, 3:476–7.
326 Ibid., 3:476. Mukhtār famously claims that "there are no objects (*ʿamr*) possessed by past communities that will not be possessed by us."
327 Ibid., 3:477. 328 Ibid., 3:475. 329 Ibid., 3:476. 330 Ibid., 3:479–82.
331 ʿUmayr does not fulfill his promise to withdraw from the fight and reaches out to Ibn al-Ashtar only when the outcome is certain.

respective positions.[332] Ibn al-Ashtar then makes a speech laying out Ibn Ziyād's crimes, particularly his refusal to peacefully resolve the conflict with Ḥusayn. The battle culminates with Ibn al-Ashtar leading a charge that breaks the center of the Syrian forces. Ibn Ziyād is killed in the course of the fighting, and his body is identified by its musky scent. The narrative ends with a report detailing Mukhtār's vague (and incorrect) predictions about the outcome of the battle, which his supporters interpret as evidence of his veracity.[333]

Fall (67/687)[334]

Al-Ṭabarī relates a two-battle variant of the "final defeat" narrative (4.1b), which begins with Muṣʿab b. al-Zubayr's appointment as the new governor of Baṣra.[335] The city is teeming with disgruntled Kūfan exiles such as Shabath b. Ribʿī, who publicly implore him for help. He agrees to march against Mukhtār, and in preparation he recalls al-Muhallab b. Abī Ṣufra, who is on campaign against the Azāriqa. Muḥammad b. al-Ashʿath personally delivers the message, adding that "slaves and non-Arab clients have seized control of our women, children, and dependents."[336] Al-Muhallab quickly returns to the city. The Baṣran army is organized according to tribe, with the Kūfans making up an independent unit with their own leadership. In Kūfa, meanwhile, Mukhtār blames the exiles for the impending conflict and places Aḥmar b. Shumayṭ in charge of his forces (explicitly referred to as the "Shīʿa"). In the ensuing battle, the Baṣrans, led by al-Muhallab, decimate the Kūfan army, killing many of Mukhtār's key supporters,

332 The Syrian disparages ʿAlī, accuses the Kūfans of fighting without an Imām, and rejects their offers of arbitration given their past refusal to honor such agreements. The Kūfan demands vengeance for Ibn Ziyād's role in the killing of Ḥusayn and his non-Arab followers at Karbalāʾ.

333 Al-Ṭabarī, 3:482.

334 Al-Ṭabarī includes a number of variant narrative elements for this segment of the core structure. In one version of the "final defeat" narrative (4.1c), Mukhtār remains loyal to Ibn al-Zubayr until the latter's appointment of Muṣʿab as governor of Baṣra (ibid., 3:495–6). He is then defeated in a single battle because of his own cowardice on the cusp of victory. An alternate version of the "Mukhtār's death" narrative claims that he is killed during a small skirmish outside the fort after a siege of four months (ibid., 3:496). This is followed by a "surrender/execution" narrative in which Muṣʿab initially decides to spare the 700 Arabs and execute the non-Arabs. He changes his mind when some unnamed companions remind him that all of these men share the same religion.

335 Ibid., 3:483–90. 336 Ibid., 3:484.

including Ibn Shumayṭ. Muṣʿab issues orders to hunt down the retreating men and execute any prisoners. Al-Ṭabarī emphasizes the extreme brutality of the Kūfan tribal leaders on the Baṣran side, who deem it more permissible to spill the blood of Mukhtār's supporters than that of "Turks or Daylamites."[337] After the battle, Mukhtār thwarts Muṣʿab's efforts to transport his army to Kūfa on boats. He rallies his remaining supporters and prepares for a final confrontation at Ḥarūrāʾ. The Kūfans are again routed, forcing Mukhtār to take refuge in the fort in Kūfa.[338]

Al-Ṭabarī's version of the "Mukhtār's death" narrative (4.2a) centers on the siege of the fort.[339] The encircled men are compelled to buy water from peddlers at extortionate prices, and subsist on supplies smuggled in by their wives. Muṣʿab then tightens the siege, searching women before allowing them to pass. As conditions inside the fort deteriorate, Mukhtār leads a series of small raids, during which he is pelted with stones and filthy water from the rooftops. Eventually, he decides to launch a final, likely fatal, attack, and is joined by only nineteen of his followers. He warns the rest that if they surrender, they will face execution. At this point, al-Ṭabarī also relates Mukhtār's explanation of his motivations to al-Sāʾib.[340] Specifically, Mukhtār notes the seizure of various parts of the Muslim world by men whom he considers his equals in terms of lineage – that is, Marwān and Ibn al-Zubayr. He claims superior legitimacy, however, based on his commitment to the Prophet's family, and concludes by ridiculing al-Sāʾib for his gullibility and urging him to fight for personal glory. Mukhtār is killed in the ensuing skirmish.

At the start of al-Ṭabarī's "surrender and execution" narrative (4.3b), Bujayr b. ʿAbd Allāh al-Muslī, a non-Arab client, reiterates Mukhtār's warning about the consequences of surrender.[341] The men ignore him and throw themselves at the mercy of their enemies. Bujayr then makes an eloquent argument for forgiveness, drawing parallels with previous conflicts and emphasizing the common bonds of religion. As in most other sources, Muṣʿab is inclined to pardon the men, but some Kūfan tribal leaders insist on retribution.[342] He eventually orders the prisoners'

[337] Ibid., 3:485–6.
[338] Ibid., 3:489. Al-Ṭabarī's "final defeat" narrative is followed by two reports about a group of extremist (*ghālin*) Shīʿa.
[339] Ibid., 3:490–2. [340] Ibid., 3:491. [341] Ibid., 3:492–3. [342] Ibid., 3:492.

execution, rejecting a final offer by Mukhtār's men to march against the Syrians. Bujayr requests and is granted a death apart from the others.[343]

Interpretive Framework

Al-Ṭabarī's treatment of Mukhtār's revolt mirrors those of al-Balādhurī and al-Dīnawarī in that it emphasizes a tribal/ethnic interpretive framework. At the very start of his narrative, al-Ṭabarī makes a distinction between those with tribal standing and those described as clients or slaves. During his time in the Ḥijāz, Mukhtār insists on an oath of allegiance commensurate with his tribal status, vows to fight only men of distinguished lineage, and demands respect on a par with Ibn al-Zubayr's other supporters. After his return to Kūfa, Mukhtār recruits figures who are associated with the Shīʿa but also possess high tribal standing, such as ʿAbīda b. ʿAmr al-Baddī and Ibn al-Ashtar. Once in power, Mukhtār continues to make overtures to tribal leaders. The early period of his rule includes only a few revenge accounts with almost no mention of the killing of prominent tribal figures, including those associated with the events of Karbalāʾ. Mukhtār even agrees to abandon his non-Arab supporters if the tribal leaders agree to fight with him against his enemies. He only turns on these elites in the wake of their failed rebellion. Before his death, Mukhtār explicitly acknowledges his material motivations, describing his lineage as equal to those of other caliphal contenders and asking his men to fight for the glory of their names. In the process, his religious discourse is exposed as a cover for an overtly political agenda.

The reports preserved by al-Ṭabarī consistently describe Mukhtār's non-Arab[344] supporters as "clients and slaves" who are hostile to tribal

343 A similar sentiment (described in less detail) is ascribed to Musāfir b. Saʿīd b. Nimrān, who is also killed separately (ibid., 3:492–3). Two further reports merit mention. In the first, ʿUbayd Allāh b. al-Ḥurr (among others) urges Muṣʿab to spare the lives of some of the 6,000 prisoners (ibid., 3:496). He advises turning the Arabs over to their kin as a favor, returning the slaves to their owners so that they might work, and killing only the non-Arab clients for their "disbelief." Muṣʿab rejects this proposal, and the account ends with a poem that condemns the execution. In the second report, a charlatan attempts to deceive the Banū Hamdān by producing a letter allegedly written by Ibn al-Ḥanafiyya to Mukhtār (ibid., 3:495). The narrator discredits the man, who then turns his attention to "slaves." The point here is quite apparent: the Hamdān are easily swayed by those who claim to represent the family of the Prophet, and they are exceeded in naïveté only by slaves.

344 For al-Ṭabarī, this term likely included individuals of Persian, Turkish, or Daylamite origin.

leaders and adamantly oppose his repeated overtures for Arab support. Mukhtār's decision to grant non-Arabs access to financial resources previously reserved exclusively for Arabs ultimately leads to a citywide uprising. Non-Arabs are even segregated from the larger Arab Muslim population in the army, where they constitute their own units under their own leaders. Non-Arab prisoners are uniformly executed by their captors even when they possess a safe-conduct. This severity contrasts with the treatment of Arab prisoners, who are generally released after the conclusion of hostilities. These reports highlight the underlying social tensions that dominated the Muslim world at this time. For al-Ṭabarī, it was these tensions that initially fueled Mukhtār's movement and later undermined it.

Religious considerations are marginal to, though not absent from, al-Ṭabarī's depiction of Mukhtār's movement. The Shī'a are mentioned at numerous points, but their beliefs do not influence the shape of the broader narrative. In many instances, they simply serve as objects of ridicule or mockery. Their veneration of the purported chair of 'Alī, for example, is viewed with disdain even by their own leaders, most notably Ibn al-Ashtar. Mukhtār tolerates or even endorses some of their problematic beliefs, but only when this enables him to secure an immediate political gain. He is thus willing to take advantage of Surāqa's testimony regarding angels on piebald horses in public while expressing his skepticism in private. Whereas other sources link Mukhtār to the doctrine of *badā'*, al-Ṭabarī associates it with extremist elements among his supporters. Mukhtār's religious program is thus reduced to two elements: calling for vengeance for the family of the Prophet and affirming the Imāmate of Ibn al-Ḥanafiyya. The former helps him consolidate his control of Kūfa, particularly after the elite uprising, whereas the latter legitimizes him through association with a distant charismatic figure.

The primary role of religion in al-Ṭabarī's text lies in explaining the general cohesiveness of Mukhtār's movement. At the start of his organizational efforts, Mukhtār recognizes that religious sentiments provide a means for bringing together a wide coalition of non-Arabs and Arabs. In the case of non-Arabs, his call for revenge for the Prophet's family aligns with their hostility toward the tribal leaders who participated in the campaign against Ḥusayn.[345] Mukhtār also draws on Shī'ī sympathies

[345] Al-Ṭabarī strongly suggests that most of the non-Arabs in Kūfa were partial to Shī'ī religious beliefs.

in appealing to Arab supporters. When he enters Kūfa, he targets influential members of the Banū Hamdān, who remain loyal to him throughout the narrative.[346] They even attack fellow tribesmen during the elite uprising, privileging religious affiliation over tribal affinity. In his recruitment of Ibn al-Ashtar, Mukhtār references the latter's father's strong support of ʿAlī and forges a letter from Ibn al-Ḥanafiyya. After Mukhtār's defeat, Kūfan tribal leaders justify their brutality by arguing that their Arab and non-Arab opponents' adherence to Shīʿī religious beliefs outweighs their tribal affiliations. In all of these cases, religion provides insight into Mukhtār's movement without affecting the overall narrative.

A final point to consider involves al-Ṭabarī's propensity for viewing local developments within a regional political framework. This perspective is evident in his depiction of Mukhtār's final speech, in which Mukhtār compares himself to the Zubayrids and the Umayyads. It is also reflected in the elaborate descriptions of Mukhtār's expansion efforts in the Ḥijāz and Baṣra. On numerous occasions, al-Ṭabarī invokes the larger context of caliphal politics. He explains, for example, the underlying causes of the battle between Ibn al-Ashtar and Ibn Ziyād as well as the political rivalries that led to Muṣʿab's appointment as governor of Baṣra. In contrast to other sources that view Mukhtār's rule as a local phenomenon, al-Ṭabarī presents it as part of a broad upheaval within the Muslim world shaped by tribal politics and changing ethnic demographics.

I al-Masʿūdī (d. 346/957)

Al-Masʿūdī's *Murūj al-dhahab* presents a single, smooth account of Mukhtār's rebellion featuring nine narrative elements in chronological order.

The Ḥijāz	Sedition	Rule	Fall
1.1a, 1.2a	2.1a, 2.6c	3.1a, 3.2a	4.1a, 4.2a, 4.3b

The elements are listed in the order of their appearance in the text.

346 Al-Ṭabarī even includes a report that mocks the Banū Hamdān for their propensity to be duped by swindlers who claim to represent the Prophet's family (3:448). See also n. 343 in this chapter.

The Ḥijāz (61–4/680–4)

Al-Mas'ūdī folds the "Ibn al-Zubayr oath" narrative (1.1a) into his discussion of the initial conflict between Ibn al-Zubayr and the Umayyads.[347] In al-Mas'ūdī's telling, Mukhtār takes the oath of allegiance to Ibn al-Zubayr without requesting anything in return. Soon thereafter, the Umayyad army leaves the region after learning of the death of the caliph, Yazīd I b. Mu'āwiya. Ibn al-Zubayr is then able to secure the oath of allegiance from the people of Iraq and names Ibn Muṭī' as his governor of Kūfa. This report is followed by a version of the "return to Kūfa" narrative (1.2a) in which Mukhtār offers to recruit an army of Kūfan Shī'a to fight the Umayyads.[348] Ibn al-Zubayr gives him permission to travel to the city and implement his plan. It is worth noting that both of the narrative elements in this period unambiguously maintain Mukhtār's loyalty to Ibn al-Zubayr.

Sedition (64–6/684–5)

Al-Mas'ūdī's discussion of Mukhtār's rebellion is highly condensed. It starts with an abridged variant of the "entry and recruitment" narrative (2.1a) in which Mukhtār pretends to mourn the deaths of a number of Ṭālibids and their followers.[349] He then summons the Kūfans to avenge the blood of the Prophet's family. At this point, al-Mas'ūdī transitions into the "rebellion" narrative (2.6a), as Mukhtār secures the support of the Shī'a, marches on the fort, and expels Ibn Muṭī' from the city.[350] He also distributes the remaining contents of the treasury among the unnamed people. In a letter to Ibn al-Zubayr, Mukhtār justifies his actions by disparaging Ibn Muṭī' as a weak and feckless leader. He renounces his allegiance only after Ibn al-Zubayr condemns his financial policies and refuses to confirm him as governor.

Rule (66–7/685–6)

Al-Mas'ūdī's portrayal of Mukhtār's rule in Kūfa is unique. After his break with Ibn al-Zubayr, Mukhtār offers his support, along with a large monetary gift, to 'Alī b. Ḥusayn, the fourth Imām of the Twelver Shī'a.[351] The 'Alid responds by publicly denouncing Mukhtār in the Prophet's mosque in Medina and by accusing him

347 Al-Mas'ūdī (2009), 4:101–4.
348 Ibid., 4:104. These same details are repeated later in al-Mas'ūdī's account (4:120).
349 Ibid., 4:104. 350 Ibid., 4:104–5. 351 Ibid., 4:105.

of false sympathy for the family of Abū Ṭālib. Mukhtār next writes to Ibn al-Ḥanafiyya with a similar offer.[352] 'Alī b. Ḥusayn counsels his uncle to reject the overture, dismissing Mukhtār as a political opportunist who manipulates the public's affection for the Prophet's family for personal gain. Ibn 'Abbās, by contrast, advises Ibn al-Ḥanafiyya to delay his response given the potential danger posed by Ibn al-Zubayr. In the end, Ibn al-Ḥanafiyya remains silent on the matter.

In the ensuing part of al-Mas'ūdī's text, Mukhtār consolidates his position in Kūfa by recruiting new supporters with Shī'ī proclivities. After publicly affirming the Imāmate of Ibn al-Ḥanafiyya, Mukhtār claims to receive knowledge of the unknown and revelation through an angel.[353] He also begins to pursue and punish Ḥusayn's killers. Al-Mas'ūdī here alludes to the killing of 'Umar b. Sa'd, described as the man in charge of the campaign against Ḥusayn, but offers no concrete details.[354] These revenge killings prove incredibly popular among the Kūfans, and bolster Mukhtār's base of support.

The most detailed narrative element in al-Mas'ūdī's chronicle is a variant of the "Ibn al-Ḥanafiyya siege" narrative (3.1a), which opens with Ibn al-Zubayr's imprisonment of Ḥasan b. Muḥammad b. al-Ḥanafiyya[355] (d. 95/714?). After Ḥasan escapes and takes refuge with his father in Mecca, Ibn al-Zubayr blockades the Banū Hāshim and threatens to burn them alive. He even gathers firewood to convey the seriousness of his intentions. The account now shifts to Kūfa, where Abū 'Abd Allāh al-Jadalī musters, on Mukhtār's orders, 4,000 Kūfan cavalry for a rescue mission. Mukhtār worries, however, that such a large force might prod Ibn al-Zubayr to act on his threat more quickly and decides instead to send a smaller detachment of cavalry.[356] They arrive in Mecca undetected, and successfully evacuate the Banū Hāshim. As in other sources, Ibn al-Ḥanafiyya forbids the Kūfans to fight in the sanctuary unless they are attacked first, but Ibn al-Zubayr is unaware of this order. The report concludes with a statement from

352 Ibid. 353 Ibid., 4:106. 354 Ibid.

355 Ibid., 4:107–9. For Ḥasan's political views and his importance in theology, see *EI²*, s.v. "Al-Ḥasan b. Muḥammad b. al-Ḥanafiyya" (J. van Ess). See also al-Ziriklī, 2:212.

356 Al-Mas'ūdī (2009), 4:108.

'Urwa b. al-Zubayr[357] (d. 93–4/711–13) in which he claims that his brother only intended to frighten Ibn al-Ḥanafiyya.[358]

At this point, al-Mas'ūdī inserts a series of reports directly pertaining to the Kaysānī Shī'a. He notes that they uphold the Imāmate of Ibn al-Ḥanafiyya but mentions a few areas of disagreement.[359] The most important controversy surrounds Ibn al-Ḥanafiyya's death: some Kaysānīs confirm it, whereas others believe that he remains alive and hidden on the mountain of Raḍwā.[360] Another dispute involves the origin of the name Kaysāniyya.[361] One group claims that it stems from Mukhtār, who was given the nickname Abū 'Amra Kaysān by 'Alī b. Abī Ṭālib. Others contend that Kaysān was the name of one of Mukhtār's leading supporters. Al-Mas'ūdī here refers readers interested in Kaysānī theological doctrines to his (now lost) heresiography. He then acknowledges many famous Kaysānī poets and presents long quotations from their works.[362] The next two sections document the hostility between Ibn al-Zubayr and the Banū Hāshim. The first relates Ibn 'Abbās's criticism of Ibn al-Zubayr, which leads to the former's exile and eventual death in Ṭā'if.[363] The second depicts Ibn al-Ḥanafiyya defending his father, 'Alī, and himself against Ibn al-Zubayr's disparaging polemical attacks.[364]

After a long discussion of political events in Syria, al-Mas'ūdī returns to Kūfa for an isolated, one-battle variant of the "Ibn Ziyād battle/elite uprising" narrative (3.2a).[365] The account picks up after the defeat of the Tawwābūn at 'Ayn al-Warda. The Umayyad army led by Ibn Ziyād marches toward Mawṣil and meets Ibn al-Ashtar at the Khāzir River. The subsequent Kūfan victory, which is not portrayed in detail, is facilitated by the defection of the Qays, who still harbor resentment from their defeat

357 For his life and his scholarly importance, see *EI*², s.v. "'Urwa b. al-Zubayr" (G. Schoeler). See also Ibn Sa'd, 5:136–9; al-Ziriklī, 4:226.

358 For this report, al-Mas'ūdī directs readers to another book, entitled *Ḥadā'iq al-adhhān*, which focuses on the virtues of the family of the Prophet: see al-Mas'ūdī (2009), 4:109. At the conclusion of the narrative, al-Mas'ūdī quotes Ibn al-Zubayr's threat to burn Ibn al-Ḥanafiyya unless he surrenders by sunset. Ibn al-Ḥanafiyya is only saved by the timely arrival of Abū 'Abd Allāh al-Jadalī.

359 Ibid., 4:109. 360 Ibid. 361 Ibid., 4:110. 362 Ibid., 4:110–12.

363 Ibid., 4:112.

364 Ibid., 4:113. This exchange is also mentioned by al-Ya'qūbī (see section F).

365 Ibid., 4:135–6.

at Marj Rāhiṭ.[366] Ibn al-Ashtar sends Ibn Ziyād's head to Mukhtār, who forwards it to Ibn al-Zubayr (as opposed to Ibn al-Ḥanafiyya) as a sign of his continued loyalty.

Fall (67/687)

Al-Masʻūdī's account of Mukhtār's fall from power features a typical variant of the one-battle "final defeat" narrative (4.1a).[367] The proximate cause of the conflict is Ibn al-Zubayr's appointment of Muṣʻab as the new governor of Iraq. This leads to a military confrontation near Ḥarūrā' in which both sides suffer heavy casualties. In the end the Baṣrans are victorious, and Mukhtār is forced to retreat to the fort in Kūfa.

Al-Masʻūdī then offers his version of the death narrative (4.2a),[368] in which Mukhtār leads a group of his supporters out of the fort each day on small raids. These men are explicitly identified as members of the *khashabiyya* from among the Kaysānī Shīʻa, but there is no discussion of their particular beliefs. Mukhtār is killed during one of these skirmishes. He is beheaded, and then a mob tears apart his body.

At the start of al-Masʻūdī's "surrender and execution" narrative (4.3b), Muṣʻab refuses to grant a safe-conduct to the remaining 7,000 men in the fort.[369] When they continue to fight with stubborn resolve, however, he relents and guarantees their safety in return for their surrender. He then violates the agreement and executes them anyway, referring to them disparagingly as the *khashabiyya*. It is worth noting that al-Masʻūdī describes these rebels as having fought sincerely to avenge Ḥusayn.

Interpretive Framework

Al-Masʻūdī situates Mukhtār's rebellion in an interpretive framework informed by regional political rivalries. The motivations of individuals are mostly ascribed to narrow self-interest. Along these lines, Mukhtār is cast as a political partisan who continues to espouse his loyalty to Ibn al-Zubayr even after seizing control of Kūfa. The primary cause of their falling out is fiscal policy. It is only after this break that Mukhtār seeks alternate ʻAlid sources of

366 Recall that the other sources disagree over whether ʻUmayr followed through on his pledge to withdraw from battle.

367 Al-Masʻūdī (2009), 4:137. 368 Ibid., 4:137–8. 369 Ibid., 4:138.

authority in an act of blatant political opportunism. Mukhtār's subsequent actions are pragmatic measures designed to maintain power, and their religious symbolism is subordinate to his political agenda. His conflict with Ibn Ziyād is framed within a larger regional conflict with no hint of religious motivations. After Ibn al-Ashtar's victory near Mawṣil, Mukhtār sends Ibn Ziyād's head to Ibn al-Zubayr, perhaps as an overture toward reconciliation. The rescue mission to Ibn al-Ḥanafiyya is driven by the 'Alid's ambiguous response to Mukhtār's offers of fealty. Other figures are depicted in equally calculating political terms. Ibn al-Zubayr is ready to burn the Banū Hāshim until he is confronted by a large Kūfan cavalry, while Muṣ'ab violates his promise of safe-conduct when it proves expedient.

Al-Mas'ūdī's focus on broad political issues is coupled with a cynical view of religious claims. Mukhtār manipulates religious sentiment throughout the text. After his return to Kūfa, he manifests sadness in order to win the Shī'ī support that fuels his rebellion. This stratagem is followed by pragmatic attempts to secure the backing, first, of 'Alī b. Ḥusayn and then Ibn al-Ḥanafiyya. These important 'Alids, as well as Ibn 'Abbās, repeatedly decry his lack of belief, and condemn, explicitly and implicitly, his utilitarian call for avenging the family of the Prophet. Mukhtār's revenge killings of people complicit in Ḥusayn's death are likewise a transparent attempt to garner public support. Al-Mas'ūdī's criticism does not extend to important 'Alids or to the wider Shī'ī community, with one notable exception: the Kaysānī Shī'a are excoriated for defending Mukhtār even after his death. Finally, al-Mas'ūdī rarely enables Mukhtār to articulate his own desires or beliefs. This treatment contrasts with other sources, in which he announces his intentions at critical moments such as his initial flight from Kūfa or just prior to his death.

A final point worth mentioning centers on the almost complete lack of tribal or ethnic factors in al-Mas'ūdī's account. Unlike most other sources, al-Mas'ūdī does not even allude to the non-Arab identities of Mukhtār's supporters. The tribal elites are also absent from the narrative, with no indication of an uprising in Kūfa or complaints about Mukhtār's preference for non-Arabs or former slaves. Recall that the Kūfan exiles are often portrayed as lobbying for a Baṣran military campaign and, in the course of the final battle, as being particularly brutal in their treatment of Mukhtār's supporters. All of these details are replaced in al-Mas'ūdī's chronicle by an interpretive framework centered on regional and caliphal politics.

IV Interpretive Frameworks: Localities, Tribes, and Religion

Four primary interpretive frameworks pervade historical depictions of Mukhtār (see Table 2.4). The first framework highlights tensions between Arab tribal elites and non-Arabs (both clients and slaves). It lies at the heart of the accounts of al-Balādhurī, al-Dīnawarī, and al-Ṭabarī and constitutes a secondary lens in the work of Ibn A'tham. For these authors, Mukhtār channels the growing power and consequent demands of non-Arab populations that had been systematically denied status and financial benefits. He is opposed by Arab leaders invested in the maintenance of the existing tribal system. The latter are embodied by figures such as Shabath b. Rib'ī, who routinely represents their interests in their confrontations with Mukhtār. The tribal/ethnic framework is particularly noticeable in reports of military encounters, in which tribal leaders execute non-Arab prisoners while sparing the lives of Arabs. In negotiations before their revolt and in their appeals for Baṣran intervention, tribal leaders regularly express their anger about the elevation of non-Arabs to positions of authority. They also mention Mukhtār's decision to grant non-Arabs stipends from communal Muslim property. These arguments are decisive in convincing the Baṣrans to march against Kūfa. In the final encounter with Mukhtār, the tribal elites are vicious in their treatment of Mukhtār's men and later demand the execution of all prisoners despite reasonable objections. For historians working within this interpretive framework, Mukhtār represents shifting demographics and growing divisions within the Muslim community. Although the tribal elites are victorious in the short term, Mukhtār foreshadows the end of their dominance.

A second interpretive framework that informs discussions of Mukhtār's rebellion centers on its religious dimensions. Historians writing from this perspective – in particular Ibn A'tham and al-Ya'qūbī, but also al-Balādhurī, Pseudo-Ibn Qutayba, al-Ṭabarī, and al-Mas'ūdī – tend to equate Mukhtār's supporters with the Shī'a. In some cases, pro-Shī'ī sentiment is conveyed without the explicit use of this term. The contingent of cavalry that Mukhtār sends to the Ḥijāz, for example, is referred to as the *khashabiyya*, while another supporting group is called the *saba'iyya*. A number of historians (e.g. al-Balādhurī, Pseudo-Ibn Qutayba, and al-Mas'ūdī) openly discuss the sincerity of Mukhtār's religious claims, particularly his calls for avenging the family of the Prophet. They also debate whether his revenge killings were

Table 2.4 – *The Interpretive Frameworks for Mukhtār's Rise and Fall*

	Tribal/ethnic	Religious	Regional/political	Propagandist
Ibn A'tham al-Kūfī	X (secondary – opposition)	X (dominant – movement)		
Ibn Sa'd				X (Zubayrids and 'Alids)
Akhbār al-dawla				X ('Abbāsids)
al-Balādhurī	X (dominant – motivation)	X (secondary – manipulation)		
Ps.-Ibn Qutayba		X (secondary – personal)	X (dominant – caliphal politics)	
al-Ya'qūbī		X (dominant)	X (secondary – ambition)	
al-Dīnawarī	X (dominant)		X (secondary – ambition)	
al-Ṭabarī	X (dominant)	X (secondary – manipulation)	X (secondary – ambition)	
al-Mas'ūdī		X (secondary – manipulation)	X (dominant – caliphal politics)	

Each author's dominant interpretive framework is highlighted in dark gray and any secondary framework(s) in light gray.

motivated by belief or fueled by a political agenda. Some historians (e.g. al-Balādhurī, al-Ṭabarī) go so far as to combine the religious and tribal/ethnic interpretive frameworks. In these works, Mukhtār's non-Arab supporters are essentially indistinguishable from the Shī'a. They claim that Mukhtār has knowledge of the future, accept the idea that God can change his mind (*badā'*), and venerate a chair for its association with 'Alī. Some historians utilize these reports to draw unfavorable connections between the Shī'a and certain segments of the population. In addition to non-Arabs, the Banū Hamdān are singled out for their general gullibility. Other historians – particularly those with Shī'ī sympathies – (Ibn A'tham, al-Ya'qūbī) describe Mukhtār and his followers as holding deviant and false beliefs that are not representative of "mainstream" Shī'ism. Overall, historians invested in a religious framework portray Mukhtār as the leader of a Shī'ī revolutionary movement regardless of his actual sincerity.

The third interpretive framework at play in the sources places Mukhtār's revolt within a broader regional struggle between the Umayyads in Syria and the Zubayrids in the Ḥijāz. For Pseudo-Ibn Qutayba and al-Mas'ūdī, and to a smaller degree for al-Ya'qūbī, al-Dīnawarī, and al-Ṭabarī, Mukhtār represents a third center of power with ambitions to extend the reach of his authority. This motivation is evidenced by his efforts to recruit followers in Baṣra (the "Baṣran expansion" narrative) or to secure territory in the Ḥijāz through utilitarian (and sometimes false) overtures toward Ibn al-Zubayr and Ibn al-Ḥanafiyya. Historians invested in a regional framework devote considerable space to political and military developments in other locations. Al-Ṭabarī, for example, provides long descriptions of the initial conflict between the Umayyads and Ibn al-Zubayr as well as a detailed register of military encounters near Mawṣil. These writers attribute Mukhtār's downfall to the changing political situation in Baṣra. After Muṣ'ab is appointed governor, Kūfan tribal leaders successfully petition him to march against Mukhtār through appeals grounded in the maintenance of the status quo.

The fourth and final interpretive framework integrates Mukhtār into larger narratives that focus on other historical figures or movements. The two sources that best fit in this category – Ibn Sa'd and the *Akhbār al-dawla al-'Abbāsiyya* – are only interested in Mukhtār for secondary reasons. Ibn Sa'd uses Mukhtār to better understand the rivalry between Ibn al-Ḥanafiyya (the ʿAlids) and Ibn al-Zubayr (the Zubayrids). He first mentions Mukhtār's decision to break with Ibn al-Zubayr and then recounts his repeated efforts to win the support of Ibn al-Ḥanafiyya. This framing is hardly surprising given that Ibn Saʿd places these reports under the biography of Ibn al-Ḥanafiyya. The *Akhbār al-dawla al-ʿAbbāsiyya*, for its part, utilizes Mukhtār's history to buttress the legitimacy of the ʿAbbāsids (specifically Ibn ʿAbbās) and their agents (in this case Bujayr).

V Notes on Historiography

The case of Mukhtār b. Abī ʿUbayd illustrates the applicability of the model proposed in Chapter 1. In concrete terms, the accounts adhere to the rhetoricized approach, which privileges the creation of meaning over verbatim reporting. The historians present a relatively stable core structure that they populate with narrative elements formed through considerable rhetorical embellishment. These elements are woven together into interpretive frameworks that convey authorial purpose. My analysis has found no discernible differences between historical sources grouped according to genre (chronography vs. prosopography vs. biography).

This particular case study is, in many ways, a useful starting point for the application of my historiographical model. First, a majority of the sources considered in this chapter are chronographies, which are, by their very nature, vested in a linear narrative. The pertinent historical accounts are, therefore, concentrated in a few locations with connective commentary that reinforces the author's intent. This makes it possible to identify a stable core structure and to deduce the authors' various interpretive frameworks. The analysis also features some prosopographical sources. These, however, are more difficult to parse than are the chronographies, since Mukhtār is typically discussed in relation to other important figures, particularly Ibn al-Ḥanafiyya. Second, the sources in this chapter reveal no substantive differences in the approaches employed by Sunnī and Shīʿī historians, respectively. This homogeneity may be a result of Mukhtār's uniqueness in that he attracts the attention of historians across communal boundaries for whom his portrayal lacks real theological stakes. This is not the case with figures such as ʿAlī b. Abī Ṭālib, who are contested by different groups, or with figures such as Ḥusayn, who are situated at the core of group identity.

The next two case studies complicate the issues of genre and communal affiliation in order to demonstrate the broader utility of the rhetoricized model of historical writing. In terms of source material, Chapters 3 and 4 focus largely on biographical and prosopographical works, according a reduced role to chronographies. In terms of subject matter, these chapters examine well-known Shīʿī Imāms discussed extensively by both Sunnī and Shīʿī historians. The subsequent analyses will highlight the utility of my model across genres while exposing the fallacy of established assumptions about the qualitative differences between Sunnī and Shīʿī historical writing.

3 *The Life of Mūsā b. Ja'far al-Kāẓim (d. 183/799)*

This second case study demonstrates the applicability of my historiographical model across communal boundaries through an examination of the life of the seventh Imām of the Twelver Shī'a, Mūsā b. Ja'far al-Kāẓim. Two preliminary points merit mention. First, most of the sources that discuss al-Kāẓim (both Twelver and non-Twelver) are either biographical or prosopographical in nature. These are historical genres whose rhetoricized characteristics are well known among modern scholars.[1] Second, there is considerable disparity in the amount of pertinent historical material between Twelver and non-Twelver sources. Twelver writers offer extensive biographies in line with al-Kāẓim's importance as the Imām at a time of crisis and division. The non-Twelver sources handle al-Kāẓim with a lighter touch. Sunnī accounts cast him as a scholar of good repute, while Zaydī reports compare him unfavorably to his contemporary rival (and the subject of Chapter 4), Yaḥyā b. 'Abd Allāh (d. 187/803).

The chapter opens by outlining the core structure of al-Kāẓim's biography that is shared by every source regardless of its genre or the communal affiliation of its author. This is followed by a two-part analysis that reflects the nature of the extant source material. The first section focuses on the non-Twelver sources and adheres to a relatively straightforward structure. It catalogues narrative elements and then identifies the primary interpretive frameworks that shape the corpus of Sunnī and Zaydī accounts. The second section turns to Twelver sources and examines the evolving depictions of al-Kāẓim's life chronologically, ordered by the death dates of the individual writers. The focus in this section is on detailed Twelver representations of al-Kāẓim, in contrast to the generality of non-Twelver works. Despite differences in the treatment of al-Kāẓim by non-Twelver and Twelver sources, the chapter establishes a unity between their historical approaches.

[1] Cooperson, *Classical Arabic Biography*, 1–24.

I The Core Structure: The Life of Mūsā al-Kāẓim

Mūsā al-Kāẓim b. Ja'far b. Muḥammad b. 'Alī b. Ḥusayn b. 'Alī b. Abī Ṭālib was born near Medina between 127/745 and 129/746–7.[2] His mother Ḥumayda was of Berber or Andalusian origin and was purchased from a slave dealer by his father, Ja'far al-Ṣādiq (d. 148/765).[3] Numerous Twelver accounts emphasize Ḥumayda's special qualities, specifically the divine intervention that ensured that she was still a virgin at the time of her sale.[4] There are few details regarding al-Kāẓim's childhood; those that exist are mentioned by Twelver scholars to establish his right to the Imāmate. In one representative example, he is reported to have spoken from the cradle and to have instructed one of his father's followers to change the name the latter had given his newborn daughter.[5] In another, he is described as serious in outlook and not inclined to frivolous play.[6] These scattered traditions are meant to elevate al-Kāẓim's status above that of his brothers.

The succession crisis that followed al-Ṣādiq's death produced five important factions.[7] The forebears of the Ismā'īlīs held that al-Ṣādiq had appointed his eldest son, Ismā'īl, as his successor. When Ismā'īl apparently predeceased his father, they either denied his death or claimed that the Imāmate had passed to Ismā'īl's son (al-Ṣādiq's grandson) Muḥammad. A second group, referred to as the Samṭiyya or Shumayṭiyya, turned to another of al-Ṣādiq's sons, Muḥammad, as al-Ṣādiq's successor, but they had little lasting impact on the historical record. The Nawūsiyya, a third faction, claimed that al-Ṣādiq had not died, and awaited his return as the Mahdī. The fourth group, initially perhaps the most populous, rallied to al-Ṣādiq's eldest surviving son, 'Abd Allāh al-Afṭaḥ (d. 148/765), and were known as the Faṭḥiyya. When 'Abd Allāh died shortly after his father without an heir, most Faṭḥīs acknowledged al-Kāẓim as the Imām. A significant portion continued to uphold 'Abd Allāh's legitimacy and counted Mūsā as

[2] Ibn Kathīr (1997), 13:623; al-Mufīd, *Irshād*, 288; al-Khaṭīb al-Baghdādī, 13:29; Ibn al-Jawzī, 9:87. For a summary of his life, see also *EI*^{2}, s.v. "Mūsā al-Kāẓim" (E. Kohlberg).

[3] Al-Iṣbahānī, 413. [4] Al-Kulaynī, 1:476–7.

[5] He had initially named his child either 'Ā'isha or al-Ḥumayrā' ('Ā'isha's nickname). Al-Kulaynī, 1:310; al-Mufīd, *Irshād*, 290.

[6] Al-Kulaynī, 1:311; al-Mufīd, *Irshād*, 290.

[7] For these divisions, see al-Nawbakhtī, 77–86; al-Qummī, 79–88; al-Baghdādī, 87–90; al-Shahrastānī, 273–4, 278–80.

the eighth Imām, after ʿAbd Allāh, but most disavowed their previous choice and accepted Mūsā as the seventh Imām. In supporting al-Kāẓim, they joined a fifth group that had immediately affirmed Mūsā's Imāmate, finding him superior to ʿAbd Allāh in terms of religious knowledge. This fifth group were the forebears of the Twelver Shīʿa.

Mūsā al-Kāẓim spent his life in Medina, with the exception of two periods of imprisonment. The first took place during the reign of the caliph al-Mahdī (r. 158–69/775–85), but he was quickly released and allowed to return home.[8] Al-Kāẓim was arrested a second time by the caliph Hārūn al-Rashīd (r. 170–93/786–809), who eventually sent him to Baghdad, where he died in 183/799.[9] His body was displayed in public to confirm his death before being interred in a cemetery in northwest Baghdad.[10] Most of his followers acknowledged ʿAlī b. Mūsā al-Riḍā (d. 203/818) as his successor, but some denied al-Kāẓim's death and awaited his return as the Mahdī. Such rejectionism was hardly novel, but it was exacerbated in this instance by the high millennial expectations of the period. This group was collectively called the Wāqifiyya as a result of their "stopping" the Imāmate with al-Kāẓim.[11]

This biographical account of al-Kāẓim is common to most of the historical sources across temporal, communal, and genre lines. In other words, it represents the "core structure" identified in Chapter 1 as a key component of the rhetoricized model of Muslim historical writing. Historians likely assumed that this structure was known to their audiences, who both authorized and expected literary flourishes and anecdotal elaboration to endow these events with meaning. This creation of meaning, informed by probability ("it could have happened") and verisimilitude ("it seems true"), took precedent over the literal recording of historical details.

8 Al-Ṭabarī, 4:588; Ibn Kathīr (1997), 13:623; al-Khaṭīb al-Baghdādī, 13:32; Ibn al-Jawzī, 9:87; Ibn al-Athīr, 6:75.

9 Al-Yaʿqūbī, 2:360; al-Kulaynī, 1:486; al-Ṭabarī, 4:647; Ibn Bābawayh, *ʿUyūn*, 1:81, 85; al-Mufīd, *Irshād*, 288, 298–392; al-Khaṭīb al-Baghdādī, 13:33; Ibn al-Jawzī, 9:88; Ibn al-Athīr, 6:164; Ibn Kathīr (1997), 13:624. Al-Masʿūdī (1973), 4:216, gives a date of 186/802.

10 Al-Yaʿqūbī, 2:360; al-Iṣbahānī, 417; al-Khaṭīb al-Baghdādī, 13:33; Ibn Bābawayh, *ʿUyūn*, 1:79–82, 85.

11 For these, see Pseudo-Nāshiʾ al-Akbar, 47; al-Nawbakhtī, 86–9; al-Qummī, 89–93; al-Baghdādī, 90–2; al-Shahrastānī, 275–8.

II The Non-Twelver Sources

This section focuses on the eight sources listed in Table 3.1 that were authored by Sunnī[12] and Zaydī[13] historians. The analysis is organized around four categories of narrative elements (see Table 3.2) scattered through the core structure: (i) introductory descriptions, (ii) life as a free man, (iii) release from prison, and (iv) final imprisonment and death. The initial part of the section catalogues variants of the narrative elements. These are shaped by literary devices, elaborations, and embellishments, which often lend similar accounts dramatically

Table 3.1 – *The Non-Twelver Sources for Mūsā al-Kāẓim*

Aḥmad b. Sahl al-Rāzī (d. late third/ninth century) Zaydī Shī'ī	*Akhbār Fakhkh* Chronography
al-Ṭabarī (d. 310/923) Sunnī	*al-Tārīkh* Chronography
al-Iṣbahānī (d. 356/967) Zaydī Shī'ī	*Maqātil al-Ṭālibiyyīn* Biography/prosopography
al-Khaṭīb al-Baghdādī (d. 463/1071) Sunnī	*Tārīkh Baghdād* Prosopography
'Alī b. Bilāl (fl. fifth/eleventh century) Zaydī Shī'ī	*al-Maṣābīḥ* Biography/prosopography
Ibn al-Jawzī (d. 591/1201) Sunnī	*al-Muntaẓam* Prosopography
Ibn al-Athīr (d. 630/1233) Sunnī	*al-Kāmil fī al-tārīkh* Chronography
Ibn Khallikān (d. 681/1282) Sunnī	*Wafayāt al-a'yān* Prosopography

[12] The references for the Sunnī accounts are as follows: al-Ṭabarī, 4:588 and 647; al-Khaṭīb al-Baghdādī, 23:29–33; Ibn al-Jawzī, 9:87–9; Ibn al-Athīr, 6:85 and 164; Ibn Khallikān, 5:308–10.

[13] The references for the Zaydī accounts are as follows: al-Rāzī, 136 and 227; 'Alī b. Bilāl, 470 and 482; al-Iṣbahānī, 413–18.

Table 3.2 – *Summary of Narrative Categories in the Non-Twelver Sources*

Category	Narrative elements	Observations
Introductory Descriptions	A single narrative highlighting al-Kāẓim's piety, patience, and generosity	The description of al-Kāẓim offered here reappears to differing degrees in the later Sunnī historical tradition.
Life as a Free Man	(1) Descendant of ʿUmar (2) Debt collector (3) Cucumber farmer and locusts (4) Freed slave	
Release from Prison	(1) al-Mahdī and Q47:22 (2) *Ḥabashī* dream	Narrative 1 includes two variants. In the first al-Mahdī recites Q47:22 on his own and is reminded of the bonds of kinship, whereas in the second ʿAlī b. Abī Ṭālib appears to al-Mahdī in a dream.
Final Imprisonment and Death	(1) Prophet's grave (2) Caliph and mule (3) al-Sindī's sister (4) Prison letter (5) Short death accounts (6) Barmakid plot	Narrative 5 consists of condensed statements that simply affirm al-Kāẓim's death in prison. The one exception depicts al-Sindī b. Shāhik's organizing of a public examination of al-Kāẓim's body. Narrative 6 is long and detailed, beginning with the causes of al-Kāẓim's arrest and ending in his burial.

different meanings.[14] The second part of the section identifies interpretive frameworks which, as discussed in Chapter 1, are the primary means for conveying authorial intent. The most important and influential of these frameworks are found in al-Iṣbahānī's *Maqātil* and al-Khaṭīb al-Baghdādī's *Tārīkh*.

A The Narrative Elements

Introductory Descriptions

This category of elements consists of minor details about al-Kāẓim. The first report ascribes his nickname (al-'Abd al-Ṣāliḥ, "the upright servant") to his extensive and continuous prayers.[15] Specifically, he is said to have remained in a state of prostration in the Prophet's mosque for the entirety of the night. A second account emphasizes al-Kāẓim's habit of responding to hostility with acts of generosity and kindness. And a final report mentions his routine distribution of purses full of money to the needy, a custom that was so widely known that it became proverbial.

Life as a Free Man

The second category encompasses accounts that depict al-Kāẓim's experiences as a free man in Medina. The non-Twelver sources mention four episodes that fit this category. The first concerns a descendant of 'Umar b. al-Khaṭṭāb (r. 13–23/634–44) who is known to slander and curse 'Alī.[16] Some of al-Kāẓim's companions offer to kill the man, but he rejects this idea. Instead, he discovers the location of the man's farm in Medina and rides out to it on his donkey, trampling crops in the process. When al-Kāẓim reaches the man's house, he finds him despondent because of the damage to his field. He addresses him in a lighthearted manner, asking how much of a loss he has incurred from the damage and how much profit he had anticipated. The man initially refuses to answer but then estimates a net profit of 300 *dīnār*s, which al-Kāẓim gives him before leaving. The man's behavior changes after this incident: he becomes deferential and respectful toward al-Kāẓim. When

[14] For the previous case study, the variants were listed in the appendix instead of the main text.

[15] Al-Khaṭīb al-Baghdādī, 13:29; Ibn Khallikān, 5:308 (explicitly quoting al-Khaṭīb).

[16] Al-Iṣbahānī, 413–14; al-Khaṭīb al-Baghdādī, 13:30.

al-Kāẓim's companions later marvel at this change, he recounts the story and asks whether his plan was not better than their proposed murder.

The second element in this category is related by a man who travels to Medina in order to collect an overdue debt.[17] When the collection proves difficult, he visits al-Kāẓim's estate on the outskirts of Medina to complain about the situation. Upon his arrival, he is first greeted and fed before al-Kāẓim appears and inquires about the purpose of his visit. After he explains his situation, al-Kāẓim compensates him for the outstanding debt (300 *dīnār*s). This narrative highlights al-Kāẓim's proverbial generosity, a theme that, as previously mentioned, is also central to the category of introductory descriptions.

Generosity also features in the third narrative element, which concerns a farm near Medina that produces cucumbers, melons, and gourds.[18] One year, just as the crops are ripening, they are destroyed by a swarm of locusts. The farmer is sitting by the road, lamenting his loss (120 *dīnār*s, including the price of two camels), when al-Kāẓim passes by and questions him about his sad countenance. After learning of the disaster, al-Kāẓim gives him 150 *dīnār*s to cover both his losses and his expected profit. The cucumber farmer is understandably overjoyed, and asks al-Kāẓim to pray for him. The narrative concludes with al-Kāẓim first reciting an invocation (which results in continued good fortune for the farmer) and then recounting a Prophetic tradition.

The final episode in this category relates a series of encounters between al-Kāẓim and a slave in the Ḥijāz.[19] At the start of the account, al-Kāẓim and his companions set up camp in a barren valley in the Ḥijāz known as Sāya.[20] In the morning, they are approached by a black slave, who presents al-Kāẓim with a gift of food, a mix of flour and clarified butter known as *'aṣīda*. He returns two more times with firewood and fire. Al-Kāẓim records the name of the slave and the name of his owner. He instructs the narrator to hold on to the paper until he asks for it. The traveling party eventually reaches al-Kāẓim's estate, where it remains for a time before setting out for Mecca. After completing the minor pilgrimage (*'umra*), al-Kāẓim sends one of his companions, Ṣā'id, to seek out in secret the location of a certain man. Ṣā'id

[17] Al-Khaṭīb al-Baghdādī, 13:29–30. An identical account is transmitted by al-Mufīd (*Irshād*, 296).
[18] Al-Khaṭīb al-Baghdādī, 13:30–1. [19] Ibid., 13:31–2; Ibn al-Jawzī, 9:87.
[20] Yāqūt, 3:202–3.

does so, but he is detected in the process. It turns out that the man is an avid partisan of al-Kāẓim. He covertly follows Ṣā'id and reaches a visibly displeased al-Kāẓim, who asks him about the price of one of his slaves – the one who had previously brought him gifts. The man offers him all his property, but al-Kāẓim insists on purchasing the slave for a fair price. The narrative concludes with al-Kāẓim emancipating the slave and then buying him a large farm.

Release from Prison

The next category of accounts in the non-Twelver sources focus on al-Kāẓim's release from prison following his initial arrest. In the first of these reports, al-Mahdī explains his decision to free the 'Alid by invoking Q47:22. This is, in fact, the most commonly cited anecdote pertaining to al-Kāẓim within the entirety of the Sunnī historical tradition. Both variants of this narrative element are ascribed to al-Rabī' b. Yūnus (d. 170/786), who served as chamberlain for al-Manṣūr (r. 136–58/754–75) and al-Mahdī.[21]

The first version begins with al-Rabī' observing al-Mahdī's performance of the night prayer.[22] In the course of the Qur'ānic recitation, the caliph reaches a particular verse, Q47:22, which cautions against the breaking of ties with kin.[23] After he completes his prayer, al-Mahdī orders al-Rabī' to bring him Mūsā. The command leaves al-Rabī' confused as to whether the caliph desires his own son Mūsā (the future caliph al-Hādī [r. 169–70/785–6]) or Mūsā al-Kāẓim. He eventually reasons that al-Mahdī must be asking for the latter, and transports him to court. The caliph greets al-Kāẓim, recounts his recitation of Q47:22 in the prayer, and expresses his fear of potentially severing their bonds of kinship. He promises to release al-Kāẓim if the latter takes an oath renouncing rebellion. Al-Kāẓim readily agrees and is then allowed to return to Medina.

In the second version of this narrative element, al-Mahdī does not recite Q47:22 in his evening prayer.[24] Instead, he has a dream in which 'Alī b. Abī Ṭālib (d. 40/661) appears and utters the verse as a warning. The caliph then summons al-Rabī' in the middle of the night,

21 *EI*^{2}, s.v. "Al-Rabī' b. Yūnus" (A. S. Atiya); al-Ziriklī, 3:15.

22 Al-Ṭabarī, 4:588.

23 Q47:22 reads: "Would you then, if you were given the command, work corruption in the land and sever your ties of kinship?"

24 Al-Khaṭīb al-Baghdādī, 13:32.

frightening him in the process. As the chamberlain approaches, he overhears al-Mahdī reciting the verse to himself and is ordered to bring Mūsā al-Kāẓim. When the ʿAlid enters, al-Mahdī embraces him, seats him at his side, and relates his dream. He asks al-Kāẓim to swear that he will never rebel against him or his children. Al-Kāẓim assures him that this is not his intention. Al-Mahdī then instructs al-Rabīʿ to give al-Kāẓim 3,000 *dīnār*s and return him to his family in Medina. The account ends with the observation that al-Rabīʿ carried out these orders that same night, and by morning al-Kāẓim had already left the city.

The second narrative element in this category involves al-Rashīd and seems to take place during al-Kāẓim's second period of imprisonment (likely between 179/795 and 183/799). The account opens with ʿAbd Allāh b. Mālik al-Khuzāʿī[25] (d. second/eighth century) summoned to court by al-Rashīd with such haste that he is unable to dress properly.[26] This leaves him quite unsettled. When he arrives at the caliphal residence, he finds al-Rashīd seated on a carpet, silent and unresponsive. As the silence stretches out, ʿAbd Allāh is gripped by terror. Finally, al-Rashīd asks him whether he knows the reason for the summons. ʿAbd Allāh replies that he does not. The caliph then relates a dream in which a black (*ḥabashī*) man bearing a spear commanded him to release al-Kāẓim under threat of death. ʿAbd Allāh asks three times whether he should free al-Kāẓim from prison. Al-Rashīd finally responds, ordering that al-Kāẓim be given 3,000 *dirham*s and the choice of whether to stay in Baghdad or return to Medina. When ʿAbd Allāh reaches the prison, al-Kāẓim is frightened by his appearance in the middle of the night, reasoning that such a visit could only bode ill for him. ʿAbd Allāh conveys al-Rashīd's orders and expresses his astonishment at the turn of events. Al-Kāẓim then reveals that he recently had a dream in which the Prophet taught him a prayer that would precipitate his release. The account ends with the text of the prayer.

Final Imprisonment and Death

The final narrative category discusses the causes of al-Kāẓim's second imprisonment and death. It includes the largest number of accounts,

[25] According to al-Masʿūdī, ʿAbd Allāh b. Mālik was in charge of al-Rashīd's household as well as the *shurṭa*. See al-Masʿūdī (1973), 4:206; Ibn Khallikān, 5:309.

[26] Ibn Khallikān, 5:309. This narrative is first cited by al-Masʿūdī (1973), 4:206–7.

some of which focus on isolated incidents while others incorporate multiple encounters into a single, cohesive report.

The first narrative element features a notably hostile exchange between al-Rashīd and al-Kāẓim.[27] The incident takes place during the caliph's visit to the grave of the Prophet in Medina following his completion of the Ḥajj. As the caliph makes his way through the city, he is surrounded by prominent tribesmen and Qurashī notables, including al-Kāẓim. When he reaches the tomb, al-Rashīd loudly declares, "Peace unto you, O Messenger of God, O cousin!" The wording is meant to humble those around him by invoking 'Abbāsid kinship with the Prophet. Al-Kāẓim then proclaims, "Peace unto you, O father," highlighting the superiority of 'Alid claims to Muḥammad. The slight leads the irate caliph to accuse al-Kāẓim of excessive pride.

Similar tension informs a second element associated with al-Rashīd's visit to Medina.[28] The episode begins with a number of important locals gathered on the outskirts of the city to greet al-Rashīd. Al-Kāẓim rides out on a mule to join them, and is questioned by al-Faḍl b. al-Rabī'[29] (d. 208/824) about the appropriateness of his mount.[30] The chamberlain notes that such an animal will neither help him secure favors nor allow him to escape pursuit. Al-Kāẓim responds that he has taken a moderate stance on the matter: the honor of the occasion certainly exceeds the lowliness of a donkey, but it does not reach the lofty heights of a horse. The narrative illustrates al-Kāẓim's restraint, but it also hints at his unwillingness to submit to or acknowledge al-Rashīd's authority. Many writers cite this incident together with the hostile exchange described earlier as the cause of al-Kāẓim's arrest.

The third and fourth narrative elements in this category center on al-Kāẓim's experiences in prison. In the third narrative,[31] al-Kāẓim is remanded to the custody of al-Sindī b. Shāhik[32] (d. 204/819), whose

[27] Al-Khaṭīb al-Baghdādī, 13:32; Ibn al-Jawzī, 9:88; Ibn al-Athīr, 7:164; Ibn Khallikān, 5:309.
[28] Al-Iṣbahānī, 414.
[29] Al-Faḍl b. al-Rabī' b. Yūnus and his father were longstanding officials (serving in a variety of offices) for the 'Abbāsids. See al-Ziriklī, 5:148; *EI*[3], s.v. "Al-Faḍl b. al-Rabī'" (J. Turner).
[30] Al-Mufīd's more detailed Twelver account in *Irshād*, 297–8, replaces al-Faḍl with his father.
[31] Al-Khaṭīb al-Baghdādī, 13:32–3; Ibn al-Athīr, 6:164.
[32] Al-Sindī b. Shāhik was a client of al-Manṣūr who held high posts during the reigns of al-Rashīd and al-Amīn. For the former, he served as the chief of

unnamed sister is placed in charge of his care. Al-Kāẓim's extensive prayer regimen, which spans the night and much of the day, convinces her of his innocence and prompts her to observe that a people who opposes such a righteous servant of God (*al-'abd al-ṣāliḥ*) will surely fail. The fourth element[33] quotes a letter that al-Kāẓim sends to al-Rashīd from prison. In it, he contrasts the hardship of his days with the ease and comfort of the caliph's days. He then notes that they will be united on a day that will not be transient when God will render final judgment. Both of these narrative elements foreground al-Kāẓim's piety and forbearance.

Most non-Twelver reports on the circumstances of al-Kāẓim's death are quite brief. Two of the three Zaydī authors (al-Rāzī and 'Alī b. Bilāl) do not mention al-Kāẓim's death at all. Among Sunnī authors, al-Ṭabarī simply states that al-Kāẓim died in Baghdad in 183/799 and offers no further explanation, thereby suggesting natural causes.[34] In a similar manner, al-Khaṭīb al-Baghdādī mentions al-Kāẓim's death in custody but implicitly dismisses the possibility of poisoning.[35] He notes that al-Sindī b. Shāhik summoned prominent figures from Baghdad to inspect al-Kāẓim's body and verify his death. Ibn al-Jawzī and Ibn al-Athīr report that al-Kāẓim died in prison but make no comment on the cause.[36] Finally, Ibn Khallikān acknowledges the possibility of poisoning but prefaces it with the phrase "It is said," thereby conveying his skepticism of this claim.[37] Overall, most of the non-Twelver sources are either silent on the details of al-Kāẓim's death or attribute it to natural causes.

There is, however, one detailed non-Twelver narrative element that offers a comprehensive explanation of al-Kāẓim's death.[38] The report begins with al-Rashīd's decision to have his son Muḥammad, the future caliph al-Amīn (r. 193–8/809–13), placed under the tutelage of Ja'far b. Muḥammad b. al-Ash'ath[39] (d. after 148/765). Yaḥyā b. Khālid al-

"police" (*shurṭa*). See *EI*[2], s.v. "Mu'ammar b. 'Abbād" (H. Daiber); Crone, *Slaves on Horses*, 194–5.

33 Al-Khaṭīb al-Baghdādī, 13:33; Ibn al-Jawzī, 9:88; Ibn al-Athīr, 6:164.

34 Al-Ṭabarī, 4:647. 35 Al-Khaṭīb al-Baghdādī, 13:33.

36 Ibn al-Athīr, 6:164; Ibn al-Jawzī, 9:88. 37 Ibn Khallikān, 5:310.

38 Al-Iṣbahānī, 414–18.

39 Al-Tustarī lists Ja'far b. Muḥammad as a transmitter and companion of al-Ṣādiq. He maintained a physical distance from al-Kāẓim because of his official position with the 'Abbāsids, presumably in Baghdad. See also al-Ṭabarī, 4:433, 437, 449, and 5:16.

Barmakī[40] (d. 190/805) views this arrangement as a potential threat to his family's status and influence. In order to counter it, he ingratiates himself with Ja'far b. Muḥammad, a known partisan of Mūsā al-Kāẓim, and forwards exaggerated reports of Ja'far's disloyalty and Shī'ī leanings to al-Rashīd. He also targets al-Kāẓim through the latter's heavily indebted nephew 'Alī b. Ismā'īl b. Ja'far (d. presumably second/eighth century). Specifically, he sends 'Alī money, flatters him, and asks him to travel to Baghdad to meet with al-Rashīd. When al-Kāẓim learns of these developments, he offers to pay 'Alī's debts and asks him not to make orphans of his (al-Kāẓim's) children. 'Alī rejects the overture and travels to Baghdad, where he testifies that al-Kāẓim receives large sums of money from followers in every part of the Muslim world. The extent of his wealth, 'Alī claims, is such that he is able to produce 60,000 *dīnār*s in cash with little trouble.[41] Yaḥyā al-Barmakī further embellishes these charges before taking them to al-Rashīd. In exchange for his testimony, 'Alī is granted 200,000 *dirham*s. As he waits for the money, however, he is stricken by a sickness that makes his entrails burst out. This prompts him to observe that money is useless to a dead man.[42]

The second part of this "Barmakid plot" narrative begins with al-Rashīd's arrival in Medina in 179/795 to visit Muḥammad's grave prior to the Ḥajj. When he approaches the tomb, al-Rashīd addresses the Prophet and justifies his impending arrest of al-Kāẓim on the grounds of the latter's "sowing dissent" and "shedding blood." Al-Kāẓim is then taken into custody. The caliph orders the preparation of two litters and dispatches each with a contingent of cavalry. The first is sent to Kūfa without al-Kāẓim, whereas the second, carrying al-Kāẓim, heads to Baṣra. This ploy is meant to conceal al-Kāẓim's true location. He is ultimately remanded to the care of 'Īsā b. Ja'far b. al-Manṣūr[43] (d. 172/789), the 'Abbāsid governor of Baṣra, and remains there for a

40 For the Barmakids, see *EI*², s.v. "Al-Barāmika" (W. Barthold and D. Sourdel). Al-Rashīd purged the family from power in 187/803.

41 According to 'Alī b. Ismā'īl, al-Kāẓim offered to buy an estate for 30,000 *dīnār*s in cash. The owner, however, wanted a different type of money which al-Kāẓim was able to produce in short order. The point of the allegation is that al-Kāẓim had access to incredible wealth. See al-Iṣbahānī, 415.

42 Al-Tustarī briefly discusses the controversy over the identity of the family member who betrays al-Kāẓim. The chief candidates are 'Alī and his brother Muḥammad, both of whom are al-Kāẓim's nephews. See al-Tustarī, 7:367–8.

43 'Īsā b. Ja'far was a cousin of al-Rashīd and a grandson of al-Manṣūr. See al-Khaṭīb al-Baghdādī, 11:158; al-Ziriklī, 5:102.

year. At this point, ʿĪsā informs al-Rashīd that he has no credible evidence of the charges against al-Kāẓim. In fact, spies sent to eavesdrop on his prayers in hopes of hearing curses against al-Rashīd or the ʿAbbāsids have only heard him asking God for forgiveness. ʿĪsā threatens to release al-Kāẓim unless al-Rashīd makes alternative arrangements for his imprisonment.

Al-Kāẓim is then transported from Baṣra to Baghdad, where he is held for an extended time by al-Faḍl b. al-Rabīʿ, who repeatedly disregards orders to kill his prisoner. Al-Rashīd now transfers al-Kāẓim to the custody of al-Faḍl b. Yaḥyā al-Barmakī[44] (d. 193/808). In time, however, al-Kāẓim wins the sympathy of al-Faḍl al-Barmakī, who also refuses to arrange his murder. Al-Rashīd is particularly enraged when he learns of the comfortable circumstances of al-Kāẓim's imprisonment. The discovery prompts him to send his servant Masrūr[45] (d. after 219/834) from his capital in Raqqa to Baghdad to investigate the situation further. Masrūr confirms the reports and then delivers letters to al-Sindī b. Shāhik and ʿAbbās b. Muḥammad[46] (d. 186/802). The latter is placed in charge of the city and ordered to flog al-Faḍl al-Barmakī, while the former is given custody of al-Kāẓim. Meanwhile, al-Rashīd convenes a huge gathering in Raqqa in which he derides and curses al-Faḍl al-Barmakī for his disobedience. In order to defuse the situation, Yaḥyā al-Barmakī, al-Faḍl's father, secretly promises to eliminate al-Kāẓim in exchange for a caliphal pardon for his son.

In the next part of the account, Yaḥyā al-Barmakī hastens to Baghdad, citing bureaucratic matters related to taxation. Numerous rumors begin to spread about the real purpose of his visit. Upon arrival, Yaḥyā orders al-Sindī to wrap al-Kāẓim in a carpet and have him trampled to death. The report includes a passage in which al-Kāẓim asks al-Sindī to summon one of his retainers to wash his corpse. He notes that members of Prophet's family provide their own dowers,

44 Al-Faḍl b. Yaḥyā al-Barmakī is generally ascribed pro-ʿAlid views, as reflected in his interactions with al-Kāẓim. See *EI*², s.v. "Al-Barāmika" (W. Barthold and D. Sourdel).

45 Masrūr was a eunuch in the service of al-Rashīd. See al-Ṭabarī's index, where he is identified as Masrūr al-Khādim al-Kabīr.

46 ʿAbbās b. Muḥammad b. ʿAlī b. ʿAbd Allāh was a brother of the caliphs al-Saffāḥ and al-Manṣūr. He was particularly active during the reigns of al-Manṣūr and al-Mahdī. See *EI*², s.v. "Al-ʿAbbās b. Muḥammad" (K. V. Zettersteen); al-Khaṭīb al-Baghdādī, 12:124–5; al-Ziriklī, 3:264–5.

perform pilgrimages on behalf of each other, and shroud their own dead.

After al-Kāẓim's death, prominent public figures and jurists are summoned to verify that there are no marks on the body.[47] It is then put on display and accompanied with a public proclamation of the following statement: "This is Mūsā b. Ja'far, who has died. Look at him." A variant version of the announcement on the authority of some Ṭālibids reads as follows: "This is Mūsā b. Ja'far, who the *rawāfiḍ* claim has not died. Look at him." Al-Kāẓim is buried in the Qurashī Hāshimī cemetery in Baghdad.

B Interpretive Frameworks

The non-Twelver narrative elements support three interpretive frameworks. Although this section describes the frameworks as independent and self-standing, they were often combined together within a given historical work.

Exemplar

The first interpretive framework in the non-Twelver sources depicts al-Kāẓim as an exemplary figure imbued with characteristics generally associated with revered religious scholars. The two most frequently recurring qualities are his pious devotion to God and his generosity. Al-Kāẓim's piety is principally evident in the first narrative category, in whose reports his nickname, al-'Abd al-Ṣāliḥ, stems from his extensive devotion to prayer. A similar tendency informs the "al-Sindī's sister" narrative, which describes al-Kāẓim's daily prayer routine and concludes with a condemnation of people who would mistreat such a man – namely, the 'Abbāsid caliphs. While not directly about prayer and worship, the "caliph and mule" narrative portrays al-Kāẓim as indifferent to the allures of the material world. He refuses to adhere to the expectations of caliphal ceremony because he neither desires reward nor fears death. This fearlessness is also central to the "prison letter" narrative, which culminates with al-Kāẓim's warning to al-Rashīd of a final reckoning on the Day of Judgment.

[47] These include al-Haytham b. 'Adī (d. between 206/821 and 209/824), a Kūfan transmitter of historical reports with a low reputation among religious scholars. He was also a regular companion to the 'Abbāsid caliphs from al-Manṣūr to al-Rashīd. See *EI*^{2}, s.v. "Al-Haytham b. 'Adī" (C. Pellat).

The non-Twelver sources are also vested in reports of al-Kāẓim's generosity. The narrative elements in the introductory descriptions category note that al-Kāẓim's openhandedness became proverbial in his lifetime thanks to his propensity to distribute purses of money to those in need. This idea finds further support in the second category, which details al-Kāẓim's generous support of individuals in difficult circumstances. In the "debt collector" narrative, a visitor is unable to secure the repayment of a loan and takes his troubles to al-Kāẓim, who first offers him hospitality and then compensates him for the outstanding debt. Here al-Kāẓim functions as a means of last resort in times of need, a role usually reserved for the caliph.

A more complicated view of al-Kāẓim informs the "descendant of 'Umar" narrative. The primary antagonist is an unnamed man whose enmity toward the 'Alids is such that al-Kāẓim's companions resolve to kill him. Al-Kāẓim forbids this act of violence and instead visits the man on his farm, trampling his crops in the process. He then compensates the man for both his material losses and his expected profits. This act of charity transforms the man from an enemy into a friend.[48] At the end of the narrative, al-Kāẓim asks his companions rhetorically whether his strategy was not better than their planned recourse to violence. The episode epitomizes al-Kāẓim's propensity for generosity and kindness toward even his most implacable opponents.

The relationship between piety and generosity is developed further in two other narrative elements. In the "cucumber farmer and locusts" narrative, a despondent farmer affirms al-Kāẓim's special status with God (*baraka*) after receiving compensation for his ruined crops. In this case, al-Kāẓim's generosity is associated with his access to divine favor. An even clearer amalgamation of piety and generosity is found in the "freed slave" narrative. Recall that al-Kāẓim refuses to accept the slave owner's offer to gift him the slave, citing a Prophetic tradition transmitted through his (al-Kāẓim's) forebears. This incident combines a number of al-Kāẓim's exemplary qualities: his kindness to the slave, his pious integrity in interactions with the owner, and his generosity in buying a farm for his newly freed devotee.

[48] There is some ambiguity here for a modern reader, since it seems that al-Kāẓim created the very situation that allowed him to win the allegiance of the farmer. Whether this aspect of the report was similarly problematic for a premodern audience is unclear.

Finally, the "Barmakid plot" narrative demonstrates al-Kāẓim's exemplary piety during the course of events leading to his death. His virtue is first apparent in his attempts to convince 'Alī b. Ismā'īl to remain in Medina rather than travel to Baghdad as an informant. Although 'Alī never makes his intentions clear, al-Kāẓim intuits his relative's material motivations and appeals to their kinship. Al-Kāẓim's special standing with God is evidenced by 'Alī's painful death at the end of the episode. After his arrest, al-Kāẓim wins over three separate jailors, who frustrate the caliph's attempts to arrange his murder. 'Īsā b. Ja'far b. al-Manṣūr assigns him a number of spies, who find his prayers humble and self-effacing. Al-Kāẓim has a similar effect on both al-Faḍl b. al-Rabī' and al-Faḍl al-Barmakī. Even al-Sindī b. Shāhik, his eventual executioner, treats him with reverence as they discuss his impending burial rites.

Kinship

A second interpretive framework at play in non-Twelver depictions of Mūsā al-Kāẓim involves the relationship of the 'Abbāsids to the 'Alids, which oscillates between a desire for unity and a deep-rooted competition. In both variants of the "al-Mahdī and Q47:22" narrative, the caliph's anger is mitigated by a Qur'ānic verse that calls for the kind treatment of relatives. The pull of kinship, however, is offset by political struggles between the two branches of the family. Thus, al-Mahdī agrees to release al-Kāẓim only after making him swear off future rebellions. This episode underscores the suspicions that complicated any potential reconciliation among the Banū Hāshim.

A more pessimistic view of 'Abbāsid–'Alid relations is found in the narrative describing the tense exchange between al-Kāẓim and al-Rashīd at the Prophet's grave. Al-Rashīd eagerly extols his connection to the Prophet in the company of prominent Medinans. The claim exemplifies 'Abbāsid efforts to present themselves as the rightful heirs to Muḥammad. However, al-Rashīd is upstaged by al-Kāẓim, who loudly refers to the Prophet as his "father." The effectiveness of this retort reflects the degree to which 'Alid lineage appeared to hold greater sway in the eyes of the general population. The 'Alids' ability to lay claim to the Prophet contributed to their propaganda efforts against the 'Abbāsids and fueled the deterioration of familial relations between the two groups. Overall, this narrative element helps explain the persistence of 'Alid–'Abbāsid hostility despite the Qur'ānic emphasis on kinship. Many Sunnī authors preserve both of these narratives, identifying the exchange at the Prophet's grave as the proximate cause for al-Kāẓim's second arrest.

Court Politics

The final interpretive framework embedded in the non-Twelver sources stems from the "Barmakid plot" narrative, in which al-Kāẓim is a victim of larger intrigues at the 'Abbāsid court. At the center of these intrigues is Yaḥyā al-Barmakī, who fears a loss of political influence as a consequence of al-Rashīd's decision to entrust the education of his son al-Amīn to Ja'far b. Muḥammad, a partisan of al-Kāẓim. Through a complicated set of maneuvers, he convinces al-Rashīd to arrest al-Kāẓim during a visit to the Ḥijāz. Although the arrest is certainly predicated on preexisting 'Abbāsid suspicions of the 'Alids, it results mainly from power struggles within the 'Abbāsid court.

Political considerations continue to predominate in the narrative after al-Kāẓim's initial arrest. Al-Rashīd creates an elaborate diversion to keep the general population unaware of the 'Alid's location. Al-Kāẓim is then passed among a series of influential figures in the 'Abbāsid state. The first of these is a member of the ruling family – 'Īsā b. Ja'far b. al-Manṣūr, a cousin of al-Rashīd – who threatens to release his prisoner for lack of any evidence of wrongdoing. Al-Kāẓim is then sent to Baghdad, where he stays with al-Faḍl b. al-Rabī' for an extended period. Despite his high rank at the 'Abbāsid court, al-Faḍl does not comply with instructions to execute al-Kāẓim. The third jailor is al-Faḍl b. Yaḥyā al-Barmakī, the son of the man who arrested al-Kāẓim in the first place. He, too, refuses to kill al-Kāẓim, and instead provides him with comfortable quarters. These developments reflect al-Rashīd's difficulties in ruling from his capital in Raqqa in northern Syria, as he is defied not just by members of his own family (who may be influential in their own right) but also by administrators directly dependent on him for their authority. Eventually, al-Rashīd orders a public flogging of al-Faḍl al-Barmakī, which finally compels al-Faḍl's father, Yaḥyā, to arrange al-Kāẓim's death. The entire episode illustrates the limitations of al-Rashīd's power. He is capable of wielding great authority, but this sometimes requires considerable personal investment. His difficulties with al-Kāẓim speak to the complicated power dynamics of the early 'Abbāsid state.

The end of the "Barmakid plot" narrative highlights the overall political environment of the period. The examination of al-Kāẓim's body by local notables and jurists in Baghdad points to the caliph's worries about potential rumors of foul play. Along the same lines, Yaḥyā al-Barmakī is concerned with the public's perception of al-Kāẓim's death. Thus he falsely claims that his visit to Baghdad is prompted by fiscal matters, and later orders al-Kāẓim to be wrapped in a carpet and trampled to conceal physical marks that might raise suspicions. The corpse is then placed on the bridge in Baghdad to preempt possible Shī'ī or popular assertions that he is still alive.

C *Pious Exemplar or Political Puppet?*

The narrative choices made by non-Twelver authors in their depictions of Mūsā al-Kāẓim's life are summarized in Table 3.3. The Sunnī sources generally adhere to a common set of themes, focusing, in particular, on al-Kāẓim's exemplary qualities and lineage. The sole Zaydī source adds the element of court intrigue and political machinations. The discussion that follows is divided into two parts. The first documents the emergence of a broad consensus regarding al-Kāẓim among Sunnī scholars. The second introduces a few additional Zaydī authors to better understand al-Kāẓim's place within the Zaydī historical tradition.

The Sunnī Frameworks

Sunnī authors offer a very limited treatment of al-Kāẓim's life. The earliest extant Sunnī source to discuss al-Kāẓim in any detail is al-Ṭabarī's historical chronicle, which includes very few biographical details. Al-Kāẓim first appears in the year 169/785 with a version of the "al-Mahdī and Q47:22" narrative in which the caliph is reminded of his obligations to kin. In this account, al-Mahdī's decision to seek reconciliation with the 'Alids is not ascribed to a dream but rather to an epiphany during prayer. In return, he asks al-Kāẓim to promise that he will not rebel against al-Rashīd or his children. This account aligns with many of al-Ṭabarī's depictions of 'Abbāsid–'Alid relations, in which familial tensions are attributed to political competition and court intrigue.[49] Al-Ṭabarī's only other reference to al-Kāẓim is a brief death notice in 183/799 that implicitly rejects foul play. The report makes

[49] This is also true of the third case study (see Chapter 4).

Table 3.3 – *The Non-Twelver Narrative Elements and Interpretive Frameworks*

	al-Ṭabarī (d. 301/922)	al-Iṣbahānī (d. 356/967)	al-Khaṭīb (d. 463/1071)	Ibn al-Jawzī (d. 591/1201)	Ibn al-Athīr (d. 630/1233)	Ibn Khallikān (d. 681/1282)
Introductory Descriptions						
ʿAbd Sāliḥ/piety (E)			X			X (al-Khaṭīb)
Proverbial generosity (E)		X	X			X (al-Khaṭīb)
Kindness to enemies (E)		X	X	X		X (al-Khaṭīb)
Life as a Free Man						
Descendant of ʿUmar (E)		X	X			
Debt collector (E)			X			
Cucumber farmer/locusts (E)			X			
Freed slave (E)			X	X		
Release from Prison						
al-Mahdī and Q47:22 (K)	X (no dream)		X (dream)	X (dream)	X (no dream)	X (dream/al-Khaṭīb)
Ḥabashī dream (E)						X
Final Imprisonment and Death						
Prophet's grave (K)			X	X	X	X (al-Khaṭīb)
Caliph and mule (E)		X				
al-Sindī's sister (E)			X		X	
Prison letter (E)			X	X	X	
Short death accounts	X (no poison)		X (prison, no poison)	X (prison, no poison)	X (prison, no poison)	X (prison, maybe poison)
Barmakid plot (CP)		X				
Interpretive Framework	Kinship	Court politics/ Exemplar	Exemplar/ Kinship	Kinship/Exemplar	Kinship/Exemplar	Kinship/Exemplar

Historical chronicles are highlighted in dark gray, biographies and prosopographies in light gray. The narratives are categorized as pertaining to the frameworks of exemplariness (E), kinship (K), and court politics (CP).

no mention of a second imprisonment, possible poisoning, or any examination of al-Kāẓim's body.[50]

Al-Khaṭīb al-Baghdādī projects an exemplary image of al-Kāẓim through a series of anecdotes that foreground his generosity and piety. Al-Kāẓim fits the traditional profile of a distinguished scholar unconcerned with material wealth and engaged in copious acts of worship. This portrayal contrasts with that of Twelver Shī'ī authors, discussed in the next section, who elevate al-Kāẓim far beyond the rank of a scholar to that of a divinely inspired Imām. Al-Khaṭīb provides a few narratives that emphasize the importance of kinship, but these are primarily of an explanatory nature. Al-Kāẓim's first release from prison, for example, is explained through a version of the "al-Mahdī and Q47:22" narrative, which (unlike al-Ṭabarī's account) depicts 'Alī appearing in a dream to rebuke the 'Abbāsid caliph for his ill treatment of kin.[51]

It is worth noting that al-Khaṭīb's biography exerted considerable influence on the subsequent Sunnī historical tradition.[52] Thus, later sources often document al-Kāẓim's personal qualities but seldom provide explanations for his second imprisonment. The contentious exchange between the caliph and al-Kāẓim near the Prophet's grave is occasionally quoted but rarely identified as the cause of his arrest. These sources acknowledge al-Kāẓim's death in prison but offer no further details.

Ibn al-Jawzī's treatment of al-Kāẓim exemplifies al-Khaṭīb's lasting historiographical importance. After basic facts regarding birth and offspring, Ibn al-Jawzī confirms al-Kāẓim's elevated standing with a report about his generosity and kindness toward enemies and an allusion to the narrative of the freed slave. He then explores the 'Abbāsid–'Alid relationship through al-Mahdī's decision to release al-

[50] As discussed in the next section, roughly contemporaneous annalistic Shī'ī accounts are equally scarce in detail. Al-Ya'qūbī notes al-Kāẓim's death in the custody of al-Sindī and the subsequent examination of his body without necessarily suggesting murder. Al-Mas'ūdī, on the other hand, seems to suspect poison and includes a dream account that conveys al-Kāẓim's favored position with God.

[51] It is al-Khaṭīb al-Baghdādī's variant of this episode that predominates in the later Sunnī historical tradition.

[52] The most prominent element preserved by al-Khaṭīb al-Baghdādī (but not quoted in either the biographical or the annalistic Sunnī sources under consideration) is the "descendant of 'Umar" narrative. This narrative persists in the Twelver Shī'ī sources without holding any particular polemical importance.

Kāẓim (the "al-Mahdī and Q47:22" narrative) and al-Rashīd's anger toward him (the "Prophet's grave" narrative). Although the latter report sheds light on 'Abbāsid–'Alid animosity, it is not presented as the direct cause of al-Kāẓim's arrest. During his imprisonment in Baghdad, al-Kāẓim writes to al-Rashīd (the "prison letter" narrative), warning him to fear God on the Day of Judgment. He then dies of natural causes. Overall, Ibn al-Jawzī follows al-Khaṭīb in utilizing an interpretive framework that centers on exemplary piety but also gestures toward 'Abbāsid–'Alid tensions.

Moving into the seventh/thirteenth century, Ibn al-Athīr and Ibn Khallikān are representative of the interpretive approaches of later Sunnī chronographical and prosopographical works. Ibn al-Athīr follows al-Ṭabarī by offering the variant of the "al-Mahdī and Q47:22" narrative in which the caliph releases al-Kāẓim after reciting the verse in ritual prayer. He then explains the second arrest with reference to the "Prophet's grave" narrative. In these reports, Ibn al-Athīr's focus on kinship is perhaps due to the general centrality of 'Abbāsid–'Alid relations in historical chronicles. Ibn al-Athīr also cites the "prison letter" and "al-Sindī's sister" narratives, which unambiguously uphold al-Kāẓim's piety. It is noteworthy that Ibn al-Athīr does not mention poisoning.

Ibn Khallikān's collection of biographies includes an entry on al-Kāẓim that quotes large sections of al-Khaṭīb's text. Specifically, he preserves all of al-Khaṭīb's narrative elements in the first category as well as the "al-Mahdī and Q47:22" and "Prophet's grave" narratives. He also records a second dream account, the "*ḥabashī* dream" narrative, that ties al-Kāẓim's preferential status with God to his kinship with the Prophet. This narrative is ascribed to al-Mas'ūdī (a Twelver Shī'ī author discussed in the next section), a connection that might account for Ibn Khallikān's claim that al-Kāẓim was poisoned.[53]

[53] Nearly a century later al-Dhahabī (d. 748/1347) included al-Kāẓim in his *Tārīkh al-islām*, a prosopographical source organized chronologically by period. Given his familiarity with al-Khaṭīb al-Baghdādī's work, al-Dhahabī's adherence to al-Khaṭīb's interpretive framework is not surprising. He follows previous biographers in emphasizing al-Kāẓim's piety, kindness (even toward his enemies), and generosity. He then offers a mix of anecdotes to support this characterization. The "cucumber farmer and locusts" narrative, for example, establishes al-Kāẓim's generosity, whereas the "prison letter" narrative demonstrates his devotion to God. Among the biographers, al-Dhahabī is unique in addressing the reasons for al-Kāẓim's second arrest. He explains that

The Sunnī historical tradition views al-Kāẓim through interpretive frameworks that either focus on his exemplary characteristics (primarily in the prosopographies and biographies) or integrate him into a larger story of imperial kinship (primarily in the chronicles). The former tend to present him as part of a class of scholars with remarkable acumen and personal qualities. The latter are chiefly interested in the frayed relationship between the branches of the Prophet's family. Subsequent Sunnī chroniclers remained committed to the perspective of 'Abbāsid–'Alid rivalry, but also reflected the influence of the exemplary framework. This confluence contributed to the gradual emergence of a hybrid portrait in which al-Kāẓim was both a victim of 'Abbāsid–'Alid competition and a pious exemplar.

The Zaydī Framework

Al-Iṣbahānī's *Maqātil al-Ṭālibiyyīn* is the only Zaydī work that includes a complete and detailed biography of al-Kāẓim. The reason for his absence from other Zaydī sources is fairly straightforward: they do not consider al-Kāẓim an Imām. In fact, he is widely criticized by the Zaydīs for his alleged political quietism. Al-Iṣbahānī's inclusion of al-Kāẓim stems from the overall purpose of his text, which is to document the murders of prominent Ṭālibids under the Umayyad and early 'Abbāsid caliphs.

Al-Iṣbahānī carefully balances the Zaydī dismissal of al-Kāẓim's religious claims with an affirmation of his elevated status as a descendant of the Prophet. He accomplishes this goal through a number of narrative elements that are also prevalent in the Sunnī sources. For example, al-Iṣbahānī cites a version of the "descendant of 'Umar" narrative that resembles that of al-Khaṭīb and demonstrates al-Kāẓim's proverbial generosity and his propensity for responding with kindness to the hostility of his opponents. In addition, al-Iṣbahānī is the only non-Twelver author to preserve a version of the "caliph and mule" narrative, in which al-Kāẓim displays both his piety and his indifference to the trappings of power. On the whole, these reports resemble the Sunnī sources in depicting al-Kāẓim as a model of scholarly piety.

caliphs do not tolerate being addressed in the way in which al-Kāẓim spoke to al-Rashīd in the "Prophet's grave" narrative. Finally, al-Dhahabī describes al-Kāẓim's imprisonment as comfortable, and rejects the claims that he was poisoned. Like previous accounts, al-Dhahabī's biography highlights the dual themes of exemplary piety and kinship. See al-Dhahabī, yrs 181–90: 417–19.

The most important and detailed of al-Iṣbahānī's reports, however, is the "Barmakid plot" narrative, which is not mentioned by the Sunnī writers despite indications that they had access to it.[54] This narrative element centers on the role of 'Abbāsid court politics in al-Kāẓim's arrest and eventual murder. Specifically, it attributes the hostility between al-Rashīd and al-Kāẓim to Yaḥyā al-Barmakī's attempts at consolidating power. Al-Kāẓim is almost entirely passive in the chain of events leading to his death. His only active intervention involves a failed attempt to convince his nephew to stay in Medina and not betray him to the caliph. Al-Kāẓim then becomes a pawn in the conflict between different centers of power in the 'Abbāsid state. At times, he inadvertently exacerbates these tensions when sympathetic jailors resist caliphal orders for his execution. Al-Kāẓim is finally killed by Yaḥyā al-Barmakī in an attempt to rehabilitate his son's position at court.

Al-Iṣbahānī's interpretive framework is firmy centered on court politics. This contrasts sharply with the frameworks of the Sunnī sources, which highlight either al-Kāẓim's exemplary qualities or 'Abbāsid–'Alid kinship. This is not to say that al-Iṣbahānī is exclusively interested in political intrigue. In addition to including the exemplary accounts mentioned previously, he weaves al-Kāẓim's piety into the very fabric of the "Barmakid plot" narrative. This bifurcated depiction likely stems from the Zaydī belief in the collective authority of the family of the Prophet, which extends even to those members who did not attain the Imāmate. In other words, al-Iṣbahānī fits al-Kāẓim within a general Zaydī veneration of 'Alids while simultaneously rejecting Twelver claims about his religious authority.

Other Zaydī authors offer a more vociferously negative portrayal of al-Kāẓim, comparing him unfavorably to his Ḥasanid contemporary Yaḥyā b. 'Abd Allāh (discussed in Chapter 4). The most influential of these sources is Aḥmad b. Sahl al-Rāzī's (d. late third/ninth century) relatively early account of the rebellion of Ṣāḥib Fakhkh al-Ḥusayn b. 'Alī b. al-Ḥasan[55] (d. 169/786), entitled *Akhbār Fakhkh*.[56] According to al-Rāzī,

[54] This is suggested by the fact that one of al-Iṣbahānī's sources for the narrative is Yaḥyā b. al-Ḥasan al-'Alawī, who is also cited as a source by al-Khaṭīb al-Baghdādī. Therefore, either al-Khaṭīb had only limited access to Yaḥyā's accounts or he consciously chose to omit this report.

[55] EI^2, s.v. "Al-Ḥusayn b. 'Alī, Ṣāḥib Fakhkh" (L. Veccia Vaglieri).

[56] Al-Rāzī, 136 and 227. For more on al-Rāzī's account, see Modarressi, *Tradition and Survival*, 143–4, and al-Kulaynī, 1:366.

al-Kāẓim refused to join al-Ḥusayn b. 'Alī's uprising, arguing that his participation would lead to the deaths of all of Ja'far al-Ṣādiq's sons.[57] This excuse prompted al-Ḥusayn to observe that only the wicked hide disbelief while manifesting faith. The text contrasts al-Kāẓim's political passivity with Yaḥyā b. 'Abd Allāh's position on the front lines of the rebellion.[58]

'Alī b. Bilāl's (d. fifth/eleventh century) biography of al-Ḥusayn b. 'Alī also emphasizes al-Kāẓim's failings. In the run-up to the rebellion at Fakhkh, Yaḥyā b. 'Abd Allāh rides to al-Kāẓim's estate to lobby for support.[59] He is kept waiting for a long time before being granted an audience. Yaḥyā then explains the situation, noting the ill treatment of the 'Alids at the hands of the new 'Abbāsid governor. In spite of this persecution, al-Kāẓim refuses to back the rebellion, and Yaḥyā returns to Medina in frustration. The disparity between the active Yaḥyā and the passive al-Kāẓim is quite clear. But 'Alī b. Bilāl's account goes one step further and makes al-Kāẓim explicitly complicit with 'Abbāsid oppression as he stands with them on the battlefield at Fakhkh[60] and later accompanies them as they punish the defeated 'Alids.[61] Yaḥyā, by contrast, retreats from the battle, escapes with caravans of pilgrims, and continues to foment rebellion across the Muslim world.

Al-Kāẓim is not a central figure in the Zaydī historical tradition. With the exception of al-Iṣbahānī's biographical entry, Zaydī authors mention al-Kāẓim only in the context of his inaction during the uprising at Fakhkh, which thoroughly discredits him among the Zaydī Shī'a and makes his rehabilitation virtually impossible. He also pales in comparison to Yaḥyā b. 'Abd Allāh. Whereas the latter is hailed as a legitimate Imām who participated in one rebellion, organized a second rebellion (in Daylam), and ordered his brother Idrīs to launch a third rebellion (in North Africa), al-Kāẓim is at best reluctant to rebel and at worst complicit with 'Abbāsid tyranny.

[57] Al-Rāzī, 136.

[58] The comparison is more explicit in a later account, in which Yaḥyā is called the best Ḥasanid and al-Kāẓim the best Ḥusaynid of the time. This is, in itself, a laudatory tradition, but it reveals the continual comparison of the two figures, with al-Kāẓim always falling short because of his failure to support the rebellion. See ibid., 227.

[59] 'Alī b. Bilāl, 470. [60] Ibid., 482. [61] Ibid., 485–6.

III The Twelver Shīʿī Sources

Twelver Shīʿī biographies of Mūsā al-Kāẓim are considerably more elaborate than those of non-Twelver sources. Over time, these biographies evolved to support a theological framework grounded in the Twelver Shīʿī conception of the Imāmate. This evolution, however, does not mean that they were fabricated wholesale; rather, they reflected a rhetoricized approach to historiography, in which the authorial creation of meaning was shaped by the material and political circumstances of the Twelver community at the time of composition. As will become clear, the key ingredient in this process was the production of plausible, verisimilar accounts that reinforced existing themes in accordance with the historiographical model described in Chapter 1.

Table 3.4 lists the Twelver Shīʿī sources under consideration in this chapter. This is not a comprehensive register of Twelver works that cover al-Kāẓim's life, as biographical material is scattered throughout myriad legal and theological texts. In many cases, authors utilize accounts of the lives of the Imāms to make doctrinal points. Ibn Bābawayh's reports of al-Kāẓim, for example, specifically lay the groundwork for an affirmation of al-Riḍā's Imāmate.[62] Given the wide dispersal of biographical material, it has been necessary to make difficult choices about the inclusion or exclusion of specific works. The following analysis includes three texts that contain relatively complete biographies of al-Kāẓim (Ibn Bābawayh's *ʿUyūn*, al-Mufīd's *Irshād*, and al-Irbilī's *Kashf*); three collections of traditions (al-Kulaynī's *Kāfī*, Ibn Bābawayh's *Amālī*, and al-Mufīd's *Ikhtiṣāṣ*); and two historical chronicles (al-Yaʿqūbī's *Tārīkh* and al-Masʿūdī's *Murūj*). These works constitute a useful cross-section of the most influential Twelver Shīʿī sources despite some notable omissions, such as al-Barqī's (d. 274/887) *Maḥāsin*.[63]

With the exception of the two annalistic works (al-Yaʿqūbī and al-Masʿūdī), these sources follow a fairly well-established form. Their primary interest lies in affirming al-Kāẓim's status as Imām by imbuing him with special qualities that far exceed the piety and generosity

62 Cooperson, *Classical Arabic Biography*, 76–100.

63 Given these limitations, it is difficult to make broad historiographical conclusions. Still, the following analysis documents changes in Twelver Shīʿī depictions of al-Kāẓim through the elaboration or excision of some key narrative elements.

Table 3.4 – *The Twelver Shī'ī Sources for Mūsā al-Kāẓim*

al-Ya'qūbī (d. 283/897)	*al-Tārīkh* Chronography
al-Kulaynī (d. 329/941)	*al-Uṣūl min al-Kāfī* Collection of traditions
al-Mas'ūdī (d. 345/956)	*Murūj al-dhahab* Chronography
Ibn Bābawayh (d. 381/991)	*al-Amālī* Collection of traditions *'Uyūn akhbār al-Riḍā* Biography/collection of traditions
al-Shaykh al-Mufīd (d. 413/1022)	*al-Ikhtiṣāṣ* Collection of traditions *al-Irshād* Biography
al-Irbilī (d. 717/1317)	*Kashf al-ghumma* Biography

attributed to him in non-Twelver (i.e. Sunnī) accounts. The biographies generally begin by documenting al-Ṣādiq's designation of al-Kāẓim as his successor, then offer evidence of his distinctive virtues, and conclude with accounts of his death. The confirmation of death is particularly important given the emergence of a group that claimed that al-Kāẓim was alive, or would return from the dead as the promised Mahdī/Qā'im.

The approach utilized in the examination of the Twelver Shī'ī sources differs from that applied to the non-Twelver sources. The previous section on non-Twelver works first listed narrative elements, then proposed interpretive frameworks, and finally determined their use by individual authors. The Twelver sources, however, offer more complex narratives of al-Kāẓim's life, with later sources adding new layers of material to the core structure. In an effort to trace this process of accretion, the remainder of this chapter examines the Twelver Shī'ī works chronologically. The narrative elements of each text are first identified, with an emphasis on changes and additions over time. These elements are organized into five categories: (1) generosity accounts, (2) knowledge accounts, (3) miracles, (4) confrontations with power, and (5) accounts of imprisonment and death. This is followed by a general assessment of each text. The section ends with a discussion of the dominant interpretive frameworks used in these sources and their relationship to the shifting fortunes of the Twelver Shīʿī community.

A *Twelver Shīʿī Texts*

al-Yaʿqūbī (d. 283/897)

Al-Yaʿqūbī's historical chronicle, the earliest Twelver Shīʿī source under consideration, provides a minimalistic treatment of al-Kāẓim devoid of narrative elements from the second or third categories (pertaining to knowledge and miracles, respectively).[64] After mentioning al-Kāẓim's death in the year 183/799, al-Yaʿqūbī relates a report belonging to narrative category 5, in which al-Rashīd's servant Masrūr summons prominent figures in Baghdad to identify the body and refute rumors of foul play.[65] This is followed by a succinct summary of al-Kāẓim's final rites and his burial in the Qurashī cemetery in western Baghdad.[66] There is nothing particularly remarkable about the death account.

Al-Yaʿqūbī's discussion then turns to al-Kāẓim's distinguished qualities and high status. In one of these narrations, al-Kāẓim contrasts the powerful with the oppressed.[67] This report is ostensibly about al-Kāẓim's knowledge, but it functions primarily as a critique of the ʿAbbāsids. In another account, an unnamed companion approaches al-Kāẓim in prison and suggests that he appeal to a third party to intervene on his behalf before al-Rashīd.[68] Al-Kāẓim vehemently rejects this idea, observing that one should only turn to God for help. This report falls into narrative category 4 (confrontations with power) and hints at al-Kāẓim's unwillingness to compromise his religious principles for material gain – in this case, release from prison. Al-Yaʿqūbī's remaining accounts consist of brief statements that either reinforce al-Kāẓim's exemplary characteristics (narrative category 1) or confirm his death (narrative category 5). Given the cursory nature of

[64] Al-Yaʿqūbī, 2:360–1. [65] Ibid., 2:360. [66] Ibid. [67] Ibid., 2:361.
[68] Ibid.

this material, it is not included in Table 3.6. Although al-Ya'qūbī mentions 'Abbāsid efforts to dispel rumors of murder or poisoning, he does not assess the validity of these accusations. This lack of interest in the details of al-Kāẓim's burial contrasts with its importance to later Twelver Shī'ī authors.

al-Kulaynī (d. 329/941)

Al-Kulaynī's compendium of Twelver Shī'ī traditions, entitled *al-Uṣūl min al-Kāfi*, encompasses extensive material detailing the lives of the Imāms. The analysis that follows utilizes biographical traditions drawn primarily from two sections of al-Kulaynī's work. The first focuses on al-Kāẓim's efforts at establishing his legitimacy,[69] while the second contains a biographical sketch of his life.[70] It also makes use of traditions that discuss the Imāms' foreknowledge of their deaths[71] and present proofs of al-Kāẓim's designation as Imām.[72]

Narrative Category 1 Generosity Accounts

Al-Kulaynī preserves no narratives that address al-Kāẓim's generosity (narrative category 1). This absence may be connected to the fact that al-Kulaynī's text predates the earliest appearance of these accounts in the non-Twelver sources. Al-Iṣbahānī, for example, relates a version of the "descendant of 'Umar" narrative some decades after al-Kulaynī, and al-Khaṭīb al-Baghdādī's "debt collector" narrative is first attested in the fifth/eleventh century. It is possible that such accounts were either unavailable to al-Kulaynī or not in general circulation. The lack of generosity narratives may also stem from their potential disjuncture with Twelver Shī'ī historical assumptions. An emphasis on al-Kāẓim's proverbial generosity suggests access to considerable wealth, a characteristic that contradicts idealized images of the pious poverty of the Imāms. This recurring theme in Twelver Shī'ī biographical works is explored in greater detail below.

Narrative Category 2 Knowledge Accounts

Most of al-Kulaynī's accounts highlight the depth and scope of al-Kāẓim's knowledge. Three reports cast al-Kāẓim as a distinguished

69 Al-Kulaynī, 1:351–67. 70 Ibid., 1:476–86. 71 Ibid., 1:258–9.

72 Ibid., 1:307–11. In this category of traditions, al-Kāẓim performs actions or manifests qualities that al-Ṣādiq has ascribed to his successor. Similar accounts are abundant in the biographies of other Twelver Imāms.

scholar and ascribe to him expertise in various areas of acquired knowledge. The first of these involves a Christian wanderer who prays to God for proper guidance.[73] After encounters with prominent Christian and Jewish scholars, he is directed to al-Kāẓim, from whom he requests an interpretation of Q44:1–4.[74] Al-Kāẓim offers a pro-Shīʿī gloss of the verses and then asks the wanderer a series of questions about Jesus and Mary. The man is unable to answer, so al-Kāẓim produces the answers himself, specifying the name of Mary's mother, the time and date of Jesus' conception and birth, the name of the river along which Mary gave birth, and the circumstances surrounding her vow of silence. He then discloses information about the wanderer's forebears. This display of erudition convinces the wanderer to embrace Islam and to adopt the name ʿAbd Allāh. There is a hint of the supernatural in the report, but most of the information provided by al-Kāẓim is theoretically available through research and study.

The theme of knowledge also informs a second report, in which a nun and a monk visit al-Kāẓim.[75] Like the wanderer in the previous narrative, they consult him on religious matters and he questions them back. The nun quickly converts to Islam, but the monk is more hesitant. He tells the Imām about his experiences with an Indian holy man who could travel to Jerusalem and back in a single day and night. This is followed by a digression in which al-Kāẓim points out that there are seven special names of God that allow individuals to traverse large distances very quickly. The jinn Āṣif, for example, invoked one of these names to transport the throne of Sheba to Solomon. The monk relates that he tracked the holy man to a small monastery in India, where God miraculously provided for his material needs. The holy man sent him to Medina with instructions for securing a meeting with al-Kāẓim. In the course of their conversation, al-Kāẓim answers all of the monk's questions, and even reveals the name of the Indian holy man – Mutammam b. Fayrūz. The monk, however, is unable to answer any of al-Kāẓim's questions, many of which involve mystical knowledge of God. At the end of the narrative, the monk converts to Islam and accepts al-Kāẓim as his Imām.

73 Ibid., 1:478–81.
74 Q44:1–4 reads: "[1] Ḥā, Mīm. [2] By the Manifest Book! [3] Indeed We sent it down on a blessed night, and indeed We have been warning [mankind]. [4] Every definitive matter is resolved in it."
75 Al-Kulaynī, 1:481–4.

A third knowledge report begins with the two narrators, Hishām b. Sālim al-Jawālīqī (d. after 148/765) and Muḥammad b. 'Alī b. Nu'mān (fl. mid second/eighth century),[76] expressing their doubts about the claim to the Imāmate of 'Abd Allāh b. Ja'far, al-Kāẓim's brother, because of his inability to adequately answer a tricky legal question.[77] As they debate their next move, Hishām observes a stranger across the street who signals to him to follow. Hishām is troubled by the gesture, given widespread rumors that 'Abbāsid spies in Medina have been ordered to find and kill al-Ṣādiq's successor. Nevertheless, he follows the man alone to the home of Mūsā al-Kāẓim, who tries to assuage his fear and confusion. The next part of the narrative relates an exchange during which Hishām accepts al-Kāẓim as the legitimate Imām. He then secretly shares his experience with others, who are also convinced by al-Kāẓim's legal expertise. As in the two previous examples, this account centers on a type of knowledge that is theoretically within the reach of any dedicated scholar.[78]

Four other narrative elements in al-Kulaynī's text forward a conception of al-Kāẓim's knowledge that is more weighted toward the supernatural, particularly through his prediction of future events. In the first, one of al-Kāẓim's companions, Abū Khālid al-Zubālī,[79] fears for the Imām's life on the eve of his first imprisonment during al-Mahdī's caliphate.[80] Al-Kāẓim reassures him of his safety and promises to meet him on a specific date at a given location. Abū Khālid arrives at the spot on the designated day but, as the sun descends, he begins to doubt the Imām's appearance. At that very moment, al-Kāẓim's party emerges from the

[76] The first narrator is Hishām b. Sālim al-Jawālīqī, a prominent Kūfan theologian who transmitted reports from al-Ṣādiq and al-Kāẓim. See Modarressi, *Tradition and Survival*, 269–71; al-Najāshī, 2:399; al-Tustarī, 10:559–63. The second narrator is Muḥammad b. 'Alī b. Nu'mān, a Kūfan jurist and theologian who was called Mu'min al-Ṭāq by his fellow Shī'a and Shayṭān al-Ṭāq by his enemies. He was a money changer and a client of the Bajīla. See Modarressi, *Tradition and Survival*, 338–9; al-Najāshī, 2:203–4; al-Tustarī, 9:464–71. In al-Tustarī's version of this narrative, Muḥammad b. 'Alī is explicitly referred to as Mu'min al-Ṭāq.

[77] Al-Kulaynī, 1:351. 'Abd Allāh is unable to provide an adequate justification for his ruling on an issue involving *zakāt*.

[78] Al-Kāẓim's awareness of Hishām's doubts can plausibly be attributed to his general knowledge of the uncertainty prevalent among al-Ṣādiq's companions; this information is not necessarily of supernatural provenance.

[79] Al-Tustarī (11:303) identifies Abū Khālid as a companion of al-Kāẓim and then recounts this incident.

[80] Al-Kulaynī, 1:477–8.

direction of Baghdad. The Imām then mildly reproaches Abū Khālid for his lack of faith, ascribes his doubts to Satan, and predicts a second arrest that will culminate in his death.

In the second report, Isḥāq b. ʿAmmār[81] (d. before 181/797) overhears al-Kāẓim predict his own death and wonders silently whether the Imām possesses such information about his followers.[82] Al-Kāẓim is instantly aware of these thoughts, and chastises Isḥāq for his skepticism. He then reveals that Isḥāq will die within two years and that his family will be rent by internal feuds that will leave it in abject poverty. The clearly startled Isḥāq pleads with al-Kāẓim to forgive him for his lack of faith. The report concludes by confirming the accuracy of the Imām's predictions. In this encounter, al-Kāẓim models two supernatural abilities: knowledge of the future and clairvoyance.

The final two reports that demonstrate al-Kāẓim's knowledge of the future concern the failed revolt at Fakhkh. The first records an exchange between the leader of the rebellion, al-Ḥusayn b. ʿAlī, and al-Kāẓim in the days preceding the battle.[83] Having secured control of Medina, al-Ḥusayn solicits the oath of allegiance from al-Kāẓim. The Imām responds by counseling him to avoid the mistakes of Muḥammad al-Nafs al-Zakiyya[84] (d. 145/762), who had pressured al-Ṣādiq to support his rebellion. He refuses to take the oath, urges al-Ḥusayn to fight well in the name of God, and predicts his death in battle. The episode manages to balance contradictory depictions of al-Kāẓim. He supports al-Ḥusayn b. ʿAlī's rebellion but avoids personal involvement because of his foreknowledge of its failure.

The second Fakhkh account preserves an icy correspondence between al-Kāẓim and Yaḥyā b. ʿAbd Allāh.[85] The exchange of letters begins with Yaḥyā ascribing al-Kāẓim's refusal to support the rebellion to personal ambition. He also draws a comparison between al-Kāẓim's attitude toward al-Ḥusayn b. ʿAlī and al-Ṣādiq's attitude toward al-

[81] Abū Yaʿqūb Isḥāq b. ʿAmmār b. Ḥayyān was a Kūfan money changer and a client of the Banū Taghlib. He is known as a companion and transmitter of al-Ṣādiq and al-Kāẓim. See Modarressi, *Tradition and Survival*, 299; al-Najāshī, 1:193–4; al-Tustarī, 1:757–70.

[82] Al-Kulaynī, 1:484. [83] Ibid., 1:366.

[84] Al-Ziriklī, 6:220; *EI*[2], s.v. "Muḥammad b. ʿAbd Allāh b. al-Ḥasan al-Muthannā b. al-Ḥasan b. ʿAlī b. Abī Ṭālib, called al-Nafs al-Zakiyya" (F. Buhl).

[85] Al-Kulaynī, 1:366–7. Modarressi (in *Tradition and Survival*, 144) mentions this episode when discussing al-Rāzī's depiction of the strained relations between al-Kāẓim and Yaḥyā b. ʿAbd Allāh.

Nafs al-Zakiyya. In his response, al-Kāẓim disavows any desire for power, rejects the charge that he is preventing others from joining the rebellion, and questions Yaḥyā's religious knowledge. He then exhorts Yaḥyā to obey the caliph in order to avoid certain death. Al-Kāẓim's letter is intercepted by the 'Abbāsids and reaches al-Rashīd, who is thereby reassured of his loyalty. The narrator implies that al-Kāẓim had foreknowledge of the letter's fate and drafted it in order to protect himself in the aftermath of the rebellion's failure. This interpretation has the effect of transforming al-Kāẓim's response from a gesture of passive surrender to one of cautious dissimulation. The narrative counters Zaydī accusations of quietism and complicity with the 'Abbāsids by framing al-Kāẓim's actions as a reasonable outgrowth of his knowledge of the future.

Narrative Category 3 Miracles

Al-Kulaynī includes two narrative elements in which al-Kāẓim performs miracles, acts that constitute a radical break with the laws of nature. These feats have no logical explanation and exceed the relative plausibility of predicting the future or reading minds. The first miracle account involves a Christian woman in Mecca who is despondent after the death of her cow, the sole means of sustenance for her orphaned children.[86] Al-Kāẓim asks her whether she would be happy if the cow returned to life. He then performs a two-cycle prayer and recites an inaudible invocation before prodding the cow with a stick and ordering it to rise up, which it does. The woman is overjoyed, and al-Kāẓim quietly slips away.

The second miracle report involves al-Kāẓim's interactions with an ascetic, who is identified as Ḥasan b. 'Abd Allāh and praised for his fearless and principled devotion to Islam.[87] One day, al-Kāẓim approaches Ḥasan at the mosque and lauds his good conduct while also lamenting his lack of true understanding (*ma'rifa*). The Imām advises him to seek knowledge by studying traditions with prominent Medinan scholars. Ḥasan does so, but when he later returns to al-Kāẓim, the Imām systematically refutes all of these traditions and sends him away. The ascetic sinks into despair, and again beseeches al-Kāẓim for guidance. This time, al-Kāẓim teaches him about the Imāmate, tracing it from 'Alī through Ja'far al-Ṣādiq and then naming

[86] Al-Kulaynī, 1:484. [87] Ibid., 1:352–3.

himself as the Imām of the age. Ḥasan asks for clear proof, and al-Kāẓim instructs him to tell a tree standing some distance away that the Imām wishes it to approach. The tree physically uproots itself and moves until it is standing before al-Kāẓim, who then gestures for it to return to its place. After seeing this miracle, Ḥasan accepts al-Kāẓim as the Imām and devotes himself to silent worship.

Narrative Category 4 Confrontations with Power

The only narrative in al-Kulaynī's text in which al-Kāẓim directly confronts ʿAbbāsid authority is set in prison just prior to his death.[88] This report begins with al-Sindī b. Shāhik summoning eighty prominent men to view the conditions of al-Kāẓim's imprisonment. Al-Sindī points out al-Kāẓim's comfortable living quarters and derisively dismisses rumors of mistreatment. He then allows the gathered men to question al-Kāẓim. The Imām first affirms that he is being treated well, but then reveals that he has recently been fed seven poisoned dates that will cause him to turn green the following day and die the day after that. Upon hearing this, al-Sindī trembles with fear. The confrontational aspects of this account are subtle. Although al-Kāẓim confirms the gist of al-Sindī's claims, he also displays an awareness of ʿAbbāsid machinations and an unwillingness to let them pass unchallenged.

On the whole, al-Kulaynī depicts al-Kāẓim as exercising restraint in his dealing with the caliphs. This is often a result of his foreknowledge of the outcome of rebellions against al-Mahdī and al-Rashīd. Thus, al-Kulaynī responds to Zaydī accusations of al-Kāẓim's complicity (or outright treason) by emphasizing the pointlessness of sacrificing innocent lives in a doomed endeavor. Although the Imām remains explicitly nonconfrontational, his access to divine favor is evidenced by both his extensive knowledge and his ability to perform miracles.

Narrative Category 5 Imprisonment and Death

Al-Kulaynī presents a series of brief reports that summarize the details of al-Kāẓim's death.[89] He notes that the Imām was arrested by al-Rashīd in Medina prior to the Ḥajj in Shawwāl of 179/795. He was initially sent to Baṣra, where he was held by ʿĪsā b. Jaʿfar b. al-Manṣūr, before being transferred to Baghdad, where he remained in the custody

[88] Ibid., 1:258–9. This account is also included in narrative category 5.
[89] Ibid., 1:476.

of al-Sindī b. Shāhik until his death in Rajab of 183/799.[90] Al-Kulaynī identifies the cause of death as poisoning by means of seven tainted dates, echoing the narrative described in the previous section.[91]

Although these accounts agree with many aspects of the "Barmakid plot" narrative found in the non-Twelver sources, they are noticeably devoid of historical context. There is no indication that al-Kāẓim was the victim of Yaḥyā al-Barmakī's efforts to discredit his rivals at the 'Abbāsid court. The Imām's prison history is also condensed, as he is transferred directly from 'Īsā in Baṣra to al-Sindī in Baghdād, with no mention of al-Faḍl al-Barmakī. The one element of the "Barmakid plot" narrative that al-Kulaynī preserves in detail concerns al-Kāẓim's betrayal by a member of his family.[92] In al-Kulaynī's telling, al-Kāẓim is aware of the intentions of his nephew Muḥammad b. Ismā'īl b. Ja'far al-Ṣādiq (d. before 183/799)[93] and attempts to dissuade him through an appeal to kinship and promises of financial support. When questioned about these efforts, al-Kāẓim explains that he is reluctant to sever familial bonds with his nephew, as this would prompt God to shorten his life. However, Muḥammad rejects his uncle's appeals, travels to Baghdad, and testifies that al-Kāẓim has set himself up as a rival caliph in Medina. Al-Rashīd rewards him with 100,000 *dirhams*, but he is immediately stricken with diphtheria and dies before receiving the money.

The differences between the depictions of familial betrayal offered by al-Kulaynī and al-Iṣbahānī suggest that the two represent independent accounts. First, they disagree on the identity of the 'Alid traitor, as al-Iṣbahānī names 'Alī b. Ismā'īl rather than Muḥammad b. Ismā'īl. Second, al-Iṣbahānī's account asserts that the primary rationale for the betrayal involved financial difficulties, a factor that is downplayed in al-Kulaynī's narrative. Third, the substance of the accusations differs: Muḥammad b. Ismā'īl describes al-Kāẓim as a rival caliph, whereas 'Alī b. Ismā'īl highlights his extravagant wealth. Fourth, al-Kulaynī presents the incident in isolation, while al-Iṣbahānī integrates it into a larger narrative involving court intrigue. In terms of similarities, both narratives mention al-Kāẓim's unsuccessful efforts to dissuade his nephew, and both document his subsequent death.

90 For examples of al-Kulaynī's propensity for succinct death narratives, see ibid., 1:476 and 486.

91 Ibid., 1:258–9. 92 Ibid., 1:485–6. 93 Al-Tustarī, 9:115–18.

Assessment

Loyalty and faith in the Imām are a primary theme in al-Kulaynī's depiction of al-Kāẓim. In the narratives featuring al-Kāẓim's prediction of his own release from prison and the fate of Isḥāq's family, for example, the Imām scolds his followers for entertaining any doubts about the scope of his knowledge. Bear in mind that al-Kulaynī was writing only a few decades after the disappearance of the twelfth Imām, when the community was in the throes of a full-blown crisis.[94] His emphasis on loyalty and faith was likely directed at those Twelver Shīʿa who were tempted to convert to Zaydī or Ismāʿīlī Shīʿism because of the uncertainty surrounding the occultation of the twelfth Imām. These narratives reframed the crisis as a test: Satan was tempting believers to abandon the Imām of the age.

Another major theme that pervades al-Kulaynī's text concerns the nature and provenance of al-Kāẓim's knowledge. This issue was intrinsically tied to the Twelver doctrine of the Imāmate and divided the community from the earliest period onward. One position held to a rationalist understanding of the Imām's role, arguing that knowledge was acquired through study, while the other claimed that God directly endowed the Imām with all requisite knowledge.[95]

Al-Kulaynī provides potential support for both of these views. In the narratives involving the Christian wanderer, the nun and the monk, and Hishām and Muḥammad's doubts about the Imāmate, al-Kāẓim showcases his mastery of a vast range of religious knowledge. In the first two, he expertly responds to his interlocutors' questions and then asks them his own questions, which they are unable to answer. In the third, al-Kāẓim explicitly predicates his claim to the Imāmate on his knowledge, juxtaposing it with that of his brother ʿAbd Allāh. The source of this knowledge remains unspecified. It is certainly possible that al-Kāẓim received it directly from God. It is equally plausible, however, that it was the product of prolonged study of materials passed down from the Prophet.

The other reports in the category of knowledge accounts unambiguously endorse the idea of divine inspiration. The narratives concerning al-Kāẓim's predictions of his future release from prison and the

94 Modarressi, *Crisis and Consolidation*, 66–105.
95 On this debate, compare Modarressi, *Crisis and Consolidation*, 19–51, with Amir-Moezzi, *Divine Guide*, chapters 2–4.

dissolution of Isḥāq's family attribute to al-Kāẓim knowledge of the future and the ability to read the thoughts of his followers. In his exchanges with al-Ḥusayn b. 'Alī and Yaḥyā b. 'Abd Allāh over the rebellion at Fakhkh, al-Kāẓim predicts the 'Abbāsids' victory and protects himself through a letter that he knows will fall into enemy hands. He also attempts to dissuade his nephew Muḥammad b. Ismā'īl from betraying him in Baghdad despite his awareness of the futility of these efforts. The image of al-Kāẓim as the recipient of divine favor is further amplified by miracle accounts in which he reanimates a dead cow and prompts a tree to walk.

A final theme in al-Kulaynī's reports involves justifying al-Kāẓim's apolitical views while maintaining his credentials as an oppositional figure. Al-Kulaynī frames al-Kāẓim's refusal to participate in the rebellion at Fakhkh as a consequence of his divinely inspired foresight. He is not complicit with 'Abbāsid power; rather, he is unwilling to throw away his life on an ill-conceived uprising. Such a portrayal contests Zaydī reports that ascribe al-Kāẓim's purported support of the 'Abbāsids to naked political ambition. Likewise, al-Kulaynī's explanation of al-Kāẓim's letter to Yaḥyā b. 'Abd Allāh turns a disconcertingly quietist letter into a ploy to ensure the Imām's safety in the aftermath of the failed rebellion. In these accounts, al-Kāẓim is cast as a careful and reasonable Imām, sympathetic to al-Ḥusayn b. 'Alī but reluctant to follow him into disaster. Lest he be perceived as completely passive, the narrative about al-Sindī's plot to poison him places al-Kāẓim in direct conflict with the 'Abbāsids as he publicly exposes their involvement in his impending death. In the process, al-Kāẓim demonstrates a willingness to confront the 'Abbāsids in particularly important contexts. His caution, then, is a product of thoughtful political calculation.

Al-Kulaynī's defense of al-Kāẓim against Zaydī attacks may help explain the absence of narrative elements belonging to category 1 (generosity accounts). The non-Twelver sources are comfortable with acknowledging the Imām's access to considerable financial resources as a precondition of his generosity. Al-Kulaynī, by contrast, is eager to avoid the potential complications and criticisms associated with wealth. This sensitivity likely stems from the apparent tension between the image of an oppressed 'Alid Imām, on the one hand, and that of a wealthy patron, on the other. Later Twelver scholars are more at ease with this tension, but in the time of al-Kulaynī, the critiques of other

Shīʿī groups may have rendered a portrayal that embraces both facets untenable.

The themes of loyalty, knowledge, supernatural abilities, and political confrontation recur in varying combinations in subsequent Twelver Shīʿī sources. Al-Kulaynī's text represents an early Twelver Shīʿī interpretation of al-Kāẓim, particularly that of the Twelver community in Qumm still recovering from the shock of the Imām's occultation.[96] It does not, however, necessarily reflect the views of other Twelver Shīʿī communities, such as that in Baghdad. As will become clear below, later generations crafted strikingly different depictions of al-Kāẓim by omitting or elaborating narrative elements to suit their particular needs.

al-Masʿūdī (d. 345/956)

Al-Masʿūdī discusses Mūsā al-Kāẓim in two passages located under the caliphate of al-Rashīd. The first is the "*ḥabashī* dream" narrative, which was previously mentioned among the prison-release accounts in the non-Twelver sources.[97] In this version, a black figure appears to al-Rashīd in a dream and threatens to impale him with a spear unless he sets al-Kāẓim free. After the caliph awakens, he orders al-Kāẓim's release, gives him 30,000 *dirham*s, and permits him to return to Medina. Al-Kāẓim is startled by al-Rashīd's decision. He then reveals to the narrator that he had a dream in which the Prophet taught him a prayer that he promised would end his imprisonment. The report concludes with the text of the prayer.

Al-Masʿūdī's text is the earliest extant source to include this narrative, but it was later quoted in both Twelver and non-Twelver sources. There are certainly more potent accounts of confrontation, but in this case al-Kāẓim manages to defy the caliph through a direct intervention from God via the Prophet. His uttering of the prayer has an immediate effect, precipitating the appearance of the threatening figure in al-Rashīd's dream. This is a far cry from the "al-Mahdī and Q47:22" narrative, in which the caliph is simply reminded of his duty to kin. There are, however, some problematic dimensions to this report, at

[96] This context influences a range of contemporaneous Twelver texts, some of which exhibit far greater supernatural tendencies. See, for example, al-Barqī's *Maḥāsin*. Although al-Kulaynī settled in Baghdād, his scholarly perspective remained grounded in Qumm.

[97] Al-Masʿūdī (1973), 4:206–7.

least from a Shīʿī perspective. First, the Imām exhibits palpable fear when he is approached by the narrator in the middle of the night. And second, he is surprised at the turn of events, despite the Prophet's guarantee about the efficacy of the prayer. These reactions are not typical of Twelver Shīʿī Imāms, who usually manifest apathy or joy in the face of death and convey complete trust in God's power.

Al-Masʿūdī's final mention of al-Kāẓim is an unattributed death announcement.[98] He notes that the Imām died in Baghdad in 186/802 during the fifteenth year of al-Rashīd's reign. There is no reference to imprisonment, but the cause is clearly specified as poisoning. Al-Masʿūdī directs readers to another, no longer extant, work in which he discusses the circumstances and consequences of al-Kāẓim's death. The unavailability of this text limits al-Masʿūdī's value as a Twelver Shīʿī source.

Ibn Bābawayh (d. 381/991)

In his *ʿUyūn akhbār al-Riḍā*, Ibn Bābawayh preserves a version of al-Kāẓim's biography that differs significantly from that of al-Kulaynī. This divergence stems from the purpose of his work, which is to establish the legitimacy of al-Riḍā's Imāmate.[99] This goal shapes the very structure of the book. In the first three chapters, al-Kāẓim serves as a conduit for detailing the circumstances of al-Riḍā's birth. The next three chapters contain a series of reports that confirm al-Kāẓim's designation of al-Riḍā as his successor. It is only in chapters 7 and 8 that Ibn Bābawayh presents biographical information specific to al-Kāẓim. The first of these recounts his interactions with the ʿAbbāsid caliphs al-Hādī and al-Rashīd, whereas the second focuses on his death.

Narrative Category 1 Generosity Accounts

Ibn Bābawayh offers no accounts of al-Kāẓim's generosity. A likely reason for this absence was discussed in the section on al-Kulaynī: generosity narratives suggest access to considerable wealth, but acknowledging that al-Kāẓim was rich would open him to Zaydī charges that he was motivated by personal ambition. The first Twelver author to

[98] Ibid., 4:216.

[99] Ibn Bābawayh also cites these accounts in other works that are not as specialized as the *ʿUyūn*. See Ibn Bābawayh, *Amālī*, 130–2, 335–8.

include this type of information in his biography of al-Kāẓim was al-Shaykh al-Mufīd, discussed later in this chapter.

Narrative Category 2 Knowledge Accounts

Ibn Bābawayh includes only one narrative element that directly addresses the issue of knowledge. The report in question features one of the founders of the Ḥanafī law school, Abū Yūsuf (d. 182/798), who requests al-Mahdī's permission to question al-Kāẓim on a legal issue, confident that he will fail to provide an adequate answer.[100] The issue concerns the difference between a pilgrim seeking shade during the Ḥajj (which is not permitted) and finding shelter in the shade of a tent (which is permitted). Al-Kāẓim turns the question around and asks Abū Yūsuf about the difference between a menstruating woman making up for missed prayers (not required) and making up for missed days of fasting (required). Abū Yūsuf responds that the difference is based on God's commands. Al-Kāẓim applies the same reasoning to the matter of the pilgrim and shade. The ruling is affirmed by both al-Mahdī and Abū Yūsuf. It is noteworthy that Ibn Bābawayh's single knowledge account involves a legal question, in contrast to the more fantastical knowledge reports mentioned by al-Kulaynī.

Narrative Category 3 Miracles

Ibn Bābawayh's work contains a single report of al-Kāẓim performing a miracle. For reasons that will become apparent, it also belongs to narrative category 4 (confrontations with power). The episode centers on a dinner during which al-Rashīd plans to embarrass and belittle al-Kāẓim.[101] To this end, he hires a charmer (*muʿazzim*), who devises a trick so that whenever al-Kāẓim reaches for a piece of bread, it flies away. This greatly amuses al-Rashīd. Then al-Kāẓim commands the image of a lion embroidered on a curtain to "Seize the enemy of God!" The lion comes to life and swallows the charmer. This so shocks and frightens the members of the gathering, including the caliph, that they faint. After they regain consciousness, al-Rashīd asks al-Kāẓim to have the image of the lion restore the man. Al-Kāẓim responds that the cane of Moses did not return the canes or ropes that it had swallowed from

[100] Ibn Bābawayh, *ʿUyūn*, 1:64. For Abū Yūsuf, see al-Ziriklī, 8:193; *EI*[3], s.v. "Abū Yūsuf" (B. Wheeler).

[101] Ibn Bābawayh, *ʿUyūn*, 1:78.

the pharaoh's sorcerers. It is at this point that the enraged caliph resolves to poison al-Kāẓim.

The "lion and charmer" narrative conveys al-Kāẓim's utter disregard for the potential repercussions of his actions. The miracle is itself an overt act of defiance that personifies the Imām's latent power and highlights his ability and even willingness to confront the caliph. This fierce attitude is one of the hallmarks of Ibn Bābawayh's depiction of al-Kāẓim. In most cases, however, it is expressed through conventional means, such as conversation or debates, rather than miracles.[102]

Narrative Category 4 Confrontations with Power

A considerable portion of Ibn Bābawayh's text consists of reports of al-Kāẓim's confrontations with 'Abbāsid power.[103] These narratives counter claims of the Imām's weakness or complicity, attributing his occasional passivity to an acceptance of God's will. His political quietism is not born of fear, but rather results from his adherence to a predetermined course of events. Al-Kāẓim gets the better of his opponents (usually the caliphs al-Mahdī and al-Rashīd), treats them with scorn and indifference, and staunchly refuses to accord them any special treatment.

The most detailed narrative element in this category relates an extended conversation between al-Kāẓim and al-Rashīd.[104] The account offers minimal context, plunging immediately into the text of their exchange. Al-Rashīd first asks al-Kāẓim whether he considers himself to be the legitimate caliph and thereby entitled to collect taxes (*kharāj*). The Imām responds by counseling the caliph to ignore slanderous rumors and relating a Prophetic tradition in which relatives rekindle their mutual affection through a physical embrace. The two men hug, and al-Rashīd's attitude softens. He asks al-Kāẓim to answer some questions without resorting to cautionary dissimulation (*taqiyya*). Al-Kāẓim agrees to do so in return for a guarantee of protection or safe-conduct. In the course of the ensuing conversation, al-Kāẓim establishes the following points: (i) Abū Ṭālib was closer than 'Abbās in kinship to the Prophet,[105] (ii) Fāṭima had a greater

102 Al-Kulaynī, by contrast, confines al-Kāẓim's miracles to private settings involving people in need of material comfort or spiritual guidance.

103 Six of these narratives are analyzed in this section. The "lion and charmer" narrative discussed in the preceding section also falls into this category.

104 Ibn Bābawayh, *'Uyūn*, 1:66–70.

105 The caliph proposes that the 'Abbāsids and the 'Alids share an equal lineage with the Prophet given that each branch is descended from one of the Prophet's uncles ('Abbās for the 'Abbāsids and Abū Ṭālib for the 'Alids). Al-Kāẓim replies

right than ʿAbbās to inherit from the Prophet,[106] (iii) the ʿAlids are entitled to claim the Prophet as their forebear,[107] and (iv) Fāṭima is a legitimate genetic link between the ʿAlids and the Prophet.[108] At the end of the conversation, al-Rashīd violates his promise of immunity and orders al-Kāẓim's arrest.

Ibn Bābawayh preserves two versions of another confrontation account, in which the ʿAbbāsids acknowledge their status as usurpers.[109] In the more comprehensive of these reports, al-Ma'mūn (r. 198–218/813–33) recalls his first meeting with al-Kāẓim during a trip to Medina with his father, al-Rashīd.[110] The narrative begins in a makeshift court in Medina, where heralds announce the lineage of individuals who seek an audience with al-Rashīd. The caliph grants each petitioner a sum of money commensurate with his social standing. Near the end of the session, al-Kāẓim enters the court, and al-Rashīd treats him with great respect. He questions al-Kāẓim about his many dependents and learns of his considerable financial difficulties. The caliph then promises to settle his debts and to provide enough additional funds to finance the marriages of his many charges. Al-Kāẓim expresses his hope that al-Rashīd will follow through on his words. After he leaves the court, al-Kāẓim informs al-Ma'mūn that he will one day become caliph and asks him to treat his son al-Riḍā kindly.

that the ʿAlid link is closer since the Prophet's father ʿAbd Allāh and Abū Ṭālib were full brothers whereas ʿAbbās had a different mother.

106 The caliph asks why the ʿAlids claim to be the heirs of the Prophet when Abū Ṭālib predeceased Muḥammad whereas ʿAbbās was still alive at the Prophet's death. Al-Kāẓim offers two responses. First, he states that an uncle has no share in inheritance in the presence of a son or a daughter (i.e. Fāṭima). Second, he invokes Q8:72 to argue that those who, like ʿAbbās, did not emigrate to Medina with the Prophet lost their rights to inheritance.

107 The caliph asks why the ʿAlids allow people to refer to them as "sons" of the Prophet when they are actually descendants of ʿAlī. Al-Kāẓim notes that according to the rules of kinship, the Prophet could marry the daughter of an ʿAbbāsid but he could not marry the daughter of an ʿAlid.

108 The caliph asks for Qur'ānic proof of the ʿAlids' claim that they are of the Prophet's progeny, since such a designation generally extends through sons and not daughters. Al-Kāẓim begins with Q6:84–5 and draws a parallel between Maryam's role as the link between Jesus and the Israelite prophets and Fāṭima's role as the link between the ʿAlids and Muḥammad. He then cites the incident of the mutual cursing (*mubāhala*) (through Q3:61) and the events at the Battle of Uḥud (through Q21:60).

109 Ibn Bābawayh, *ʿUyūn*, 1:72–5.

110 For a shorter version of this narrative, see ibid., 1:75–6, and *Amālī*, 335–6.

Some time later, al-Ma'mūn questions al-Rashīd about his deference toward al-Kāẓim. The caliph affirms al-Kāẓim as the legitimate Imām and acknowledges that the 'Abbāsids hold power only through brute force. He then sends the 'Alid a very small sum of money with a note in which he (falsely) claims financial straits. Al-Ma'mūn is displeased by this decision, but al-Rashīd argues that 'Abbāsid interests are best served by al-Kāẓim's poverty. These events are witnessed by the singer Mukhāriq (d. 231–2/845–6), who, infuriated by al-Rashīd's words, goads the caliph into granting him 30,000 *dīnār*s and a large estate. When Mukhāriq later offers these as a gift to al-Kāẓim, he refuses to accept them. This narrative serves two purposes. First, it counters reports of al-Kāẓim's excessive wealth. And second, it places confirmation of al-Kāẓim's status as the legitimate heir of the Prophet in the mouths of two 'Abbāsid caliphs.

Lest al-Kāẓim appear weak in the face of 'Abbāsid power, Ibn Bābawayh also presents two narrative elements in which he directly confronts the ruling caliph. In the first, al-Kāẓim receives word that al-Hādī plans to move against him.[111] His family and friends counsel him to hide in order to evade capture or even death. In response, a smiling al-Kāẓim recites a poem about the futility of those who seek to triumph over God. He then utters a prayer asking for God's help against al-Hādī. Soon after, news arrives of al-Hādī's sudden and unexpected death. At the next family gathering, an unnamed relative composes verses extolling God's responsiveness to the prayers of the upright and virtuous.

In another confrontation narrative, an angry al-Rashīd orders his chamberlain, al-Faḍl b. al-Rabī', to summon al-Kāẓim to court for immediate execution.[112] When al-Faḍl reaches al-Kāẓim's house (which he describes as a ruin), he is met by two threatening swordsmen, who direct him to a back room. He delivers the caliph's summons to the Imām. An openly disdainful al-Kāẓim complies, citing a Prophetic tradition about the necessity of obeying rulers in a period of cautionary dissimulation (*taqiyya*). He then recites a prayer and assures al-Faḍl that he, al-Kāẓim, will not be harmed on that day. When they finally reach al-Rashīd's court, the caliph's demeanor is completely transformed. He honors al-Kāẓim, asks him why he does not visit more

[111] Ibn Bābawayh, *'Uyūn*, 1:64–6, and *Amālī*, 336–7.
[112] Ibn Bābawayh, *'Uyūn*, 1:62–4.

often, and gives him a great amount of money. The Imām criticizes the caliph's love of the material world and explains that he accepts the money only in order to fund ʿAlid marriages. Some time later, al-Faḍl questions the caliph about his sudden change in attitude. Al-Rashīd recounts a vision (or a dream) of soldiers threatening to attack the palace if al-Kāẓim is harmed. The report ends with the Imām teaching al-Faḍl the text of his prayer.

A similar inversion of the power relationship between caliph and Imām informs two accounts associated with al-Kāẓim's death, which thus fit in both this narrative category and the next one (imprisonment and death). The first is a nearly identical version of the report involving poisoned dates found in al-Kulaynī's text.[113] Recall that, in this narrative, al-Sindī b. Shāhik summons prominent men to observe the conditions of al-Kāẓim's imprisonment. The Imām confirms that he is being treated well but also reveals that he has been poisoned, suggesting foreknowledge of his death and an unwillingness to allow the ʿAbbāsids to absolve themselves of responsibility for his murder.

The second confrontational death account involves a botched poisoning attempt that results in the demise of an unfortunate dog.[114] At the start of this report, al-Rashīd sends al-Kāẓim a plate of dates, one of which he has personally poisoned using a needle and thread. He orders his servant to make sure that the ʿAlid consumes all of the fruit by himself. When al-Kāẓim receives the plate, he begins to eat the dates using a toothpick. Just then, one of al-Rashīd's favorite dogs breaks free of his gold chains, and al-Kāẓim tosses him the tainted fruit before finishing off the rest. The poor dog dies a horrible, painful death. The caliph is both enraged by the loss of his pet and frustrated by his inability to harm al-Kāẓim.

The narrative then shifts to a point three days before al-Kāẓim's death when he informs his prison guard, al-Musayyab b. Zuhayr[115] (d. second/eighth century), of his plans to travel to Medina in order to designate al-Riḍā as his successor. Al-Musayyab is understandably skeptical. The Imām chastises him for his lack of faith and reveals that he will use the same name of God that allowed the jinn Āṣif to

[113] Ibn Bābawayh, *ʿUyūn*, 1:79, and *Amālī*, 132.
[114] Ibn Bābawayh, *ʿUyūn*, 1:82–5.
[115] Al-Musayyab b. Zuhayr was a confidant of al-Rashīd who was charged with holding al-Kāẓim. Al-Tustarī (10:78) cites this particular incident as proof of his Shīʿī beliefs.

retrieve Sheba's throne for Solomon.[116] He utters the name and vanishes. Some time later, he reappears and refastens his own chains. The implication here is fairly straightforward: al-Kāẓim is capable of escaping from prison at any time. In the remainder of the report, the Imām details the circumstances of his death, gives instructions about his burial, and prohibits al-Sindī b. Shāhik from performing his funeral rites. When al-Kāẓim is near death, al-Musayyab observes and recognizes the image of al-Riḍā in the room. The new Imām washes and shrouds his father's corpse while al-Sindī b. Shāhik and others simulate the proper movements without actually touching the body. Al-Riḍā thus establishes his legitimacy as the rightful Imām. In both parts of the "poisoned dog" narrative, al-Kāẓim exposes the illusory nature of 'Abbāsid authority.

Ibn Bābawayh's final confrontation account, the "*ḥabashī* dream" narrative, is preserved in two independent versions. The first resembles al-Mas'ūdī's account, described previously, but is told from a different perspective and with an inverted sequence of events.[117] The report opens with a frightened al-Kāẓim in prison. He performs a four-cycle prayer and recites an invocation seeking God's help. A black swordsman then appears to al-Rashīd in a dream and demands al-Kāẓim's release. The caliph wakes up in terror and orders his unnamed chamberlain to bring the 'Alid to him. The chamberlain finds al-Kāẓim fearful and anxious at being summoned at such a strange hour. He is explicitly described as weeping, sullen, and sad. After reaching the court, al-Kāẓim is asked about and describes the prayers he performed the previous night. Al-Rashīd then sets him free, presenting him with many gifts and making him one of his boon companions. The encounter ends with al-Kāẓim teaching the caliph the text of his useful invocation. The Imām's situation remains stable for a period until al-Rashīd arrests him for a second time, placing him in the custody of al-Sindī b. Shāhik and ultimately ordering his murder.[118]

[116] Note the parallels between this report and the report involving a nun and a monk mentioned previously in the discussion of al-Kulaynī's knowledge accounts.

[117] Ibn Bābawayh, *'Uyūn*, 1:76–7.

[118] Ibid., 1:77. Ibn Bābawayh's *Amālī* (338) contains a slight variant of this account in which the caliph orders the preservation of the prayer and then confines al-Kāẓim to a (presumably comfortable) residence with no mention of a second arrest or poisoning.

Al-Kāẓim plays a more confident and confrontational role in Ibn Bābawayh's second version of this narrative.[119] In this report, a terrified al-Faḍl b. al-Rabīʿ is called to court by al-Rashīd in the middle of the night. After al-Faḍl regains his composure, the caliph instructs him to give al-Kāẓim many valuable gifts and to permit him to return to Medina. When the surprised al-Faḍl hesitates and asks for a confirmation of these commands, the caliph angrily recounts the dream with the swordsman. At the prison, al-Faḍl finds al-Kāẓim in prayer and conveys al-Rashīd's orders. The Imām, who displays no sign of fear or anxiety, refuses the gifts, maintaining that they are the common property of the Muslim community. He eventually relents, in order to avoid the caliph's anger, but then bestows the gifts on al-Faḍl. At the end of the account, al-Kāẓim describes a dream in which the Prophet appeared to him and affirmed the injustice of his imprisonment. He also recited Q21:111,[120] instructed al-Kāẓim to perform a series of prayers and fasts, and taught him the invocation that resulted in his release.[121]

These two related dream narratives offer contrasting depictions of al-Kāẓim. In the first, he is weak, afraid of death, and uncertain about the efficacy of his own prayers. In the second, he is strong and confident in a manner that aligns with Ibn Bābawayh's other confrontation narratives. This disparity will be discussed in greater detail in the assessment of Ibn Bābawayh's text later in this section.

Narrative Category 5 Imprisonment and Death

Ibn Bābawayh provides seven narrative elements that focus on al-Kāẓim's death.[122] Three of these have been discussed already: the "poisoned dates" narrative, in which al-Kāẓim displays knowledge of his impending death;[123] the "poisoned dog" narrative, in which he

[119] Ibn Bābawayh, *ʿUyūn*, 1:60–1.

[120] Q21:111 reads: "And I know not – maybe it is a trial for you and an enjoyment for a while."

[121] The text of the invocation is different in the two versions of the "*ḥabashī* dream" narrative.

[122] There is an eighth account (Ibn Bābawayh, *ʿUyūn*, 1:81) related by a number of unnamed Medinans, which simply restates the basic facts surrounding al-Kāẓim's death. Many of these reports seem designed to refute the Wāqifī claim that al-Kāẓim was still alive and in occultation.

[123] Ibn Bābawayh, *ʿUyūn*, 1:79, and *Amālī*, 132.

exercises agency in the events leading to his death;[124] and the narrative in which he is betrayed by a family member.[125]

The first of Ibn Bābawayh's distinctive reports centers on al-Kāẓim's vigorous prayer routine in prison. There are two variants of this narrative. In the first, al-Rashīd asks al-Faḍl b. al-Rabī' about a piece of cloth that he sees each day from the roof of his palace, which overlooks the prison. Al-Faḍl replies that it is not cloth but rather al-Kāẓim, who prostrates himself in prayer from sunrise to noon. Al-Rashīd then lists al-Kāẓim's many virtues, prompting al-Faḍl to ask why such a man is in prison. The caliph responds that al-Kāẓim poses a serious threat to 'Abbāsid authority.

The second version of the "cloth" narrative substitutes the figure of al-Faḍl b. al-Rabī' for that of the caliph.[126] In this account, the narrator recalls al-Faḍl pointing to a spot on the ground of a distant house. At first, the narrator believes that it is a piece of cloth, but he quickly realizes that it is the form of a man in prayer. Al-Faḍl identifies the man as al-Kāẓim and then details the latter's daily prayer ritual, which stretches through the day and the night. After hearing this, the narrator cautions al-Faḍl to refrain from harming the 'Alid lest he bring misfortune upon himself. Al-Faḍl notes that he has received orders to kill al-Kāẓim but has repeatedly refused to carry them out. Al-Kāẓim is later transferred to the custody of the Barmakids (i.e. al-Faḍl b. Yaḥyā al-Barmakī), but al-Faḍl b. al-Rabī' continues to send him food each day. On the fourth day, however, the daily rations are provided by his new jailor, al-Faḍl al-Barmakī. At this point, al-Kāẓim raises his hands to the sky and testifies that he would have been guilty of killing himself had he eaten tainted food prior to this point. As in the accounts involving poisoned dates and the caliph's poisoned dog, al-Kāẓim here is firmly in control of the circumstances of his death.

Ibn Bābawayh's variation of the "Barmakid plot" narrative shares a number of features with al-Iṣbahānī's more comprehensive and

124 Ibn Bābawayh, *'Uyūn*, 1:82–5.

125 Ibn Bābawayh's version of the betrayal narrative (ibid., 1:60) is similar to al-Kulaynī's account, with one notable difference: the 'Alid informant is identified as Muḥammad b. Ja'far al-Ṣādiq (upheld as the successor to al-Ṣādiq by the Shumayṭiyya) rather than Muḥammad b. Ismā'īl b. Ja'far al-Ṣādiq.

126 Ibn Bābawayh, *'Uyūn*, 1:76–8, and *Amālī*, 130–2. The *Amālī* provides a more elaborate account of al-Kāẓim's transfer to the custody of al-Faḍl al-Barmakī and his examination by the doctor.

detailed account.[127] The summary that follows expands only on those parts not mentioned in the earlier discussion.

In this version of the narrative, al-Kāẓim's arrest is a result of ʿAbbāsid court intrigues surrounding al-Rashīd's succession.[128] At the start of the account, Yaḥyā al-Barmakī feels threatened by al-Rashīd's decision to entrust the education of his son Muḥammad, the future caliph al-Amīn, to Jaʿfar b. Muḥammad b. al-Ashʿath. He resolves to first win his rival's trust and then expose him to the caliph as a traitor. One day, after al-Rashīd presents Jaʿfar with 20,000 *dīnārs*, Yaḥyā al-Barmakī insinuates that Jaʿfar is a partisan of al-Kāẓim who, in the manner of the Shīʿa, sends a fifth of his earnings to the Imām. He encourages the caliph to test Jaʿfar's loyalty by challenging him to produce the full sum of the gift that night. Although Jaʿfar b. Muḥammad passes the test, the incident is indicative of Yaḥyā's efforts at undermining his rival.[129]

The next part of the report documents the betrayal of ʿAlī b. Ismāʿīl b. Jaʿfar al-Ṣādiq.[130] Recall that in previous versions, Yaḥyā al-Barmakī provides ʿAlī b. Ismāʿīl with financial gifts in exchange for testifying against his uncle al-Kāẓim. ʿAlī rejects al-Kāẓim's attempts to dissuade him from this course of action and dies while awaiting his promised reward. Ibn Bābawayh's version of this incident includes significantly more (and sometimes different) historical context. First, the betrayal takes place in a year in which al-Rashīd performs the Ḥajj. This allows Yaḥyā al-Barmakī to personally pressure ʿAlī b. Ismāʿīl to accompany the caliphal caravan back to Baghdad.[131] Second, the account mentions a gradual deterioration in al-Kāẓim's relationship with his nephew. It also does not discuss ʿAlī's gruesome death, ending instead with al-Kāẓim's plea to not make orphans of his children.

127 Whereas al-Iṣbahānī's composite narrative is drawn from multiple sources, Ibn Bābawayh relies almost entirely on the reports of Muḥammad b. Sulaymān al-Nawfalī. Cooperson argues that Ibn Bābawayh did not have access to al-Iṣbahānī's text, and, instead, utilized a number of common sources. See Cooperson, *Classical Arabic Biography*, 87–90. For al-Nawfalī, see EI^2, s.v. "Al-Nawfalī" (C. Pellat).

128 Ibn Bābawayh, *ʿUyūn*, 1:57–9.

129 Although al-Iṣbahānī alludes to Yaḥyā al-Barmakī's efforts to discredit Jaʿfar, he offers no concrete examples.

130 Ibn Bābawayh, *ʿUyūn*, 1:59–60.

131 In al-Iṣbahānī's account, Yaḥyā summons ʿAlī to meet the caliph in Baghdad.

The final part of Ibn Bābawayh's narrative includes an elaborate description of al-Kāẓim's arrest and its immediate aftermath. As in al-Iṣbahānī's version, al-Rashīd approaches the Prophet's grave and announces his plan to arrest al-Kāẓim for inciting communal strife and bloodshed.[132] He then sends out two identical caravans, one toward Baṣra with al-Kāẓim and another, empty, in the direction of Kūfa to conceal the 'Alid's true location.[133] Here Ibn Bābawayh interjects an extended anecdote about an ultimately unsuccessful conspiracy designed to expose partisans of al-Kāẓim in the caliphal retinue. After a short stay in Baṣra in the custody of 'Īsā b. Ja'far, al-Kāzim is secretly transported to Baghdad, where he is remanded to the custody of al-Sindī b. Shāhik and kept in harsh conditions. At one point he is temporarily freed, in a possible allusion to the threatening dream narratives that prompt the caliph to order al-Kāẓim's release. Al-Kāẓim is eventually poisoned by tainted dates on the direct order of the caliph.[134]

Ibn Bābawayh discusses two further incidents that relate to al-Kāẓim's death but lie outside the scope of the "Barmakid plot" narrative. In the first, 'Umar b. Wāqid[135] (d. second/eighth century) recalls being summoned by al-Sindī b. Shāhik and questioned about his links to al-Kāẓim.[136] After receiving assurances about his safety, 'Umar divulges the names of his associates and other Shī'ī sympathizers. Informed in this manner, al-Sindī gathers around fifty of al-Kāẓim's companions, shows them the Imām's body, and asks them to testify that there are no signs of violence or foul play. They then perform al-Kāẓim's death rites, led by al-Sindī, and bury the body. At the end of the account, 'Umar b. Wāqid expresses astonishment at Wāqifī claims that al-Kāẓim is alive and in occultation.

Ibn Bābawayh's final narrative presents a more colorful description of al-Kāẓim's burial. The report opens with al-Sindī b. Shāhik parading

132 Ibn Bābawayh, *'Uyūn*, 1:60. 133 Ibid., 1:70–2.

134 A number of elements central to al-Iṣbahānī's version of the "Barmakid plot" narrative are missing from Ibn Bābawayh's version. Most notably, there is no mention of al-Kāẓim's transfer to the custody of al-Faḍl al-Barmakī or the subsequent chain of events that results in al-Faḍl's beating and public condemnation. Yaḥyā al-Barmakī is likewise absent from Ibn Bābawayh's account of al-Kāẓim's death.

135 Al-Tustarī (8:231) identifies 'Umar b. Wāqid as a Sunnī but nonetheless cites him as an eyewitness to al-Kāẓim's burial in order to discredit Wāqifī claims.

136 Ibn Bābawayh, *'Uyūn*, 1:79–81.

al-Kāẓim's coffin through Baghdad accompanied by a herald, who hurls insults at the Imām and summons people to view his corpse.[137] When Sulaymān b. Abī Jaʿfar (al-Manṣūr)[138] (d. after 199/814) hears of this spectacle, he commands his family and servants to seize the body, by force if necessary, when it reaches the western part of Baghdad. He then places al-Kāẓim at an intersection with a new herald, who summons people to pay their respects. The body is washed, perfumed, and shrouded before burial in the Qurashī cemetery. Al-Rashīd disavows knowledge of al-Sindī's actions and thanks Sulaymān for his intervention.

Assessment

As mentioned previously, al-Kulaynī endows al-Kāẓim with both knowledge that extends into the supernatural and an ability to precipitate miracles through prayer. He also depicts him as avoiding direct conflict with the ʿAbbāsids except in cases in which they attempt to mislead people (e.g. by claiming innocence in his murder). Ibn Bābawayh similarly affirms the Imām's knowledge and miraculous abilities, but he breaks with al-Kulaynī in emphasizing al-Kāẓim's eagerness to confront the ʿAbbāsids. In one instance (al-Kāẓim's debate with al-Rashīd), al-Kāẓim deftly establishes that the ʿAlids are closer in kinship to the Prophet than the ʿAbbāsids are, and then exposes al-Rashīd's perfidy through the latter's violation of a safe-conduct. In another case (the "lion and charmer" narrative), al-Kāẓim demonstrates the extent of his powers by commanding the image of a lion to consume an enemy. There are other episodes in which al-Kāẓim calls on God to intervene on his behalf either to facilitate the demise of an opponent, as in the case of al-Hādī's death, or to secure his release from prison by frightening the caliph with menacing dreams. In still other accounts, such as those involving ʿAbbāsid attempts to poison him, the Imām exposes the hollowness of ʿAbbāsid authority by determining the parameters of his own death and then arranging his burial rites in accordance with Twelver Shīʿī expectations. Whereas al-Kulaynī describes al-Kāẓim as fearful and cautious, Ibn Bābawayh presents him as confident and disdainful of ʿAbbāsid power.

137 Ibid., 1:81–2.

138 Sulaymān b. Abī Jaʿfar was the son of the second ʿAbbāṣid caliph, al-Manṣūr. He survived into the reign of al-Maʾmūn. See al-Ṭabarī, index.

The reasons for Ibn Bābawayh's markedly confrontational portrayal of al-Kāẓim are difficult to establish with certainty, but three possible explanations come to mind. First, it is tempting to suggest that Ibn Bābawayh was influenced by his exposure to Mu'tazilī ideas, which advocated an activist conception of the Imāmate. Second, it is possible that Ibn Bābawayh was responding to Zaydī accusations that al-Kāẓim was complicit in 'Abbāsid oppression. Al-Kulaynī addressed this criticism through narratives in which al-Kāẓim predicted the failure of the 'Alid uprising at Fakhkh, his foreknowledge explaining and excusing his inaction. By contrast, Ibn Bābawayh simply recasts the Imām in an oppositional role without mentioning his unwillingness to back previous rebellions. The fact that al-Kāẓim does not seize actual power reflects divine will rather than cowardice or complicity. In one narrative (in which al-Faḍl b. al-Rabī' is sent to al-Kāẓim's house to bring him to court), al-Kāẓim justifies his response to a caliphal summons as a necessary act in a period of cautionary dissimulation (*taqiyya*). In this case, al-Kāẓim teaches the Twelver Shī'ī community that compliance is preferable to bloodshed in the face of overwhelming power. Third, Ibn Bābawayh lived in Baghdad under the Būyids, who explicitly patronized a newly empowered and confident Shī'ī community. A view of the Imām as careful and cautious was no longer meaningful or pertinent, so he was reimagined as an oppositional figure. In the terms of the model presented in Chapter 1, Ibn Bābawayh elaborated existing narrative elements to fit a new interpretive framework.

Ibn Bābawayh preserves one report that seems to contradict his confrontational portrait of al-Kāẓim. This is the first variant of the "*ḥabashī* dream" narrative, in which al-Kāẓim is skeptical of the efficacy of the prayer that the Prophet teaches him in a dream. He also weeps in terror when the jailor approaches to set him free. This is a far cry from other narratives, in which al-Kāẓim's disdain of the 'Abbāsids is palpable and his confidence unbounded. Ibn Bābawayh's decision to include this account is somewhat puzzling. The text seems to be a relic of a fundamentally different and much earlier depiction of al-Kāẓim.[139] Ibn Bābawayh diminishes this narrative's significance, however, by including a second, quite different, version of the same encounter in which al-Kāẓim is far more combative.

139 Although al-Kulaynī does not cite the "*ḥabashī* dream" narrative, it reflects his view of the Imām as a pious figure who exhibits a cautious fear of the 'Abbāsids.

A final point to consider pertains to the larger goal of Ibn Bābawayh's biographical reports, namely, the repudiation of the Wāqifīs, who denied al-Kāẓim's death and expected him to reappear at an appropriate time to establish a just state. Ibn Bābawayh counters these claims through elaborate reports of al-Kāẓim's death and burial. In one, al-Sindī b. Shāhik gathers al-Kāẓim's associates to identify his body, prepare it for burial, and physically place it in the grave. Another depicts a citywide procession and a street brawl over the treatment of al-Kāẓim's body. The most important of these accounts, however, is the "poisoned dog" narrative, in which al-Riḍā travels to Baghdad to prepare his father's body for burial. By doing so, he fulfills the Twelver Shīʿī expectation that every Imām's funeral rites be performed by his successor.[140]

Al-Kulaynī and Ibn Bābawayh provide the two interpretive frameworks that predominate in Twelver depictions of al-Kāẓim. Al-Kulaynī concentrates on the areas of knowledge and miracles, downplaying the Imām's willingness to challenge ʿAbbāsid authority. Ibn Bābawayh, by contrast, emphasizes al-Kāẓim's fearlessness and brazen defiance of the ʿAbbāsid caliphs. He also invests the Imām with enough power to expose the vacuous nature of ʿAbbāsid rule.

al-Shaykh al-Mufīd (d. 413/1022)

Al-Shaykh al-Mufīd's biography of al-Kāẓim draws on the knowledge accounts and miracles recorded by al-Kulaynī while scaling back the confrontational attitude depicted by Ibn Bābawayh. The following analysis focuses on al-Mufīd's *Kitāb al-irshād*, which details the lives of eleven Imāms and provides evidence of the existence and disappearance of the twelfth. Al-Mufīd's is the first extant Twelver work to provide a complete biography of al-Kāẓim, utilizing seemingly contradictory elements from multiple sources.

[140] Ibn Bābawayh also preserves a series of accounts (not discussed in this chapter) that attribute Wāqifī claims to greed. He notes that al-Kāẓim faced considerable financial constraints in helping the poor. Had he spent large amounts of money on those in need, his expenditures would have verified the slanders of his enemies in al-Rashīd's eyes. Instead, he gave the money to a small number of agents to distribute secretly on his behalf. Ibn Bābawayh, *ʿUyūn*, 1:91–2.

Narrative Category 1 Generosity Accounts

In contrast to al-Kulaynī and Ibn Bābawayh, al-Mufīd presents two generosity accounts that feature prominently in non-Twelver biographical works. The first is the "debt collector" narrative (also cited by al-Khaṭīb al-Baghdādī), in which al-Kāẓim compensates a man unsuccessfully seeking the repayment of a debt.[141] In this report, as previously mentioned, al-Kāẓim plays a role generally reserved for the caliph. The second generosity account is the "descendant of 'Umar" narrative, in which the Imām dissuades his companions from killing a critic and then wins his support through nonviolent means.[142] This element is also preserved by al-Iṣbahānī (who wrote before al-Mufīd) and al-Khaṭīb (who wrote after al-Mufīd) with identical chains of transmission. Al-Mufīd's version is distinguished by al-Kāẓim's observation that "I was sufficient for the evil within him."[143]

Al-Mufīd's generosity accounts indicate the availability of a corpus of material that transcended communal boundaries. Despite some minor differences between the reports of al-Mufīd and al-Khaṭīb, they adhere to a similar structure and convey nearly identical content. The same textual overlap is evident, to a lesser extent, in al-Mufīd's confrontation narratives.

Narrative Category 2 Knowledge Accounts

There are five narrative elements in al-Mufīd's biography of al-Kāẓim that center on the Imām's knowledge. The first of these is the narrative, mentioned by al-Kulaynī, that recounts al-Kāẓim's success in winning the loyalty of his father's companions Hishām and Muḥammad.[144] As noted previously, this episode hints at supernatural knowledge but is primarily concerned with establishing the Imām's mastery of the law. It is his ability to answer a legal question that stumped his brother 'Abd Allāh that convinces the Shī'a to endorse his claim to the Imāmate.

A second knowledge account relates an exchange between al-Kāẓim and Muḥammad b. al-Ḥasan al-Shaybānī (d. 189/805) on the issue of pilgrims seeking shade during the Ḥajj.[145] Recall that Ibn Bābawayh also cites an incident in which a prominent Ḥanafī scholar questions

[141] Al-Mufīd, *Irshād*, 296. [142] Ibid., 297.

[143] Al-Khaṭīb offers a more restrained and less elaborate account. Al-Iṣbahānī presents an abbreviated version but retains most of the important details. For those reports, see the relevant discussions in the first part of this chapter.

[144] Al-Mufīd, *Irshād*, 291–2. [145] Ibid., 297–8.

al-Kāẓim about a similar issue. There are four reasons to treat al-Mufīd's account as an independent report. First, al-Mufīd's chain of transmission shows no overlap with that of Ibn Bābawayh.[146] Second, Ibn Bābawayh's account features a different Ḥanafī scholar, Abū Yūsuf, and a different ruling caliph, al-Mahdī. Third, the two narratives do not focus on quite the same legal question. The issue addressed in Ibn Bābawayh's report concerns the difference between shade provided by a camel and that provided by a tent, whereas al-Mufīd's account compares the shade of a camel to natural shade of any provenance. Finally, al-Kāẓim responds to the question differently in each account. In Ibn Bābawayh's text, the Imām offers parallel legal examples to prove that divine will always trumps human reason. In al-Mufīd's account, al-Shaybānī laughs derisively at al-Kāẓim's view that a camel's shade is not permissible whereas natural shade is. This prompts al-Kāẓim to ask whether al-Shaybānī scoffs at the example of the Prophet. The Imām then showcases his mastery of Prophetic traditions while also critiquing one of the central tenets of Sunnī legal theory, analogical reasoning. In this instance, then, al-Mufīd appears to embellish the narrative element with a new context and content to support his own framework.

Al-Mufīd also presents a number of narratives that frame al-Kāẓim's knowledge in more supernatural terms. In one such account, Abū Baṣīr[147] (d. 150/767) asks al-Kāẓim to identify qualities unique to an Imām.[148] After affirming the necessity of a formal designation from his predecessor, al-Kāẓim emphasizes that an Imām must know the future and possess the ability to converse with each person in their own language. He then promises to supply Abū Baṣīr with proof before the end of their meeting. Shortly thereafter a man from Khurāsān enters the room and begins to speak to al-Kāẓim in Arabic. When the Imām responds in Persian, the astonished man apologizes for assuming that

[146] Ibn Bābawayh's chain runs as follows: ʿAlī b. Ibrāhīm b. Hāshim – Ibrāhīm b. Hāshim – ʿUthmān b. ʿĪsā – his companions. Al-Mufīd's chain is the following: Abū Zayd – ʿAbd al-Ḥamīd.

[147] This is most likely Yaḥyā b. Abī Qāsim al-Asadī, who was considered a trustworthy transmitter from al-Bāqir, al-Ṣādiq, and al-Kāẓim. See al-Najāshī, 2:411, and al-Tustarī, 11:14–24. He is also the subject of a knowledge account forwarded by al-Irbilī (3:57). There is a smaller possibility that the name refers to Layth b. al-Bakhtarī, who was a companion of and transmitter of legal reports from al-Ṣādiq and al-Kāẓim. See al-Tustarī, 8:622–32.

[148] Al-Mufīd, *Irshād*, 293.

al-Kāẓim did not understand his native tongue. Al-Kāẓim then turns to Abū Baṣīr and makes the maximalist claim that the Imāms are fluent in all human and nonhuman (i.e. animal, plant) languages.

Al-Mufīd's final two knowledge elements combine the Imām's awareness of the future with the imperative for Twelvers to remain faithful to him. These accounts recall al-Kulaynī's emphasis on loyalty as well as Ibn Bābawayh's depiction of a supremely confident Imām. Both center on the figure of 'Alī b. Yaqṭīn (d. 182/798), a staunch supporter of al-Ṣādiq and al-Kāẓim, who held a number of important administrative posts under the 'Abbāsids.[149] The first begins with al-Rashīd giving Ibn Yaqṭīn numerous garments, including a particularly expensive and striking black cloak.[150] Ibn Yaqṭīn sends them to al-Kāẓim along with a fifth of his wealth, as required by Twelver Shī'ī law.[151] The Imām returns the cloak and instructs Ibn Yaqṭīn to keep it safe, saying that he will have need of it in the future. The narrative then jumps forward in time. Ibn Yaqṭīn dismisses one of his servants, who seeks revenge by accusing him of being a secret partisan of al-Kāẓim. The servant informs al-Rashīd that Ibn Yaqṭīn forwards the Imām money and gifts, making particular mention of the black cloak. Al-Rashīd summons Ibn Yaqṭīn and asks him to produce the cloak. Ibn Yaqṭīn describes the degree of care he devotes to the maintenance of the cloak and sends a servant to retrieve it. Its arrival allays the caliph's anger and dispels his suspicions. The dismissed servant is flogged and dies soon after.

The second narrative featuring Ibn Yaqṭīn conveys a similar message. This report concerns a dispute in the early Twelver Shī'ī community over the proper method for wiping the feet during the ritual ablution.[152] The disagreement centers on whether one should wipe the feet from the ankles to the toes or vice versa. Ibn Yaqṭīn writes to al-Kāẓim, asking for clarification. The Imām responds by ordering him to perform the ablution in a manner that breaks with established Twelver Shī'ī practice: instead of wiping the feet, as the Shī'a typically do, Ibn Yaqṭīn is told to wash his feet in the manner of the Sunnīs. Ibn Yaqṭīn is confused by al-Kāẓim's instructions but nonetheless complies

149 Madelung, "Treatise," 18–19, n. 2.
150 Al-Mufīd, *Irshād*, 293–4.
151 This refers to a tax associated primarily with the Shī'a known as *khums*. For its roots in early Shī'ism, see Hayes, "Alms and the Man"; *EI*², s.v. "Khums" (R. Gleave). For a classical treatment, see al-Ṭūsī, *Mabsūṭ*, 1:236–8.
152 Al-Mufīd, *Irshād*, 294–5.

with them. Some time later, al-Rashīd again receives information regarding Ibn Yaqṭīn's sympathy for al-Kāẓim. He is uncertain about the charge in view of Ibn Yaqṭīn's history of impeccable service. On the advice of an unnamed source, the caliph decides to observe him perform the ablution to ascertain his true loyalties. He is reassured when Ibn Yaqṭīn washes, rather than wipes, his feet, and vows to ignore any future slanders. Soon thereafter, Ibn Yaqṭīn receives a new letter, in which al-Kāẓim outlines an ablution procedure that conforms to Twelver Shīʿī practice.

In both of these accounts, al-Kāẓim uses his knowledge of the future to protect his partisan from harm. It is important to note that Ibn Yaqṭīn obeys the Imām in spite of his misgivings. It is this obedience that saves his life, reinforcing the importance of loyalty and faith.

Narrative Category 3 Miracles

Al-Mufīd's biography of al-Kāẓim includes two narrative elements involving miracles. The first is identical to al-Kulaynī's account in which the Imām wins over an ascetic known for his religious devotion by first challenging him to acquire true knowledge and then miraculously commanding a tree to uproot itself and move.[153] Although the miracle is an important final step in the ascetic's conversion, he is initially attracted to al-Kāẓim's mastery of religious knowledge.

A similar tone informs al-Mufīd's second miracle account, which describes al-Kāẓim's encounter with a lion on the road from Medina to his estate outside the city.[154] In this report, al-Kāẓim approaches the lion, which bows down to him and speaks in a strange language, unintelligible to the narrator.[155] The Imām then turns toward Mecca, utters an inaudible prayer, and points to the lion, which again speaks in the same strange language for some time. Once the prayer is completed, the lion departs. Some time later, the narrator gathers the courage to ask for an explanation. The Imām replies that the lion's spouse was having difficulties in pregnancy and wanted him to mediate a prayer for her well-being. The lion also wanted to know whether the cub would be

153 Ibid., 292–3. 154 Ibid., 295–6.

155 The narrator is identified as Abū al-Ḥasan ʿAlī b. Sālim (Abī Ḥamza) al-Baṭā'inī (d. 201/816 or 202/817), a Kūfan client of Anṣār who lived in Baghdad and transmitted reports from al-Ṣādiq and al-Kāẓim. He also served as a financial agent for al-Kāẓim and later became a leader of the Wāqifīs. See al-Najāshī, 2:69–70; al-Tustarī, 7:268–77; Modarressi, *Crisis and Consolidation*, 183–7.

a male or a female. After receiving al-Kāẓim's help, the lion promised that his fellow beasts would never attack the Imām, his descendants, or their followers.

It may be argued that the lion narrative fits into the category of knowledge accounts, since it ascribes to the Imām the ability to speak with animals. Recall that in the narrative that portrays al-Kāẓim conversing in Persian, he explicitly claims that the Imāms know the languages of all living beings. In that instance, however, al-Kāẓim demonstrates proficiency in a human language that can be learned through books and study. The case of the lion is quite different, as no instruction manuals enable conversation with lions. In addition to highlighting the Imām's linguistic skills, this narrative demonstrates his complete and absolute fearlessness. At the end of the report, al-Mufīd attests to the wide circulation of countless similar accounts.

Narrative Category 4 Confrontations with Power

Four of al-Mufīd's narrative elements relate to al-Kāẓim's confrontations with power. As all of these elements have been discussed previously, this section focuses on those features that are distinctive to al-Mufīd. It is worth noting that two of these confrontation narratives are preserved in al-Mufīd's collection of traditions, *al-Ikhtiṣāṣ*, as opposed to his biographical work, *al-Irshād*.[156]

The first confrontation account is an expanded version of the debate between al-Kāẓim and al-Rashīd previously cited by Ibn Bābawayh.[157] It begins with al-Rashīd angrily showing al-Kāẓim a scroll that contains a series of allegations. He is particularly concerned by al-Kāẓim's purported acceptance of taxes (*kharāj*), which is tantamount to a rival claim to the caliphate. The list of charges also includes key theological elements associated with the Twelver conception of the Imāmate, such as required obedience to the Imām and the cursing of those of the Prophet's companions who opposed ʿAlī.[158] Instead of addressing these theological matters, al-Kāẓim asserts his right to accept financial gifts (*khums*) and notes the hardships imposed on him by his enemies. He also denies receiving any money that might be designated as *kharāj*. The narrative then relates the same questions and

156 This might suggest that genre differences influenced his decisions to include or exclude certain texts.
157 Al-Mufīd, *Ikhtiṣāṣ*, 48–53.
158 By comparison, Ibn Bābawayh's narrative is limited to financial matters.

answers pertaining to kinship that are found in Ibn Bābawayh's text. In their final exchange, not reproduced by Ibn Bābawayh, the caliph asks about al-Ṣādiq's legal reasoning, which allows al-Mufīd (via al-Kāẓim) to expound on Twelver jurisprudence. Al-Kāẓim is eventually given a monetary gift and allowed to return to his family.

Al-Mufīd's second confrontation narrative recalls one variant of Ibn Bābawayh's "*ḥabashī* dream" narrative.[159] Recall that Ibn Bābawayh offers two versions of this report: the first shows al-Kāẓim as fearful and weak, whereas the second portrays him as confident and powerful. Al-Mufīd includes the latter version in which the Imām is dismissive of ʿAbbāsid authority. The former may have been prevalent in the early fourth/tenth century during the lifetimes of al-Kulaynī and al-Masʿūdī, and tenable as late as the end of that century in the lifetime of Ibn Bābawayh. In the early fifth/eleventh century, however, al-Mufīd omits it altogether given its disjuncture with his understanding of the proper behavior and demeanor of an Imām.

The third confrontation account is an expanded version of the narrative in which al-Rashīd visits Medina either before or after performing the Ḥajj, and Medinan notables gather to welcome him on the outskirts of the city.[160] Al-Kāẓim joins the delegation on his mule, prompting al-Rabīʿ[161] to question him about the appropriateness of greeting the caliph on such a lowly mount. In his response, al-Kāẓim extols moderation and downplays the honor of meeting al-Rashīd.

The fourth and final element in this category is a variant of al-Kāẓim's exchange with al-Rashīd at the Prophet's grave.[162] There is a notable lack of overlap between al-Mufīd's account and al-Khaṭīb's later version, but they agree on the broad outlines of the event: al-Rashīd visits the Prophet's grave and proudly addresses him as "cousin," which prompts al-Kāẓim to refer to him as "father." In contrast to the non-Twelver version, in which al-Rashīd publicly rebukes al-Kāẓim for his pride, al-Mufīd's account simply notes the caliph's anger.

[159] Al-Mufīd, *Ikhtiṣāṣ*, 53–4. Both al-Mufīd and Ibn Bābawayh cite al-Faḍl b. al-Rabīʿ as their source. Ibn Bābawayh quotes more of the prayer that the Prophet teaches al-Kāẓim and cites a different chain of transmission.

[160] Al-Mufīd, *Irshād*, 297.

[161] Note that al-Iṣbahānī replaces al-Rabī with his son al-Faḍl b. al-Rabīʿ. See al-Iṣbahānī, 414.

[162] Al-Mufīd, *Irshād*, 298.

Al-Rashīd's silence in al-Mufīd's text makes the Imām's victory less ambiguous.

Narrative Category 5 Imprisonment and Death

Al-Mufīd offers a single narrative element connected to al-Kāẓim's imprisonment and death that closely aligns with al-Iṣbahānī's "Barmakid plot" narrative.[163] This account includes all of the basic features described previously (see also Table 3.5), with one notable exception. Whereas al-Iṣbahānī states that Yaḥyā al-Barmakī had al-Kāẓim rolled in a carpet and trampled, al-Mufīd identifies his cause of death as poisoning. Specifically, Yaḥyā al-Barmakī orders al-Sindī b. Shāhik to serve the Imām tainted dates that lead to his death three days later. Al-Mufīd thus incorporates Twelver expectations of poisoning into a narrative that originally did not feature poisoning at all.[164]

Al-Mufīd's version of this narrative element also contains a few details that foreground al-Kāẓim's exemplary qualities. Two of these merit further discussion. In the first, al-Kāẓim informs his companions that his nephew 'Alī b. Ismā'īl will betray him to al-Rashīd. When they then ask why he treated 'Alī with such kindness and generosity on the eve of his departure, he responds with a Prophetic tradition instructing individuals to do their utmost to preserve the bonds of kinship. This speaks to both his forbearance and his knowledge of the future. Instead of expressing hopelessness, the Imām is here more concerned with the fates of others than with his own. A second unique detail in al-Mufīd's account involves a spy who overhears al-Kāẓim thanking God for fulfilling his request for time to devote exclusively to worship. This rationale transforms his prolonged imprisonment from a punitive measure into a blessing.

Assessment

Al-Mufīd's depiction of al-Kāẓim shares many features with those of al-Kulaynī and Ibn Bābawayh. In terms of knowledge, al-Mufīd quotes

[163] Ibid., 298–302.

[164] Muḥammad al-Nawfalī (see n. 127 in this chapter) is the likely source for the central elements of the "Barmakid plot" narrative, as he is explicitly cited by both al-Mufīd and al-Iṣbahānī, whose accounts align quite closely. Ibn Bābawayh, by contrast, offers quite a different rendering of the causes and circumstances of al-Kāẓim's arrest. It is unclear whether al-Mufīd appropriated his account directly from al-Iṣbahānī or whether he had independent access to al-Nawfalī's original text.

Table 3.5 – *The Barmakid Plot Narrative*

	al-Iṣbahānī (d. 356/967) *Maqātil*	Ibn Bābawayh (d. 381/991) *'Uyūn*	al-Mufīd (d. 413/1022) *Irshād*
Narrative detail			
Ibn al-Ash'ath	X	X (money trick)	X
'Alid informant	X ('Alī b. Ismā'īl)	X ('Alī b. Ismā'īl)	X ('Alī b. Ismā'īl)
al-Rashīd's prayer at the Prophet's grave	X	X	X
Arrest with two litters	X	X	X
Transfer from 'Īsā to al-Faḍl b. al-Rabī'	X	X (no transfer; freed)	X
Transfer from al-Faḍl b. al-Rabī' to al-Faḍl al-Barmakī	X		X
Beating of al-Faḍl al-Barmakī	X		X
Transfer to al-Sindī b. Shāhik	X	X (re-arrest)	X
Death through Yaḥyā al-Barmakī	X (carpet)		X (poison)
Shroud conversation with al-Sindī	X		X
Examination of body	X		X
Bridge and announcement	X		X
Burial in Qurashī cemetery	X		X

his own version of the narrative in which al-Kāẓim's legal expertise is the basis for his claim to the Imāmate in the eyes of two of his father's followers, Hishām and Muḥammad. He also records an encounter in which the Imām uses Prophetic traditions to refute a prominent Ḥanafī jurist, al-Shaybānī. These reports involve knowledge that is accessible to normal human beings. Like al-Kulaynī, however, al-Mufīd extends the Imām's abilities beyond the mundane, associating him with the supernatural. On two occasions, al-Kāẓim demonstrates extraordinary linguistic mastery. In the first instance, he explains to a companion that the Imām must know the languages of all living beings, and immediately provides evidence of this ability by addressing a foreign visitor in Persian. In the second case, al-Kāẓim converses with a lion and then intercedes with God on its behalf. The latter account, in particular, suggests that the Imām's knowledge flows directly from God. How else could he learn the language of animals? In another miraculous narrative, al-Kāẓim demonstrates his extensive knowledge to an ascetic while also commanding a tree to walk toward him. It is the combination of knowledge and miracles that convinces the ascetic of the Imām's claims.

In addition to languages, al-Mufīd regularly points to al-Kāẓim's knowledge of the future. In its most basic form, this manifests in the Imām's prediction of the arrival of a Persian-speaking pilgrim. In other cases, however, it is meant to reinforce communal loyalty. For al-Kulaynī, these narrative elements are largely punitive in that the Imām discerns the doubts of his followers and then scolds them for their lack of faith. Al-Mufīd, by contrast, cites cases in which loyalty and faith are the keys to salvation. For example, al-Kāẓim instructs Ibn Yaqṭīn to perform the ablution in a manner that does not align with Shī'ī practice. The directive confuses Ibn Yaqṭīn, but he puts aside his doubts and complies with the Imām's orders. This ultimately saves his life when al-Rashīd tests his allegiance by observing his ablution. The Imām knows the future and acts in the interests of his supporters. Their reciprocal responsibility consists of faithfully following his instructions.

Al-Mufīd's biography aligns with that of Ibn Bābawayh in its portrayal of al-Kāẓim's challenges to 'Abbāsid authority. The "Prophet's grave" narrative depicts al-Kāẓim undermining al-Rashīd's efforts to extol his familial connection to Muḥammad. A more subtle form of confrontation is embedded in the "caliph and mule" narrative, in which al-Kāẓim refuses to accord al-Rashīd any special deference. The narrative of al-Kāẓim's debate with al-Rashīd shows the Imām deflecting charges of treason and providing proofs of the close kinship between the Prophet and the ʿAlids. In the "*ḥabashī* dream" narrative, al-Kāẓim is fearless in the face of death and disdainful of the caliph's gifts.[165] On other occasions, the Imām does not directly confront the ʿAbbāsids but exhibits firm control over his personal affairs. This is evident in the Ibn Yaqṭīn narratives, where al-Kāẓim protects his companions against the caliph's suspicions. It is even more apparent in al-Mufīd's version of the "Barmakid plot" narrative, in which al-Kāẓim's imprisonment is God's response to his prayers for isolation. These accounts lack any sense of victimhood.

Al-Mufīd incorporates conspicuous justifications of Twelver Shīʿī theological views into seemingly unrelated reports. In the case of the "Persian language" and "ascetic and tree" narratives, al-Kāẓim foregrounds two central tenets of Twelver Shīʿism: he addresses the scope of the Imām's knowledge, and confirms the superiority of the Prophet's family. At the start of al-Kāẓim's debate with al-Rashīd, the caliph accuses him of claiming obligatory obedience and promoting the cursing of ʿAlī's opponents. Al-Kāẓim does not deny these charges; instead, he offers evidence for the Imām's right to collect funds from his followers. A similar financial right is mentioned in the narrative involving Ibn Yaqṭīn and the black cloak, in which Ibn Yaqṭīn sends a fifth of his money and gifts to the Imām as *khums*. The debate with al-Rashīd ends with al-Kāẓim providing, at the caliph's request, an explanation of the legal views of Jaʿfar al-Ṣādiq. Legal methods are also central to al-Kāẓim's encounter with al-Shaybānī through his condemnation of analogical reasoning.

A final notable characteristic of al-Mufīd's biography is his use of material not found in previous Twelver sources.[166] This includes two generosity narratives and one confrontation narrative. In the "debt collector" narrative, al-Kāẓim performs a function generally reserved for the caliph by satisfying the claims of a frustrated creditor. This report also emphasizes the Imām's concern for social justice and his

[165] Recall that the other variant of this narrative depicts al-Kāẓim as cowering in fear for his life.

[166] It is, of course, possible (though not probable) that Twelver sources included this material but that these sources are now lost. A vast majority of the texts from this period do not survive into the present.

willingness to use personal funds to rectify financial inequity. In the "descendant of 'Umar" narrative, the Imām's generosity secures the support of a man who has routinely disparaged him. Perhaps the most notable aspect of this encounter, however, is al-Kāẓim's claim that he is sufficient to dispel the evil within him.[167] This statement frames his generosity as a natural outgrowth of his position as the Imām of the age. Al-Mufīd also cites a version of the "Prophet's grave" narrative in which al-Kāẓim embarrasses al-Rashīd by invoking 'Alid kinship. These three narrative elements, first recorded by al-Mufīd but later found in Sunnī biographical works, represent an area of potential overlap between the textual worlds and networks of Twelver and non-Twelver scholars.

'Alī b. 'Īsā al-Irbilī (d. 717/1317)

Jumping forward 300 years, 'Alī b. 'Īsā al-Irbilī builds his biography of al-Kāẓim around large sections of earlier written works. The most important of these is al-Mufīd's *Irshād*, which he quotes in full and supplements with selected accounts from other sources. The discussion below focuses mainly on this new material to illuminate the ways in which al-Irbilī elaborates, embellishes, and alters elements previously deployed by al-Mufīd.

Narrative Category 1 Generosity Accounts

In addition to the "debt collector" and "descendant of 'Umar" narratives described previously, al-Irbilī cites a version of the "cucumber farmer and locusts" narrative, in which al-Kāẓim provides compensation for crop damage.[168] The account, identical to a report preserved by al-Khaṭīb al-Baghdādī, highlights al-Kāẓim's generosity but lacks any overt supernatural elements. This feature may partly explain its prevalence in non-Twelver sources.

Narrative Category 2 Knowledge Accounts

Al-Irbilī includes numerous elements that focus on al-Kāẓim's knowledge. A comprehensive examination of each would require considerable additional space. This section therefore covers only a representative sampling

[167] This line is absent from al-Khaṭīb al-Baghdādī's version of the "descendant of 'Umar" narrative.

[168] Al-Irbilī, 3:10–11.

of these narratives. Bear in mind that in addition to the reports presented below, al-Irbilī incorporates the entirety of al-Mufīd's knowledge accounts.

Al-Irbilī elaborates several different aspects of al-Kāẓim's knowledge. Some of his reports illustrate the Imām's use of powerful prayers,[169] whereas others note his awareness of the needs of his companions[170] and the exact amounts of money brought to him from outside sources.[171] Three texts feature death predictions, including a variant of the narrative in which al-Kāẓim foretells the fate of Isḥāq b. ʿAmmār's family, first cited by al-Kulaynī.[172] The future also figures prominently in a report in which al-Kāẓim foresees a locust infestation that will prevent a farmer (one of his followers)[173] from purchasing his annual allotment of dates.[174] Another such account is a variant of al-Kulaynī's prison-release prediction narrative, related through a different chain of transmission.[175] Two other reports endow al-Kāẓim with the ability to obtain information instantaneously. In the first, the Imām urges a man to return to his home, which has apparently collapsed in the rain.[176] In the second, al-Kāẓim notifies a visitor from Rayy of his brother's death in Kūfa and instructs him to treat the brother's widowed wife kindly in order to secure a share of the inheritance.[177]

Some of al-Irbilī's knowledge narratives show curious similarities to those found in previous sources. In one account, for example, al-Kāẓim speaks Chinese, and then notes that a legitimate Imām has mastery over the language of every being with a soul.[178] The parallels with the "Persian language" and "lion" narratives are fairly straightforward. A more complicated report involves a North African man who meets al-Kāẓim in Medina.[179] The Imām is already aware of the man's problem (a terrible fight with his brother). He informs the man of his brother's death and warns him of the consequences of breaking the

[169] Ibid., 3:42–4. [170] Ibid., 3:46–7. [171] Ibid., 3:49.

[172] For al-Kulaynī's account as reproduced by al-Irbilī, see ibid., 3:47. For other reports of the Imām's death predictions, see ibid., 3:47–8, 3:50–1.

[173] The man is identified as Ibrāhīm b. ʿAbd al-Ḥamīd (d. after 183/799), a Kūfan client of the Banū Asad who transmitted from al-Ṣādiq but was also associated with al-Kāẓim and al-Riḍā. There are indications that he was a Wāqifī, and he is listed as the author of a *Kitāb al-nawādir* as well as an *ʿaṣl* (a Shīʿī literary genre containing the sayings of the Imāms). See al-Najāshī, 1:98–9; Tustarī, 1:219–26.

[174] Al-Irbilī, 3:51. [175] Cf. ibid., 3:41–2; al-Kulaynī, 1:477–8.

[176] Al-Irbilī, 3:45. [177] Ibid., 3:46. [178] Ibid., 3:54. [179] Ibid., 3:52–3.

bonds of kinship.[180] This narrative gestures to a series of reports that focus on kinship (e.g. the narrative of the nephew's betrayal) and supernatural knowledge (e.g. the narrative of Ibn Yaqṭīn and the black cloak). In the area of law, al-Irbilī includes a report in which Abū Yūsuf and al-Shaybānī devise a plan to humiliate al-Kāẓim, who is in prison, through a complicated legal question, but are instead astonished when he predicts the death of one of his jailors.[181] This recalls previous narratives about al-Kāẓim's interactions with Ḥanafī jurists as well as the narrative featuring the demise of Isḥāq b. 'Ammār's family.

Perhaps the most striking and unique narrative element preserved by al-Irbilī involves the Ṣūfī Shaqīq b. Ibrāhīm al-Balkhī[182] (d. 194/810), who visits Mecca in the year 149/767 for the Ḥajj.[183] As he performs the rites of pilgrimage, Shaqīq repeatedly encounters al-Kāẓim in the guise of a Ṣūfī who responds to his thoughts with appropriate Qur'ānic passages, demonstrates his piety, and offers religious counsel. After he completes the Ḥajj, Shaqīq is sitting near the Ka'ba, when al-Kāẓim appears in his regular clothes and is immediately surrounded by throngs of people. It is only then that Shaqīq recognizes his true identity. The episode concludes with some poetry in which Shaqīq recounts his subsequent experiences with al-Kāẓim. Overall, the report adopts a supernatural view of the Imām's knowledge that highlights his religious credentials.[184]

Narrative Category 3 Miracles

Al-Irbilī mentions five narratives in which al-Kāẓim performs miracles. Two of these, featuring the conversion of an ascetic and a conversation with a lion, are taken directly from al-Mufīd and depict miracles tied to the Imām's knowledge (narrative category 2) in that (i) the ascetic is initially attracted by al-Kāẓim's intellect and (ii) al-Kāẓim demonstrates fluency in lion language.

In the first of the new miracle accounts, al-Kāẓim meets a despondent pilgrim whose donkey has died outside Medina.[185] The Imām says,

[180] Ibid. [181] Ibid., 3:55–6. [182] For Shaqīq al-Balkhī, see al-Ziriklī, 3:171.

[183] Al-Irbilī, 3:4–7. Algar, in "Imam Musa," documents the transmission history of this report, which seems to have originated in the fourth/tenth century in a (now lost) text authored by Abū Muḥammad Ḥasan b. 'Abd al-Raḥmān al-Rāmhurmuzī (d. ca. 360/907).

[184] It also differs from similar narratives mentioned by al-Kulaynī, which often conclude with the Imām scolding his companions for their lack of faith.

[185] Al-Irbilī, 3:54–5.

"Perhaps it is not dead," and the man accuses him of mockery, but then al-Kāẓim recites a prayer and the donkey comes back to life. The man later asks about the miracle and is told not to question that which he will never understand. This report bears a strong resemblance to the narrative of the resurrected cow, in that the Imām helps relieve distress caused by the loss of an important animal. The donkey narrative, however, involves a Muslim pilgrim who is skeptical of al-Kāẓim, whereas the cow narrative features a Christian woman who immediately welcomes his help.

The second new miracle account demonstrates al-Kāẓim's superiority over his brother ʿAbd Allāh.[186] It begins with the Imām placing a stack of firewood in the middle of a room in his house. He then convenes a small gathering of the Shīʿa that includes ʿAbd Allāh. After the guests arrive, al-Kāẓim ignites the wood and sits in the center of the fire (presumably on the coals), relating Prophetic traditions for an hour. When he is done, he brushes the ashes from his clothes and challenges his brother to do the same. This account is a clear polemic against the Faṭḥī Shīʿa, who upheld ʿAbd Allāh's Imāmate.

A third new account lies on the boundary between narrative categories 3 (miracles) and 4 (confrontations), as al-Kāẓim performs a miracle that openly defies the ʿAbbāsid caliph.[187] At the start of the report, al-Rashīd sends al-Kāẓim a tray of manure that has been shaped to resemble figs.[188] When the Imām raises the cover, however, the tray is full of real figs, which he eats with pleasure, returning the remainder to the caliph. Al-Rashīd observes that they have the appearance of real fruit, but when he places one in his mouth, it is transformed back into manure. The confrontational aspects of this miracle narrative are self-evident.[189]

Narrative Category 4 Confrontations with Power

Al-Irbilī preserves seven narrative elements that depict al-Kāẓim's confrontations with power. The "Prophet's grave" and "caliph and

[186] Ibid., 3:53–4.

[187] In this respect, it resembles the lion and charmer narrative in which the miracle is itself an act of confrontation.

[188] Al-Irbilī, 3:56–7.

[189] Al-Irbilī expresses doubts about the reliability of this account, questioning whether al-Rashīd would stoop to such a disgraceful level given his awareness of al-Kāẓim's status. He also notes the disparity between al-Kāẓim's response, on the one hand, and his belief in cautionary dissimulation and his reputation for forbearance, on the other.

mule" narratives are quoted directly from al-Mufīd. A third report in this category is the account of the figs and manure discussed in the previous section. The four remaining narratives are versions of reports found in earlier sources.

The first is a variant of the narrative related by Ibn Bābawayh in which al-Kāẓim is untroubled to hear of the caliph al-Hādī's ill intentions.[190] He rejects the advice of his family and friends to go into hiding, instead uttering an invocation that is seemingly answered with al-Hādī's sudden death. The text ends with a line of poetry praising the efficacy of prayer.[191] The second account is a summary of al-Kāẓim's debate with al-Rashīd in which the Imām confirms the strength of 'Alid claims to the Prophet.[192] This version lacks many of the details found in Ibn Bābawayh's and al-Mufīd's earlier reports, such as (i) an introductory explanation for the debate, (ii) a logical progression of questions, and (iii) al-Rashīd's ultimate concession. The narrative concludes with the simple statement that al-Kāẓim died in prison.

Al-Irbilī's final two confrontation narratives appear in non-Twelver sources but are not mentioned in any of the previous Twelver Shī'ī sources under consideration. The first of these is the "al-Mahdī and Q47:22" narrative, in which 'Alī appears to the caliph in a dream and rebukes him for mistreating his kin. The second is the "prison letter" narrative, wherein al-Kāẓim warns al-Rashīd of a final reckoning on the Day of Judgment.[193] Both of these elements feature prominently in Sunnī biographies of al-Kāẓim. They are first cited by al-Khaṭīb al-Baghdādī and then recur almost universally in the works of later Sunnī writers. The reason for their ubiquity may stem from their ambiguity. Whereas al-Irbilī supplements these episodes with reports that confirm the Imām's elevated standing and document his subtle resistance to 'Abbāsid power, the non-Twelver sources utilize them in isolation to cast al-Kāẓim as a typical pious scholar.

190 Al-Irbilī, 3:59–60.
191 By contrast, Ibn Bābawayh offers six lines of poetry. See Ibn Bābawayh, *'Uyūn*, 1:65–6.
192 Al-Irbilī, 3:60–1.
193 Al-Irbilī quotes this narrative from two different authorities: from al-Junābadhī at 3:11 and from Ibn al-Jawzī at 3:59.

Narrative Category 5 Imprisonment and Death

Al-Irbilī preserves al-Mufīd's version of the "Barmakid plot" narrative in its entirety (see Table 3.5), along with smaller accounts that provide additional context. At the very end of the "debate with al-Rashīd" narrative, for example, al-Irbilī identifies al-Kāẓim's nephew Muḥammad b. Ismāʿīl b. Jaʿfar and brother Muḥammad b. Jaʿfar as potential ʿAbbāsid informants. This is an implicit reference to the narrative preserved by al-Kulaynī and Ibn Bābawayh in which a member of the Imām's family visits al-Rashīd and accuses al-Kāẓim of setting up a rival caliphate. Al-Kulaynī[194] names the informant as al-Kāẓim's nephew Muḥammad b. Ismāʿīl, whereas Ibn Bābawayh[195] specifies al-Kāẓim's brother, Muḥammad b. Jaʿfar. There are no other new or distinguishing elements in al-Irbilī's version of al-Kāẓim's imprisonment and death.

Assessment

The most notable feature of al-Irbilī's biography is its piecemeal quotation of other sources. Al-Mufīd is the dominant voice in al-Irbilī's composition, providing the baseline portrait of al-Kāẓim that is either tempered or elaborated by elements drawn from other texts. Recall that al-Mufīd combined al-Kulaynī's focus on knowledge, loyalty, and miracles with Ibn Bābawayh's emphasis on confrontation. Al-Irbilī adds material that supports each of these tendencies but ultimately accentuates the Imām's supernatural qualities over his role as a figure of resistance.

The majority of al-Irbilī's non-Mufīd reports fall under the first three narrative categories. In terms of generosity accounts (category 1), he includes the narratives involving the cucumber farmer and the debt collector, which reflect al-Kāẓim's concern for those in need.[196] Al-Irbilī also offers many more knowledge accounts (category 2) than do his predecessors. Al-Mufīd's reports fall evenly on the spectrum between legal (potentially learned) knowledge and supernatural (divinely inspired) knowledge. Al-Irbilī shifts this balance decisively by including accounts that ascribe the Imām's knowledge to a supernatural link with God. The narratives in which the Imām announces the

194 Al-Kulaynī, 1:485–6. 195 Ibn Bābawayh, *ʿUyūn*, 1:60.

196 Although not present in the previous Twelver sources under consideration, these episodes are found in the Sunnī works discussed earlier in this chapter.

collapse of a distant house and the death of an absent brother demonstrate his instantaneous awareness of events in far-off places. The narrative featuring a follower who has quarreled with his brother goes even further, as al-Kāẓim warns him of impending doom. Other narrative elements reinforce established ideas such as the Imām's access to all languages (the "Chinese language" narrative), his knowledge of the future (his prediction of a locust swarm and of the death of a jailor), and his ability to read minds (the narrative of his interactions with Shaqīq al-Balkhī). Al-Irbilī also preserves two knowledge accounts mentioned by al-Kulaynī but absent from Ibn Bābawayh and al-Mufīd, in which al-Kāẓim predicts his own release from prison and the destruction of Isḥāq b. 'Ammār's family. Finally, al-Irbilī quotes three reports in which al-Kāẓim performs miracles (category 3). The "resurrected donkey" narrative resembles a previous miraculous account, that of the resurrected cow, and the narrative in which al-Kāẓim sits on hot coals explicitly targets the Faṭḥī Shī'a. The last miracle account, involving the transformation of manure into figs, showcases the Imām's control over nature itself in a direct encounter with the caliph.

In contrast to the first three narrative categories, which undergo a proliferation and expansion in al-Irbilī's work, the fourth narrative category, confrontations with power, remains largely static. Al-Irbilī takes some such accounts from al-Mufīd (e.g. the "Prophet's grave" and "caliph and mule" narratives), but he ignores the more aggressive reports related by Ibn Bābawayh (e.g. the "poisoned dog" and "*ḥabashī* dream" narratives). His other confrontation narratives are quite tame. The account of al-Kāẓim's prediction of al-Hādī's death (also quoted by Ibn Bābawayh) depicts him as unafraid of 'Abbāsid plots, but it does not place him in direct conflict with the caliph. In the "al-Mahdī and Q47:22" narrative, the Imām's freedom results from 'Alī b. Abī Ṭālib's appearance in the caliph's dream. Al-Kāẓim then swears, as a precondition of his release, that he has no plans to rebel. Even al-Irbilī's version of the debate with al-Rashīd removes much of the friction between the Imām and the caliph in favor of a pared-down exchange over 'Alid lineage. In the "prison letter" narrative, al-Kāẓim is portrayed as a scholar (as opposed to a rebel) fulfilling his duty to remind the caliph of the consequences of his actions. The one episode that presents al-Kāẓim in a potentially confrontational light is the "figs and manure" narrative. Al-Irbilī, however, expresses his doubts about its reliability, deeming it out of line with al-Kāẓim's known espousal of cautionary dissimulation (*taqiyya*).

B Interpretive Frameworks: Supernatural Imām or Confrontational Imām

The last step in the rhetoricized historiographical model outlined in Chapter 1 involves the identification of the dominant interpretive frameworks put forward by individual authors. These are particularly evident in Twelver biographical or compilatory works. They are less obvious in historical chronicles (i.e. those of al-Yaʿqūbī and al-Masʿūdī), which offer only brief accounts of al-Kāẓim with an emphasis on the circumstances of his death.[197] The brevity of these latter works likely results from their universalist structure, which, as noted in Chapter 2, tends to emphasize larger political themes. Put differently, chronographic works are often influenced by the tension between an imperial ʿAbbāsid historiography and the personal proclivities of individual writers. This premise seems to hold for al-Yaʿqūbī's and al-Masʿūdī's minimalist treatments of al-Kāẓim.

A vast majority of the Twelver Shīʿī material about al-Kāẓim is preserved in either biographical works or in collections of traditions with sections specifically devoted to biographical topics. The narrative elements in these texts (see Table 3.6) convey two distinct interpretive frameworks. The first highlights the Imām's supernatural connection to God, whereas the second accentuates his unyielding opposition to the ʿAbbāsid caliphs. The remainder of this section documents the use of these frameworks by individual Twelver writers.

Al-Kulaynī's portrayal of al-Kāẓim is heavily weighted in favor of the supernatural interpretive framework. The Imām is endowed with an almost infinite knowledge drawn directly from a divine source. There are isolated accounts in which al-Kāẓim reveals information that he may have learned from his forebears through books. In the majority of reports, however, he is able to predict the future, read the thoughts of his followers, and access obscure historical facts. These supernatural elements are reinforced by miracle narratives in which, for example, al-

197 While it is true that al-Masʿūdī's work contains the first extant appearance of the "*ḥabashī* dream" narrative, this report does not survive into the later Twelver tradition, perhaps because of its depiction of the Imām as fearful and weak.

Table 3.6 – *The Twelver Shīʿī Narrative Elements for Mūsā al-Kāẓim*

	Narrative category	al-Yaʿqūbī	al-Kulaynī	al-Masʿūdī	Ibn Bābawayh	al-Mufīd	al-Irbilī
	1. Generosity Accounts						
	Debt collector					X (Irshād)	X
	Cucumber farmer and locusts						X
	Descendant of ʿUmar					X (Irshād)	X
	2. Knowledge Accounts						
	Christian wanderer		X				
	Nun and monk		X				
	Debate with Abū Yūsuf				X		
	Debate with al-Shaybānī					X (Irshād)	X
	Hishām and Muḥammad		X			X (Irshād)	X
?	Collapsing house prediction						X
?	Brother's death prediction						X
?	Chinese language						X
?	Persian language					X (Irshād)	X
S	Prison release prediction		X				X
S	Isḥāq's family prediction		X				X and X (pt) X [illegible]
S	Ibn Yaqṭīn and black cloak					X (Irshād)	X
S	Locust swarm prediction						X
S	Ibn Yaqṭīn and ablution					X (Irshād)	X
S	Correspondence with Yaḥyā		X				
S	Exchange with al-Ḥusayn b. ʿAlī		X				
S	Quarrel with brother						X
S	Debate with Abū Yūsuf and al-Shaybānī						X
S	Shaqīq al-Balkhī						X
	3. Miracles						
	Ascetic and tree		X			X (Irshād)	X
	Hot coals						X
	Resurrected cow		X				
	Resurrected donkey						X
	Conversation with lion					X (Irshād)	X
4	Figs and manure						X
4	Lion and charmer				X		

Narrative category		al-Yaʿqūbī	al-Kulaynī	al-Masʿūdī	Ibn Bābawayh	al-Mufīd	al-Irbilī
4. Confrontations with Power							
	Refusal of human intercession	X					
	al-Hādī's death prediction				X		X
	Encounter with al-Maʾmūn				X		
	al-Mahdī and Q47:22						X
	Prophet's grave					X (Irshād)	X
	Caliph and mule					X (Irshād)	X
	Debate with al-Rashīd				X	X (Ikhtiṣāṣ)	X
	Ḥabashī dream			X	X – 2	X (Ikhtiṣāṣ)	
	Caliphal summons and dream				X		
5	Prison letter						X and X
5	Poisoned dog				X		
5	Poisoned dates		X		X		
3	Figs and manure						X
3	Lion and charmer				X		
5. Imprisonment and Death							
	Betrayal by family member		X		X		X
	Barmakid plot				X (person)	X (Irshād)	X
	Cloth mistaken for al-Kāẓim				X – 2 (al-Rashīd, al-Faḍl b. al-Rabīʿ)		
4	Prison letter						X and X
4	Poisoned dog				X		
4	Poisoned dates		X		X		
	Funeral procession				X		
	Associates washing body				X		
	Narratives on imprisonment	Yes	Yes (al-Sindī)	No (silent)	X – 2 (al-Sindī, Faḍl al-Barmakī)	X (Irshād) (Sindī)	X (al-Sindī)
	Narratives featuring poison	No (silent)	Yes	Yes	Yes – 2 (al-Rashīd, Faḍl al-Barmakī)	Yes (Irshād) (Yaḥyā al-Barmakī/al-Sindī)	Yes (Yaḥyā al-Barmakī/al-Sindī)
	Narratives of body being examined	X (Masʿūdī)			X (Sulaymān b. Abī Jaʿfar)		

The (s) in the first column of knowledge accounts indicates supernatural knowledge. Numbers in the first column denote narratives that fit in other categories.

Kāẓim restores a cow to life or commands a tree to move. Al-Kulaynī also asserts the necessity of faith and loyalty on the part of the Imām's followers and warns of the dire consequences of disbelief. Thus, al-Kāẓim reacts with displeasure to even small doubts in the minds of his followers. In dealing with the ʿAbbāsids, he exercises patience and a reasoned caution. Thanks to his awareness of the future, he refuses to participate in failed rebellions, and secures the safety of his followers.

Ibn Bābawayh, by contrast, depicts al-Kāẓim first and foremost as a figure of overt and clear resistance to ʿAbbāsid power using the confrontational interpretive framework. He does retain some of al-Kulaynī's material, highlighting al-Kāẓim's knowledge and his ability to perform miracles, but these isolated reports are eclipsed by the Imām's repeated clashes with the ʿAbbāsid caliphs. Even in instances in which he ultimately concedes to their demands, he does so in a combative and disdainful manner that emphasizes his resistance. This tendency is particularly apparent in imprisonment and death narratives in which al-Kāẓim easily thwarts ʿAbbāsid schemes until the moment that is divinely designated for his death. Quite simply, Ibn Bābawayh's al-Kāẓim is in supreme command of every situation, and utterly fearless in his interactions with caliphal power. Such an attitude allows him to expose the hollow nature of ʿAbbāsid authority: in one report, he mocks a caliphal summons, but then complies with it in order to model proper behavior during a period of cautionary dissimulation (*taqiyya*).

The move from the supernatural framework of al-Kulaynī to the confrontational framework of Ibn Bābawayh tracks the changing circumstances of the Twelver Shīʿī community in Baghdad. Operating within the parameters of rhetoricized historiography, each writer appropriated and/or embellished existing narrative elements to produce an interpretive framework that was meaningful and relevant for his particular community.

Al-Kulaynī was writing at a time not far removed from the initial disappearance of the twelfth Imām in 260/874. This development raised significant doubts among Twelvers and precipitated defections to rival Shīʿī groups (the Zaydīs and the Ismāʿīlīs).[198] Al-Kulaynī tackled these doubts directly by focusing on the critical importance of faith and loyalty to the Imām. The Twelver community also found itself

[198] Modarressi, *Crisis and Consolidation*, 95–105.

in a politically compromised position in the early fourth/tenth century. In order to survive, it distanced itself from political activism and adopted a quietist orientation. The Zaydīs relentlessly attacked this strategy as evidence of cowardice and complicity. Al-Kulaynī answered these charges by advocating for cautionary dissimulation (*taqiyya*) as the only reasonable approach in the face of overwhelming military might. Al-Kāẓim symbolized the efficacy of this strategy through his obstinate refusal to participate in the rebellion at Fakhkh and through his dealings with the ʿAbbāsids.

From 334/945 to 447/1055, Baghdad was ruled by the Būyids, a Shīʿī dynasty that generously patronized Shīʿī scholars and instituted the public commemoration of Shīʿī religious festivals. Būyid rule signaled a dramatic shift in the political fortunes of the Twelver Shīʿa, as they were no longer targets of official persecution. Ibn Bābawayh's confrontational framework fit a Twelver community that was by now a century removed from the occultation crisis and relatively free to operate in Baghdad. It also countered Zaydī claims that the Imāms were complicit with caliphal power. In Ibn Bābawayh's formulation, the Imām combined the activist credentials of the Zaydī Imāms with a deeper understanding of God's intentions. His compliance modeled appropriate behavior in periods of oppression, while his fearlessness conveyed the proper attitude at times of safety and confidence.

Although al-Mufīd, too, lived in Baghdad during the Būyid period, his depiction of al-Kāẓim conflates the supernatural and confrontational frameworks. He includes reports that reinforce the central themes put forward by al-Kulaynī. Faith and loyalty, for example, retain their critical importance, as the Imām utilizes his knowledge of the future to save the lives of those companions who obey his instructions. He also speaks with animals and commands trees in clear displays of his miraculous abilities. Al-Mufīd supplements these supernatural accounts with affirmations of the Imām's political courage. Thus, al-Kāẓim challenges the ʿAbbāsids' attempts to predicate their legitimacy on their kinship with the Prophet. Al-Mufīd, however, does not go so far as Ibn Bābawayh in his depiction of the Imām's confrontational nature. There are certainly reports of the Imām's fearlessness, but nothing replicating the boldness of his actions in the narratives of the poisoned dog and the caliphal summons conveyed to his home by al-Faḍl b. al-Rabīʿ. Overall, al-Mufīd offers a composite biography that markedly favors the supernatural framework over the confrontational one.

Al-Mufīd was a critical figure in the history of Twelver Shī'ism. As the head of the community in Baghdad, he trained an entire generation of students, including, most prominently, al-Sharīf al-Murtaḍā[199] (d. 436/1044). Al-Mufīd's influence was particularly evident in theology, where he helped introduce Mu'tazilī concepts into Twelver Shī'ism, and in law, where he laid the foundation for a rationalist legal system. Al-Mufīd accepted most of the central premises of Mu'tazilism, but he remained committed to a different notion of the Imāmate. Specifically, he upheld the special status of the Imāms, affirming their ability to intercede for the faithful on the Day of Judgment. This position might explain al-Mufīd's preference for the supernatural framework, especially with respect to the Imām's knowledge and his interventions on behalf of his followers. Al-Mufīd's text also reflects his interest in theology and law. In a number of reports, al-Kāẓim directly addresses theological controversies or articulates legal points for the caliph or his companions. These statements are often unique to al-Mufīd's version of a given report, suggesting their later insertion. The utility of such ascriptions is self-evident: they legitimize al-Mufīd's views through their association with the Imāms. Al-Mufīd thus advocates for his theological and legal views via a reformulation of previous historical materials.

Three centuries later, al-Irbilī represents a further development in al-Kāẓim's biography, with the growth of knowledge-related and miraculous narrative elements at the expense of confrontational ones. Al-Irbilī was a scholar and bureaucrat who spent the last fifty years of his life in Baghdad. His links with Sunnī scholars may explain his acknowledged use of material from writers such as al-Khaṭīb al-Baghdādī and Ibn al-Jawzī. Al-Irbilī appears to have downplayed his Shī'ī inclinations, perhaps because of his employment in the bureaucracy or perhaps in order to maintain his social position. This tendency, in turn, might explain his emphasis on the Imām's special qualities and his dismissal of aggressively activist accounts. Such a possibility is most apparent in his rejection of the "figs and manure" narrative as contradicting al-Kāẓim's strict adherence to cautionary dissimulation (*taqiyya*). It may also shed light on his decision to add materials weighted toward the first three narrative categories. Al-Irbilī was

199 For al-Sharīf al-Murtaḍā, see *EI*^{2}, s.v. "Al-Sharīf al-Murtaḍā" (C. Brockelmann); Abdulsater, *Shī'ī Doctrine*.

rebalancing elements of al-Kāẓim's biography to better align with the Twelver Shīʿī community's position in late seventh/thirteenth- and early eighth/fourteenth-century Baghdad.

In closing, it is important to note that the comparison of these four biographical works does not represent a linear evolution in Twelver Shīʿism for a number of reasons. First, it focuses on works written by scholars who spent large portions of their lives in Baghdad. This fact places a significant limitation on the generalizability of my claims to the Twelver Shīʿī community at large. Second, there are too few data points to make broad conclusions. In addition to their limited number, the authors are not distributed evenly across time. The first three writers lived within a hundred years of each other, whereas the fourth flourished three centuries later. Third, there was a diversity of beliefs within the Twelver Shīʿī community that included a spectrum of views regarding the nature and scope of the Imāmate. The four selected texts do not cover that wide range, so any generalizations carry a considerable risk of distortion.

Even with these reservations in mind, it is nonetheless possible to derive historically useful information from the source texts. Specifically, they offer insight into some of the seminal ideas circulating among Twelver scholars in Baghdad. The ideas ingrained in each biography embody debates over the nature of the Imām's authority and the community's relationship to political power. The texts also reveal the influence of political and social changes on Twelver Shīʿī historical memory, as biographies were subtly revised to make sense of present-day circumstances. These are not trivial matters: they explicate a marginalized community's sense of self and the ways in which it legitimized its interactions with governmental authority. The biographies may not represent the authoritative views of the Twelver Shīʿa, but they shed light on the questions that were being debated among the scholars of the time. Such conclusions are rightfully narrow in scope, but they gesture toward wider implications.

IV Notes on Historiography

The first section of this chapter focused on non-Twelver historical depictions of Mūsā al-Kāẓim. Sunnī historical chronicles utilized al-Kāẓim in a familiar manner – namely, to highlight the deterioration of the relationship between the ʿAbbāsids and the ʿAlids. Many chroniclers integrated

Table 3.7 – *The Interpretive Frameworks for Mūsā al-Kāẓim*

	Framework 1	Framework 2
Sunnī	Exemplar	Kinship
Zaydī	Court politics	N/A
Twelver	Supernatural	Confrontational

these familial tensions into a broad narrative detailing the rise and fall of 'Abbāsid power. Sunnī prosopographical works, by contrast, incorporated al-Kāẓim into a wider community of pious scholars. They showcased his generosity and piety, even in the direst of situations, such as imprisonment. Zaydī authors focused almost exclusively on court and caliphal politics, citing al-Kāẓim's refusal to support the rebellion at Fakhkh to compare him unfavorably with Yaḥyā b. 'Abd Allāh. They also used him to accuse the Twelvers of cowardice, pride, and complicity with 'Abbāsid tyranny.

It is worth considering the ways in which Twelver frameworks of al-Kāẓim (see Table 3.7) differ from their non-Twelver counterparts. It is true that Twelver biographies were partly influenced by theological concerns, and thus included elements of hagiography. This is most apparent in the long lists of reports in which Imāms formally designate their successors.[200] But are the Twelver sources really that different from the non-Twelver sources? Both reflect an interest in chronology and provide the same basic outline of al-Kāẓim's life, documenting his lineage, birth, two imprisonments, death, and burial. In the rhetoricized model outlined in Chapter 1, this shared timeline represents the core structure that authors assume is known to their respective audiences. Twelver Shī'ī writers built on this structure by appropriating malleable narrative elements to craft interpretive frameworks that were shaped by political and social conditions. In times of persecution, the Imām assumed a passive role in order to prevent bloodshed, whereas in times of empowerment, he displayed an aggressive confidence.

The reason for the Twelver focus is fairly clear. Given his position as an Imām, al-Kāẓim carried considerable weight for the Twelver

[200] For the Shī'ī concept of *naṣṣ* (designation), see Haider, *Shī'ī Islam*, 41–8.

community: every statement established a legal norm, and every action modeled proper behavior. He was too important to be used as a vehicle for discussing kinship (as in some Sunnī chronicles) or court politics (as in the Zaydī sources). As a point of comparison, recall that Twelver depictions of Mukhtār (see Chapter 2) were virtually indistinguishable from non-Twelver ones, embodying frameworks centered on both religious tensions and court politics. In other words, the apparent distinctiveness of the Twelver historical accounts in the case of al-Kāẓim is a direct consequence of the subject matter. As this chapter has shown, stepping back and examining these historical reports with a focus on authorial approach reveals commonalities that transcend communal identity.

One of the central claims of this book is that Muslim historians as a whole operated within the presuppositions of rhetoricized historiography. The implications of this claim, discussed in Chapter 1 and actualized in Chapter 2, merit repetition at this point. In the classical and late antique world, historians were expected to configure known narrative elements into new interpretive frameworks that produced meanings that were significant for their audiences. In some cases this meant the creation of new accounts, but in most cases it involved less radical transformations that retained the basic content of existing reports (i.e. their narrative elements). This process was shaped by the conditions of plausibility and verisimilitude. In the case of al-Kāẓim, authors did not simply create a fictitious biography to fit their theological views (a basic assumption of hagiography); rather, they tinkered with known narratives to highlight a particular point or to dismiss another. In other words, they employed literary devices for rhetorical effect, altering speeches or dialogues, inserting new details, or placing an episode in differing contexts. These changes facilitated the creation of five quite disparate biographies of al-Kāẓim, in each of which the meaning of his life (i.e. interpretive framework) was reconfigured for a new time and a new audience. Twelver and non-Twelver writers employed a common approach to historical material. The former were not, in some essential way, less reliable or more polemical than the latter. Transcending such an essentialist view requires a modeling of historical writing that rejects the limited horizons of atomistic analysis.

Overall, the first two case studies, in Chapters 2 and 3, suggest that the proposed historiographical model is not limited by genre or by the communal affiliations of individual historians. The rhetoricized nature of the material is discernible in a range of sources (chronographies, prosopographies, and biographies) authored by a diverse array of scholars. This chapter demonstrates the fundamental similarity in approach between non-Twelver (i.e. primarily Sunnī) and Twelver historians. The latter are often referenced in modern studies, but typically in a dismissive manner that marginalizes their utility. Zaydī historical works, by contrast, are rarely cited by contemporary scholars at all.[201] The final case study (Chapter 4) addresses this lacuna by focusing mainly on Zaydī works to examine a period in the life of a particularly important Zaydī Imām. In the process, it further showcases the broad applicability of the model at the heart of this study.

201 The one possible exception is al-Iṣbahānī's *Maqātil al-Ṭālibiyyīn*.

4 *The Last Years of Yaḥyā b. ʿAbd Allāh (d. 187/803)*

In Chapters 2 and 3, the application of a rhetoricized model of historical writing generated useful correctives to ingrained assumptions about Islamic historiography. These case studies revealed the similarity in historical approach across genres and the fallacy of dismissing or marginalizing historical works on the basis of the partisan loyalties of their writers. This chapter applies the proposed model to the case of Yaḥyā b. ʿAbd Allāh, a prominent Zaydī Imām who appears in a wide range of historical sources. The analysis reinforces many of the conclusions of the previous chapters while extending the material scope of this study to the largely underutilized historiographical corpus of the Zaydī Shīʿa.

The chapter focuses on the last eleven years of Yaḥyā's life as presented in twelve Muslim historical works composed between the third/ninth and ninth/fifteenth centuries (see Table 4.1). The first section identifies the core structure common to most depictions of this period of Yaḥyā's life. The second section discusses the Sunnī sources, in which Yaḥyā is deployed as a secondary character in a larger ʿAbbāsid narrative. The third section turns to the Zaydī sources, which affirm Yaḥyā's place as a legitimate Zaydī Imām despite his apparent complicity with ʿAbbāsid power. They also utilize Yaḥyā to elaborate their doctrine of the Imāmate. A final (and very brief) section examines a single Twelver Shīʿī source that seems to bridge the gap between the Sunnī and Zaydī accounts.

In comparison with the revolt of Mukhtār (Chapter 2) or the life of al-Kāẓim (Chapter 3), the core structure for Yaḥyā's last years is quite sparse. This results from the fact that non-Zaydī sources primarily employ an interpretive framework that minimizes Yaḥyā's importance. Despite this scarcity, a clear core structure is still readily apparent across historiographical traditions. As in the other case studies, the nature of the source material dictates the application of the model and the consequent structure of the analysis. The discussion of the Sunnī

Table 4.1 – ***The Sources for Yaḥyā b. ʿAbd Allāh's Last Years***

Ibn Saʿd (d. 230/845) Sunnī	*al-Ṭabaqāt al-kubrā* Prosopography
al-Balādhurī (d. 278/892) Sunnī	*Ansāb al-ashrāf* Prosopography
al-Yaʿqūbī (d. 284/897) Imāmī Shīʿī	*al-Tārīkh* Chronography
Aḥmad b. Sahl al-Rāzī (d. late third/ninth century) Zaydī Shīʿī	*Akhbār Fakhkh* Chronography
al-Ṭabarī (d. 310/923) Sunnī	*al-Tārīkh* Chronography
al-Iṣbahānī (d. 356/967) Zaydī Shīʿī	*Maqātil al-Ṭālibiyyīn* Biography/prosopography
al-Nāṭiq Yaḥyā b. al-Ḥusayn (d. 424/1033) Zaydī Shīʿī	*al-Ifāda* Biography/prosopography
ʿAlī b. Bilāl (fl. fifth/eleventh century) Zaydī Shīʿī	*al-Maṣābīḥ* Biography/prosopography
al-Khaṭīb al-Baghdādī (d. 463/1071) Sunnī	*Tārīkh Baghdād* Prosopography
Ibn al-Athīr (d. 630/1233) Sunnī	*al-Kāmil fī al-tārīkh* Chronography
al-Nuwayrī (d. 733/1332) Sunnī	*Nihāyat al-arab* Encyclopedic work
Ibn Kathīr (d. 774/1373) Sunnī	*al-Bidāya wa-l-nihāya* Chronography

sources begins with a listing of shared narrative elements along with their chief variants. This is followed first by a summary of the accounts of individual writers and then by a discussion of the two main Sunnī interpretive frameworks. Such a structure fits the limited scope of the Sunnī historical material. The Zaydī sources, by contrast, are more voluminous and contain complex narrative elements. The staggering diversity of these works necessitates a detailed author-by-author analysis.

I The Core Structure: From Yaḥyā's Rebellion to his Death

Yaḥyā b. 'Abd Allāh b. Ḥasan b. Ḥasan b. 'Alī b. Abī Ṭālib was a younger paternal half-brother to the 'Alid rebels Muḥammad al-Nafs al-Zakiyya (d. 145/762–3) and Ibrāhīm b. 'Abd Allāh (d. 145/762–3). His mother was Qurayba bt. Rukay' b. Abī 'Ubayda.[1] The exact year of his birth is unknown, but he was left orphaned by his father's imprisonment and death on the orders of the 'Abbāsid caliph al-Manṣūr (r. 136–58/754–75) before his brothers' revolt in Iraq.[2] There is very little information regarding Yaḥyā's childhood. He was raised along with his half-brother Idrīs (d. 175/791) in the household of the sixth Twelver Imām Ja'far b. Muḥammad al-Ṣādiq (d. 148/765), who oversaw his education and designated him as one of his legatees.[3]

Yaḥyā first rose to prominence during the rebellion of Ṣāḥib Fakhkh al-Ḥusayn b. 'Alī (d. 169/786) in Medina. The Zaydī sources attribute the revolt to the policies of the new 'Abbāsid caliph al-Hādī (r. 169–70/785–6), most notably the forcible relocation of many 'Alids to Medina and the appointment of a hostile governor, 'Umar b. 'Abd al-'Azīz al-'Umarī (d. after 169/786), over the Ḥijāz. Yaḥyā was one of the main catalysts of the revolt, leading a small party that seized control of the Prophet's mosque prior to the morning prayer.[4] After the 'Abbāsids crushed the rebels at Fakhkh, many 'Alids fled to Mecca, 6 miles away, and escaped by mixing with crowds of pilgrims. Yaḥyā and Idrīs were among the survivors. They initially traveled with supporters from the Banū Khuzā'a to Abyssinia. Here the chronology of Yaḥyā's movements becomes muddled, with stops in the Ḥijāz, Yemen (where he purportedly won the support of Muḥammad b. Idrīs al-Shāfi'ī[5] [d. 204/820]), Armenia, and Baghdad.[6] At some point before 176/791–2, Yaḥyā reached Iran and organized his own rebellion.

1 Ibn Sa'd, 5:442; al-Nāṭiq, 97; al-Iṣbahānī, 388; 'Alī b. Bilāl, 490.

2 Al-Iṣbahānī, 178–84. 3 Al-Nāṭiq, 97; al-Iṣbahānī, 388–9.

4 For Yaḥyā's role in the uprising, see Haider, *The Origins of the Shī'a*, 207–10. For the larger uprising, see al-Rāzī, 134–52.

5 For al-Shāfi'ī, see *EI*², s.v. "Al-Shāfi'ī" (E. Chaumont).

6 See, for example, al-Rāzī, 190–7, and 'Alī b. Bilāl, 492–3. For a meticulous reconstruction of Yaḥyā's post-Fakhkh travels, see Maher Jarrar's preface to his edition of al-Rāzī's *Akhbār Fakhkh*.

Yaḥyā's appearance in Iran marks the start of the period under consideration in this chapter. The subsequent events, though cited by almost every source, are scant in detail. Yaḥyā arrived in Daylam and began recruiting local supporters to his cause.[7] The year of his revolt is generally identified as 176/791–2.[8] The caliph Hārūn al-Rashīd (r. 170–93/786–809) responded by dispatching a large army to the region.[9] Yaḥyā never actually engaged the ʿAbbāsids in battle, and instead negotiated an agreement of safe-conduct (*amān*).[10] The reasons for this decision are disputed, but most sources mention betrayal by a regional leader and then describe Yaḥyā's return to Baghdad.[11] At some point over the next decade, Yaḥyā was arrested by al-Rashīd, an act that most historians deemed a violation of the *amān* agreement.[12] Yaḥyā died in 187/803, though the circumstances and location of his death remained in dispute.[13] For obvious reasons, the Zaydī sources devote considerably more attention than do non-Zaydī sources to Yaḥyā's movements between 176/791 and 187/803.

7 Ibn Saʿd, 5:442; al-Balādhurī, 3:353; al-Rāzī, 184–5; al-Ṭabarī, 4:628; al-Iṣbahānī, 390; al-Nāṭiq, 99; ʿAlī b. Bilāl, 492–3; al-Khaṭīb al-Baghdādī, 14:115; Ibn al-Athīr, 6:125; al-Nuwayrī, 22:89 and 25:40; Ibn Kathīr (1932–9), 9:167.

8 Al-Ṭabarī, 4:628; Ibn al-Athīr, 6:125; al-Nuwayrī, 22:89 and 25:40; Ibn Kathīr (1932–9), 9:167.

9 Ibn Saʿd, 5:442; al-Balādhurī, 3:353; al-Rāzī, 185–6; al-Ṭabarī, 4:628; al-Iṣbahānī, 390–2; al-Nāṭiq, 99–100; ʿAlī b. Bilāl, 493–4; Ibn al-Athīr, 6:125; al-Nuwayrī, 22:89 and 25:40; Ibn Kathīr (1932–9), 9:167.

10 Ibn Saʿd, 5:442; al-Balādhurī, 3:353; al-Rāzī, 207–12; al-Ṭabarī, 4:628–9; al-Iṣbahānī, 392–4; al-Nāṭiq, 100; ʿAlī b. Bilāl, 494–5; al-Khaṭīb al-Baghdādī, 14:115; Ibn al-Athīr, 6:125; al-Nuwayrī, 22:89 and 25:40; Ibn Kathīr (1932–9), 9:167.

11 Al-Rāzī, 198–207; al-Ṭabarī, 4:629; al-Iṣbahānī, 392 and 394; al-Nāṭiq, 99–100; ʿAlī b. Bilāl, 494; al-Khaṭīb al-Baghdādī, 14:115 (with no mention of the regional leader); Ibn al-Athīr, 6:125; al-Nuwayrī, 22:89 and 25:40; Ibn Kathīr (1932–9), 9:167.

12 Al-Rāzī, 214; al-Ṭabarī, 4:629–30; al-Iṣbahānī, 396–400; al-Nāṭiq, 103; ʿAlī b. Bilāl, 501; Ibn al-Athīr, 6:125; al-Nuwayrī, 22:89 and 25:40; Ibn Kathīr (1932–9), 9:167.

13 Every source places his death in Baghdad, with the exception of Ibn Saʿd (5:442). See al-Balādhurī, 3:353; al-Rāzī, 228–34; al-Ṭabarī, 4:631; al-Iṣbahānī, 401–3; al-Nāṭiq, 107; ʿAlī b. Bilāl, 503; al-Khaṭīb al-Baghdādī, 15:116; Ibn al-Athīr, 6:125; al-Nuwayrī, 22:89 and 25:40; Ibn Kathīr (1932–9), 9:168.

II The Sunnī Sources

The narrative elements summarized in this section are drawn from seven Sunnī historical works (see Table 4.1), which range from biographical dictionaries to historical chronicles.[14] These elements, which elaborate the core structure outlined above, consist of five episodes: (1) Yaḥyā's rebellion against al-Rashīd, (2) Yaḥyā's encounter with a member of the Zubayrid family, (3) al-Rashīd's invalidation of the *amān* agreement, (4) the fall of the Barmakid family (ca. 187/803),[15] and (5) Yaḥyā's death. The section begins by describing each narrative element along with its main variants. It then examines the ways in which Sunnī writers utilized these narratives to construct their interpretive frameworks.

A Narrative Elements

The Rebellion Narrative

The most detailed version of the narrative element depicting Yaḥyā's rebellion[16] starts with his arrival in Daylam, where he tries to rally local support. When al-Rashīd learns of this activity, he sends al-Faḍl b. Yaḥyā al-Barmakī[17] (d. 193/808) to the region at the head of a large army and with considerable additional resources at his disposal. At this point, some reports mention al-Rashīd's appointment of new governors for Ṭabaristān and Jurjān.[18] A special emphasis is placed on al-Faḍl al-Barmakī's maintenance of an unimpeded channel to the caliph during the campaign. Upon reaching Daylam, al-Faḍl camps at a place known as Ashabb (in Ṭālaqān) and initiates a correspondence with

[14] These accounts are as follows: Ibn Sa'd, 5:492; al-Balādhurī, 3:353; al-Ṭabarī, 4:628–33 and 658–9; al-Khaṭīb al-Baghdādī, 14:115–16; Ibn al-Athīr, 6:125–6 and 175–6; al-Nuwayrī, 22:89, 22:97, and 25:40; Ibn Kathīr (1932–9), 9:167–8 and 189.

[15] For the Barmakids, see EI^2, s.v. "Al-Barāmika" (W. Barthold and D. Sourdel). The relevant family members are Yaḥyā b. Khālid b. Barmak and his two sons al-Faḍl and Ja'far.

[16] Ibn Sa'd, 5:422; al-Balādhurī, 3:353; al-Ṭabarī, 4:628–9; Ibn al-Athīr, 6:125; al-Nuwayrī, 22:89 and 25:40; Ibn Kathīr (1932–9), 9:167.

[17] EI^2, s.v. "Al-Faḍl b. Yaḥyā al-Barmakī" (D. Sourdel).

[18] Al-Muthanna b. al-Ḥajjāj b. Qutayba b. Muslim was appointed over Ṭabaristān and 'Alī b. al-Ḥajjāj al-Khuzā'ī over Jurjān: see al-Ṭabarī, 4:628. For al-Muthanna, see Bosworth, *'Abbasid Caliphate*, 116, n. 441, and for 'Alī b. al-Ḥajjāj, see ibid., 116, n. 442.

Yaḥyā that alternates between threats and promises. He also offers the "King of Daylam" an enormous bribe of 1,000,000 *dirhams* in exchange for abandoning Yaḥyā. Although he is soon coerced into accepting an agreement of safe-conduct (*amān*), Yaḥyā secures a few concessions. He stipulates that the agreement be written by the caliph in his own hand and witnessed by important members of the Banū Hāshim, including ʿAbd al-Ṣamad b. ʿAlī[19] (d. 185/801), ʿAbbās b. Muḥammad[20] (d. 186/802), Muḥammad b. Ibrāhīm[21] (d. 184/800), and Mūsā b. ʿĪsā[22] (d. 183/799). Al-Rashīd eagerly accepts these terms and lavishes honors and gifts on Yaḥyā both before and after his arrival in Baghdad. The narrative ends by noting the growth of a friendship between al-Faḍl al-Barmakī and Yaḥyā b. ʿAbd Allāh, which perhaps foreshadows the events of 187/803 described later in this section.

There is a variant[23] of this element that is ascribed to a work entitled *Nasab al-Ṭālibiyyīn* by the Shīʿī scholar Yaḥyā b. Muḥammad al-ʿAlawī (d. 376/986).[24] It differs from the standard version in two ways. First, it mainly focuses on Yaḥyā's activities in Daylam and conveys little interest in al-Faḍl al-Barmakī. And second, it emphasizes

19 ʿAbd al-Ṣamad b. ʿAlī b. ʿAbd Allāh b. ʿAbbās was a paternal uncle of al-Manṣūr who served the dynasty in a number of roles. He was appointed governor of Mecca and Medina on multiple occasions and was briefly placed in charge of the *shurṭa* in Baṣra. In 163/780, he was removed from the governorship of Jazīra after two years in the post and imprisoned. After his release from prison in 166/783, he served as governor of Syria for a short period. See al-Ṭabarī, index.

20 ʿAbbās b. Muḥammad b. ʿAlī b. ʿAbd Allāh b. ʿAbbās was the brother of al-Saffāḥ and al-Manṣūr. The latter appointed him to the governorship of Syria and entrusted him with leadership of a campaign against the Byzantines in 138–9/756–7. He briefly served al-Rashīd as governor of Jazīra and died in Baghdad. See al-Ziriklī, 3:264–5; al-Ṭabarī, index.

21 Muḥammad b. Ibrāhīm b. Muḥammad b. ʿAlī al-ʿAbbāsī was governor of Mecca or Medina six times between 150/767 and 178/795. He also led the Ḥajj twice (149/766 and 178/795), conducted the annual raid against the Byzantines in 152/769, and reportedly held prisoners during the reign of al-Manṣūr. See al-Ziriklī, 5:293; al-Ṭabarī, index.

22 Mūsā b. ʿĪsā b. Mūsā served al-Manṣūr and al-Mahdī as governor of Mecca, Medina, Yemen, Egypt, and Kūfa in a long career that stretched through 180/796. He also took part in the military campaign against Ṣāḥib Fakhkh in 169/786. See al-Ziriklī, 7:326; al-Ṭabarī, index.

23 Al-Khaṭīb al-Baghdādī, 14:115.

24 This is likely Yaḥyā b. Muḥammad b. Aḥmad b. Zubāra al-ʿAlawī al-Ḥusaynī, a Shīʿī (probably Imāmī) scholar and theologian from Nīshāpūr who held the post of *naqīb* (leader) for the Banū Hāshim. He is said to have authored works on ritual law, legal theory, and the Imāmate. See Bernheimer, *The ʿAlids*, 81–3; al-Najāshī, 2:414–5l; Ibn al-Murtaḍā, 114.

the importance of a clause in the *amān* agreement that extends protection to seventy of Yaḥyā's unnamed followers. For reasons that will become clear later, this variant is particularly popular in the Zaydī sources.

The Zubayrid Encounter Narrative

The second narrative element explains the change in al-Rashīd's attitude toward Yaḥyā after his arrival in Baghdad. It consists of two variants, both of which are first recorded by al-Ṭabarī and later mentioned by other Sunnī writers in abridged form. There is a degree of overlap between this element and the narrative describing the breaking of the *amān*, discussed in the next section, particularly in sources that conflate Yaḥyā's appearances before al-Rashīd.

In the first variant, Yaḥyā is brought before the court in chains.[25] The caliph, al-Rashīd, mocks him while denying rumors of his mistreatment in prison. Yaḥyā responds by exposing his tongue, which is clearly discolored by some kind of poison. He then appeals to the close kinship between the 'Alids and the 'Abbāsids, asking al-Rashīd to desist from imprisoning and torturing him. Just as the caliph appears to soften, 'Abd Allāh b. Muṣ'ab al-Zubayrī[26] (d. 184/800) intervenes and accuses Yaḥyā of sedition and rebellion. In the course of his accusation, he refers to Medina as "our Medina," which prompts Yaḥyā to question his use of this phrase ("Who are you?") and to note that the city's importance derives from its association with the Prophet and not with al-Zubayr[27] (d. 36/656). Yaḥyā then returns to his initial line of argument, observing that the 'Alids and the 'Abbāsids have equal claims against each other. 'Abd Allāh b. Muṣ'ab's slander, he argues, is intended only to divide the two branches of the Prophet's family.

25 Al-Ṭabarī, 4:629–30; Ibn Kathīr (1932–9), 9:167–8.

26 Some sources substitute Bakkār b. 'Abd Allāh b. Muṣ'ab (d. 195/811) for his father, but this is clearly a mistake. 'Abd Allāh b. Muṣ'ab was appointed at various times to the governorships of Medina and Yemen. He was succeeded by his son and lived out his last years in Baghdad as a boon companion of al-Rashīd. Bakkār remained governor of Medina from 181/797 to 193/809, long after Yaḥyā b. 'Abd Allāh had died. For Bakkār b. 'Abd Allāh, see al-Ṭabarī, 5:16; *EI*², s.v. "Yaḥyā b. 'Abd Allāh" (W. Madelung); al-Ziriklī, 2:60; Bosworth, *'Abbasid Caliphate*, 121, n. 461. For 'Abd Allāh b. Muṣ'ab, see Ibn Sa'd, 5:500; al-Khaṭīb al-Baghdādī, 10:171–4; al-Ziriklī, 4:138; *EI*², s.v. "Yaḥyā b. 'Abd Allāh" (W. Madelung).

27 For al-Zubayr, see *EI*², s.v. "Al-Zubayr b. al-'Awwām" (I. Hasson).

At this point, Yaḥyā shifts the direction of the conversation. He recalls that ʿAbd Allāh b. Muṣʿab approached him after the defeat of Muḥammad al-Nafs al-Zakiyya and recited a poem that cursed the ʿAbbāsid caliph al-Manṣūr. He also encouraged Yaḥyā to continue the fight in Baṣra. This counteraccusation leads to an extended argument that culminates in Yaḥyā quoting lines from the purported poem. ʿAbd Allāh b. Muṣʿab denies the charge and offers to take an oath to establish his innocence. Yaḥyā asks al-Rashīd to administer a specific oath formula that includes the following words: "May I be deprived of God's strength and power and abandoned to my own strength and power if I really said that." The caliph then forces a reluctant ʿAbd Allāh to take this version of the oath. On his way home, he falls off his horse and is struck by a form of semi-paralysis that leads to his death.

The second variant[28] of this element is narrated by the ʿAlid ʿAbd Allāh b. ʿAbbās b. Ḥasan b. ʿUbayd Allāh b. ʿAbbās b. ʿAlī (d. late third/ninth century).[29] It begins with ʿAbd Allāh and his father receiving permission to enter the court on a day on which al-Rashīd is in a foul mood. This is considered a significant honor. Al-Faḍl b. al-Rabīʿ[30] (d. 208/824), the chamberlain, then informs the caliph that ʿAbd Allāh b. Muṣʿab is at the door, requesting a private audience. The narrator's father suggests that this is a ruse devised by al-Faḍl b. al-Rabīʿ to curtail al-Rashīd's fondness for his ʿAlid cousins. When ʿAbd Allāh b. Muṣʿab is finally ushered to court, he claims to have encountered agents of Yaḥyā b. ʿAbd Allāh in Medina calling for revolution. Al-Rashīd summons Yaḥyā, who emphasizes the close bonds of kinship between the ʿAlids and the ʿAbbāsids and questions the credibility of any Zubayrid accusations. At this point, both Yaḥyā and ʿAbd Allāh b.

28 Al-Ṭabarī, 4:631–3.

29 More is known about his father ʿAbbās b. al-Ḥasan (d. early third/ninth century), a poet of high repute, who moved from Medina to Baghdad, where he became a boon companion of al-Rashīd and al-Maʾmūn. See al-Khaṭīb al-Baghdādī, 12:125–6.

30 Al-Faḍl b. al-Rabīʿ b. Yūnus was first appointed chamberlain after his father became al-Manṣūr's *wazīr*. During al-Rashīd's reign, al-Faḍl did not disguise his animosity toward the Barmakids, and is often ascribed a pivotal role in their downfall. He was appointed *wazīr* by al-Rashīd and al-Amīn (r. 193–7/809–13) beginning in 187/809. After al-Maʾmūn's (r. 197–218/813–33) return to Baghdad, al-Faḍl went into hiding until he was pardoned. See al-Ziriklī, 5:148; *EI*[2], s.v. "Al-Faḍl b. al-Rabīʿ" (D. Sourdel).

Muṣ'ab recite short prayers and take oaths that resemble those in the first variant – promising to forsake God's strength and power and be abandoned to their own strength and power if untruthful.[31] Al-Rashīd then imprisons Yaḥyā and, after some hesitation, permits 'Abd Allāh (the narrator) and his father to return home.

Later that night, 'Abd Allāh b. Muṣ'ab dispatches a servant to request a meeting with the narrator's father in an effort to convince him to testify against Yaḥyā. The father sends his son in his stead, cautioning him that his life may be at risk. Upon arrival, however, the narrator sees women mourning in the courtyard and quickly learns of 'Abd Allāh b. Muṣ'ab's death.[32] He informs his father, who is overjoyed at this turn of events. They are both then summoned to appear before al-Rashīd. The narrator's father speaks first, praising God for preserving the close bonds of kinship between the 'Alids and the 'Abbāsids. Yaḥyā, who is brought from prison, expresses similar sentiments, denies any seditious intentions, and disparages both 'Abd Allāh b. Muṣ'ab and al-Faḍl b. al-Rabī' for their duplicity. Al-Rashīd grants him 100,000 *dīnār*s and sets him free.

The details common to the two variants of this narrative element are (i) the competing accusations of Yaḥyā and 'Abd Allāh b. Muṣ'ab, (ii) the taking of oaths that involve a renunciation of God's power and strength, and (iii) the subsequent death of 'Abd Allāh b. Muṣ'ab. The most striking difference between them concerns the presence or omission of the elegy for al-Nafs al-Zakiyya. In addition, the second variant is more unambiguous in its denial of the substance of 'Abd Allāh b. Muṣ'ab's accusations.

The *Amān* Break Narrative

The third narrative element in the Sunnī sources documents al-Rashīd's attempts to annul his *amān* agreement with Yaḥyā. There are two main variants of this episode, one preserved by al-Ṭabarī and the other by al-Khaṭīb al-Baghdādī. The latter is particularly distinctive in that it relates two separate meetings with jurists and includes the poisoning accusation referenced in the previous section.

31 In contrast to the first variant, Yaḥyā does not accuse 'Abd Allāh b. Muṣ'ab of reciting an elegy for al-Nafs al-Zakiyya.

32 The cause of death is identical to that in the first version: 'Abd Allāh b. Muṣ'ab suffers from abdominal pain and paralysis after falling off his mount.

In the first variant, al-Rashīd convenes a meeting of prominent jurists, including, most notably, Muḥammad b. al-Ḥasan al-Shaybānī[33] (d. 189/805) and Abū Bakhtarī Wahb b. Wahb[34] (d. 200/816), for the express purpose of invalidating the safe-conduct.[35] Al-Shaybānī unequivocally upholds the agreement, going so far as to claim that it would remain in effect even if Yaḥyā were to organize a new rebellion. Al-Rashīd then turns to Abū Bakhtarī, who cancels the *amān* with no explanation or justification. This prompts the caliph to tear the document in half and later appoint Abū Bakhtarī to the post of chief judge.

The second variant connects al-Rashīd's frustrations with the agreement to a stipulation that also protects seventy of Yaḥyā's supporters without explicitly identifying them.[36] The caliph is particularly upset at Yaḥyā's refusal to divulge all seventy names at once. Instead, Yaḥyā waits until al-Rashīd arrests one of his followers and then secures his release by claiming him as one of the seventy. The caliph summons a number of important jurists and then, in their presence, presses Yaḥyā for names. When Yaḥyā again refuses to comply, al-Rashīd angrily threatens to repudiate the agreement. The argument inspires the narrator[37] to recite a line of poetry in appreciation of Yaḥyā's cleverness, which further enrages al-Rashīd. At this point, Abū Bakhtarī grabs the *amān* and tears it in half. The caliph, however, is still uncertain and asks Abū Yūsuf[38] (d. 182/798) for a ruling on the safe-conduct. To the

33 Al-Shaybānī was one of the architects of the Ḥanafī law school. See *EI*², s.v. "Al-Shaybānī" (E. Chaumont).

34 Abū Bakhtarī was born and raised in Medina and moved to Baghdad during the reign of al-Rashīd. His first appointment as a judge was in eastern Baghdad. He later held the same post in Medina before becoming governor after Bakkār b. ʿAbd Allāh's removal in 193/809. Abū Bakhtarī's reliability as a transmitter was suspect. See al-Khaṭīb al-Baghdādī, 3:456–61; Ibn Khallikān, 6:37–42; al-Ziriklī, 8:126.

35 Al-Ṭabarī, 4:631; Ibn al-Athīr, 6:125–6; al-Nuwayrī, 25:40; Ibn Kathīr (1932–9), 9:167.

36 Al-Khaṭīb al-Baghdādī, 14:115–16.

37 The narrator is identified as ʿAbd al-Raḥmān b. ʿAbd Allāh b. ʿUmar b. Ḥafṣ al-ʿUmarī (d. 186/802), who was a judge in Medina but spent most of his life in Baghdad. His reputation as a transmitter is generally negative. See al-Khaṭīb al-Baghdādī, 10:230–4.

38 This account replaces Muḥammad al-Shaybānī (mentioned by most other sources) with Abū Yūsuf, another seminal figure in the Ḥanafī law school. For Abū Yūsuf, see *EI*², s.v. "Abū Yūsuf" (J. Schacht).

caliph's dismay, Abū Yūsuf affirms its validity and further asserts that Yaḥyā cannot be compelled to reveal any names.

Some days later, al-Rashīd convenes the jurists for a second meeting. This time Yaḥyā's countenance has changed dramatically, and he looks yellow. The caliph addresses him but receives no reply. He then turns to the jurists and asks, "Do you not see that I speak to this man and he does not answer?" The jurists gather around Yaḥyā, who exposes a tongue that has turned green and robbed him of the ability to speak. Al-Rashīd denies poisoning him, and even takes an oath on his authority as caliph to this effect. He notes that if he wished Yaḥyā dead, he could simply order his execution. When the narrator turns back to Yaḥyā, he finds him lying face down on the ground, motionless.

Both variants of this narrative element feature al-Rashīd's gathering of the jurists and Abū Bakhtarī's invalidation of the *amān*. They differ regarding the identities of the jurists present, the number of gatherings, and the possibility that Yaḥyā was poisoned.

The Barmakids' Fall Narrative

Perhaps the most famous and disputed episode in al-Rashīd's reign involved the sudden purge of the Barmakid family.[39] According to most sources, the caliph's anger was mainly directed at Ja'far b. Yaḥyā al-Barmakī, who was executed near the end of 186/802. His father, Yaḥyā al-Barmakī (d. 190/805), and brother al-Faḍl were imprisoned, and the family's property was seized. The cause of the family's fall was debated for centuries, and remains an open question. The fourth narrative element in the Sunnī sources offers a possible explanation for the caliph's anger that directly implicates Yaḥyā b. 'Abd Allāh. Two versions of this element are preserved by al-Ṭabarī (under the year 187/803), and a third is recorded much later by al-Nuwayrī (under the year 185/801).

The first variant opens with al-Rashīd placing Yaḥyā under arrest and remanding him to the custody of Ja'far al-Barmakī.[40] One night, Ja'far summons Yaḥyā for questioning. As the conversation progresses, Yaḥyā denies any wrongdoing and beseeches Ja'far to fear God and not act in a manner that will make him an enemy of the Prophet. Ja'far is

[39] For the Barmakids, see *EI*[2], s.vv. "Al-Barāmika" (W. Barthold and D. Sourdel) and "Al-Faḍl b. Yaḥyā al-Barmakī (D. Sourdel).

[40] Al-Ṭabarī, 4:658; Ibn al-Athīr, 6:175–6; al-Nuwayrī, 22:97; Ibn Kathīr (1932–9), 9:189.

ultimately won over by this argument and agrees to set him free. Yaḥyā, however, pleads that he cannot travel without fear of being caught and returned to prison, prompting Jaʿfar to order one of his agents to accompany Yaḥyā to safety. News of this development reaches al-Faḍl b. al-Rabīʿ, the chamberlain, through an informant. Sensing an opportunity to undermine his rival, al-Faḍl notifies al-Rashīd, who rebukes him with the words, "What does this have to do with you?" and suggests that Jaʿfar may have acted in accordance with the caliph's orders. The caliph then invites Jaʿfar for dinner, at the conclusion of which he asks about Yaḥyā. Jaʿfar lies and says that he is in prison in fetters. The caliph pushes further and asks, "On my life?" At this point, Jaʿfar realizes that al-Rashīd knows the truth and admits that he has released Yaḥyā. The caliph ostensibly praises him but secretly vows to kill him.

The second variant begins with a stranger appearing in court and requesting a private meeting with the caliph.[41] Al-Rashīd asks him to wait, completes his other business, and then motions for him to approach. The stranger, however, insists on complete privacy, so al-Rashīd clears the court of family members and servants. The stranger first requests a guarantee of safe-conduct, which al-Rashīd readily grants, and then reveals that he has seen Yaḥyā b. ʿAbd Allāh in a caravanserai in Ḥulwān, a town in Khurāsān. Upon further questioning, the stranger offers a physical description of Yaḥyā, his retinue (whose members all bore notes guaranteeing their safety), and his distinctive method of prayer.[42] Al-Rashīd, convinced that the visitor is telling the truth, questions him about his identity. The man states that he is a descendant of the Khurāsānīs who brought the ʿAbbāsids to power, originally from Marv but now residing in Baghdad. Al-Rashīd then asks whether he would be willing to submit to a test of loyalty. After the stranger agrees, the caliph gives him a purse containing 2,000 *dīnār*s and tells him to conceal it. He then summons his slaves and

[41] Al-Ṭabarī, 4:658–9.

[42] Yaḥyā is here described as performing the *ʿaṣr* prayer in a manner consistent with Twelver Shīʿī law, immediately after his *ẓuhr* prayer and with the first two cycles elongated and the last two cycles abbreviated. For the Sunnī position on the relevant prayer timings, see Ibn Qudāma, 1:300–5. For the Zaydī position, see Ibn Miftāḥ, 2:140–5. For a good comparative discussion of differences in the timings of the *ẓuhr* and *ʿaṣr* prayers and the requirements for the third and fourth prayer cycles, see al-Ṭūsī, *Khilāf*, 1:257–61 (timings) and 1:337–8 and 1:341–3 (structure).

orders the man beaten and paraded around town as an example for those who slander members of the caliph's court. This ruse provides cover for al-Rashīd as he plots against the Barmakids.

The start of the third variant mirrors that of the first in that Yaḥyā is remanded to the custody of Jaʿfar al-Barmakī.[43] One night, in a state of drunkenness, Jaʿfar incorrectly informs al-Rashīd that Yaḥyā is dead. He does so partly because he is drunk and partly because he knows the news will make the caliph happy. Jaʿfar then tells his father, Yaḥyā al-Barmakī, what he has done. Yaḥyā is utterly despondent and concludes that the family now has two equally unappealing options: they can kill the ʿAlid and thereby be assured of hellfire, or they can release him and suffer the wrath of the caliph. Yaḥyā al-Barmakī decides to send Yaḥyā b. ʿAbd Allāh to Khurāsān with a letter requesting asylum from the governor, ʿAlī b. ʿĪsā b. Māhān (d. 196/812).[44] He is unaware, however, of the longstanding animosity between ʿAlī and his sons Jaʿfar and al-Faḍl. Once Yaḥyā reaches Khurāsān, ʿAlī b. ʿĪsā secretly forwards Yaḥyā al-Barmakī's letter to al-Rashīd, prompting the subsequent purge.

The details common to these variants are Jaʿfar al-Barmakī's decision to release Yaḥyā b. ʿAbd Allāh from prison and al-Rashīd's secret acquisition of this knowledge. Although the second variant does not directly mention Jaʿfar, it strongly suggests that he was responsible for Yaḥyā's release. The biggest difference between the three variants concerns the means by which the information reaches the caliph. The first mentions the chamberlain, al-Faḍl b. Rabīʿ, who is eager to undermine the Barmakids at court. The second involves an anonymous stranger. The third implicates a provincial governor, ʿAlī b. ʿĪsā, who has a strained relationship with the Barmakids.

The Death Narrative

The Sunnī sources offer very brief descriptions of Yaḥyā's death, which differ in terms of location (whether he died in prison) and cause (whether he was poisoned). The brevity of these death reports, which often consist of a single sentence, evidence a general lack of

43 Al-Nuwayrī, 22:97 and 25:40.

44 ʿAlī b. ʿĪsā b. Māhān was governor of Khurāsān under al-Rashīd. He later played a key part in convincing al-Amīn to depose al-Maʾmūn from caliphal succession. He died in battle against al-Maʾmūn's forces. See al-Ziriklī, 4:317; *EI*², s.v. "Ibn Māhān" (D. Sourdel).

interest in this subject. It also noteworthy that most writers severely constrict the eleven-year period between Yaḥyā's return to Baghdad in 176/791 and his death in 187/803. They often insert a short death announcement immediately after his arrest without commenting on the length of his imprisonment.

B The Sunnī Sources Interpreted

The Sunnī Accounts

Sunnī depictions of Yaḥyā's rebellion and its aftermath selectively populate an established core structure with combinations of the five narrative elements described in the previous section and listed in Table 4.2. In some instances, the writers change the order of narrative elements or embellish their details. In others, they combine narrative elements into composite versions that complicate the larger account. The discussion that follows focuses narrowly on the unique features of each writer's treatment of Yaḥyā. The content and structure of the Sunnī sources are summarized in Table 4.3.

Ibn Saʿd and al-Balādhurī

Ibn Saʿd[45] and al-Balādhurī[46] provide short summary accounts that incorporate two of the five narrative elements listed in Table 4.2 (1a and 5). These reports are so brief and condensed that they are difficult to contextualize in terms of ʿAbbāsid political developments. Both writers tend to focus on issues of culpability and blame. Ibn Saʿd distinctively claims that Yaḥyā died peacefully in Medina and that al-Rashīd upheld his end of the *amān* agreement. This version of events exonerates the caliph and salvages his relationship with Yaḥyā. Al-Balādhurī, by contrast, presents Yaḥyā as a rebel who is forced to accept an agreement of safe-conduct whose scope is limited to the preservation of his life, with no stipulation to prevent his imprisonment. Soon thereafter, the caliph arrests Yaḥyā and remands him to the custody of a loyal ʿAbbāsid client, where he remains until his – presumably natural – death. Overall, Ibn Saʿd rejects the possibility of animosity between the ʿAlids and the ʿAbbāsids, whereas al-Balādhurī exhibits a marked preference for the ʿAbbāsids.

[45] Ibn Saʿd, 5:442. [46] Al-Balādhurī, 3:353.

Table 4.2 – *The Sunnī Narrative Elements for Yaḥyā b. ʿAbd Allāh*

Element	Common details	Variants
1. Rebellion	(1) Yaḥyā's arrival in Daylam (2) Gathering of followers (3) The acceptance of an *amān*	(a) al-Rashīd dispatches al-Faḍl. In some instances, there is a suggestion that Yaḥyā was coerced into accepting the *amān*. (b) There is a strong focus on Yaḥyā's seventy followers.
2. Zubayrid encounter	(1) ʿAbd Allāh b. Muṣʿab al-Zubayrī accuses Yaḥyā of sedition (2) The swearing of oaths involving a renunciation of God's power and strength (3) The death of ʿAbd Allāh b. Muṣʿab	(a) Yaḥyā accuses al-Zubayrī of having mourned the death of al-Nafs al-Zakiyya with a poem. Some accounts include the possibility of poisoning (visible on Yaḥyā's tongue). (b) The story is told from the perspective of an ʿAlid at court. There is no mention of poetry or al-Nafs al-Zakiyya.
3. *Amān* break	(1) al-Rashīd's gathering of prominent jurists (2) Abū Bakhtarī's invalidation of the *amān*.	(a) There is one meeting. In some instances, al-Zubayrī appears and accuses Yaḥyā of sedition. (b) There are two meetings. The first focuses on Yaḥyā naming his seventy companions and culminates in the tearing of the *amān*. The second suggests poisoning (tongue).

Table 4.2 (*cont.*)

Element	Common details	Variants
4. Barmakids' fall	(1) Yaḥyā's release from prison by Ja'far al-Barmakī (2) al-Rashīd's secret knowledge of the release	(a) There is usually an exchange in which Yaḥyā convinces Ja'far to release him. The news reaches al-Rashīd through his chamberlain, al-Faḍl b. al-Rabī' (from an undisclosed source). Al-Rashīd hides his surprise and later confronts Ja'far, secretly vowing to kill him. (b) The information arrives via a mysterious stranger who informs only al-Rashīd. The caliph plans a ruse in which the stranger is secretly rewarded but publicly beaten to keep the matter secret. (c) Drunk, Ja'far lies to al-Rashīd that Yaḥyā is dead. The Barmakids try to smuggle Yaḥyā to Khurāsān, but the governor of the province betrays them to al-Rashīd.
5. Death	An often brief acknowledgment of Yaḥyā's death	No variants, but the accounts differ on two points: the location of Yaḥyā's death (Medina or Baghdad; in prison or free) and the cause of it (poisoning or not).

al-Ṭabarī

Al-Ṭabarī's elaborate account of Yaḥyā's rebellion and death is distinctive in two ways.[47] The first pertains to his version of the "*amān* break" narrative, in which al-Shaybānī and Abū Bakhtarī evaluate the validity of the agreement. According to al-Ṭabarī, the meeting of jurists concludes with Bakkār b. 'Abd Allāh b. Muṣ'ab accusing Yaḥyā of "dividing the community," "opposing our orders," and "seeking our caliphate."[48] The 'Alid then questions his credentials, exclaiming, "Who are you?" Instead of progressing to a full-blown argument, however, the encounter is curtailed by al-Rashīd's laughter. The caliph decides to release Yaḥyā, observing that he looks ill and that people might suspect foul play should he die in prison. Interestingly, Yaḥyā himself acknowledges that his sickness predates his arrest. This account rejects the possibility of poisoning and clearly situates Yaḥyā's death outside prison. Al-Ṭabarī's second distinctive feature is his use of the second variant of the "Zubayrid encounter" narrative. No other Sunnī author mentions this report, which attributes 'Abbāsid–'Alid tensions to outside political forces. Overall, al-Ṭabarī provides the most detailed versions of seven of the ten variants of the narrative elements identified above.

al-Khaṭīb al-Baghdādī

Al-Khaṭīb al-Baghdādī's account includes the only two elements – the "rebellion" and "*amān* break" narratives – that directly focus on Yaḥyā b. 'Abd Allāh.[49] His use of these reports, however, had no discernible impact on subsequent Sunnī historians, who expressed a clear preference for al-Ṭabarī's version of these events. Al-Khaṭīb al-Baghdādī's portrait of Yaḥyā is far from flattering. This is particularly evident in his description of Yaḥyā's death, where, despite an earlier allusion to poisoning (Table 4.2, element 3b), he decisively rejects reports of foul play. Al-Khaṭīb al-Baghdādī also provides an epilogue in which a prominent 'Alid[50] refuses to lead Yaḥyā's funeral prayers, citing the legitimacy of al-Rashīd's anger toward him. This report

47 Al-Ṭabarī, 4:628–33 and 658–9. Ibn al-Jawzī (d. 597/1201) essentially summarizes al-Ṭabarī's version of narrative elements 1a and 3a in his *al-Muntaẓam*, 9:15–17.

48 Al-Ṭabarī, 4:631.

49 Al-Khaṭīb al-Baghdādī, 14:115–16.

50 The man named here, 'Abbās b. al-Ḥasan b. 'Alī, is not widely attested in the sources.

validates the caliph's criticism and places it outside the narrow context of 'Abbāsid–'Alid rivalry.

Later Writers

Ibn al-Athīr's discussion of Yaḥyā begins with his version of the rebellion narrative.[51] Although he retains much of al-Ṭabarī's wording, Ibn al-Athīr excises details about provincial administration, geographical locations, and the intermediary steps involved in setting the terms of the *amān*. The account then abruptly shifts from Yaḥyā's lavish reception in Baghdad to the stark statement that "al-Rashīd imprisoned him and he died in prison." The omission of the "Zubayrid encounter" narrative means that the reader is given no clear explanation for the change in Yaḥyā's fortunes. The announcement of Yaḥyā's death is followed by a succinct version of the "*amān* break" narrative, which lacks the complexity of al-Ṭabarī's report. Ibn al-Athīr contrasts al-Shaybānī's refusal to appease the caliph with Abū Bakhtarī's eagerness to curry favor with him. The "Barmakids' fall" narrative appears much later in Ibn al-Athīr's text (under the year 187/803), and it incorporates much of the language and phrasing of al-Ṭabarī's account.

Al-Nuwayrī offers two renderings of the relevant portion of Yaḥyā's life. The first begins with a version of the rebellion narrative, dated to 176/791, which mirrors similar reports from al-Ṭabarī and Ibn al-Athīr.[52] Al-Nuwayrī mentions Yaḥyā's death in a statement that resembles that of Ibn al-Athīr in its brevity and abruptness. The narrative describing the fall of the Barmakids occurs later in al-Nuwayrī's work under the year 185/801, in two forms. The first (Table 4.2, element 4a) is the more common variant, highlighting al-Faḍl b. al-Rabī''s attempt to undermine the Barmakids. Here, too, al-Nuwayrī's text bears a striking resemblance to the accounts preserved by al-Ṭabarī and Ibn al-Athīr. The second variant (Table 4.2, element 4c) is unique to al-Nuwayrī and identifies 'Alī b. 'Īsā as the informant who told al-Rashīd of Yaḥyā's release. In both cases, Yaḥyā is a pawn in a larger political game involving 'Abbāsid elites.

Later in his encyclopedic work, al-Nuwayrī returns to the subject of Yaḥyā in a volume that focuses on Ṭālibid rebellions against the Umayyads and the 'Abbāsids.[53] He again gives a combination of the rebellion and death narratives. In this instance, however, al-Nuwayrī

[51] Ibn al-Athīr, 6:125–6 and 175–6. [52] Al-Nuwayrī, 22:89 and 25:40.
[53] Ibid., 22:97.

includes an "*amān* break" narrative virtually identical to that of Ibn al-Athīr.[54] Recall that in al-Nuwayrī's previous discussion, the "Barmakids' fall" narrative was separated from the other reports and presented in a different year. In this second case, by contrast, his version directly follows the violation of the safe-conduct. This repetition suggests that al-Nuwayrī preferred his account of the purge of the Barmakids (element 4c) to the other available variants (elements 4a and 4b).

Ibn Kathīr's discussion of Yaḥyā includes an extended treatment of the rebellion narrative that, like those of Ibn al-Athīr and al-Nuwayrī, closely aligns with that of al-Ṭabarī.[55] It is followed by a composite of the "*amān* break" and "Zubayrid encounter" narratives. Recall that in al-Ṭabarī's version of the latter, everyone, including Yaḥyā, adamantly denies any possibility of foul play. In Ibn Kathīr's report, al-Rashīd invalidates the *amān* and then refutes rumors of poisoning. Yaḥyā remains silent on the subject, instead appealing to the caliph on the basis of kinship. At this point, Ibn Kathīr transitions into the "Zubayrid encounter" narrative, but he mistakenly replaces ʿAbd Allāh b. Muṣʿab with the latter's son Bakkār.[56] The report ends with Bakkār's death and Yaḥyā's release from prison.

This is, of course, problematic, given that Yaḥyā is apparently freed in the same court session during which his safe-conduct is invalidated. Perhaps as a result of this confusion, Ibn Kathīr reports that Yaḥyā was quickly re-imprisoned and remained in custody until his death a month later. Finally, Ibn Kathīr's version of the "Barmakids' fall" narrative occurs much later in his text (under the year 187/803), and it focuses, as is typical, on court intrigues.

Sunnī Interpretive Frameworks

Yaḥyā Marginalized

Most of the narrative elements outlined in Table 4.2 portray Yaḥyā as a secondary character in a wider historical drama.[57] The first variant of

[54] The parallel suggests either that both scholars were relying on a common source or (more likely) that al-Nuwayrī drew heavily on the work of his predecessor.

[55] Ibn Kathīr (1932–9), 9:167–8 and 189.

[56] This cannot be correct, as Bakkār outlived Yaḥyā by a number of decades. See n.26 in this chapter.

[57] The two exceptions are the second variant of the rebellion narrative and the "*amān* break" narrative.

Table 4.3 – *The Sunnī Interpretive Frameworks for Yaḥyā b. ʿAbd Allāh*

	Rebellion		Zubayrid encounter		*Amān* break		Barmakids' fall			Death	Framework
	a	b	a	b	a	b	a	b	c		
Ibn Saʿd	X									X (no prison)	Marginal
al-Balādhurī	X									X (prison)	Marginal
al-Ṭabarī	X		X (tongue)	X	X (no poison)		X	X		X (no prison)	Marginal
al-Khaṭīb al-Baghdādī		X	X (no tongue)			X (tongue)				X (prison)	Central/marginal
Ibn al-Athīr	X				X		X			X (prison)	Marginal
al-Nuwayrī (I)	X						X		X	X (prison)	Marginal
al-Nuwayrī (II)	X				X				X	X (prison)	Marginal
Ibn Kathīr	X		X		X (poison?)		X			X (prison)	Marginal

the rebellion narrative is primarily concerned with changes in local administration. Al-Ṭabarī's version of Yaḥyā's revolt is preceded by the statement that al-Rashīd appointed al-Faḍl al-Barmakī to govern a number of provinces in the eastern regions of the 'Abbāsid empire. Al-Ṭabarī also recounts al-Rashīd's delegation of provincial posts to military commanders. The expedition to neutralize Yaḥyā thus becomes a vehicle to explain administrative turnover. This narrative element also reveals political alignments in the upper echelons of the 'Abbāsid court, particularly through a description of al-Faḍl's efforts to secure a direct line of communication with al-Rashīd. Once Yaḥyā appears, he provides a convenient explanation for the fates of several key figures. The most famous of these are the members of the Barmakid family, whose fall from grace is explicitly tied to the close friendship that develops between Yaḥyā and al-Faḍl al-Barmakī. The narrative's emphasis on the strength of the *amān* also prefigures a conflict between the caliph and the jurists (discussed later in this section). Yaḥyā is thereby reduced to a stock figure devoid of any real agency in the events surrounding him.

A framework of marginalization also informs both variants of the "Zubayrid encounter" narrative. Some versions feature a dramatic moment in which Yaḥyā proves al-Rashīd's nefarious intentions by revealing that his tongue has turned green. This moment, however, is subordinate to the larger focus of the narrative: the accusations of sedition. After recounting the episode, al-Ṭabarī offers alternative explanations for al-Zubayrī's death, openly questioning the story of the oaths and minimizing the impact of Yaḥyā's triumph. It appears, then, that al-Ṭabarī's interest in this report stems from al-Zubayrī's involvement. Yaḥyā is only a secondary consideration.

The "Zubayrid encounter" narrative also addresses the relationship between the 'Abbāsids and the 'Alids. In many versions of the first variant, Yaḥyā argues that kinship should transcend squabbles over political power and concedes that each side has committed wrongs against the other. The animosity between the two branches of the family, he claims, is caused by outside forces, such as the Zubayrids, with their own agendas. A similar idea is conveyed by the 'Alid narrator of the second variant, who describes his presence in court as an honor precariously predicated on al-Rashīd's whims. In these reports, Yaḥyā is either a marginal figure or a metonym for 'Abbāsid–'Alid relations.

In the first variant of the "*amān* break" narrative, Yaḥyā's imprisonment provides an arena for comparing two prominent Sunnī jurists, Muḥammad al-Shaybānī and Abū Bakhtarī. The former, a student of both Abū Ḥanīfa[58] (d. 150/767) and Abū Yūsuf,[59] is a founder of the Ḥanafī law school and a scholar of considerable repute. Although he was appointed by al-Rashīd to the judgeship of Raqqa, al-Shaybānī had a contentious relationship with the caliph. Abū Bakhtarī, by contrast, is routinely disparaged in the Sunnī sources as an unreliable transmitter and a liar.[60] He also served as a chief judge, replacing Abū Yūsuf in Baghdad, and was appointed governor of Mecca and Medina at various times. Al-Shaybānī risks al-Rashīd's anger by refusing to invalidate the safe-conduct under any circumstances. His refusal gives Abū Bakhtarī an opening to win caliphal favor by declaring the agreement void. The incident, while ostensibly about Yaḥyā, is actually concerned with differentiating between these two jurists. It ascribes al-Shaybānī's diminished position within the ʿAbbāsid state[61] to his staunch integrity. It also explains al-Rashīd's appointment of Abū Bakhtarī to numerous important administrative and juridical posts.

The "Barmakid's fall" narrative identifies Yaḥyā b. ʿAbd Allāh as the cause of the family's removal from power. The first variant focuses on court intrigues, pitting the Barmakids against the chamberlain, al-Faḍl b. al-Rabīʿ. Jaʿfar al-Barmakī's decision to release Yaḥyā enables al-Faḍl (who hears of it through an unnamed source) to undermine the family's standing with al-Rashīd. Upon receiving the information, however, the caliph criticizes the chamberlain for exceeding his station – perhaps because al-Rashīd does not want to be exposed as ignorant of his underlings' actions. Regardless, the caliph's learning the truth leads to a tense encounter with Jaʿfar al-Barmakī over dinner and a secret plan to purge the Barmakids. The second variant retains the focus on court politics but removes al-Faḍl from the picture altogether, instead positioning al-Rashīd against the Barmakids. In the third variant, it is the regional governor ʿAlī b. ʿĪsā b. Māhān, motivated by a general distrust of the Barmakids, who informs al-Rashīd of Yaḥyā's release. In all three

[58] For Abū Ḥanīfa, see *EI*^{2}, s.v. "Abū Ḥanīfa al-Nuʿmān" (J. Schacht).
[59] For Abū Yūsuf, see n.38 in this chapter.
[60] Ibn Khallikān, 6:37–42; al-Khaṭīb al-Baghdādī, 13:456–61.
[61] This is not necessarily a negative description, as government appointments were viewed with suspicion by later jurists.

versions, Yaḥyā is a pawn in the machinations of figures at the highest strata of the ʿAbbāsid state.

Finally, the paucity of narratives in the Sunnī sources concerning Yaḥyā's death underscores his general insignificance. Their primary disagreement centers on whether he died inside or outside prison. The possibility of poisoning is sometimes referenced in the course of the narrative elements relating to the encounter with al-Zubayrī and the Barmakids' fall, but it is rarely mentioned in concert with imprisonment. Most historians offer variations of a single line of text, which states simply that al-Rashīd imprisoned Yaḥyā until he died. This brevity betrays a lack of interest in Yaḥyā as an independent historical figure. His importance is predicated almost entirely on his connection with jurists, governors, and members of the caliphal court.

Yaḥyā at the Center

There are two notable exceptions to the marginalization framework that informs the depiction of Yaḥyā b. ʿAbd Allāh in most Sunnī sources: the second variant of the rebellion narrative and the second variant of the "*amān* break" narrative. Among Sunnī scholars these episodes are recorded only by al-Khaṭīb al-Baghdādī, and they reflect the general tenor of the Zaydī sources described in section III.

Al-Khaṭīb al-Baghdādī's version of the rebellion narrative focuses on Yaḥyā himself, as opposed to the broader landscape of ʿAbbāsid caliphal politics. This focus is reflected in the absence of al-Faḍl al-Barmakī as an intermediary between al-Rashīd and Yaḥyā. The account also speaks of Yaḥyā's followers, noting their number – seventy – and their securing of personal guarantees of safety from al-Rashīd. This variant makes no mention of any provincial administrator or governor. It is exclusively interested in affirming the iron-clad validity of the agreement of safe-conduct, and repeatedly confirms the clause that extended its coverage to Yaḥyā's inner circle. Al-Khaṭīb al-Baghdādī explicitly ascribes this narrative element to Yaḥyā b. Muḥammad al-ʿAlawī, suggesting an ʿAlid Shīʿī provenance for the account.[62]

In his variant of the "*amān* break" narrative, al-Khaṭīb al-Baghdādī highlights al-Rashīd's frustration at Yaḥyā's refusal to divulge the names of his supporters. Instead of contrasting al-Shaybānī's integrity with Abū Bakhtarī's opportunism, this report highlights the breakdown in

[62] For al-ʿAlawī, see n.24 in this chapter.

relations between al-Rashīd and Yaḥyā. During the first meeting of the jurists, Abū Yūsuf[63] does not rule on the validity of the *amān*, but only states that the caliph cannot compel Yaḥyā to reveal any names. The second meeting focuses almost exclusively on Yaḥyā's health. He is initially unable to speak because of a discoloration of his tongue due to poisoning, and he later collapses altogether. Al-Rashīd pleads innocence, but the text strongly intimates that this is a lie. In contrast to his marginality in the first variant of this element, here Yaḥyā is the clear protagonist of the story.

The Ghost in the Machine

Six of the seven Sunnī historians (see Table 4.3) who discuss the period between Yaḥyā's rebellion and his death marginalize his importance. Their accounts of the rebellion focus on the roles of high 'Abbāsid officials and governors. The most important such individual is al-Faḍl b. Yaḥyā al-Barmakī, but others also figure prominently in these reports. The revolt is used to explain changes in provincial appointments or to foreshadow subsequent political developments (i.e. the fall of the Barmakids). Sunnī historians frame Yaḥyā's encounter with 'Abd Allāh b. Muṣ'ab as representative of the breakdown of ties between the 'Abbāsids and the 'Alids. Each time Yaḥyā succeeds in appealing to al-Rashīd's sense of family and kinship, outside forces in the form of 'Abd Allāh b. Muṣ'ab or al-Faḍl b. al-Rabī' manage to subvert the reconciliation. In their reports of the breaking of the *amān*, Sunnī writers contrast the integrity of one jurist, al-Shaybānī, with the opportunism of another, Abū Bakhtarī, in order to explain their differing relationships with 'Abbāsid power. Yaḥyā fades into the background of these accounts with little to no agency. Sunnī sources also reference Yaḥyā in their accounts of the Barmakids, but again his role is subordinate to the main story: Ja'far al-Barmakī's decision to release him provides the family's enemies with the means to undermine their power and position. Yaḥyā's marginal status in the Sunnī sources is further accentuated through their apparent lack of interest in his death.

Al-Khaṭīb al-Baghdādī is the only Sunnī historian who treats Yaḥyā himself as a figure of central importance. This is particularly apparent in his reports of the rebellion and the controversy over the safe-conduct in which Yaḥyā and his seventy followers exercise considerable leverage

[63] Note again the substitution of Abū Yūsuf for al-Shaybānī.

over al-Rashīd. It is worth noting that the first of these narratives is explicitly ascribed to a Shīʿī source and bears a close resemblance to Zaydī accounts, as will be seen in section III. The remainder of al-Khaṭīb al-Baghdādī's biography aligns with Yaḥyā's portrayal in the other Sunnī sources.

III The Zaydī Sources

Zaydī accounts of this period of Yaḥyā's life are considerably more detailed than their Sunnī counterparts. Rather than casting him as a marginal actor in a grand ʿAbbāsid narrative, Zaydī writers emphasize Yaḥyā's standing as an Imām. For the Zaydī Shīʿa, a legitimate Imām must satisfy a number of conditions. These include ʿAlid descent through Ḥasan or Ḥusayn, the organization of an armed rebellion against tyrannical power, and a litany of personal attributes, including but not limited to scholarly excellence.[64] Zaydī authors debated the relative importance of these conditions through the centuries. These debates produced ambiguity regarding the status of prominent ʿAlids who did not meet all the necessary criteria for the Imāmate, particularly those who never achieved power or those who appeared complicit with tyrannical leaders. Yaḥyā b. ʿAbd Allāh falls squarely within both of these categories.

Zaydī reports of Yaḥyā consist of fluid, overlapping anecdotes that emphasize certain aspects of his personality. In this they differ from the Sunnī accounts, which rely on a small number of relatively discrete narrative elements in which Yaḥyā plays a secondary role. Although the Zaydī sources retain the core structure outlined in the first section of this chapter, their distinctive characteristics complicate any analysis. First, subtle shifts in chronology allow their writers to introduce several narrative elements concerning Yaḥyā's time in prison. Second, greater attention is given to the reasons for al-Rashīd's anger toward Yaḥyā, while less emphasis is placed on elements involving other figures (e.g. the encounter with ʿAbd Allāh b. Muṣʿab). Finally, Zaydī authors devote substantial space to Yaḥyā's death.

Proper examination of the Zaydī sources requires a different approach from the one taken in the previous section. The long, composite accounts and frequent textual diversions of Zaydī works are not

64 See Haider, "Zaydism," and *Shīʿī Islam*, 103–21.

suited to piecemeal analysis. For this reason, the following discussion tackles the Zaydī sources in a holistic manner. The narrative elements in each source are classified under three headings: (1) Yaḥyā's rebellion, (2) al-Rashīd's turn, and (3) prison life and death. These three chronological segments, which make up the core structure, provide the scaffolding for the subsequent analysis. The section concludes with a discussion of the central interpretive frameworks in the Zaydī sources.

A The Zaydī Accounts

Aḥmad b. Sahl al-Rāzī

The most comprehensive Zaydī treatment of the last eleven years of Yaḥyā's life is found in Aḥmad b. Sahl al-Rāzī's *Akhbār Fakhkh*, a text chiefly concerned with the events surrounding al-Ḥusayn b. ʿAlī's 169/786 rebellion in Medina. In the wake of the ʿAlid's defeat, al-Rāzī details the movements of Yaḥyā b. ʿAbd Allāh and his brother Idrīs. The information in these long sections recurs regularly in later Zaydī sources.

Yaḥyā's Rebellion

Zaydī depictions of Yaḥyā's rebellion are far more elaborate than their Sunnī equivalents. Whereas my analysis of the Sunnī sources combined the events preceding the rebellion and the acceptance of a safe-conduct under the single heading of the rebellion narrative, the Zaydī accounts require a more nuanced approach that distinguishes between multiple narrative elements.

The first relevant account preserved by al-Rāzī is a radical variant of the Sunnī rebellion narrative that establishes the basic parameters of Yaḥyā's organizational efforts while adding important details that shift the focus from al-Faḍl al-Barmakī and provincial politics to the increasing desperation of Yaḥyā's situation.[65] At the start of the account, Yaḥyā arrives in Daylam with seventy loyal followers, whom he then sends across the Muslim world to gather support. The text explicitly identifies sixteen scholars who decide to back the rebellion, including the famed jurist al-Shāfiʿī. These developments worry al-Rashīd to the extent that he swears off alcohol and dresses exclusively in rough wool. He then dispatches al-Faḍl b. Yaḥyā al-Barmakī at the head of an army

[65] Al-Rāzī, 184–98.

of 70,000 men[66] and offers Justān, the king of Daylam and Yaḥyā's protector, and his retinue large sums of money to abandon Yaḥyā. When al-Faḍl reaches Ṭālaqān, he lavishes further gifts on Justān and hints at significantly greater riches, but Justān initially refuses this overture. In the meantime, al-Rashīd begins a correspondence with Yaḥyā in which he promises him a safe-conduct and money in exchange for his surrender. Al-Rāzī quotes the text of a long, detailed letter in which Yaḥyā unequivocally rejects this proposal.

At this point, al-Rāzī transitions to a new narrative element that highlights the unreliability of Yaḥyā's supporters.[67] In this report, Abū Bakhtarī,[68] who is in Ṭālaqān as part of al-Faḍl's army, uses threats and coercion to summon important local leaders from the regions surrounding Daylam. He forces them to take oaths denying Yaḥyā b. ʿAbd Allāh's lineage and labeling him as one of the caliph's runaway slaves. This prompts Justān to ask Yaḥyā to verify his identity, given the overwhelming number of oaths to the contrary. In response, Yaḥyā first appeals to Justān on logical grounds, asking why the caliph would promise Justān such extravagant financial rewards for the return of a slave. Second, he offers Justān a lock of hair to send to Mecca and Medina, where people will affirm his identity. And third, he asks Justān to dispatch messengers to local cities to investigate whether the oaths were secured through intimidation. Justān's desire for wealth, however, renders him obstinate. Finally, Yaḥyā requests a face-to-face meeting with the oath-takers. Justān accepts this proposal and convenes a gathering with the help of Abū Bakhtarī. During the meeting, Yaḥyā delivers a passionate speech that almost convinces the oath-takers to recant. In the end, however, they are overcome by fear and remain silent. Yaḥyā forgives them for their weakness and, lacking any other options, agrees to the *amān*.[69]

Al-Rāzī's third narrative element describes the procurement and central stipulations of Yaḥyā's safe-conduct agreement.[70] Some of

[66] Note that the Sunnī sources put the size of the army at 50,000.
[67] Al-Rāzī, 198–207.
[68] Recall that Abū Bakhtarī is the jurist who invalidates the safe-conduct for al-Rashīd in both Sunnī and Zaydī accounts.
[69] In a later part of al-Rāzī's text (213), Justān receives his reward but is then struck with intense guilt and regret. His military commanders depose him and replace him with a slave who, like many others, was converted to Islam by Yaḥyā. The episode concludes with the slaves building a mosque over the house in which Yaḥyā resided during his time in Daylam.
[70] Al-Rāzī, 207–12.

this material resembles the contents of the Sunnī reports, in that al-Faḍl serves as an intermediary between Yaḥyā and al-Rashīd and the agreement is witnessed by the same members of the Banū Hāshim.[71] The narrative features the full text of the *amān*, which includes the following provisions: (i) an extension of the safe-conduct to seventy of Yaḥyā's unnamed followers, (ii) a guarantee of security from all of al-Rashīd's affiliates and associates, (iii) permission to live anywhere in the Muslim world without restriction or surveillance, and (iv) severe penalties for al-Rashīd in the event of violation (e.g. the automatic triple divorce of all his wives, the freeing of all his slaves, and the invalidation of his oath of authority). Al-Rashīd accepts all of these terms. Yaḥyā secures a similar safe-conduct from al-Faḍl al-Barmakī.

The final element in this section describes Yaḥyā's arrival in Baghdad.[72] Al-Rashīd arranges a lavish welcome and houses him in a large residence. He also orders prominent members of the Banū Hāshim to honor him and presents him with 400,000 *dīnārs* as a gift.

al-Rashīd's Turn

Al-Khaṭīb al-Baghdādī is the only Sunnī historian to posit a reason for al-Rashīd's imprisonment of Yaḥyā, explicitly mentioning the ʿAlid's refusal to identify his followers by name. By contrast, al-Rāzī and the other Zaydī writers discuss this subject at great length as a means for assessing the extent of Yaḥyā's active resistance.

Al-Rāzī's first explanation for al-Rashīd's anger centers on Yaḥyā's activities in Medina.[73] In the prototypical version of this episode, Yaḥyā settles in the Ḥijāz and distributes his newly acquired wealth to family members and other prominent Arabs. The assumption here is that the money is used to compensate ʿAlids who fell into debt after their defeat at Fakhkh in 169/786. This development alarms Bakkār b. ʿAbd Allāh b. Muṣʿab, the governor of the region, who writes to al-Rashīd and

[71] Al-Rāzī's text differs with respect to one name. It replaces al-Ṭabarī's "Muḥammad b. Ibrāhīm" with "Ibrāhīm b. Muḥammad." Jarrar (al-Rāzī, 207) identifies the latter as Ibrāhīm b. Muḥammad al-Mahdī b. ʿAbd Allāh al-Manṣūr (b. 162/779–224/839). This is unlikely, given Ibrāhīm's young age at the time of the *amān* agreement. The correct name is probably Muḥammad b. Ibrāhīm, with the reversal due to a scribal or transmission error. For Ibrāhīm b. Muḥammad, see al-Khaṭīb al-Baghdādī, 6:140–5; al-Ziriklī, 1:59–60.

[72] Al-Rāzī, 213–14. [73] Ibid., 214.

reports that Yaḥyā has set himself up as a rival caliph.[74] The persistence of these letters eventually effects a change in the caliph's attitude toward Yaḥyā.

A second explanation for al-Rashīd's anger relates to the previously mentioned argument between Yaḥyā and 'Abd Allāh b. Muṣ'ab al-Zubayrī at the 'Abbāsid court. Al-Rāzī offers three versions of this "Zubayrid encounter" narrative. The first is virtually identical to the reports preserved in the Sunnī sources and features a bemused narrator admiring Yaḥyā's ability to divert suspicion from himself by accusing 'Abd Allāh of composing an elegy for Muḥammad al-Nafs al-Zakiyya.[75] The account quotes large chunks of the purported poem and ends with the oath that results in 'Abd Allāh's death. The second version simply summarizes the incident, offering only one line of the seditious poem.[76] The third version is distinguished by its description of 'Abd Allāh's funeral.[77] Specifically, Masrūr[78] (d. after 219/834) relates three burial attempts that fail because of the sudden appearance of sinkholes. This detail underscores Yaḥyā's power and piety at 'Abd Allāh's expense.

Al-Rāzī's third explanation focuses on Yaḥyā's refusal to disclose the identities of the seventy companions protected by the *amān*.[79] In the main account, al-Rashīd asks jurists and other prominent Qurashīs to convince Yaḥyā, who is already in prison, to divulge the names of his followers.[80] The caliph tells them that he wishes to avoid inadvertently violating the terms of the safe-conduct. Yaḥyā recognizes this as a ruse and argues that revealing this information would make him complicit in his followers' deaths. The jurists relay this answer to al-Rashīd, who admits that he intends to kill the named men. The account then skips forward to the next day, when al-Rashīd convenes a second meeting. This time Yaḥyā is brought to the court and does not answer any

74 In a second version (214–15), al-Rāzī summarizes Bakkār's accusation while preserving the wider framework of this account.
75 Ibid., 215–22. 76 Ibid., 222. 77 Ibid., 232–3.
78 Masrūr, a servant of the Banū Hāshim, was given considerable responsibilities during al-Rashīd's reign. See, for example, al-Ṭabarī, 5:124 (taking custody of a prisoner) and 5:207 (leading a contingent of cavalry that protected Mecca during the Ḥajj). According to al-Ṭabarī (5:213), Masrūr was still alive during the reign of al-Mu'taṣim (r. 218–27/833–42).
79 There is some overlap between this narrative element and al-Khaṭīb al-Baghdādī's variant of the *amān* narrative.
80 Al-Rāzī, 225–7.

questions. Instead, he sticks out a yellowed tongue that indicates poisoning. Al-Rashīd argues that this a trick, but the truth is inadvertently revealed by his servant Masrūr.[81]

Al-Rāzī preserves two variants of the narrative element in which al-Rashīd invalidates the *amān*. In the first, narrated by Muḥammad al-Shaybānī, the caliph gathers several jurists for the express purpose of securing a justification for Yaḥyā's execution.[82] Al-Shaybānī examines the safe-conduct agreement and rules that there are no possible means for its nullification. This infuriates al-Rashīd, who strikes al-Shaybānī on the head with an inkpot. The other jurists offer similar opinions, albeit with less emphatic language to avoid the caliph's wrath. The only exception is Abū Bakhtarī, who states that if al-Faḍl al-Barmakī testifies that he acted with false intentions at the time of the agreement, his testimony would be grounds for its annulment. Al-Rashīd then summons the Barmakids (Yaḥyā and his sons Jaʿfar and al-Faḍl) and asks al-Faḍl whether he concluded the agreement with false intent. Al-Faḍl adamantly denies this and defends his honesty. The caliph asks him the same question three times, growing increasingly agitated. Abū Bakhtarī realizes that he is making dangerous enemies of the Barmakids, so he intervenes, tearing the agreement in half and assuming responsibility for Yaḥyā's fate.

To this point, al-Rāzī's account is quite similar to versions preserved in the Sunnī sources, albeit with some additional details, such as the inkpot. Its distinctiveness stems from Yaḥyā's response to Abū Bakhtarī's actions. Specifically, he unleashes a scathing critique of the jurist, questioning both his lineage and his integrity. He then beseeches al-Rashīd to fear God and refrain from tyranny by quoting a series of Qur'ānic passages (Q25:27–8 and Q40:52). The caliph notes that Yaḥyā did not refer to him with the appropriate title as "the Commander of the Faithful" and asks the jurists whether this omission is grounds for discarding the safe-conduct. Yaḥyā replies that the Prophet was content with being called Muḥammad by his followers even though God named him "the Messenger of God." If a modest appellation was sufficient for the Prophet, Yaḥyā asks, why is it not sufficient for al-Rashīd? Such combative descriptions of Yaḥyā are

[81] The naming issue is also mentioned in the next section as part of a narrative in which an imprisoned Yaḥyā cooks food for the caliph.

[82] Al-Rāzī, 223–5.

absent from the Sunnī sources, where he is either silent or absent throughout this episode.

Al-Rāzī's second variant of the "*amān* break" narrative closely resembles the first in terms of structure.[83] It begins with the jurists assembled in front of a fettered Yaḥyā. Muḥammad al-Shaybānī again emphatically confirms the agreement, prompting al-Rashīd to strike him with an inkpot. Abū Bakhtarī then proposes a means of annulment that involves al-Faḍl al-Barmakī, but he ultimately tears the agreement in half himself. In response, Yaḥyā severely criticizes Abū Bakhtarī and appeals directly to the caliph. An argument ensues over Yaḥyā's use of the caliph's first name. This report is primarily distinguished by an extended discussion of al-Shaybānī's regret over not contesting Abū Bakhtarī in a more aggressive manner. Even as his colleagues reassure him that he had no real choice, al-Shaybānī expresses his fear of punishment in the afterlife.

Prison Life and Death

A key feature of the Zaydī accounts is their depiction of Yaḥyā's experiences in prison. Al-Rāzī offers two narrative elements that fit in this category. The first is similar to the "Barmakids' fall" narrative mentioned in the Sunnī sources, whereas the second describes an incident involving food that foregrounds Yaḥyā's piety.

Al-Rāzī's variant of the "Barmakids' fall" narrative opens with Yaḥyā in the custody of Ja'far al-Barmakī in Baghdad.[84] Al-Rashīd asks about the 'Alid, and curses when Ja'far replies that he is healthy and well. The caliph's reaction is meant to communicate his desire for Yaḥyā's death. The exchange prompts Ja'far to summon Yaḥyā from prison with the intention of killing him. Before he can do so, however, Yaḥyā makes a speech in which he warns Ja'far of the punishment that awaits him in the hereafter, asks him to choose God over al-Rashīd, and proposes fleeing to a distant region outside the 'Abbāsid empire. These words move Ja'far, who returns Yaḥyā to his cell and takes some time to consider the situation. During their second meeting, Ja'far confesses to having committed many sins. He asks whether these sins would be forgiven if he were to release Yaḥyā. Yaḥyā says that all sins other than polytheism are forgivable as long as an individual is truly repentant, does not repeat the sin, and subsequently fulfills his religious

[83] Ibid., 234–5. [84] Ibid., 236–9.

obligations. Jaʿfar frees Yaḥyā on the condition that he proceeds to Byzantine territory, remains there for the duration of al-Rashīd's reign, and travels alone without revealing his identity to anyone. He is given papers to guarantee his safety along the way.

Before he reaches Byzantium, however, Yaḥyā is captured by the ʿAbbāsid governor of the border region, Muḥammad b. Khālid b. Barmak (d. after 187/803), who is Jaʿfar's uncle.[85] The discovery of Yaḥyā's identity unnerves Muḥammad, who correctly ascertains that Jaʿfar has acted on his own volition. Should al-Rashīd learn of Jaʿfar's actions, it would mean certain disaster for the entire Barmakid family. Muḥammad personally accompanies Yaḥyā to Mecca, where he informs al-Faḍl b. al-Rabīʿ of the situation on the condition that his innocence is communicated to the caliph. Al-Faḍl passes the information (and presumably Yaḥyā himself) to al-Rashīd, who is angered by the betrayal but follows the advice of his general Harthama b. Aʿyan[86] (d. 200/816) and continues to treat the Barmakids kindly until they are all present in Baghdad. He then swiftly disposes of them and seizes their wealth. Jaʿfar and al-Faḍl are killed in the initial purge,[87] whereas their father, Yaḥyā, is imprisoned and their uncle Muḥammad is spared.[88] At the end of the report, al-Rashīd accuses Yaḥyā of corrupting his officials and thereby causing their deaths. In response, Yaḥyā warns him of the afterlife and asks him to repent. He (Yaḥyā) is eventually remanded to the custody of Masrūr.

Al-Rāzī's second prison narrative takes an interest in Yaḥyā's culinary skills.[89] The account begins with al-Rashīd learning that Yaḥyā cooks his own meals in prison. He dispatches a servant, Aslam, to request some of the food. Yaḥyā sends over a bowl, which al-Rashīd eats with bread. He is so enraptured with the meal that he picks scraps of onion off the sides of the dish. Al-Rashīd then orders another servant, Masrūr, to give Yaḥyā an extravagant amount of cloth as compensation for the food. After a long pause, Yaḥyā rejects the gift,

85 Muḥammad b. Khālid b. Barmak is most famous for surviving the purge that claimed that rest of his family. He served as al-Rashīd's chamberlain from 172/788 until 179/795 when he was replaced by al-Faḍl b. al-Rabī. See al-Ṭabarī, 4:641.

86 For Harthama b. Aʿyan, see al-Ziriklī, 8:81; *EI*[2], s.v. "Harthama b. Aʿyan" (C. Pellat).

87 By contrast, most other sources report that al-Faḍl was imprisoned in Raqqa along with his father, Yaḥyā. See *EI*[2], s.v. "Al-Barāmika" (D. Sourdel).

88 For his survival, see also al-Ṭabarī, 4:662.

89 Al-Rāzī, 227–8.

noting that it is of no benefit to a prisoner awaiting execution. Instead, he beseeches the caliph to fear God, ignore slanderous accusations, and spare him. Masrūr is moved by these words but is understandably unwilling to convey them to al-Rashīd. Eventually, he returns and describes his exchange with Yaḥyā. At this point, this episode intersects with the "companion naming" narrative, as al-Rashīd promises, through Masrūr, to release Yaḥyā, grant him 1,000,000 *dīnārs*, award him estates, and allow him to live in the region of his choosing in exchange for the names of his seventy companions. Yaḥyā categorically rejects the offer.

Finally, al-Rāzī presents four narrative elements that pertain to Yaḥyā's death. The first three identify starvation as the primary cause of his demise, and a fourth, unique to al-Rāzī, suggests that he escaped the 'Abbāsids and spent the remainder of his life in hiding.

The first of al-Rāzī's three starvation narratives begins with al-Rashīd cursing Yaḥyā's jailor, Aslam, upon learning of the 'Alid's robust health.[90] Masrūr, another servant, explains to Aslam that the caliph desires the death of his enemy. Yaḥyā is then sequestered in a cell and denied food and water, but he manages to survive on some meat concealed in his trousers. Seven days later, Aslam confronts Yaḥyā while he is praying and asks him to explain the reasons for his rebellion. When Yaḥyā, who is in the middle of prayer, does not respond, Aslam curses him and calls him a bastard. After Yaḥyā completes his prayer, he physically assaults Aslam three times. The text implies that he exercised restraint, since otherwise he could have easily killed him. Yaḥyā then asks him which of his (Yaḥyā's) female forebears – illustrious figures beginning with Fāṭima bt. Muḥammad – he is accusing of adultery. Aslam scrambles away and orders his guards to search Yaḥyā for food, observing that a man denied sustenance for seven days could not have such strength. The guards discover the meat and confiscate it. Three days later Aslam returns. This time he tells the guards to remain vigilant in case he is attacked again. He finds Yaḥyā dead, his body stuck in the act of prostration but rolled on to the side. Aslam transfers him to a comfortable room to give the appearance of a natural death. Once assured that the corpse bears no incriminating marks, al-Rashīd invites witnesses to examine it.

90 Ibid., 228–30.

The second starvation narrative shares with the first the broad outlines of Yaḥyā's death, but nests them within an account of a sea voyage.[91] The narrator is an unnamed traveler on a ship from Mawṣil to Baghdad. He recalls an argument between passengers over whether Yaḥyā was killed by the sword or by starvation. One of the passengers, who identifies himself as Yaḥyā's jailor for al-Rashīd, relates a tale that largely agrees with the first starvation narrative. In this account, however, the jailor checks on Yaḥyā every three days and is surprised by his ability to survive and even prosper without sustenance. It is noteworthy that each time the jailor enters his room, Yaḥyā is in the midst of prayer. After three days, al-Rashīd orders a search of Yaḥyā's cell. After six days, he is incensed and orders another, more thorough, search, pointing out that no man could survive so many days without food or water. This time the jailors remove Yaḥyā's clothes, despite his objection that a strip search is below the dignity of a descendant of the Prophet. They then find and confiscate the hidden meat. Three days later, Yaḥyā's dead body is discovered in the act of prostration. The caliph orders it moved to hide the true circumstances of his imprisonment. The account ends when, later in the voyage, a young man pushes the jailor overboard. When the narrator scolds him, the man replies that the jailor was unremorseful about his role in the killing of a descendant of the Prophet.

Al-Rāzī's third starvation account is an addendum attached to the narratives about Yaḥyā's encounter with ʿAbd Allāh b. Muṣʿab al-Zubayrī and al-Rashīd's consumption of Yaḥyā's food.[92] In this report, al-Rashīd places Yaḥyā in the custody of Masrūr after the death and failed burial of ʿAbd Allāh b. Muṣʿab. A version of the "cooked food" narrative follows, in which al-Rashīd requests a second serving of Yaḥyā's meal. When Yaḥyā replies that he has no more food, the caliph expresses sympathy and reassures him about his safety. Yaḥyā, however, recognizes the falseness of these words and discloses his awareness of al-Rashīd's murderous intentions. He is then confined to his cell without food or water. The remainder of the episode follows the structure of the first starvation narrative.

Al-Rāzī's fourth death-related narrative element is unique in that Yaḥyā survives for many more years.[93] At the start of the report, some gravediggers are ordered to dig a pit (as opposed to a grave) in the

91 Ibid., 230–2. 92 Ibid., 233–4. 93 Ibid., 239–41.

ground. Surmising that it will be used to bury treasure, they decide to hide in a nearby tree and see what happens. In the middle of the night, a party clothed in white appears, with a man – Yaḥyā – tied to a horse, and a coffin. First the coffin is lowered into the pit, and then Yaḥyā is enclosed within it. All the while, he is beseeching al-Rashīd to fear God and final judgment. After the party departs, the gravediggers realize that they are complicit in this cruel act and decide to free the buried man. They dig up the coffin and revive Yaḥyā before refilling the pit so that it appears unaltered. The account concludes with disagreement over whether Yaḥyā eventually settled in Turkish regions outside 'Abbāsid territory or in Qūmis in Persia at the home of a supporter. The narrator favors the latter possibility, and even suggests that Yaḥyā married and raised a family.

al-Iṣbahānī

Al-Iṣbahānī's treatment of Yaḥyā b. 'Abd Allāh is similar to that of al-Rāzī, but it includes variants of narrative elements that alter Yaḥyā's image in a number of important ways. The initial section of al-Iṣbahānī's text recounts Yaḥyā's lineage, noting that he was raised by al-Ṣādiq and served as one of the executors of his will. The narrative then skips forward to Yaḥyā's rebellion.

Yaḥyā's Rebellion

There are significant parallels between al-Iṣbahānī's and al-Rāzī's accounts of Yaḥyā's activities in Daylam.[94] Al-Iṣbahānī, however, includes far fewer details, drawing primarily on narratives that describe Yaḥyā's organizational efforts, his betrayal by local notables, and his return to Baghdad. These elements are reduced to brief references: Yaḥyā appears in Daylam, he recruits supporters, he is challenged by the arrival of Faḍl al-Barmakī, his support dissipates due to bribery (without naming Justān), and he agrees to an *amān* (with no mention of the actual stipulations). The text culminates in Yaḥyā's return to Baghdad.[95]

[94] Al-Iṣbahānī, 389–90 and 392–4.

[95] Some aspects of al-Iṣbahānī's account intersect with that of al-Ṭabarī. For example, both texts depict Yaḥyā responding to a question posed by 'Abd Allāh b. Mūsā with lines of poetry ascribed to the Jewish poet Ḥuya b. Akhṭāb al-Naḍarī (d. 5/626). For Ḥuya, see al-Ziriklī, 2:292.

The most distinctive narrative element in this part of al-Iṣbahānī's text centers on the tensions between Yaḥyā and his Kūfan followers.[96] The fraying of this relationship is epitomized by Yaḥyā's interactions with one of the leaders of the Kūfan Zaydīs, Ibn Ḥasan b. Ṣāliḥ b. Ḥayy[97] (d. late second/eighth century). Al-Iṣbahānī describes Ibn Ḥasan as a "Batrī" Zaydī, meaning that he affirmed the caliphates of Abū Bakr, ʿUmar, and ʿUthmān (for the first six years of his reign) and adhered to a ritual practice that included the permissibility of date wine (*nabīdh*) and the wiping of leather socks during ablution (*masḥ ʿalā al-khuffayn*).[98] Yaḥyā's opposition to these views had serious consequences.[99]

Al-Iṣbahānī records two incidents in which Ibn Ḥasan actively undermines Yaḥyā's authority. In the first, Yaḥyā approaches his companions after completing his ritual ablution and finds that they have already begun to pray behind Ibn Ḥasan. Since he disagrees with Ibn Ḥasan's practice of wiping leather socks, Yaḥyā moves to the side and prays alone. This prompts an angry Ibn Ḥasan to observe that the Kūfan Zaydīs are sacrificing their lives for an Imām who refuses to pray with them. In the second incident, Yaḥyā receives a present of honeycomb and decides to share it with those around him. When Ibn Ḥasan objects that the honeycomb is the joint property of all the Shīʿa, Yaḥyā explains that gifts are not subject to communal rules. Instead of responding to the particulars of this explanation, Ibn Ḥasan argues that Yaḥyā's actions suggest an inclination toward injustice. Both reports epitomize the fragmentation and unreliability of Yaḥyā's Kūfan supporters.

al-Rashīd's Turn

Al-Iṣbahānī preserves four narrative elements that explain al-Rashīd's animosity toward Yaḥyā. The first two are variants of the "Zubayrid encounter" and "companion naming" narratives. Al-Iṣbahānī's version

96 Al-Iṣbahānī, 392.

97 Little is known about Ibn Ḥasan. His father was a prominent Batrī Zaydī traditionist who died in Kūfa in 168/784–5 and is found in the standard Sunnī *rijāl* works. See *EI*², s.v. "Al-Ḥasan b. Ṣāliḥ b. Ḥayy" (C. Pellat); Ibn Saʿd, 6:353; al-Mizzī, 6:177–91; al-Ziriklī, 2:193.

98 Haider, *The Origins of the Shīʿa*, 189–214.

99 This conflict is discussed in greater detail below. See also Haider, *The Origins of the Shīʿa*, 189–214 and "Yaḥyā b. ʿAbd Allāh"; Jarrar, "Aspects of Imāmī Influence."

of the former is substantially more detailed and elaborate than al-Rāzī's version.[100] At the start of the report, Yaḥyā attributes 'Abd Allāh b. Muṣ'ab's slander to a long history of hatred between the Zubayrids and the Banū Hāshim. He mentions the seditious poem only after 'Abd Allāh persists in accusing him of treason. The episode then follows a typical course. It concludes by mentioning the difficulties associated with 'Abd Allāh's burial, and even adds a section that questions his purported lineage.

Al-Iṣbahānī's version of the "companion naming" narrative,[101] in which al-Rashīd demands that Yaḥyā disclose the identities of his supporters, closely follows that of al-Rāzī.[102] In both reports, Yaḥyā categorically refuses to betray his followers. In al-Iṣbahānī's telling, he appears in court a few days later, unable to speak and very close to death. Al-Iṣbahānī places this incident near the end of Yaḥyā's biography, and explicitly affirms that he was poisoned.

Al-Iṣbahānī's variant of the narrative depicting Yaḥyā's activities in Medina begins with al-Rashīd gifting Yaḥyā 200,000 *dīnārs*.[103] Despite this act of generosity, the caliph remains secretly hostile toward the 'Alid, and aggressively seeks a justification for his imprisonment. One day, he arrests a man named Faḍāla, who is discovered soliciting support for Yaḥyā. Al-Rashīd compels Faḍāla to write to Yaḥyā, falsely informing him that he has won over most of the caliph's companions and military commanders. When the letter reaches Yaḥyā, he immediately seizes the messenger and brings him to Yaḥyā b. Khālid al-Barmakī. This act of loyalty assuages some of al-Rashīd's concerns. According to al-Iṣbahānī, however, Faḍāla had previously instructed Yaḥyā to refuse any correspondence from him. The rejection of the letter was thus a prearranged ruse designed to shield Yaḥyā from suspicion. Yaḥyā's reprieve is only temporary: al-Rashīd continues to receive reports from Medinans, particularly 'Abd Allāh b. Muṣ'ab and Abū Bakhtarī, concerning his subversive activities. Yaḥyā is eventually arrested and remanded to the custody of Masrūr in Baghdad. Al-Iṣbahānī later adds a postscript to this narrative, noting that Yaḥyā

100 Al-Iṣbahānī, 396–400. 101 Ibid., 403.

102 This narrative element partly resembles al-Khaṭīb al-Baghdādī's "*amān* break" narrative. The similarities may stem from their common ascription to 'Abd al-Raḥmān b. 'Abd Allāh al-'Umarī.

103 Al-Iṣbahānī, 394–5.

spent the money he received from al-Rashīd to settle the debts of al-Ḥusayn b. 'Alī's family.[104]

Al-Iṣbahānī includes an additional explanation for al-Rashīd's anger that is not mentioned by al-Rāzī.[105] In this report, the caliph summons Yaḥyā to answer charges of sedition and conspiracy. In court, Yaḥyā produces his copy of the safe-conduct for inspection but refuses to release one corner of it. The remarkable nature of this scene inspires an astonished observer to recall and recite a poem that infuriates al-Rashīd.[106] An exchange follows in which Yaḥyā readily acknowledges al-Rashīd's superiority in appearance, wealth, and generosity. The tone shifts, however, when the caliph asks Yaḥyā to compare 'Alid and 'Abbāsid kinship to the Prophet. After initially refusing to answer, Yaḥyā observes that the Prophet could hypothetically marry al-Rashīd's daughter but not Yaḥyā's daughter, since the latter would be considered too closely related. While this contrast establishes the superiority of the 'Alid claim to the Prophet, it also prompts al-Rashīd to return Yaḥyā to prison.

Al-Iṣbahānī's pared-down version of the "*amān* break" narrative features the familiar gathering of jurists that includes al-Shaybānī, Abū Bakhtarī, and al-Ḥasan b. Ziyād al-Lu'lu'ī[107] (d. 204/819).[108] Instead of communicating with these men directly, al-Rashīd uses Masrūr as his intermediary. As in previous versions, the only jurist willing to repudiate the agreement is Abū Bakhtarī, who predicates his decision on Yaḥyā's sedition.[109] Masrūr relays this ruling to al-Rashīd, who then orders Abū Bakhtarī to physically destroy the document. The report describes Abū Bakhtarī's hand trembling as he cuts the *amān* into strips. The caliph rewards him with an exorbitant sum of money and appoints him to the post of chief judge. He also prohibits al-Shaybānī, who upheld the safe-conduct, from issuing legal rulings for a long time. Despite their differences, al-Iṣbahānī's and al-Rāzī's

104 Ibid., 404. 105 Ibid., 395–6.

106 This detail is also present in al-Khaṭīb al-Baghdādī's "*amān* break" narrative.

107 Al-Ḥasan b. Ziyād al-Lu'lu'ī was a Kūfan Ḥanafī jurist who served briefly as a judge in Kūfa before settling in Baghdad. See al-Ziriklī, 2:191; al-Khaṭīb al-Baghdādī, 7:325–8.

108 Al-Iṣbahānī, 401.

109 The account notes that Yaḥyā had previously shown the *amān* to Mālik b. Anas (d. 179/796) and 'Abd al-'Azīz b. Muḥammad al-Darāwardī (d. 186/802), both of whom deemed it unassailable.

accounts share the same narrative structure and serve a similar end, namely, exposing al-Rashīd's duplicity.

Prison Life and Death

Al-Iṣbahānī includes two versions of the "Barmakids' fall" narrative in his work. The first is virtually identical to the second variant preserved in the Sunnī sources, in which an unidentified man secretly informs al-Rashīd of Yaḥyā's escape.[110] Al-Iṣbahānī's second version combines elements of al-Rāzī's account with the first variant found in the Sunnī sources,[111] but it is distinguished by the fact that Yaḥyā, sensing al-Rashīd's anger, asks al-Faḍl b. al-Barmakī's (rather than Ja'far's) permission to perform the Ḥajj (as opposed to seeking refuge with the Byzantines). The caliph learns of Yaḥyā's release from an unnamed informant, rather than from al-Faḍl b. al-Rabī'. The remainder of the episode proceeds as expected, with the caliph confronting al-Faḍl al-Barmakī, forcing him to admit the truth, and secretly vowing to destroy the Barmakids. The importance of these differences seems minimal, as both accounts showcase Yaḥyā's charismatic ability to win over the Barmakids.

Many of al-Iṣbahānī's reports of Yaḥyā's death are fairly brief. These statements attribute his demise to live burial under a column near al-Rashīd's residence in Raqqa,[112] strangulation by an agent who sneaks into his cell at night, poisoning, or exposure to a hungry lion.[113] Their sheer number reflects the issue's importance for Zaydī authors.

Al-Iṣbahānī's primary death narrative, which is not mentioned by al-Rāzī, features the testimony of an unnamed fellow prisoner who recounts Yaḥyā's slow starvation.[114] The report begins in the middle of the night as al-Rashīd arrives at the prison and orders Yaḥyā brought forth and struck a hundred times with a cane. All the while, Yaḥyā is beseeching al-Rashīd to remember God and their kinship to the Prophet and each other. The caliph rejects these pleas, continues the beating, and eventually returns him to his cell. He then orders the jailor to reduce Yaḥyā's already meager rations of food and water – four loaves of bread

110 Al-Iṣbahānī, 390–2. For the Sunnī variant, see Table 4.2.

111 Ibid., 394–5. For the Sunnī variant, see Table 4.2.

112 The text reads "al-Rāfiqa," which Yāqūt (3:17) identifies as a region near Raqqa on the Euphrates in present-day northern Syria. Note that Raqqa was al-Rashīd's capital for much of the year.

113 For all of these, see al-Iṣbahānī, 403.

114 Ibid., 401–3.

and eight measures (*arṭāl*, sing. *raṭl*) of water – by half.[115] The same procedure is repeated some nights later. When al-Rashīd returns a third time, Yaḥyā is sick and quite weak. The caliph orders the ration cut in half for a third time, leaving Yaḥyā with half a loaf of bread and one measure of water. He dies soon thereafter.

al-Nāṭiq bi-l-Ḥaqq Yaḥyā b. Ḥusayn

Al-Nāṭiq's biography of Yaḥyā incorporates much of the material recorded by al-Rāzī and al-Iṣbahānī. It also includes one additional narrative element that pertains to Yaḥyā's time in prison. On the whole, al-Nāṭiq constructs a clear and coherent chronology from scattered reports drawn from other Zaydī sources.

Yaḥyā's Rebellion

Al-Nāṭiq's portrayal of Yaḥyā's rebellion closely resembles previous accounts.[116] He offers a fleeting version of the narrative in which Yaḥyā arrives in Daylam with seventy loyal companions after a long period of wandering and begins to organize his rebellion. The caliph sends al-Faḍl al-Barmakī to deal with the situation. In his version of the "betrayal by local notables" narrative, al-Nāṭiq notes the decline in support for Yaḥyā but does not mention the stratagem of false oaths devised by Abū Bakhtarī.[117] Instead, he attributes the decline to the machinations of the king's wife, who fears the consequences of resisting al-Rashīd. The section ends with a brief version of Yaḥyā's return to Baghdad.[118] Al-Nāṭiq provides no details about the stipulations of the *amān* agreement.

al-Rashīd's Turn

In al-Nāṭiq's account, Yaḥyā remains in Baghdad for a time before setting out for Medina. The reason for this move is explained in the next section on Yaḥyā's imprisonment and death. In Medina, Yaḥyā distributes the money he has received from al-Rashīd to close members of his family and settles debts associated with the rebellion of al-Ḥusayn b. ʿAlī.[119] This worries the caliph, who orders Yaḥyā to return to Baghdad and then confronts him with evidence of his subversive

115 According to Lane (*Arabic–English Lexicon*, 3:1102), a *raṭl* is equal to twelve ounces.

116 Al-Nāṭiq, 99–100. 117 Ibid., 100–1. 118 Ibid., 101. 119 Ibid., 102.

activities. Specifically, he accuses Yaḥyā of dispatching agents to various parts of the Muslim world to recruit on his behalf. The fact that al-Nāṭiq does not contest these charges as slander suggests that they have some basis in truth.

Al-Nāṭiq's version of the "*amān* break" narrative is nearly identical to that of al-Iṣbahānī.[120] After Yaḥyā returns to Baghdad, al-Rashīd convenes a group of jurists to evaluate the validity of the agreement. Al-Shaybānī deems it unassailable, Ḥasan b. Ziyād affirms it quietly out of fear of offending the caliph, and Abū Bakhtarī repudiates it in order to win the caliph's favor. Al-Rashīd punishes al-Shaybānī by prohibiting him from issuing legal rulings and rewards Abū Bakhtarī by appointing him chief judge.

Most writers use the "Zubayrid encounter" and "companion naming" narratives to explain al-Rashīd's anger at Yaḥyā. Al-Nāṭiq, by contrast, discusses these reports much later in the context of Yaḥyā's imprisonment. For the sake of consistency, however, I will discuss them in the current section. Al-Nāṭiq's version of Yaḥyā's encounter with ʿAbd Allāh b. Muṣʿab begins with the latter claiming that he was approached by one of Yaḥyā's agents in Medina. Yaḥyā responds with the familiar diversion, charging ʿAbd Allāh with the composition of an elegy for al-Nafs al-Zakiyya. The remainder of the report follows the standard form. Yaḥyā recites only one line of the alleged poem, but the provocation compels the mutual oaths that culminate in ʿAbd Allāh's demise. Al-Nāṭiq admits to some disagreement regarding the actual circumstances of his death. The report concludes with al-Rashīd returning Yaḥyā to prison. In al-Nāṭiq's "companion naming" narrative, Yaḥyā is incarcerated without food or water and is repeatedly but unsuccessfully pressured by al-Rashīd to reveal the identities of his supporters.[121]

Prison Life and Death

Al-Nāṭiq relates two narrative elements pertaining to Yaḥyā's life in prison. The first is a brief variant of the "Barmakids' fall" narrative that parallels al-Iṣbahānī's second account.[122] In this version, al-Faḍl al-Barmakī gives Yaḥyā permission to travel from Baghdad to Medina without consulting al-Rashīd. This enrages the caliph and fuels his decision to remove the Barmakid family from power. Al-Nāṭiq concedes

[120] Ibid., 102–3. [121] Ibid., 107. [122] Ibid., 101.

the problematic nature of this account in view of the myriad contradictory reports.

Al-Nāṭiq's second prison narrative is not recorded by al-Rāzī or al-Iṣbahānī.[123] It relates to Yaḥyā's regular performance of a ritual prostration extending from the end of his night prayer to just before dawn. Al-Rashīd would often secretly observe him. One night, the caliph instructs Yaḥyā al-Barmakī to examine the spot where Yaḥyā b. 'Abd Allāh places his forehead during the prostration. He discovers a small white patch of moisture. After a little while, al-Rashīd orders another inspection, and this time Yaḥyā al-Barmakī reports that the patch has disappeared. The caliph then observes that Yaḥyā b. 'Abd Allāh, too, will soon disappear (i.e. die), like the white patch. Yaḥyā al-Barmakī is displeased by this comparison but conceals his sympathy for the 'Alid. Some time later, Yaḥyā is passed to the custody of the Barmakids, who treat him with leniency and respect. One day, he tells his jailor, Yaḥyā a-Barmakī, that al-Rashīd will soon have him killed. He then asks him to convey a handwritten note to the caliph after his death. The note, it is later revealed, informs al-Rashīd that he has lost the opportunity for repentance.

Instead of extended narratives, al-Nāṭiq lists a number of possible causes for Yaḥyā's death that include starvation, poisoning, strangulation, and live burial.[124] The "white patch" narrative, however, strongly suggests foul play. In the end, al-Nāṭiq attributes Yaḥyā's death to a combination of starvation and poisoning. According to this report, the caliph first denies Yaḥyā food and water, which leaves him in a weakened state, and then orders his poisoning.

'Alī b. Bilāl

'Alī b. Bilāl begins his account of Yaḥyā b. 'Abd Allāh with a lengthy description of his travels after the defeat at Fakhkh. As he journeys from region to region, Yaḥyā converts many nonbelievers and attracts widespread support. He eventually finds refuge with the Turks, but then decides to return to Daylam out of a sense of obligation to those who have taken the oath of allegiance to him.

[123] Ibid., 106–7. [124] Ibid., 107.

Yaḥyā's Rebellion

ʿAlī b. Bilāl includes all four of the rebellion narrative elements found in al-Rāzī's text. The section opens with Yaḥyā plotting a revolt with the help of seventy companions. His preparations compel al-Rashīd to dispatch al-Faḍl al-Barmakī to the region at the head of a large army.[125] ʿAlī b. Bilāl mentions the presence of Abū Bakhtarī in the ʿAbbāsid army, thereby alluding to the false oaths stratagem that turns the king of Daylam against Yaḥyā.[126] As in al-Nāṭiq's account, here, too, the king's wife is directly implicated in the betrayal. ʿAlī b. Bilāl's discussion of the stipulations of the safe-conduct agreement focuses mainly on the legal consequences of violation for al-Rashīd, such as the divorce of his wives, the freeing of his slaves, and the forfeiture of his property.[127] The section concludes with Yaḥyā's return to Baghdad, where al-Rashīd makes a false show of honoring him.[128]

al-Rashīd's Turn

ʿAlī b. Bilāl mentions two narrative elements that explain al-Rashīd's anger toward Yaḥyā. While the overall text strongly implies that al-Rashīd always intended to kill Yaḥyā, these reports provide more substantive reasons. The first is a distinctive variant of the "Medinan activities" narrative, in which Yaḥyā travels to the Ḥijāz for the Ḥajj soon after his return to Baghdad.[129] During his stay in Mecca, Yaḥyā is visited by many figures associated with the Ḥasanid branch of the ʿAlids. When his identity is revealed to the general population during the pilgrimage, a large crowd gathers around him, compelling him to flee to his home. The report reflects the extent of Yaḥyā's charisma and the breadth of his support. It is followed by the statement that some Medinans, such as the Zubayrids and al-Faḍl b. al-Rabīʿ, slandered Yaḥyā to the caliph.

The second of ʿAlī b. Bilāl's reports is a detailed variant of the "lineage comparison" narrative.[130] The substance of this text closely follows al-Iṣbahānī's version, but linguistic variations suggest a different provenance. The account starts with an argument between al-Rashīd and Yaḥyā during which the latter repeatedly references the safe-conduct. As he points to pertinent passages in the written document, however, Yaḥyā maintains his grip on one edge of the document. After a brief

125 ʿAlī b. Bilāl, 493–4. 126 Ibid., 494. 127 Ibid. 128 Ibid.
129 Ibid., 494–5. 130 Ibid., 495–7.

exchange of poetry, al-Rashīd initiates a debate in which Yaḥyā proves that the ʿAlids have a closer kinship to the Prophet than do the ʿAbbāsids. This angers the caliph, but unlike in al-Iṣbahānī's version, it does not immediately lead to Yaḥyā's imprisonment.

ʿAlī b. Bilāl relates multiple variations of the "*amān* break" narrative. The first version, recounted by Muḥammad al-Shaybānī and Masrūr at different points, includes a number of distinctive details.[131] First, the jurists are summoned by Abū Bakhtarī on al-Rashīd's behalf to assess the validity of the agreement. Second, the report includes a third jurist, ʿAbd Allāh b. Ṣakhr[132] (d. late second/eighth century?), not mentioned in any other source. Once again, Abū Bakhtarī is the only scholar willing to annul the agreement. The gathering is then adjourned. The next day, al-Rashīd sends Abū Bakhtarī the physical copy of the safe-conduct along with a letter formally soliciting his opinion. Abū Bakhtarī responds by shredding the document, after which the caliph orders Yaḥyā's arrest.

The second variant of the narrative featuring the jurists is told in its entirety by Muḥammad b. al-Shaybānī, who is at the time serving as a judge in Raqqa.[133] When al-Rashīd arrives in the city, he summons al-Shaybānī along with Abū Bakhtarī and Ḥasan b. Ziyād. The caliph asks each of them to rule on the validity of the *amān*. Al-Shaybānī upholds the agreement but Abū Bakhtarī cuts it in half with scissors that he produces from within his clothing. As in previous accounts, he labels Yaḥyā a rebel and authorizes his killing. The narrative then presents two recollections from al-Shaybānī. In the first, he reports that al-Rashīd punished him by temporarily prohibiting him from issuing legal rulings. In the second, he expresses astonishment at Abū Bakhtarī's willingness to take responsibility for Yaḥyā's execution and at the fact that he came to the meeting with scissors. ʿAlī b. Bilāl concludes the narrative by contrasting al-Shaybānī's integrity with Abū Bakhtarī's questionable morals and lineage.

131 Ibid., 497–9.

132 ʿAlī b. Bilāl describes him as a judge in Raqqa. Al-Ḥūthī, the editor, notes the difficulty in determining his identity. See ibid., 498, n. 2.

133 Ibid., 499–500. ʿAlī b. Bilāl's account has significant similarities with al-Iṣbahānī's account. The latter, however, is a composite narrative told from the perspective of an omniscient witness whereas the former includes al-Shaybānī's personal reflections.

Prison Life and Death

'Alī b. Bilāl's version of the "cooked food" narrative is introduced by an anecdote that foregrounds Yaḥyā's courage.[134] Specifically, Masrūr compares Yaḥyā's calm demeanor and silence when summoned by the caliph to the reactions of other prominent figures, who request time to set their affairs in order and ask panicked questions. The report then proceeds in a typical manner as Yaḥyā is arrested and handed over to Masrūr's custody. Eventually, al-Rashīd learns that Yaḥyā cooks for himself in prison, requests some of the food, and consumes it so avidly that he even licks the bowl. In return, he sends Yaḥyā a lavish gift of different varieties of cloth. Yaḥyā refuses it as inappropriate for a prisoner and asks for his release instead. The request momentarily saddens the caliph, but his anger soon returns and Yaḥyā remains in prison.

'Alī b. Bilāl's variant of the "white patch" narrative, though more detailed and elaborate than that of al-Nāṭiq, conveys the same basic information.[135] A conversation regarding the white patch in the spot where Yaḥyā b. 'Abd Allāh performs his nightly prostrations culminates in al-Rashīd's ominous prediction that the 'Alid is not long for this world. The report then jumps forward to the note in which Yaḥyā b. 'Abd Allāh posthumously informs al-Rashīd that he has no hope of repentance and will face God's justice. The caliph's shocked reaction confirms his culpability in Yaḥyā's death.

Whereas most Zaydī sources favor accounts that attribute Yaḥyā's death to starvation, 'Alī b. Bilāl is partial to more brutal explanations.[136] His two primary death narratives suggest that Yaḥyā was first tortured and then buried alive. The first[137] takes place during al-Ma'mūn's (r. 198–218/813–33) renovation of al-Rashīd's residence in Raqqa.[138] In the course of the excavation, workers find a column (or a rounded pit) containing a body that Ṭāhir b. al-Ḥusayn[139] (d. 207/822), al-Ma'mūn's military commander, identifies as Yaḥyā b. 'Abd Allāh. A variant of this account shifts the setting to one of al-Manṣūr's palaces in Baghdad.

134 'Alī b. Bilāl, 500–3. 135 Ibid., 504–5.

136 At one point, he acknowledges the possibility that Yaḥyā was strangled to death in prison: ibid., 503.

137 This explanation is very briefly mentioned by al-Iṣbahānī.

138 'Alī b. Bilāl, 503.

139 See al-Ziriklī, 3:221; *EI*[2], s.v. "Ṭāhir b. al-Ḥusayn" (C. E. Bosworth).

'Alī b. Bilāl's second death narrative is equally brutal.[140] In this report, the caliph al-Mu'taḍid (r. 279–89/892–902) decides to demolish part of one of al-Manṣūr's palaces to expand a mosque. During construction, workers discover a chamber filled with the bodies of men who were tortured to death. One of the bodies is stuffed into a narrow column with only the skull visible. An eyewitness comments on the impossibility of removing the corpse even in its current decayed state. The text strongly implies that this is Yaḥyā's body. The caliph orders the chamber sealed and has the mosque built around it.

B Zaydī Interpretive Frameworks

The Boundaries of the Imāmate

Zaydī portrayals of the final period of Yaḥyā's life were shaped by three dominant interpretive frameworks that reflect debates over the definition of and requirements for the Imāmate; the frameworks are summarized in Table 4.5. According to the Zaydī Shī'a, a legitimate Imām was an 'Alid, descended through Ḥasan or Ḥusayn, who exhibited the proper religious and scholarly qualities and then led a rebellion against a tyrannical ruler.[141] The first, "activist," framework centered on the requirement of rebellion; the second, "lineage," framework highlighted the importance of 'Alid descent; and the third, "personal," framework focused on a potential Imām's special qualities.

These three frameworks are complementary rather than oppositional. Instead of competing notions of the Imāmate, they reflect differences in the relative importance accorded to particular requirements. Is it possible for a candidate who falls short in one of these areas to still become Imām? Does a single moment of activism suffice, or must a candidate achieve power? Is the knowledge of an Imām rooted in his genes, or is it a product of his piety and training? These questions concern the weighting of qualifications within a common conception of the Imāmate. Given their overall congruence, it is not surprising that the Zaydī historians utilize all three of these frameworks. They differ, however, in their emphasis on a specific framework over the others. The following discussion first traces the presence of each framework in

[140] 'Alī b. Bilāl, 506. [141] Haider, *Shī'ī Islam*, 38–41.

Table 4.4 – *The Zaydī Narrative Elements for Yaḥyā b. ʿAbd Allāh*

Narrative element	al-Rāzī	al-Iṣbahānī	al-Nāṭiq	ʿAlī b. Bilāl
Yaḥyā's Rebellion				
Kūfan opposition		X		
Rebellion organization*	X	X	X	X
Betrayal by local notables*	X			X
Amān stipulations*	X (full text)	X (brief)	X (brief)	X (stipulates penalties)
Return to Baghdad*	X	X	X	X
al-Rashīd's Turn				
Medinan activities	X	X (detailed)	X	X
Distributing money	X	X	X	
Organizing rebellion		X (Faḍāla)	X (allusion to agents)	X (reverence)
Zubayrid encounter*	X	X	X	
ʿAbd Allāh b. Muṣʿab's burial	X	X		
Companion naming*	X	X	X	
Poisoned tongue	X	X		
Lineage comparison		X		X
Amān break*	X	X	X	X

Table 4.4 (*cont.*)

Narrative element	al-Rāzī	al-Iṣbahānī	al-Nāṭiq	ʿAlī b. Bilāl
Prison Life and Death				
Barmakids' fall±	X	X – 2 accounts ([1] Jaʿfar, [2] al-Faḍl)	X (al-Faḍl)	
Informant	Muḥammad al-Barmakī	(1) stranger (2) unspecified	unspecified	
Destination	Byzantium	(1) Byzantium (2) Medina	Medina	
Cooked food	X			X
White patch			X	X
Death by starvation	X			
Death by starvation, told on boat	X			
Survival thanks to gravediggers	X			
Slow starvation		X		
Starvation and poisoning			X	
Buried alive (column)				X
Buried alive (torture chamber)				X
Other		live burial, poison, strangulation, lion	live burial, strangulation	strangulation at night

± Narrative elements also found in the Sunnī sources.

the three segments of the core structure before delineating the dominant framework of each Zaydī source.

Yaḥyā's Rebellion

The narrative elements that populate this segment of Yaḥyā's life reflect all three frameworks outlined above. The activist framework is seen in Yaḥyā's efforts to organize his rebellion, which are mentioned by every Zaydī writer. Al-Rāzī and 'Alī b. Bilāl devote substantial space to this topic in the period preceding Yaḥyā's arrival in Daylam, describing his conversion of local populations and his successful recruitment of supporters. 'Alī b. Bilāl goes so far as to argue that Yaḥyā was offered sanctuary by the Turks but refused it in order to rebel against the 'Abbāsids. The Zaydī sources implicate Justān, the king of Daylam, in Yaḥyā's subsequent decision to accept the caliph's *amān*. The two earliest sources – al-Rāzī and al-Iṣbahānī – claim that the king allowed himself to be willfully misled for financial gain. The two later sources – al-Nāṭiq and 'Alī b. Bilāl – imply a similar motivation but also blame the king's wife, who either acted out of fear of the caliph (al-Nāṭiq) or was seduced by promises of wealth ('Alī b. Bilāl).

Al-Rāzī and 'Alī b. Bilāl document another form of deceit in Abū Bakhtarī's efforts to compel the region's political elites to take false oaths questioning Yaḥyā's identity. This element fits within both the activist and lineage frameworks. In the most detailed version, provided by al-Rāzī, Yaḥyā proposes a number of ways to verify his lineage, all of which are rejected by the king. Faced with the false oath-takers, Yaḥyā expresses empathy for their situation, as they and their families have been threatened with death and the seizure of their property. In the end, Yaḥyā's desire to rebel is undercut by the wavering resolve of his supporters. He is not swayed by al-Rashīd's offers of wealth and security, but is forced to accept the *amān* out of sheer necessity. The last source, 'Alī b. Bilāl, openly acknowledges the false nature of the safe-conduct agreement for both sides, noting that al-Rashīd only pretended to welcome Yaḥyā back to Baghdad.

Al-Iṣbahānī attributes the tensions between Yaḥyā and his Kūfan followers to issues of legal knowledge and integrity, an approach that reflects the personal framework. His description of the Kūfan Zaydīs as "Batrīs" implies that they accepted the validity of the reigns of the first two caliphs and adhered to ritual practices characteristic of Kūfan traditionists, such as the permissibility of date wine and the wiping of leather socks in ablution. Yaḥyā b. 'Abd Allāh, by contrast, was raised in the household of Ja'far al-Ṣādiq and thus held to beliefs and practices that resembled those of the Imāmī Shī'a, including a rejection of the first two caliphs as apostates, the prohibition of all alcoholic beverages, and the wiping of bare feet in ablution. Yaḥyā's ritual positions, associated with "Jārūdī" Zaydīs, came to predominate in the Zaydī community in the course of the third/ninth century.[142] Al-Iṣbahānī, who was partial to Jārūdī views, however, was writing in a period of transition from Batrī to Jārūdī Zaydism. His characterization of the Kūfans as Batrīs served two ends. First, it discredited them through an association with non-Shī'ī traditionists. And second, it accorded them responsibility for Yaḥyā's failure to overthrow the 'Abbāsids. Writing a century later, al-Nāṭiq and 'Alī b. Bilāl did not include this episode, since by this point Jārūdī ideas were prevalent throughout the Zaydī community.

al-Rashīd's Turn

The lineage framework exercises a powerful influence on this segment of Yaḥyā's biography. Three of the authors discussed – al-Rāzī, al-Iṣbahānī, and al-Nāṭiq – mention the "Zubayrid encounter" narrative, which casts the Zubayrids as pretenders intent on causing friction between the 'Abbāsids and the 'Alids. It also posits a clear tribal hierarchy in which the Banū Hāshim are elevated above other Qurashī tribes. The "lineage comparison" narrative further refines this hierarchy by identifying the 'Alids as the leading family among the Banū Hāshim. Al-Iṣbahānī utilizes both of these narrative elements to showcase 'Alid superiority. Al-Rāzī and al-Nāṭiq are more ambiguous, given their omission of the "lineage comparison" narrative. 'Alī b. Bilāl uses this narrative as proof of the special standing of the 'Alids, an idea that recurs throughout his text.

The activist framework is also present in this segment, particularly in depictions of Yaḥyā's resistance to the 'Abbāsids after his agreement with al-Rashīd. Al-Iṣbahānī presents the most emphatic of these reports, anchored in his version of the "Medinan activities" narrative in which one of Yaḥyā's agents, Faḍāla, is captured by al-Rashīd. The

[142] This is not the place to discuss the debate surrounding these terms. The standard view, articulated by Wilferd Madelung, is that Zaydism emerged from an amalgamation of Batrīs and Jārūdīs around the revolt of Zayd b. 'Alī (d. 122/740). In my *Origins of the Shī'a* (189–214), I argue against this view, that the terms Batrī and Jārūdī represent heresiographers' attempt to account for the evolution of Zaydī Shī'ism between the second/eighth and third/ninth centuries.

caliph tries to use Faḍāla to entrap Yaḥyā, but the two have previously made arrangements for just such a situation. Al-Iṣbahānī later relates a version of the "companion naming" narrative in which Yaḥyā stubbornly refuses to divulge the names of his supporters. Al-Nāṭiq's account is only slightly less adamant regarding the 'Alid's subversive activities. He reports both the caliph's discovery of Yaḥyā's network of agents (the "Medinan activities" narrative) and his frustration at Yaḥyā's loyalty to his followers (the "companion naming" narrative).

Al-Rāzī and 'Alī b. Bilāl replace Yaḥyā's activism with a more apologetic depiction that aligns with the personal framework. Al-Rāzī's "Medinan activities" narrative limits Yaḥyā to the charitable and commendable act of distributing money to his relatives, with no indication that he instructed his agents to subvert 'Abbāsid power. Al-Rāzī also puts forward a version of the "companion naming" narrative that focuses primarily on Yaḥyā's poisoning as opposed to his co-conspirators. 'Alī b. Bilāl goes even further in this direction, portraying Yaḥyā's time in Medina through the lens of his personal appeal: Yaḥyā attempts to maintain a low profile, but when he is recognized, crowds gather around him in large numbers. In 'Alī b. Bilāl's text, Yaḥyā exudes an irresistible charisma grounded in both his lineage and his piety.

All the Zaydī sources include a version (or multiple versions) of the "*amān* break" narrative, which showcases Yaḥyā's subversive activism. This is unsurprising, given the event's importance as a turning point in al-Rashīd's interactions with Yaḥyā. In every Zaydī account, al-Shaybānī unequivocally upholds the *amān* despite his knowledge of al-Rashīd's desired ends. His refusal to invalidate the agreement gives Yaḥyā the backing of one of the most prominent jurists of the time. The caliph then turns to Abū Bakhtarī, whose ruling is plainly motivated by the desire for material gain. The variants, to different degrees, document the horror of the other jurists at Abū Bakhtarī's actions. In one of al-Rāzī's accounts, al-Shaybānī even laments his failure to confront Abū Bakhtarī in a more direct and forceful manner. 'Alī b. Bilāl concludes his narrative with a scathing attack on both Abū Bakhtarī and his forebears. These reports explicitly contrast Yaḥyā's loyalty with al-Rashīd's treachery. They also counter claims of Yaḥyā's complicity with 'Abbāsid power. The agreement is merely a ruse designed to conceal al-Rashīd's true intentions – intentions that Yaḥyā understands and manages to evade for a short time. Yaḥyā's ability to draft an ironclad safe-conduct compels al-Rashīd to expose his own duplicity. This revelation transforms Yaḥyā's potential collaboration with ʿAbbāsid authority into a very public act of resistance.

The narrative elements in this section of Yaḥyā's biography support all three interpretive frameworks. First and foremost, they convey a special reverence for ʿAlid lineage shared by all the Zaydī sources. There is more ambiguity surrounding Yaḥyā's activism, as the writers differ in their expectations of a Zaydī Imām. The earliest source, al-Rāzī, provides limited evidence of Yaḥyā's activist efforts in Medina. The next two sources, al-Iṣbahānī and al-Nāṭiq, present him as an energetic and principled rebel. The most recent source, ʿAlī b. Bilāl, focuses almost exclusively on his personal qualities. The differences here are likely the product of the gradual standardization of the list of legitimate Zaydī Imāms over time. The debate over the status of figures in the second/eighth and third/ninth centuries who failed to establish Imāmates led to competing biographies that advocated for these figures' inclusion or exclusion.[143] Yaḥyā's case was further complicated by his acceptance of large sums of money from al-Rashīd. Although each writer described this act as a clever means of paying off the debts of other ʿAlids, some felt the need for further justification. Given such debates, the activist interpretation of Yaḥyā likely peaked with al-Iṣbahānī before fading through the course of the fifth/eleventh century.

Prison Life and Death

In the final segment of Yaḥyā's biography, Zaydī historians are again interested in dispelling evidence of his complicity with ʿAbbāsid political power – in other words, deploying the activist framework. To a lesser degree, they note his piety and personal integrity in the face of death, reflecting the personal framework.

Zaydī sources forward three narratives that depict Yaḥyā's life in prison: the "Barmakids' fall" narrative, the "cooked food" narrative, and the "white patch" narrative. The most elaborate version of the "Barmakids' fall" narrative occurs in al-Rāzī's work (the earliest of the Zaydī sources) and follows the basic structure of the Sunnī sources by focusing on the Barmakid family. The other Zaydī writers, by contrast, reduce the importance of the Barmakids relative to Yaḥyā. In the second of al-Iṣbahānī's variants, Yaḥyā attempts to escape al-Rashīd's animosity

[143] For another example of this tendency, see Haider, "Contested Life."

by performing the Ḥajj. In order to do so, however, he needs official permission to leave Baghdad, which he eventually secures from al-Faḍl al-Barmakī.[144] The Sunnī accounts detail the means through which al-Rashīd tracks Yaḥyā's movements prior to his confrontation with the Barmakids. These elements are abbreviated in the Zaydī variants, which are more concerned with Yaḥyā's actions in Medina.

The "cooked food" narrative also answers charges of complicity while simultaneously highlighting Yaḥyā's special qualities. When al-Rashīd learns that Yaḥyā cooks his own meals in prison, he asks for and receives some of the food, which he then eagerly consumes. The food is imbued with a particular charisma derived from Yaḥyā's personal touch. In the narrative, al-Rashīd tries to repay the favor through an expensive gift of cloth. Yaḥyā's refusal of the gift draws a sharp contrast between the two men and, by extension, between the 'Alids and the 'Abbāsids. Further, it undermines accusations that Yaḥyā was chiefly motivated by financial gain in his acceptance of the *amān*. Al-Rāzī further complicates this narrative by tying it to the issues of loyalty and integrity. When Yaḥyā requests his freedom instead of the cloth, the caliph promises him great financial rewards in exchange for the names of his companions. Yaḥyā again refuses, an act that speaks to his principles. 'Alī b. Bilāl does not include al-Rashīd's demand that Yaḥyā identify his agents. Instead, he focuses on Yaḥyā's piety, manifested in the food, and his lack of interest in material wealth, emphasized through a particularly detailed description of the cloth. The "cooked food" narrative is not mentioned by either al-Iṣbahānī or al-Nāṭiq.

The "white patch" narrative directly contrasts Yaḥyā's piety with al-Rashīd's cruelty. In the first part, Yaḥyā performs a prolonged prostration that extends through much of the night. Al-Rashīd is unable (or perhaps unwilling) to admire this act; rather, he views the temporary white patch left at the site of Yaḥyā's prostration as symbolic of his impending death. For the caliph, Yaḥyā is a nuisance that will quickly fade away and be forgotten. This reaction startles Yaḥyā al-Barmakī, who later develops a close bond with Yaḥyā b. 'Abd Allāh and agrees to deliver a note to the caliph in the event of the 'Alid's death. The note

[144] Recall that the Sunnī accounts claim that Yaḥyā was heading to Byzantium with the aid of Ja'far al-Barmakī.

promises al-Rashīd that he will answer for his actions in the hereafter. This narrative element is only preserved by the two later Zaydī writers, al-Nāṭiq and 'Alī b. Bilāl.

There is a relatively clear division in the use of prison life narrative elements by the Zaydī sources. The earliest writer, al-Rāzī, focuses on the issue of Yaḥyā's complicity. Thus, in his version of the "cooked food" narrative, Yaḥyā is unwilling to accept a financial deal or to compromise his followers. The latest writer, 'Alī b. Bilāl, highlights Yaḥyā's piety through particular variants of the "cooked food" and "white patch" narratives. He also confirms al-Rashīd's callousness and identifies him as Yaḥyā's murderer. The other two Zaydī writers make minimal use of prison narratives.

Zaydī authors exhibit considerable variation in their deployment of the narrative elements depicting Yaḥyā's death. Al-Rāzī includes two variant reports of Yaḥyā's starvation in prison. Both of these agree on the cause of his death and express horror at al-Rashīd's harsh treatment. Recall that he is stripped and searched despite his protestations that this violates his sanctity as a descendant of the Prophet. The variant that features a voyage goes further by justifying the subsequent murder of Yaḥyā's jailor even though he was only acting on the orders of the caliph. Al-Rāzī also includes the narrative in which Yaḥyā is saved by a group of gravediggers and then lives a full life in hiding. It seems that the idea of Yaḥyā's survival was not considered problematic in the third/ninth century.

Subsequent Zaydī scholars, however, reject this possibility and provide increasingly graphic death accounts that foreground al-Rashīd's brutality. For these writers, Yaḥyā's gruesome murder helps mitigate the uneasiness caused by his earlier acceptance of the *amān*. Al-Iṣbahānī offers a long list of potential causes for Yaḥyā's demise, including strangulation and being devoured by a hungry lion. Al-Nāṭiq is not quite as exhaustive, but his starvation account concludes with poisoning, which suggests a drawn-out and painful death. Finally, 'Alī b. Bilāl relates two disturbing accounts of live burial in which later authorities stumble upon Yaḥyā's body stuffed into a column or a narrow pit. One of these accounts is particularly grotesque, as the corpse is discovered in a large room filled with torture devices and other mutilated bodies.

The elaborate speculation surrounding Yaḥyā's death in the Zaydī sources contrasts sharply with the minimalism of the Sunnī sources. For

Zaydī writers, Yaḥyā's suffering validates his acceptance of an agreement with al-Rashīd. It shows that the safe-conduct was not the act of a man seeking luxury and financial gain, but rather a last-ditch attempt to do some good before his inevitable murder. From this perspective, Yaḥyā's painful death solidifies his revolutionary credentials.

The Rebel, the 'Alid, and the Model

Zaydī depictions of Yaḥyā b. 'Abd Allāh are decisively shaped by debates regarding the doctrine of the Imāmate, particularly with respect to lineage, activism, and personal qualities. First, the Zaydī sources affirm his activist credentials despite his apparent complicity with political power. Second, they exhibit a special reverence for his genealogy, establishing the superiority of the 'Alids over the 'Abbāsids and other Qurashī clans. Finally, they emphasize Yaḥyā's distinctive qualities, including his knowledge, piety, loyalty, and charisma. Table 4.5 outlines these efforts for each of the Zaydī sources.

The Zaydī accounts differ in the relative degree of importance they allot to the three interpretive frameworks. Al-Rāzī draws a relatively balanced portrait. He initially depicts Yaḥyā as a tireless and successful organizer with the charismatic appeal necessary to win followers. Lineage is addressed in his version of the "Zubayrid encounter" narrative and in death reports in which the humiliation of being stripped is compounded by Yaḥyā's pleas for the respect due to him as a descendant of the Prophet. There is also an extended discussion of the offspring he may have fathered after his possible escape from death. Finally, al-Rāzī documents repeated instances in which Yaḥyā refuses to divulge the names of his companions despite material incentives and physical threats. The refusal demonstrates both his loyalty to supporters and his principled resistance to tyrannical authority. This resistance is further exemplified by his drafting of an ironclad *amān* agreement that al-Rashīd can circumvent only through deceit.

Al-Iṣbahānī's reports also align with the three interpretive frameworks outlined above, albeit to a lesser degree than do those of al-Rāzī. Yaḥyā's activism is established at the start of his biographical entry and persists as a theme throughout the text. It is, in fact, clearly the dominant framework in al-Iṣbahānī's overall account. 'Alid lineage is less vital, but it exercises some influence in two narrative elements: the "Zubayrid encounter" narrative confirms the superiority of the Banū Hāshim, and the "lineage comparison" narrative definitively places the

Table 4.5 – *The Zaydī Interpretive Frameworks for Yaḥyā b. ʿAbd Allāh*

Narrative element	al-Rāzī	al-Isḅahānī	al-Nāṭiq	ʿAlī b. Bilāl
Yaḥyā's Rebellion				
Kūfan opposition		Personal		
Rebellion organization±	Activist	Activist	Activist	Activist
Betrayal by local notables±	Activist/lineage			Activist/lineage
Amān stipulations±	Activist	n/a	n/a	Activist
Return to Baghdad±	n/a	n/a	n/a	Activist
al-Rashīd's Turn				
Medinan activities	Personal	Activist	Activist	Personal
Zubayrid encounter±	Lineage	Lineage	Lineage	
Companion naming±	Activist	Activist (personal)	Personal	
Lineage comparison		Lineage		Lineage
Amān break±	Activist	Activist	Activist	Activist

Narrative element	al-Rāzī	al-Isbahānī	al-Nāṭiq	‘Alī b. Bilāl
Prison Life and Death				
Barmakids’ fall±	Personal	Activist (personal)	Personal	
Cooked food	Activist			Personal
White patch			Personal	Personal
Death by starvation	Lineage			
Death by starvation, told on boat	Lineage			
Survival thanks to gravediggers	Lineage			
Slow starvation		Personal (sympathy)		
Starvation and poisoning			Personal (sympathy)	
Buried alive (column)				Personal (sympathy)
Buried alive (torture chamber)				Personal (sympathy)
Dominant Interpretive Framework	Activist/lineage	Activist	Personal	Personal

± Narrative elements found also in the Sunnī sources.

ʿAlids above the ʿAbbāsids. Al-Iṣbahānī touches on Yaḥyā's personal qualities through a variant of the "Barmakids' fall" narrative, which speaks to Yaḥyā's charisma and piety, and a variant of the "companion naming" narrative, which demonstrates Yaḥyā's willingness to sacrifice his life for his followers. Yaḥyā's integrity is also foregrounded in his interactions with the hostile community of Batrī Zaydīs in Kūfa.

Al-Nāṭiq's portrayal of Yaḥyā closely follows the pattern established by al-Iṣbahānī. He affirms Yaḥyā's activism by detailing his organization of a rebellion, his continued efforts in Medina, and his manipulation of the safe-conduct. Although al-Nāṭiq's biography gestures to lineage in a variant of the "Zubayrid encounter" narrative, it mainly focuses on Yaḥyā's personal qualities. This focus is exemplified by the "white patch" narrative, which underscores both Yaḥyā's piety (as compared with al-Rashīd's cruelty) and his charismatic ability to win over his enemies, in this case Yaḥyā al-Barmakī.

ʿAlī b. Bilāl depicts Yaḥyā as a revolutionary (the "rebellion organization" narrative) while also extolling his ʿAlid credentials (the "lineage comparison" narrative). His primary emphasis, however, is on Yaḥyā's personal qualities, particularly his piety and charisma. These attributes recur in a series of episodes beginning with ʿAlī b. Bilāl's version of the "Medinan activities" narrative. In this report, Yaḥyā does not organize opposition so much as attempt to avoid crowds of adoring locals in Mecca. His inherent charisma is further evident in the "cooked food" and "white patch" narratives. In the former, Yaḥyā reduces al-Rashīd to tears through his refusal to accept the caliph's gift, and in the latter, he earns the sympathy of Yaḥyā al-Barmakī. The distinctive grisliness of ʿAlī b. Bilāl's death narratives secures another level of sympathy for Yaḥyā, as his tortured body is discovered years after his disappearance. This manner of death does not necessarily demonstrate piety, but it does contribute to a general sense of Yaḥyā's victimhood. ʿAlī b. Bilāl's preference for accounts pertaining to Yaḥyā's piety and other personal characteristics as opposed to his activist credentials might be the result of the emergence of an established Zaydī consensus regarding the validity of his Imāmate by the fifth/eleventh century. This meant that a personal framework was more useful than an activist one, especially in polemical encounters with Sunnī and Twelver scholars.

All of the Zaydī writers try to reconcile their perception of Yaḥyā as a legitimate Imām with his acceptance of a safe-conduct from al-Rashīd.

The classical Zaydī doctrine of the Imāmate rejects any compromise with tyrannical political power, yet Yaḥyā signed an agreement with substantial financial benefits. Zaydī writers address the issue in a number of ways. The most common explanation[145] cites the fraying of his support through bribery and coercion. A second explanation, put forward by al-Iṣbahānī and al-Nāṭiq, claims that Yaḥyā continued his subversive activities after his arrival in Baghdad. In this line of argument, the *amān* helped Yaḥyā protect his agents and provided him with the funds necessary to help his 'Alid kinsmen.[146] Yaḥyā's lack of interest in wealth is further reflected in his refusal to reveal the names of his followers in exchange for any amount of money (al-Rāzī) or to accept a present of cloth in the "cooked food" narrative (al-Rāzī, 'Alī b. Bilāl). A third explanation centers on Yaḥyā's knowledge that al-Rashīd would not honor the agreement. 'Alī b. Bilāl makes this quite clear by describing al-Rashīd as "manifesting the appearance" of generosity and honor on Yaḥyā's arrival in Baghdad. The caliph's dishonest nature is later exposed by his violation of the *amān* over the objection of Muḥammad al-Shaybānī. Through these narratives, the Zaydī writers rehabilitate a potentially problematic 'Alid who appears to have accommodated 'Abbāsid power as an active rebel embodying the characteristics of a prototypical Zaydī Imām.

IV The Imāmī Shī'ī Middle Ground

A *An Imāmī Shī'ī Account of Yaḥyā*

The early historical chronicle of the Imāmī Shī'ī scholar al-Ya'qūbī (d. 284/897) provides an account of Yaḥyā b. 'Abd Allāh's rebellion and death that falls between the marginalization of the Sunnī sources and the theological angst of the Zaydī sources.[147] Al-Ya'qūbī begins with a short explanation of Yaḥyā's acceptance of the *amān*. His description differs from those of the Sunnī sources in a number of important ways. First, al-Rashīd does not flatter Yaḥyā or attempt to win him over with material promises. Instead, he threatens the king of Daylam and demands that he surrender the 'Alid. Second, when it becomes apparent

145 Every Zaydī writer makes this argument to one degree or another.
146 The use of these funds is mentioned by all the Zaydī sources.
147 For the account, see al-Ya'qūbī, 2:353–4.

that he has no other choice, Yaḥyā seeks a safe-conduct from al-Faḍl b. Yaḥyā al-Barmakī. There is no mention of the caliph's involvement, his happiness at this turn of events, or his awarding of gifts to Yaḥyā upon his arrival in Baghdad. The text merely states that al-Faḍl al-Barmakī brought Yaḥyā to Baghdad, where he was imprisoned until he died. Unlike the Sunnī authors, al-Yaʿqūbī offers no details about provincial government. His text aligns with Zaydī reports in dismissing the charge that Yaḥyā was motivated by financial concerns.

Al-Yaʿqūbī's account then transitions into two variants of Yaḥyā's death, in which he is slowly starved to death in a prison cell. The basic structure of these reports mirrors that of numerous Zaydī sources in that Yaḥyā manages to survive for nine days without being provided food or water by concealing some meat in his trousers. The guards discover the hidden stash during a strip search, and Yaḥyā dies soon after. In the first variant, a man in a neighboring cell (a client of the Banū Hāshim) relates Yaḥyā's explicit claim that he is being starved to death. The second variant features a passenger on a ship to Baṣra who claims to have been one of al-Rashīd's servants and boasts of his role in Yaḥyā's murder. In the middle of the night, the man is tossed into the ocean by a stranger.

Al-Yaʿqūbī's narrative of Yaḥyā's rebellion and death fits between the Sunnī and the Zaydī sources. It resembles the Sunnī accounts by avoiding long digressions that attempt to justify Yaḥyā's apparent complicity with the ʿAbbāsids. As an Imāmī Shīʿa, al-Yaʿqūbī is not invested in rehabilitating Yaḥyā as a noble rebel intent on undermining ʿAbbāsid power. For him, actual political legitimacy is reserved for the rightful Imāms, represented, in this period, by Mūsā al-Kāẓim (d. 183/799). At the same time, al-Yaʿqūbī retains a degree of reverence for Yaḥyā given his descent from ʿAlī, the first Imām, through Ḥasan, the second Imām. This reverence is reflected in death narratives that showcase ʿAbbāsid brutality toward the ʿAlids. Such stories also lend credence to Imāmī Shīʿī claims that the ʿAbbāsids systematically murdered their Imāms. Overall, al-Yaʿqūbī's account balances the dismissiveness of Sunnī accounts with the polemical rehabilitation of Zaydī accounts.

V Imperial History vs. Debates on the Imāmate

The differences between the Sunnī and Zaydī Shīʿī accounts of Yaḥyā's life during and after his rebellion reflect fundamentally divergent authorial agendas. The Sunnī sources are interested in Yaḥyā only insofar as he helps explain other developments in the 'Abbāsid world. Yaḥyā plays a utilitarian role in these narratives as the reason for administrative turnover, the focus of court rivalries, and the cause for the fall of the Barmakids. Sunnī writers betray no interest in Yaḥyā as an actual historical personality. The details of his rebellion remain obscure, and the last decade of his life is reduced to one or two isolated anecdotes.[148] In many cases, Sunnī accounts simply state that he returned to Baghdad, where he remained in prison until his death. No Sunnī historian discusses his death in any detail.

In more general terms, the Sunnī sources are vested in an interpretive framework shaped by the larger tapestry of 'Abbāsid caliphal history. The central characters in this story are the 'Abbāsid caliphs, who steward the Muslim world through a period of almost universal unity before the gradual decline and disintegration of their empire.[149] This theme of overreach and decline is most evident in al-Ṭabarī's text, which provides the narrative prototype for most subsequent Sunnī accounts. 'Alid revolts are presented as challenges to 'Abbāsid authority grounded in competing claims to the legacy of the Prophet. Yaḥyā's rebellion, however, does not measure up to the efforts of al-Nafs al-Zakiyya or Ṣāḥib Fakhkh al-Ḥusayn b. 'Alī. This being the case, Sunnī writers minimize his importance and treat him as a figure of marginal importance (the "marginalization" framework). The details of his rebellion and his death do not merit serious consideration.

The Zaydī sources exist within a different conceptual world. In these reports, the 'Abbāsid caliphs play the role of tyrants in a broad struggle for the establishment of a just state. The presence of such an oppressive force is necessitated by the centrality of revolution in the Zaydī doctrine of the Imāmate. Rather than documenting the rise and fall of 'Abbāsid power, Zaydī writers are deeply invested in the lives of a particular set of early 'Alids. In Yaḥyā b. 'Abd Allāh, they must reckon with a figure generally accepted as a Zaydī Imām but saddled with a history of accommodating 'Abbāsid power. They resolve the contradiction by rehabilitating Yaḥyā in a manner that both affirms his credentials as an Imām and justifies his acceptance of a safe-conduct from the

148 The one exception is al-Khaṭīb al-Baghdādī, who presents two accounts drawn from Shī'ī sources that partly humanize Yaḥyā.

149 For more on 'Abbāsid decline in the Sunnī historical tradition, see Haider, "Community Divided."

'Abbāsid caliph. Put differently, the need to reconcile the Zaydī Imāmate with historical reality produces biographical accounts with notably apologetic elements. This dynamic finds expression in interpretive frameworks that place Yaḥyā in the mold of an ideal Imām.

VI Notes on Historiography

The depiction of the latter part of Yaḥyā's life in Sunnī and Zaydī Shī'ī sources speaks to a conception of historical writing primarily interested in the creation of meaning. In terms of the rhetoricized model outlined in Chapter 1, the sources hold to a common core structure that begins with Yaḥyā's failed rebellion in Daylam, proceeds to his acceptance of a safe-conduct, and culminates in his arrest and death. Writers work off this structure, embellishing narrative elements in accordance with their larger interpretive frameworks. These elaborate narratives cover events ranging from dramatic prison encounters to tense arguments in the caliphal court. In the process, they endow Yaḥyā's final years with multiple types of meaning. For Sunnī writers, Yaḥyā's importance rests in his interactions with other, more significant figures. For Zaydī writers, Yaḥyā represents evolving views of the nature of the Imāmate. The audience is complicit in this discourse and understands the registers embedded in the competing and sometimes contradictory depictions of Yaḥyā.

It is worthwhile, at this point, to take a step back and consider Yaḥyā in the context of the previous two case studies. The first case study (Chapter 2) involved an important figure, Mukhtār, whose rebellion did not carry deeper theological implications for any of the historians discussed in this book. For this reason, it was a relatively straightforward case for the rhetoricized model. The writers made sense of Mukhtār's rebellion through familiar frameworks focusing on social, political, and religious tensions in early Islam. The second and third case studies, on the other hand, concern individuals of theological importance to certain segments of the Shī'a. Consequently, Shī'ī writers far exceed their Sunnī counterparts in both the length and complexity of their accounts. The theological stakes certainly influenced their interpretive frameworks. Thus, in the previous case study, the changing Twelver frameworks reflected the community's evolving material position with respect to political power, whereas in this chapter the Zaydī frameworks reveal an internal theological conversation over the relative importance of particular requirements for the Imāmate in the context of communal polemics. These theological implications, however, have no discernible impact on Shīʿī approaches to historical material: Shīʿī historiography, like Sunnī historiography, is characterized by a shared core structure populated with embellished narrative elements. This conclusion is especially significant given the tendency either to deem Shīʿī historical works hopelessly polemical (in the case of Twelver sources) or to ignore them altogether (in the case of Zaydī sources).

5 *Reconsideration*

Imagine wandering through a bookstore on a lazy Saturday afternoon. The books are arranged on the shelves under different subject headings. A quick glance in the fiction section reveals stories drawn from the imagination, while the popular science section promises complicated truths in accessible form. The history section contains considerable ambiguity, with books documenting events through the perspectives of historians. It is understood that these authors reproduce the past through the lenses of their own experiences, but their work is still evaluated based on their fealty to facts. In other words, history, a scholarly construct, is evaluated against a standard of accuracy.

This modern European understanding of history has permeated contemporary scholarship on early Islam. In the past half-century, it has helped produce remarkable insights into premodern Muslim societies. Scholars – myself included – have devoted countless hours to disentangling contradictory reports of a given conflict or incident. Much of this work has involved tracing accounts back to their sources, with figures such as al-Wāqidī (d. 207/822) and al-Madā'inī (d. 225/840) occupying a central place in the reconstruction of early historical narratives.[1] Questions pertaining to chains of transmission and mechanisms for the transfer of knowledge have spawned complicated and passionate debates between historians.[2] This kind of careful, detailed research has allowed scholars to peek into the early Muslim community in its formative stages.

1 There are myriad examples of this type of scholarship. See, for example, Lecker, "Death"; the seminal studies compiled in Hinds's *Studies*; and the recent articles in Motzki, *The Biography of Muḥammad.*

2 For examples of scholarship that mine chains of transmission for historical information, see Motzki, *The Origins of Islamic Jurisprudence* and Sadeghi, "Traveling Tradition Test." For a more comprehensive survey of the field, see Donner, "Modern Approaches." For the debate over the oral vs. written transmission of sources, see Schoeler, *The Genesis of Literature*, esp. 1–9, and Cook, "Opponents of Writing." I also discuss this debate in *Origins of the Shīʿa*, 24–34.

More recent iterations of this approach have further complicated and enriched our understanding of this period through the introduction of novel sources such as non-Arabic texts and archaeological evidence.[3] These are all welcome developments, with great potential for the advancement of the field as a whole.

This book, however, is concerned with a different set of issues. If we place our hypothetical bookstore in Kūfa in the third/ninth century, what assumptions could we make about the content of specific categories of writing? In the case of science, for example, contemporary scholars have challenged longstanding claims about the plague in the early modern Muslim world while also documenting differences in the categorization of certain types of knowledge.[4] This sensitivity reflects a fairly obvious truism: societies conceptualize information in distinctive ways. In light of this fact, it is unlikely that modern European understandings of history match the attitudes of early Muslim historians. This disconnect raises a number of important questions about the craft of historical writing in the early period. What were the underlying assumptions and rules that governed the composition of historical works? Did historians place a premium on the verbatim, almost photographic, preservation of past events? Did they differentiate between multiple genres of historical writing? It is easy to imagine that precision in reports of the Prophet's actions or of the circumstances surrounding the revelation of Qur'ānic verses held a particular significance, but can we say the same of a conversation between an Umayyad caliph and a captured rebel? The former carried normative weight in myriad fields, whereas the latter represented a struggle for political and perhaps religious legitimacy.

Another set of pertinent questions concerns the audience for historical writing. Were historical texts aimed at a broad public? In the case of the tales of storytellers (*quṣṣāṣ*), they clearly were, but what about the grand historical narratives constructed by al-Ṭabarī or al-Khaṭīb al-Baghdādī?[5] If we assume – as seems likely – that these latter works were composed for scholarly elites, did historians assume a baseline of

[3] There are numerous examples of this kind of approach. For a representative sampling, see Hoyland, *Seeing Islam* and *In God's Path*; Borrut, "Remembering Karbalā'"; Munt, *Holy City*; Vacca, *Non-Muslim Provinces*.

[4] For the plague, see Stearns, *Infectious Ideas* and "New Directions." For a recent attempt to complicate conceptions of knowledge, see Melvin-Koushki, "Powers of One" and "The Quest for a Universal Science."

[5] For this genre of writing, see Armstrong's *The Quṣṣāṣ of Early Islam*, which argues that the term *qāṣṣ* is best translated as "preacher."

knowledge in their audience? This appears to have been the case in late antique historiography, where writers played off the ubiquity of certain narratives among the elite.[6] For such an audience, was it permissible, or even expected, that historians would create meaning by embellishing existing reports and creating new ones? Again, in the late antique world, it was fairly common and accepted for writers to rework meaningful narratives for polemical ends.

A final set of questions involves the methods employed by early Muslim historians. Did they create their reports wholesale, or did they have access to sets of preexisting reports that they then altered or embellished? The pervasiveness of key figures such as al-Madāʾinī in the historical tradition supports the latter possibility, with authors making their own interventions through the addition of small details, the insertion of dialogue, or the creation of context. Such changes could lead to dramatically different interpretations of a given event. The repurposing (literally) of these reports became more apparent after the fifth/eleventh century, as historians wove existing accounts into new, composite narratives. It is also possible, however, that early historians felt authorized to create reports that conveyed the importance of a given event instead of documenting its exact details. An exchange between a court official and a prisoner, for example, was meant to establish the stakes at a critical moment. It was not a verbatim reproduction of an actual conversation. It is unlikely that audiences expected such a reproduction.

These questions have no clear or easy answers. The prospects for reconstructing the scholarly presuppositions of a preindustrial Near Eastern society a thousand years ago in the absence of abundant source material seem bleak. But this alone should not prevent us from considering such issues, which are routinely discussed by historians of other periods.[7] In this book, I attempt to address this lacuna for the study of early Islam by proposing and modeling a different way of thinking about early historical writing. Its aim is not to replace other kinds of scholarship, but rather to provide an alternative space for interrogating the material that is perhaps more resonant with premodern attitudes toward historical writing.

6 See the citations in Chapter 1, particularly Van Nuffelen's *Orosius*.

7 For the late antique period, see Chapter 1. For studies of these issues in the Mamlūk period that have influenced my reading, see Hirschler, *Medieval Arabic Historiography* (on historical writing) and *The Written Word* (on audience).

The model presented in this book embodies an understanding of history that was prevalent in the late antique period and bears similarities to ideas in other premodern societies. Specifically, it rests on the premise that early Muslim historians were more concerned with preserving the meaning of a given event than they were with recording its specific details. In practice, this focus meant that authors were free to embellish and elaborate narrative elements (within certain bounds) in order to endow an event with significance. The baseline for such elaboration was the shared core structure of an event or a biography that was familiar to the scholarly audience. In the context of late antique studies, this kind of meaningful and ubiquitous narrative might be referred to as a myth. As described in Chapter 1, the core structure provided the skeletal outline for a story that was then populated with narrative elements either created by the historian or taken from existing sources and embellished appropriately. The resulting text was shaped by an interpretive framework that conveyed the author's purpose. This was neither a "fictional" account nor a "factual" rendering of the past. It was simply historical writing.

The most striking aspect of this model is its fluidity. The individual steps (core structure, narrative elements, and interpretive framework) function as malleable guidelines applicable to a range of approaches that operate outside the binary of fact vs. fiction. This flexibility is evinced by the diversity of structures and analytic methods utilized in the three case studies. These differences, in fact, embody one of the central premises of this book: namely, the rejection of a singular explanation or approach to early Muslim historiography.

Chapter 2, the most straightforward application of the proposed model, examines historical sources focusing on Mukhtār b. Abī 'Ubayd al-Thaqafī in a single section organized chronologically by writer. The sheer mass of information is such that the basic forms of the narrative elements are relegated to an appendix. After laying out the core structure, the chapter identifies the main narrative elements utilized in each text and then extrapolates their interpretive frameworks. The results are, unsurprisingly, complex, with the presentation of Mukhtār's rebellion adhering to a variety of frames that highlight ethnic, religious, and political conflict.

This initial case study is distinctive in two important ways. First, Mukhtār is a contested figure chiefly associated with an influential early communal group, the Kaysānī Shī'a. Within a century of his death, this branch of Shīʿism achieved a spectacular success through the ʿAbbāsid revolution, and was then abandoned by its leaders, the ʿAbbāsid caliphs. The fact that Mukhtār held no particular theological significance for Sunnī, Zaydī, or Twelver historians permitted them considerable latitude in repurposing his rebellion. These authors held to a common core structure, elaborated similar narrative elements, and conveyed overlapping interpretive frameworks touching on social and political developments. The lack of substantive differences between Sunnī and Shīʿī sources supports the universality of the rhetoricized historical model at the heart of this study. Second, the case study of Mukhtār draws primarily on historical chronicles. Whereas biographical works graft anecdotes together into a holistic view of an individual's life, chronicles operate within temporal limits. In the former, an author might position two reports together in order to make a broader point, but in the latter, events are placed under the years in which they occurred, thereby leaving their connection implicit or even obscure.[8] In view of the tendency of chronographic works to mute their rhetorical characteristics, it is striking that the contours of the proposed model are nonetheless apparent in this genre of historical writing.

Chapters 3 and 4 demonstrate the applicability of the rhetoricized historiographical model even in cases in which the subject holds great significance for a given community. In such instances, Sunnī and Shīʿī historians employ a common approach and differ only in terms of their interpretive frameworks. Chapter 3, like Chapter 2, first delineates the core structure of the subject's life and then identifies the narrative elements and their variants utilized in non-Twelver and Twelver sources. Given Mūsā al-Kāẓim's importance as the seventh Imām, a good portion of the case study is devoted to competing representations of al-Kāẓim among Twelver Shīʿī authors. The chapter reveals notable similarities in the portrayal of al-Kāẓim across the historical tradition. Despite their divergent interpretive frameworks, non-Twelver and Twelver authors employ the same techniques, populating a core structure with narrative elements in the production of their accounts. The former either cast al-Kāẓim as a scholarly exemplar or place him in the context of court politics, whereas the latter use his

[8] As noted in Chapter 1, although both of these genres of historical writing, biography and chronography, operate within the parameters of a rhetoricized historiography, the rhetoricized characteristics are certainly more evident in biographical works.

biography to make sense of the community's evolving political standing in Baghdad. Given their similar approaches, it is problematic and misleading to describe the non-Twelver sources as historical while dismissing the Twelver sources as hagiographic.

Chapter 4 offers perhaps the most complex use of the proposed model. Yaḥyā b. ʿAbd Allāh is certainly a well-known historical figure, both because of his lineage and because of his participation in the rebellion at Fakhkh. He is also famous for sending his brother Idrīs to North Africa, where the latter laid the foundation for the Idrīsid dynasty of Morocco. The core structure of Yaḥyā's rebellion and its aftermath remains quite stable across the entire historical tradition. In the Sunnī sources, however, Yaḥyā rarely rises to the level of other important ʿAlids, and is never seen as a legitimate threat to the ʿAbbāsid caliphs. The first part of this case study documents the five narrative elements through which Sunnī historians diminish Yaḥyā in comparison with other prominent figures. The second part employs a different approach due to the idiosyncrasies of the Zaydī sources. It analyzes each Zaydī writer's treatment of three segments of Yaḥyā's later life and then traces his deployment of narrative elements in the service of interpretive frameworks. Rather than matching a single framework to a single author, my analysis here suggests a complicated weighting of multiple interpretive frameworks within each text.

The three case studies gesture toward a few important observations about our view of historical writing in early Islam. Most importantly, they demonstrate the value of new approaches to the source material that transcend the methods and assumptions embedded in many contemporary studies. In other words, they point to a need for creativity, emerging from a realization that our particular notions of history do not necessarily translate to other societies in different periods. It is exceedingly difficult to reconstruct the scholarly presuppositions of the early Muslim world, but this difficulty does not make the exercise meaningless. A basic consideration of these complications has proven invaluable to scholars in other disciplines. This book provides a first foray in this direction for early Islam, anticipating that others will follow suit with innovative and – hopefully! – better methods and models.

On a more concrete level, the case studies point toward an overarching unity within historical writing. Such a unity directly challenges contemporary dismissals of Shīʿī historical works. As this study makes clear, Shīʿī (both Twelver and Zaydī) writers held to the same basic parameters and rules as did their Sunnī counterparts. All of these historians were invested in a truthful depiction of the past that endowed an event or an episode with meaning. If the interpretive frameworks utilized in the Sunnī works appear less polemical or somehow more "historical," this is simply a product of the dominance of these works in shaping our conception of the early period. It is not a reflection of their superiority as historical sources. Moreover, any reductionist generalizations of the Shīʿī sources are contradicted by the stark differences between Twelver and Zaydī interpretive frameworks.[9] The perspective presented in this book reveals a broad similarity in historical material across communal boundaries. It is time to stop characterizing the work of al-Khaṭīb al-Baghdādī as history while marginalizing the work of al-Mufīd as polemical hagiography. The pervasiveness of this distinction reflects the inherent limitations of the kinds of questions that dominate the field. Perhaps a reconsideration of the nature of this material will lead to new and better questions.

[9] In their biographies of al-Kāẓim, Twelver sources present competing modes of cooperation and resistance with respect to political power. They utilize interpretive frameworks in which the Imām clearly conveys his expectations of the Twelver Shīʿa. The primary issue here is the public performance of Twelver Shīʿī identity. Zaydī treatments of Yaḥyā b. ʿAbd Allāh, by contrast, are vested in internal theological disputes over the nature of the Imāmate. The interpretive frameworks offer a means for authors to debate the relative merits of different characteristics associated with the legitimate Imām. The primary issue here is the determination of a central Zaydī theological premise.

Appendix

The Narrative Elements for Mukhtār's Revolt

This appendix documents the narrative elements (including important variants) that populate the core structure of Mukhtār's (d. 67/687) revolt. It thus provides a narrative backdrop for Chapter 2 by detailing the options available to historians in their depictions of this episode.

I The Ḥijāz (61–4/680–4)

Two narrative elements are directly tied to Mukhtār's interactions with Ibn al-Zubayr (d. 72/693) in the period prior to and immediately following Yazīd I b. Mu'āwiya's (r. 60–4/680–3) death in 64/683.

A The Ibn al-Zubayr Oath Narrative (Two Variants)

The first narrative element depicts Mukhtār's interactions with Ibn al-Zubayr and consists of two primary variants. In the first (1.1a), Mukhtār pledges allegiance to Ibn al-Zubayr (this is stated outright or implied) and supports him in his subsequent conflict with the Umayyads.[1] The second and more detailed version (1.1b) begins with Ibn al-Zubayr questioning Mukhtār about Kūfa.[2] Mukhtār claims that the Kūfans declare their loyalty to the Umayyads but secretly desire an alternative, which prompts Ibn al-Zubayr to disparage them as duplicitous. Mukhtār then either offers his oath of allegiance[3] or asks for authorization to seize control of Kūfa.[4] When Ibn al-Zubayr rejects

[1] Ibn Sa'd, 5:732; al-Ya'qūbī, 2:175; al-Mas'ūdī (2009), 4:101.
[2] Ibn A'tham, 1:200–2; al-Balādhurī, 6:378–9; al-Ṭabarī, 3:402–3.
[3] Ibn A'tham, 1:200–2; al-Ṭabarī, 3:402–3. [4] Al-Balādhurī, 6:378–9.

these proposals, Mukhtār departs the city in a rage, presumably heading to Ṭā'if. He later circulates claims (prophecies?) that he will eradicate tyrants and kill those deserving of punishment. Ibn al-Zubayr dismisses Mukhtār as a deceitful soothsayer who would be the first to die if God killed the tyrants. Some time later, Mukhtār returns to Mecca and publicly shuns Ibn al-Zubayr. ʿAbbās b. Sahl al-Anṣārī (d. before 96/715) intercedes, explaining that Ibn al-Zubayr's initial indifference was due to the precariousness of the political situation and the need for public discretion. Although this explanation seems to appease him, Mukhtār nevertheless notes that Ibn al-Zubayr needs him more than vice versa. He then agrees to accompany Ibn Sahl to meet Ibn al-Zubayr later that evening. After a few pleasantries, Mukhtār offers his oath of allegiance on the condition that Ibn al-Zubayr consult him on important matters and appoint him to a high post. Ibn al-Zubayr counters with a more limited oath in which he promises to adhere to the Qur'ān and the Sunna. Mukhtār rejects this formula and forces Ibn al-Zubayr to accept his demands.

B The Return to Kūfa Narrative (Two Variants)

The other narrative element in this section concerns Mukhtār's rationale for leaving Kūfa.[5] There are two contradictory versions of this report in the available sources. In the first (1.2a), Ibn al-Zubayr authorizes Mukhtār to gather the Kūfan Shīʿa into an army capable of fighting the Umayyads.[6] Despite persistent tension, the formal break between Mukhtār and Ibn al-Zubayr occurs only much later. The second version (1.2b) focuses on Mukhtār's sense of betrayal upon realizing that Ibn al-Zubayr will not appoint him to high office.[7] In the most detailed accounts,[8] Hānī b. Abī Ḥayya (d. after 67/687) informs Mukhtār that Kūfa is primed for rebellion but warns of the dangers of civil strife. Some reports record a second similar

[5] Ibn Aʿtham, 1:252–3; Ibn Saʿd, 5:72–3; al-Balādhurī, 6:379 and 453–4; Pseudo-Ibn Qutayba, 2:31; al-Yaʿqūbī, 2:175; al-Ṭabarī, 3:404; al-Masʿūdī (2009), 4:104.
[6] Ibn Saʿd, 5:72–3; al-Balādhurī, 6:453 and 454; Pseudo-Ibn Qutayba, 2:31; al-Masʿūdī (2009), 4:104.
[7] Ibn Aʿtham, 1:252–3; al-Balādhurī, 6:379; al-Yaʿqūbī, 2:175; al-Ṭabarī, 3:404.
[8] Ibn Aʿtham, 1:252–3; al-Ṭabarī, 3:404.

encounter, in which Salama b. Marthad al-Qābiḍī (d. unknown) advises Mukhtār against direct involvement.

II Sedition (64–6/684–5)

The six narrative elements pertaining to Mukhtār's rebellion document his efforts to win over various segments of the Kūfan population. They often transition into longer reports about the rebellion itself.

A The Entry and Recruitment Narrative (Two Variants)

The first element describes Mukhtār's arrival in the city and his initial interactions with the Shīʿa. In the first variant (2.1a), Mukhtār appeals to the Shīʿa by claiming to represent Ibn al-Ḥanafiyya and calling for retaliation against those who killed Ḥusayn.[9] The sources differ dramatically in depth and detail, but they all suggest a smooth recruitment process with no mention of rivals among the Kūfan Shīʿa.

The second variant (2.1b) paints a more complicated picture of Mukhtār's recruiting activities.[10] In this version, Mukhtār takes a bath and changes his clothes before entering Kūfa. He slowly rides toward the center of town, appealing to particular tribal elements (Banū Hamdān and Banū Kinda) and pandering to specific individuals, such as ʿAbīda b. ʿAmr al-Baddī (d. after 67/687). In longer versions, Mukhtār spends much of his first day in the Friday mosque. He then slips into less conspicuous clothes and heads home where, in a meeting with the Kūfan Shīʿa, he claims to speak for Ibn al-Ḥanafiyya.[11] In one report,[12] he is told that the community has already chosen Sulaymān b. Ṣurad (d. 65/685) as its leader; in another,[13] he wins some initial support and openly criticizes Ibn Ṣurad but fails to sway the majority. In both cases, he awaits the outcome of Ibn Ṣurad's military expedition before proceeding with his plans.

9 Ibn Saʿd, 5:73–4; al-Yaʿqūbī, 2:175; al-Dīnawarī, 288; al-Masʿūdī (2009), 4:104–5.
10 Ibn Aʿtham, 1:253–5; al-Balādhurī, 7:379–80; al-Ṭabarī, 3:404–6.
11 Ibn Aʿtham, 1:253–5; al-Ṭabarī, 3:405–6. 12 Ibn Aʿtham, 1:253–4.
13 Al-Ṭabarī, 3:405–6.

B *The Kūfan Arrest Narrative (One Variant)*

The second narrative element (2.2a) documents Mukhtār's arrest at the urging of Kūfan tribal leaders and his release through the intercession of 'Abd Allāh b. 'Umar (d. 73/693).[14] At the beginning of the report, Ibn al-Zubayr appoints 'Abd Allāh b. Yazīd al-Khaṭmī (d. before 72/692) and Ibrāhīm b. Muḥammad b. Ṭalḥa b. 'Ubayd Allāh (d. 110/728) as his primary agents in Kūfa. A number of prominent Kūfans, led by 'Umar b. Sa'd (d. 66/686) and Shabath b. Rib'ī (d. 70/690), warn them of the danger posed by Mukhtār, accusing him of causing civil strife and describing him as a far greater threat than Ibn Ṣurad. Mukhtār is then arrested. Ibrāhīm wants to march him through the streets barefoot and in chains, but 'Abd Allāh argues that he is only suspected of wrongdoing and treats him gently. In prison, Mukhtār composes poetry and rhymed prose predicting his future role as the scourge of tyrants. He later praises those Shī'a who survived the defeat of the Tawwābūn and summons them to his cause.[15] At some point, he reaches out to 'Abd Allāh b. 'Umar, pleading his innocence and appealing for intercession. Ibn 'Umar writes to Ibn al-Zubayr's agents, 'Abd Allāh and Ibrāhīm, explains his familial ties with Mukhtār, and asks for the latter's release. He is freed after ten men come forward to vouch for his future behavior. In two sources, Mukhtar swears that he will not foment unrest on penalty of animal sacrifices and slave manumissions.[16] Soon thereafter, he disavows the oath as meaningless given the necessity of fighting tyrants.

C *The Feigned Sickness Narrative (Two Variants)*

There are two main variants of this narrative element. The first (2.3a) is a very brief report which states that Mukhtār avoided arrest at the hands of 'Abd Allāh b. Muṭī''s agents by feigning sickness.[17] The second, more colorful, version (2.3b) opens with Ibn Muṭī' giving an ill-advised speech in which he promises to consult the Kūfans regarding the use of their taxes and to follow the example of 'Umar and 'Uthmān.[18] Some members of the crowd, led by al-Sā'ib b. Mālik al-Ash'arī (d. 67/687),

[14] Ibn A'tham, 1:264–6; al-Balādhurī, 6:380–2; al-Ṭabarī, 3:406, 420–1, and 433–4.

[15] Al-Ṭabarī, 3:421.

[16] Al-Balādhurī, 6:381–2; al-Ṭabarī, 3:434.

[17] Al-Balādhurī, 6:385; al-Dīnawarī, 288.

[18] Ibn A'tham, 1:273–5; al-Ṭabarī, 3:435–6.

respond by demanding that no funds be sent to Ibn al-Zubayr in Mecca and that the governor rule in accordance with the example of 'Alī b. Abī Ṭālib. Ibn Muṭī' quickly acquiesces to these demands. Iyās b. Muḍārib al-'Ijlī (d. 66/685), the new head of security (*shurṭa*), blames Mukhtār for the unrest and advises his arrest to insure stability. The governor then dispatches two men, Zā'ida b. Qudāma al-Thaqafī (d. 76/690) and Ḥusayn b. 'Abd Allāh al-Hamdānī (d. after 65/685), to summon Mukhtār to court on the pretext of seeking his counsel. In conveying this message, Zā'ida secretly warns Mukhtār that the invitation is a trap. Mukhtār excuses himself by feigning sickness. Both messengers are aware of the deception but conceal it when reporting back to Ibn Muṭī'.

D The Kūfan Delegation Narrative (One Variant)

In the fourth narrative element (2.4a), a delegation of Kūfan Shī'a travel to Mecca to verify Mukhtār's ties to Ibn al-Ḥanafiyya.[19] The episode occurs after Mukhtār has secured the oath of allegiance from most of the Kūfan Shī'a, but prior to the rebellion. Multiple sources identify 'Abd al-Raḥmān b. Shurayḥ al-Shibāmī (d. 67/687) as one of the leading members of the delegation.[20] When the Kūfans question Ibn al-Ḥanafiyya about Mukhtār, he is cautious and does not answer directly. Instead, he extols the virtues of the family of the Prophet and of those who come to their aid. The Kūfans interpret this as an implicit endorsement of Mukhtār. After they return to Kūfa, a relieved Mukhtār has them testify to his veracity in front of a large public gathering, using the occasion to renew the oaths of his followers.

E The Ibrāhīm b. al-Ashtar Letter Narrative (Two Variants)

There are two variations of the fifth narrative element, which describes Mukhtār's overtures to Ibrāhīm b. Mālik al-Ashtar (d. 72/691). In the first and shorter version (2.5a),[21] Mukhtār visits Ibn al-Ashtar with a small party that includes Yazīd b. Anas al-Asadī (d. 66/686), Aḥmar b. Shumayṭ al-Bajalī (d. 67/686), 'Abd Allāh b. Kāmil al-Shākirī (d. 67/

[19] Ibn A'tham, 1:275–6; Ibn Sa'd, 5:73; al-Balādhurī, 6:384–5; al-Ya'qūbī, 2:175; al-Ṭabarī, 3:436–7.
[20] Ibn A'tham, 1:276; al-Balādhurī, 6:384–5; al-Ṭabarī, 3:436.
[21] Ibn Sa'd, 5:73–4; al-Dīnawarī, 288–9.

686), and Abū ʿAmra Kaysān (d. 67/686). He urges Ibn al-Ashtar to follow in the footsteps of his father, Mālik al-Ashtar (d. 37/658), a loyal supporter of the family of the Prophet. He then produces a letter purportedly written by Ibn al-Ḥanafiyya, requesting Ibn al-Ashtar's help. Mukhtār's companions testify to its authenticity, and Ibn al-Ashtar, expressing no reservations, takes the oath of allegiance.

The second version of this narrative (2.5b) shares most features of the first but is considerably more detailed.[22] It also differs regarding the names of Mukhtār's companions, replacing Abū ʿAmra Kaysān with other prominent Kūfans.[23] At the start of the account, Mukhtār sends a delegation of his supporters to Ibn al-Ashtar, who welcomes them and, sensing their fear, promises them safety. He agrees to join them on the condition that he is given authority. The delegation responds that Ibn al-Ḥanafiyya has already placed Mukhtār in charge. Ibn al-Ashtar remains silent, and the group departs without an answer. Three days later, Mukhtār leads them back to Ibn al-Ashtar's home with a letter allegedly written by Ibn al-Ḥanafiyya. Ibn al-Ashtar is suspicious of the letter because Ibn al-Ḥanafiyya refers to himself in it as the "Mahdī." Mukhtār, however, produces witnesses who testify to the letter's authenticity. Ibn al-Ashtar seems to accept these testimonials, but later asks ʿĀmir b. Sharāḥīl al-Shaʿbī (d. between 103/721 and 110/728) to record the names of the witnesses for him. In some accounts, he also asks al-Shaʿbī why he did not also testify regarding the letter.[24] Instead of revealing his doubts to Ibn al-Ashtar, al-Shaʿbī affirms the reputation and honesty of the witnesses.

F The Rebellion Narrative (Three Variants)

The sixth and final narrative element in this period depicts the actual events of Mukhtār's rebellion. There is considerable divergence in authorial treatments of the revolt, but they generally fall into one of three variants. The first (2.6a) is unique. Mukhtār pretends to mourn for the family of the Prophet, inciting a riotous crowd that he exploits to banish Ibn Muṭīʿ from the city's fort.[25] There is no mention of a prolonged recruitment process or a carefully organized uprising. In

22 Ibn Aʿtham, 1:277–9; al-Balādhurī, 6:385–6; al-Ṭabarī, 3:437–9.
23 Ibn Aʿtham, al-Balādhurī, and al-Ṭabarī differ on the identities of these Kūfans.
24 Ibn Aʿtham, 2:279; al-Ṭabarī, 3:438.
25 Al-Masʿūdī (2009), 4:104; al-Balādhurī, 6:453.

the second variant (2.6b), Iyās b. Muḍārib, the head of the *shurṭa*, hears rumors of the impending revolt and orders Ibn al-Ashtar to remain in his home.[26] Mukhtār then permits Ibn al-Ashtar to confront Iyās, leading to a street skirmish that results in the latter's death. This incident precipitates a larger conflict between the partisans of Ibn Muṭīʿ and the supporters of Ibn al-Ashtar and Mukhtār. The governor is eventually forced to take refuge in the fort, where he requests and is granted a safe-conduct. Mukhtār sends him a large sum of money and allows him to leave the city unharmed.

The third and most intricate version of the rebellion narrative (2.6c) relates a series of encounters between Mukhtār's men and Zubayrid loyalists.[27] According to these reports, Ibn Muṭīʿ learns, through Iyās b. Muḍārib, that Mukhtār is planning a rebellion for Rabīʿ I 66/685. The governor orders his supporters – tribal leaders including Shabath b. Ribʿī and Shamir b. Dhī al-Jawshan (d. 66/686) – to seize public spaces (*jabbānāt*) to prevent the gathering of rebels. Iyās is killed in a dramatic encounter with Ibn al-Ashtar, marking the premature start of the revolt.[28] The subsequent conflict is depicted through a number of discrete episodes. In one account, Shabath contrasts the Arab lineage of his men with the allegedly foreign origins of Mukhtār's supporters.[29] He captures a group of prisoners, sparing the life of every Arab and executing every non-Arab. In another report, Ibn al-Ashtar urges his men to disregard the lineages of their Arab opponents.[30] A third account conveys Shabath's incredulity when his soldiers criticize the recitation of only short passages of the Qur'ān in the communal prayer.[31] Despite some discrepancies regarding the movement of troops, this version of the rebellion invariably ends with the siege of the fort. Shabath first counsels Ibn Muṭīʿ to seek a guarantee of safe-conduct. He then advises him to sneak out of the fort and hide until he is able to depart the city safely. The next night Ibn Muṭīʿ makes his way to the compound of Abū Mūsā al-Ashʿarī (d. ca. 48/668) while the rest of his supporters receive safe-conducts in exchange for their oaths of

[26] Al-Dīnawarī, 290–2.
[27] Ibn Aʿtham, 2:279–91; al-Balādhurī, 6:389–95; al-Ṭabarī, 3:439–48. A very brief version of this element is preserved by al-Yaʿqūbī, 2:175.
[28] Note that in this version Mukhtār does not authorize Ibn al-Ashtar to kill Iyās prior to their encounter.
[29] Ibn Aʿtham, 2:284–5; al-Ṭabarī, 3:443.
[30] Ibn Aʿtham, 2:286–7; al-Ṭabarī, 3:446.
[31] Ibn Aʿtham, 2:284–5; al-Ṭabarī, 3:442–3.

allegiance. As in the previous variant, Ibn Muṭīʿ is given a great deal of money and permitted to flee the city.

III Rule (66–7/685–6)

The period of Mukhtār's rule includes two types of narrative elements. The first recount important political and military events, whereas the second relate to the pursuit of Ḥusayn's killers. The meaning and significance of these reports stem as much from their ordering in a text as from their content. This section only covers those revenge narratives that involve prominent figures.

A The Ibn al-Ḥanafiyya Siege Narrative (One Variant)

The most commonly cited narrative element (3.1a) in this period documents Mukhtār's efforts to aid Ibn al-Ḥanafiyya in his standoff with Ibn al-Zubayr in Mecca.[32] The conflict is precipitated by Ibn al-Zubayr's insistence on securing the allegiance of the ʿAlids in general and Ibn al-Ḥanafiyya in particular. The tension is further exacerbated with Mukhtār's seizure of Kūfa, which Ibn al-Zubayr considers proof of ʿAlid political aspirations. For their part, Ibn al-Ḥanafiyya and other important figures such as ʿAbd Allāh b. ʿAbbās (d. 68/686) refuse to take the oath of allegiance to Ibn al-Zubayr until communal consensus is reached on the identity of the legitimate caliph. Ibn al-Zubayr confines them to a small area of Mecca and threatens to burn them alive if they do not acquiesce by a certain date. At this point, Ibn al-Ḥanafiyya appeals for help to Mukhtār, who sends a staggered series of cavalry detachments under the general command of Abū ʿAbd Allāh al-Jadalī (d. after 67/687). The small size of these groups allows them to travel undetected.[33]

The Kūfans enter Mecca just before Ibn al-Zubayr's deadline. In some sources,[34] they remove their swords out of deference for the sanctity of the Kaʿba and instead carry wooden clubs, thereby earning the name *khashabiyya*. Ibn al-Ḥanafiyya forbids them to fight

[32] Ibn Aʿtham, 2:299–307; Ibn Saʿd, 5:74–6; *Akhbār al-dawla*, 99–107; al-Balādhurī, 3:474–8; al-Yaʿqūbī, 2:178–80; al-Ṭabarī, 3:472–3; al-Masʿūdī (2009), 4:107–9.

[33] Al-Masʿūdī (2009), 4:108.

[34] *Akhbār al-dawla*, 106; al-Balādhurī, 3:476; al-Ṭabarī, 3:473.

in the sanctuary, which leads to an extended impasse. There are multiple versions of the resolution of this conflict. Ibn al-Zubayr is initially confident and confrontational, given his superior numbers. According to most of the sources, however, his position deteriorates with the piecemeal arrival of squadrons of Kūfan cavalry.[35] Ibn al-Ḥanafiyya is eventually escorted out of the blockade and settles in a neighboring region, where he remains with a few Kūfan supporters for the duration of Muhktār's rule.

B The Ibn Ziyād Battle/Elite Uprising Narrative (Three Variants)

The discussion that follows presents three variants of this complicated narrative element, which combines two distinct historical events. The first variant (3.2a) describes a battle between the Kūfans and 'Ubayd Allāh b. Ziyād (d. 67/686), whereas the third (3.2c) recounts the failed revolt of the Kūfan tribal elites. The second variant (3.2b) is a composite account that includes both the battle and the revolt.

Five sources address only the conflict between Mukhtār and Ibn Ziyād (3.2a). In these reports, Ibn al-Ashtar leads the Kūfans to victory over the Umayyad army in a single battle near the Khāzir River.[36] The most prominent Umayyad casualty is Ibn Ziyād, who is widely considered responsible for Ḥusayn's killing at Karbalā'. Mukhtār sends Ibn Ziyād's head to Mecca, where the Prophet's family members rejoice at his death.[37] According to some sources, Mukhtār dispatches two armies against Ibn Ziyād, the first being a small force led by Yazīd b. Anas and the second a larger army under the command of Ibrāhīm b. al-Ashtar.[38]

Three writers include accounts that combine the "Ibn Ziyād battle" and "elite uprising" narratives (3.2b). These reports consist of three distinct parts. In the first, Mukhtār sends Yazīd b. Anas with a hand-selected force of 3,000 men to meet a large Umayyad army led by Ibn

[35] *Akhbār al-dawla*, 105–6; al-Balādhurī, 3:478; al-Ṭabarī, 3:473.
[36] Ibn Sa'd, 5:74; al-Balādhurī, 3:478; al-Mas'ūdī (2009), 4:135–7. Pseudo-Ibn Qutayba (2:31) uniquely depicts Mukhtār personally leading the Kūfans into battle.
[37] According to al-Mas'ūdī, Ibn Ziyād's head was sent to Ibn al-Zubayr rather than to Ibn al-Ḥanafiyya. This detail supports his claim that Mukhtār was an agent of Ibn al-Zubayr in the early part of his rule. See al-Mas'ūdī (2009), 4:137.
[38] Al-Ya'qūbī, 2:175–6; al-Dīnawarī, 292–6.

Ziyād.[39] Yazīd sets up camp near Mawṣil and defeats a series of small Umayyad cavalry units. Prior to these engagements, Yazīd falls gravely ill and is forced to direct his troops from a litter or platform on the battlefield. He dies a few days later. Yazīd is succeeded by his designated deputy, Waraqa b. ʿĀzib al-Asadī (d. 67/687?), who convinces the troops to return to Kūfa because of the numerical superiority of their enemies. When news of the retreat reaches Mukhtār, he orders Ibn al-Ashtar to raise a new army, gather the remnants of Yazīd's men, and again march against Ibn Ziyād.

The second part of this narrative (3.2b) chronicles the deterioration of the political situation in Kūfa. The tribal leaders, discontented with Mukhtār's rule, accuse him of favoring the non-Arab population[40] and/or of being a soothsayer.[41] Shabath b. Ribʿī conveys these grievances to Mukhtār, who promises to address them if the tribal elites agree to fight on his behalf against the Syrians. The elites reject this condition, and, soon after Ibn al-Ashtar's departure, launch their own rebellion. Mukhtār tries to negotiate with them while writing desperately to Ibn al-Ashtar and ordering his immediate return. The ploy allows Ibn al-Ashtar to reenter the city with his men prior to the outbreak of hostilities. In addition to Shabath, the sources identify Shamir b. Dhī al-Jawshan, Kaʿb b. Abī Kaʿb al-Khathʿamī (d. unknown) and Muḥammad b. al-Ashʿath (d. 68/686) as the main leaders of the rebellion. In the decisive battle at Jabbānat al-Sabīʿ, Ibn al-Ashtar leads Mukhtār's forces to victory.

The third and final part of the hybrid narrative begins a few days later with Ibn al-Ashtar's second march to Mawṣil.[42] Some writers here recount Ibn al-Ashtar's disgust with a group of Kūfan Shīʿa for their reverence of a chair they claim is connected to ʿAlī (the "ʿAlī's chair" narrative, discussed in section E below). He sets up camp at the Khāzir River across from Ibn Ziyād's larger force. At this juncture, ʿUmayr b. al-Ḥubāb al-Sulamī (d. after 67/687), a high-ranking Qaysī commander in the Umayyad army, secretly offers to defect or withdraw from the field in order to avenge Qaysī losses at the hands of the Kalb at the Battle of Marj Rāhiṭ.[43] Ibn al-Ashtar tests ʿUmayr's sincerity by asking his advice

[39] Ibn Aʿtham, 2:310–14; al-Balādhurī, 6:396–7 and 398; al-Ṭabarī, 3:451–4.
[40] Ibn Aʿtham, 2:315–18; al-Ṭabarī, 3:454–9. [41] Al-Balādhurī, 6:398–9.
[42] Ibn Aʿtham, 2:334–43; al-Ṭabarī, 3:475–82. Al-Balādhurī (6:423–7) offers a number of revenge accounts before returning to the encounter with Ibn Ziyād.
[43] According to Ibn Aʿtham, ʿUmayr approaches Ibn al-Ashtar on the night before the battle. Al-Ṭabarī suggests (though without conviction) that ʿUmayr's men

regarding whether to attack immediately or wait until his men have reinforced their positions. The sources differ on the causes of the Kūfan victory. The episode concludes with the discovery of Ibn Ziyād's body on the battlefield. His head along with those of others complicit in the death of Ḥusayn are sent to Mukhtār in Kūfa.

Only one source treats the conflict with Ibn Ziyād and the elite uprising as isolated events.[44] In his version of the battle narrative (3.2a), al-Dīnawarī mentions Yazīd b. Anas's initial campaign and death before providing a thorough account of Ibn al-Ashtar's victory at Khāzir. The rebellion of the elites (3.2c) is not discussed until much later in al-Dīnawarī's text, and his treatment of it is quite idiosyncratic. Ibn al-Ashtar, for example, has no role in quelling the unrest, and the location of the final battle is uniquely recorded as Jabbānat al-Hash āshīn.

C *The Ḥijāzī Expansion Narrative (One Variant)*

The third narrative element (3.3a) is a two-part description of Mukhtār's failed attempt to seize control of Mecca and Medina.[45] In the first part, Mukhtār writes a conciliatory letter to Ibn al-Zubayr, restating his fealty to his original oath of allegiance. This is clearly a ruse. Ibn al-Zubayr, fully aware of the deceit, tests Mukhtār's sincerity by appointing 'Umar b. 'Abd al-Raḥmān b. al-Ḥārith (d. after 66/685) as his governor of Kūfa. Upon receiving word of 'Umar's departure from Mecca, Mukhtār sends Zā'ida b. Qudāma with a contingent of cavalry to intercept the caravan. Zā'ida first offers 'Umar a large bribe (twice the cost of his expenses, or 70,000 *dirhams*), and then overtly threatens him. 'Umar eventually takes the money and flees to Baṣra.

In the second part of the Ḥijāzī expansion narrative, Mukhtār learns that the Umayyads have deployed two armies, one toward Iraq and the other toward the Ḥijāz. He worries that the Umayyads and the Zubayrids will attack him simultaneously from two directions. This

withdraw only after the tide of fighting has already turned in favor of Ibn al-Ashtar. Al-Dīnawarī views 'Umayr's withdrawal as critical to the Kūfan victory. See Ibn A'tham, 2:335; al-Dīnawarī, 293–5; al-Ṭabarī, 3:479–81.

44 Al-Dīnawarī, 292–6 (Ibn Ziyād battle) and 300–1 (elite uprising).

45 Al-Balādhurī, 6:415–16 and 419–21; al-Ṭabarī, 3:470–2.

concern prompts him to reach out to Ibn al-Zubayr a second time, again falsely offering his help against the Umayyads. Ibn al-Zubayr is rightly suspicious, but he accepts the offer on the condition that Mukhtār and his men renew their oaths of allegiance. Mukhtār then sends 3,000 men (including only 700 Arabs) under Shuraḥbīl b. Wars al-Hamdānī (d. 66/686), ostensibly to fight with Ibn al-Zubayr but with secret orders to occupy Mecca. The Zubayrid forces are led by ʿAbbās b. Sahl. The two sides meet in al-Raqam, a location near Medina,[46] and, after a series of conversations in which Shuraḥbīl refuses to march against the Umayyads at Wādī al-Qurā, Ibn Sahl discerns Mukhtār's true purpose. He waits until the Kūfans are distracted and then attacks, killing Shuraḥbīl and the bulk of his men. Mukhtār is enraged by this betrayal.

D The Baṣran Expansion Narrative (One Variant)

The fourth narrative element (3.4a) concerns Mukhtār's efforts to extend his control to Baṣra.[47] The main protagonist in this plan is al-Muthannā b. al-Mukharriba al-ʿAbdī (d. after 67/686), a supporter of Mukhtār who survived the massacre of the Tawwābūn. Al-Muthannā arrives in Baṣra on Mukhtār's orders and settles in a mosque in the district of the Tamīm, where he begins to administer the oath of allegiance to fellow tribesmen. Al-Qubāʿ al-Ḥārith b. ʿAbd Allāh b. Abī Rabīʿa (d. ca. 80/700), the Zubayrid governor of the city, learns of these activities and sends two of his senior military men, ʿAbbād b. al-Ḥusayn (d. after 80/700) and Qays b. Haytham (d. after 71/690–1), to deal with the situation. Relying heavily on the conscripted support of non-Arabs (*mawālī*), they force al-Muthannā to retreat to the district of the ʿAbd al-Qays. At this point, the head of the Azd, Ziyād b. ʿAmr al-ʿAtakī (d. after 77/696–7), approaches al-Qubāʿ, notes his obligation to protect al-Muthannā since the Azd and the ʿAbd al-Qays are allies, and demands a negotiated settlement. The governor permits al-Muthannā and his supporters to leave the city. Mukhtār later proves incapable of winning over even those few Baṣran elites who had come to al-Muthannā's aid.

[46] Yāqūt, 3:67. [47] Al-Balādhurī, 6:416–18; al-Ṭabarī, 3:467–70.

E The 'Alī's Chair Narrative (Two Variants)

The fifth narrative element in this section depicts the reverence shown by a segment of Mukhtār's supporters for a chair fraudulently associated with 'Alī.[48] As Mukhtār accompanies Ibn al-Ashtar to the outskirts of Kūfa, a group of the Shī'a parade the chair on a gray mule and beseech God through it for help against their enemies. Mukhtār seems to approve of them, whereas Ibn al-Ashtar compares them to the Israelites who worshiped the golden calf. There are two explanations for the origins of the chair. The first (3.5a) implicates Ṭufayl b. Ja'da b. Hubayra (d. after 67/686), who, in the face of financial troubles, buys a filthy chair from an oil merchant, refurbishes it, and claims that it contains a vestige of 'Alī b. Abī Ṭālib's knowledge.[49] Mukhtār purchases it for 12,000 *dirhams* and presents it to his followers after congregational prayers, drawing a direct link between it and the Ark of the Covenant. This account ends with Shabath b. Rib'ī publicly criticizing the veneration of the chair to no avail and Ṭufayl expressing regret for his actions. The second explanation (3.5b) directly incriminates Mukhtār, who demands that Ṭufayl's family surrender 'Alī's chair.[50] They have no knowledge of such a chair but, realizing that he will not accept no for an answer, produce one to appease him. The report includes the names of those who were in charge of the chair and claimed knowledge of the future through it. It also unequivocally states that Mukhtār rejected these claims.

F The Surāqa's Angels Narrative (One Variant)

The sixth narrative element (3.6a) focuses on the poet Surāqa b. Mirdās al-Bāriqī (d. 79/698).[51] After the failure of the elite uprising, Mukhtār begins to arrest and execute his opponents. Surāqa tries to win his freedom by composing poems that praise Mukhtār and his supporters. When he is brought forth for judgment, Surāqa testifies that he saw angels fighting on piebald horses alongside Mukhtār, alluding to accounts of angels aiding Muḥammad in the Battles of Badr (2/624)

[48] Al-Balādhurī, 6:413–14; al-Ṭabarī, 3:475–7.

[49] Al-Ṭabarī, 3:476–7. The veracity of this claim is predicated on the close association between Ṭufayl's father and 'Alī.

[50] Al-Balādhurī, 6:413–14; al-Ṭabarī, 3:477.

[51] Ibn A'tham, 2:319–21; al-Balādhurī, 6:401; al-Ṭabarī, 3:460–1; al-Dīnawarī, 303.

and Ḥunayn (8/630). In some accounts, Surāqa only reports the presence of mysterious figures, and Mukhtār identifies them as angels.[52] Surāqa is then compelled to testify to the general public regarding the angels. According to a few sources, Mukhtār accuses him of lying in order to save his life.[53] Surāqa is released and banished from Kūfa for fear of his corrupting influence. He takes refuge in Baṣra, where he recants his testimony and composes a series of poems that openly mock Mukhtār.

G The Shamir Revenge Narrative (Three Variants)

The seventh narrative element recounts the revenge killing of Shamir b. Dhī al-Jawshan, a figure deeply complicit in the murder of Ḥusayn. All versions of this episode begin in similar fashion, but they differ on the circumstances of Shamir's death.[54] After the suppression of the elite uprising, Shamir joins a number of prominent Kūfans who flee the city. Mukhtār sends a slave (the accounts differ regarding his name) with a contingent of cavalry specifically in pursuit of him. Although the slave manages to catch up to Shamir, he is killed in one-on-one combat.

The variants of this narrative element diverge from one another at this point. In one version (3.7a),[55] Shamir and his companions take refuge on the banks of a river. Many of them are worried about lingering in the same location for too long. Shamir, however, views this concern as cowardice and vows to remain in the same spot for three days. Meanwhile, a detachment of Kūfan cavalry sent by Mukhtār arrives under the command of Abū Kanūd ʿAbd al-Raḥmān b. ʿUbayd al-Azdī (d. after 70/689). Shamir and his fellow travelers are killed in the resulting skirmish, and their heads are sent to Mukhtār. A second version[56] (3.7b) retains many of these elements but adds an important detail. Prior to setting up camp, Shamir sends a letter to Muṣʿab b. al-Zubayr through a non-Arab courier. The letter is intercepted by ʿAbd al-Raḥmān b. ʿUbayd, who is stationed in a small town under the leadership of Abū ʿAmra Kaysān to guard against a Baṣran attack. Shamir dies in the subsequent fight, but his companions escape to

[52] Al-Balādhurī, 6:401; al-Ṭabarī, 3:461; al-Dīnawarī, 303.
[53] Ibn Aʿtham, 2:319–21; al-Ṭabarī, 3:460–1.
[54] See Ibn Aʿtham, 2:321–3; al-Balādhurī, 6:407; al-Dīnawarī, 301–2; al-Ṭabarī, 3:459–60.
[55] Ibn Aʿtham, 2:321–3. [56] Al-Balādhurī, 6:407; al-Ṭabarī, 3:459–60.

safety. In a third version[57] (3.7c), Shamir is killed by the Kūfan army just before its decisive battle against the Baṣrans (see discussion of the final battle).

H The 'Umar b. Sa'd Revenge Narrative (Two Variants)

The eighth and final narrative element of this section includes two variants of the execution of 'Umar b. Sa'd b. Abī Waqqāṣ, who remained in Kūfa under the protection of a safe-conduct acquired through one of Mukhtār's chief supporters, 'Abd Allāh b. Ja'da b. Hubayra (d. after 67/687).[58] The first version (3.8a) of this narrative begins with Ibn al-Ḥanafiyya accusing Mukhtār of hypocrisy for granting safety to the man most responsible for spilling the blood of the family of the Prophet.[59] Mukhtār then dispatches Abū 'Amra Kaysān to 'Umar with the express goal of provoking a hostile encounter. In the second version (3.8b), Mukhtār acts of his own accord, manipulating the ambiguous language of the safe-conduct to justify his pursuit of 'Umar.[60] The sources differ as to whether Mukhtār explicitly orders 'Umar's execution.[61] In either case, 'Umar's head is brought to Mukhtār and shown to 'Umar's despondent son Ḥafṣ, who is subsequently also executed and beheaded. Mukhtār observes that these deaths are not adequate compensation for the killings of Ḥusayn and his son 'Alī, and then sends the heads to Ibn al-Ḥanafiyya in Mecca. Shorter variants of this narrative simply state that 'Umar b. Sa'd was caught and killed by Mukhtār.[62]

57 Al-Dīnawarī, 301–2.
58 Ibn A'tham, 2:295–8; al-Balādhurī, 6:405–6; al-Ṭabarī, 3:459–60. Pseudo-Ibn Qutayba (2:30–1) does not explicitly mention the safe-conduct.
59 Al-Balādhurī, 6:405–6; Pseudo-Ibn Qutayba, 2:30; al-Ṭabarī, 3:465. Ibn A'tham notes Ibn al-Ḥanafiyya's complaint (2:298) but does not cite it as the cause of 'Umar's death.
60 Ibn A'tham, 2:295–8; al-Dīnawarī, 299–301.
61 Cf. Ibn A'tham (2:295–6), for whom Mukhtār's instructions lead to 'Umar's death; al-Balādhurī (6:405–6) and Pseudo-Ibn Qutayba (2:31), according to whom Mukhtār orders the execution; and al-Ṭabarī (3:464–5), who describes the execution as an accident.
62 Al-Dīnawarī, 301; al-Mas'ūdī (2009), 4:106.

IV Fall (67/687)

This section discusses narrative elements that cover three aspects of Mukhtār's fall from power: his defeat, his death, and the fate of his companions. The last of these, though arguably outside the scope of this study, offers important insights into the interpretive frameworks utilized by individual historians.

A The Final Defeat Narrative (Three Variants)

The narrative elements relating to Mukhtār's defeat on the battlefield take three different forms. The first (4.1a) features a single battle. It begins with Ibn al-Zubayr appointing his brother Muṣʿab as the new governor of Baṣra and ordering him to march against Mukhtār.[63] The two armies meet near Ḥarūrā' on the banks of the Euphrates outside Kūfa. There are disagreements about the duration of the fighting (from three days[64] to four months[65]), but Mukhtār's forces are ultimately routed, forcing him to retreat with his remaining supporters to the fort in Kūfa.[66]

The second version of the "final defeat" narrative (4.1b) features two battles. In this account, Muṣʿab decides to attack Kūfa when he learns of Mukhtār's military vulnerability.[67] He is also moved by the pleas of Kūfan exiles who have fled to Baṣra after their failed revolt.[68] In preparation for the campaign, Muṣʿab writes to al-Muhallab b. Abī Ṣufra (d. 83/703), his most trusted military commander, who is campaigning against the Azāriqa in Iran. Muḥammad b. al-Ashʿath (d. 67/687) is tasked with delivering the letter, and he personally testifies to Mukhtār's persecution of prominent tribesmen. After al-Muhallab returns to Baṣra, Muṣʿab marches out with his army, which includes distinct tribal units led by Kūfan notables. Mukhtār's forces are commanded by Aḥmar b. Shumayṭ. This first battle occurs in the proximity of Madā'in[69] or Madhār,[70] and ends with a decisive Baṣran victory. When news of the disaster reaches Mukhtār, he tries to slow the Baṣran advance by diverting water from the Euphrates canal

63 Pseudo-Ibn Qutayba, 2:32; al-Yaʿqūbī, 2:181; al-Masʿūdī (2009), 4:137.
64 Al-Yaʿqūbī, 2:181. 65 Pseudo-Ibn Qutayba, 2:32. 66 Ibid.
67 Ibn Aʿtham, 2:344–9.
68 Al-Balādhurī, 6:427–31 and 436–9; al-Dīnawarī, 304–7; al-Ṭabarī, 3:483–8.
69 Ibn Aʿtham, 2:345. 70 Al-Balādhurī, 6:454–5; al-Dīnawarī, 305.

system. He then positions his remaining forces near Ḥarūrā' between the Baṣran army and Kūfa. The fighting in this second battle is intense, and claims the lives of a number of important figures, including Muḥammad b. al-Ash'ath. As in the first version, Mukhtār is defeated and takes refuge in the fort.

The third variant of this narrative element (4.1c) ascribes responsibility for Mukhtār's defeat to his cowardice.[71] In this report, Mukhtār remains loyal to Ibn al-Zubayr until Muṣ'ab's appointment to the governorship of Baṣra.[72] The two armies meet near Madhār, a location intentionally chosen by Mukhtār based on a prophecy that predicts a great Kūfan victory. The Kūfans attack in the middle of the night and drive the Baṣrans into full retreat. Mukhtār, however, finds himself alone on the battlefield and, fearing that his forces have suffered a crushing defeat, retreats to the fort in Kūfa. When the sun rises, the Kūfans assume that their commander has died in the battle. Most of them disperse, but a group of around 8,000 stalwarts return to Kūfa, where they discover Mukhtār hiding in the fort. Meanwhile, Muṣ'ab and the Baṣrans regroup and seize control of the city.

B Mukhtār's Death Narrative (One Variant)

The narrative element describing Mukhtār's death (4.2a)[73] begins with him trapped in the central fort in Kūfa. The sources differ on the length of the siege, but there is a general consensus that it continued long enough to impact the physical and mental health of Mukhtār's supporters. A few writers mention the scarcity of water and the increasingly restrictive measures imposed by Muṣ'ab.[74] In the course of the siege, Mukhtār and his men routinely venture out and engage in small skirmishes before retreating back to safety. There are also exchanges between Mukhtār and his closest companions in which he confesses that he was primarily motivated by personal ambition.[75]

[71] Al-Ṭabarī, 3:495–6. [72] Pseudo-Ibn Qutayba, 2:32.

[73] Ibn A'tham, 2:349–52; al-Balādhurī, 6:439–41; al-Ya'qūbī, 2:180–2; al-Dīnawarī, 307–8; al-Ṭabarī, 3:490–2 and 496; al-Mas'ūdī (2009), 4:137. Pseudo-Ibn Qutayba (2:32) asserts that Mukhtār was killed in battle without mentioning the siege.

[74] Ibn A'tham, 2:349; al-Balādhurī, 6:439; al-Ṭabarī, 3:490.

[75] Ibn A'tham, 2:351; al-Balādhurī, 6:439–41; al-Dīnawarī, 307–8; al-Ṭabarī, 3:491.

Mukhtār later unsuccessfully urges his men to go out with him in a final, desperate charge.[76] He is killed during this foray.

C *The Surrender and Execution Narrative (Two Variants)*

The third and final narrative element in this segment describes the surrender and execution of those who remained in the fort after Mukhtār's death. The main protagonist in these reports is Bujayr b. 'Abd Allāh al-Muslī (d. 67/687), who urges his companions to follow Mukhtār's example, telling them that they will find no mercy from their enemies and will certainly face execution.[77] Although the sources agree that the men eventually surrender, they differ on the terms of that surrender.[78] The more detailed accounts include a long speech in which Bujayr pleads for the lives of his companions, comparing the conflict to previous instances of civil strife within the Muslim community.[79] Muṣʿab b. al-Zubayr is moved by these words, but ultimately accedes to the demands of the Kūfan tribal leaders and orders the execution of all prisoners. The less detailed accounts ascribe to Muṣʿab full responsibility for this controversial act.[80] The main discrepancy between the two variants relates to whether the men surrender unconditionally (4.3b) or with promises of a safe-conduct (4.3a).

76 Ibn Aʿtham, 2:351; al-Balādhurī, 6:439–41; al-Ṭabarī, 3:491. See also *Akhbār al-dawla*, 180.

77 *Akhbār al-dawla*, 180–1; al-Balādhurī, 6:441–3; al-Ṭabarī, 3:492. Here and below, al-Balādhurī does not identify Bujayr by name.

78 For accounts that mention a safe-conduct, see Ibn Aʿtham, 2:352; al-Yaʿqūbī, 2:181–2; al-Masʿūdī (2009), 4:138. For accounts that claim unconditional surrender, see *Akhbār al-dawla*, 180–1; Pseudo-Ibn Qutayba, 2:32; al-Ṭabarī, 3:496.

79 Ibn Aʿtham, 2:352–3; al-Balādhurī, 6:441–3; *Akhbār al-dawla*, 181–2; al-Ṭabarī, 3:492–3.

80 Pseudo-Ibn Qutayba, 2:32; al-Yaʿqūbī, 2:181–2; al-Ṭabarī, 3:496; al-Masʿūdī (2009), 4:138.

Bibliography

Abdulsater, Hussein, *Shīʿī Doctrine, Muʿtazilī Theology* (Edinburgh: Edinburgh University Press, 2018).

Akhbār al-dawla al-ʿAbbāsiyya, ed. ʿAbd al-ʿAzīz al-Dūrī and ʿAbd al-Jabbār Muṭṭalibī (Beirut: Dār al-Ṭalīʿa, 1971).

Algar, Hamid, "Imam Musa al-Kazim and Sufi Tradition," *Islamic Culture* 64 (1990), 1–14.

ʿAlī b. Bilāl, *al-Maṣābīḥ*, ed. ʿAbd Allāh b. ʿAbd Allāh b. Aḥmad al-Ḥūthī (Amman: Mu'assasat al-Imām Zayd b. ʿAlī al-Thaqāfiyya, 2002).

Amir-Moezzi, Mohammad Ali, *The Divine Guide in Early Shiʿism*, trans. David Streight (Albany: SUNY Press, 1994).

Ansari, Hassan, *L'imamat et l'Occultation selon l'imamisme* (Leiden: Brill, 2017).

Anthony, Sean, *The Caliph and the Heretic* (Leiden: Brill, 2011).

"Crime and Punishment in Early Medina," in *Analyzing Muslim Traditions*, by Harald Motzki, Nicolet Boekhoff-van der Voort, and Sean Anthony (Leiden: Brill, 2010), 385–465.

Armstrong, Lyall, *The Quṣṣāṣ of Early Islam* (Leiden: Brill, 2017).

al-Baghdādī, ʿAbd al-Qāhir b. Ṭāhir, *al-Farq bayn al-firaq*, ed. Muḥammad Fatḥī al-Nādī (Cairo: Dār al-Salām, 2010).

al-Balādhurī, Aḥmad b. Yaḥyā, *Kitāb al-jumal min ansāb al-ashrāf*, ed. Suhayl Zakkār and Riyāḍ Ziriklī, 13 vols. (Beirut: Dār al-Fikr, 1996).

al-Barqī, Aḥmad b. Muḥammad, *al-Maḥāsin*, ed. Jalāl al-Dīn al-Ḥusaynī (Tehran: Dār al-Kutub al-Islāmiyya, 1951).

Bernheimer, Teresa, *The ʿAlids* (Edinburgh: Edinburgh University Press, 2013).

Borrut, Antoine, "Court Astrologers and Historical Writing in Early ʿAbbāsid Baghdād," in *The Place to Go*, ed. Jens Scheiner and Damien Janos (Princeton: Darwin Press, 2014), 455–501.

Entre mémoire et pouvoir (Leiden: Brill, 2011).

"Remembering Karbalā'," *JSAI* 42 (2015), 249–82.

Bosworth, C. E. (trans.), *ʿAbbasid Caliphate in Equilibrium*, vol. 30 of *The History of al-Ṭabarī* (Albany: SUNY Press, 1989).

Breisach, Ernst (ed.), *Classical Rhetoric and Medieval Historiography* (Kalamazoo: Medieval Institute Publications, 1985).

Brown, Peter, *The World of Late Antiquity* (London: Thames & Hudson, 1971).
Brunt, Peter, "Cicero and Historiography," in *Greek and Roman Historiography*, ed. John Marincola (Oxford: Oxford University Press, 2011), 207–40.
Conrad, Lawrence, "Ibn A'tham and His History," *al-'Uṣūr al-Wusṭā* 23 (2015), 87–125.
Cook, Michael, "The Opponents of the Writing of Tradition in Early Islam," *Arabica* 44 (1997), 437–530.
Cooperson, Michael, *Classical Arabic Biography* (New York: Cambridge University Press, 2000).
"Probability, Plausibility, and 'Spiritual Communication' in Classical Arabic Biography," in *On Fiction and* Adab *in Medieval Arabic Literature*, ed. Philip Kennedy (Wiesbaden: Harrassowitz, 2005), 69–84.
Cox, Patricia, *Biography in Late Antiquity* (Berkeley: University of California Press, 1983).
Croke, Brian, "Historiography," in *The Oxford Handbook of Late Antiquity*, ed. Scott Fitzgerald Johnson (Oxford: Oxford University Press, 2012), 405–36.
Crone, Patricia, *Roman, Provincial, and Islamic Law* (Cambridge: Cambridge University Press, 1987).
Slaves on Horses (Cambridge: Cambridge University Press, 1980).
Daniel, Elton, "The Anonymous History of the 'Abbasid Family and Its Place in Islamic Historiography," *IJMES* 14 (1982), 419–34.
al-Dhahabī, Muḥammad b. Aḥmad, *Tārīkh al-Islām*, ed. 'Umar 'Abd al-Salām Tadmurī, 70 vols. (Beirut: Dār al-Kitāb al-'Arabī, 1987).
al-Dīnawarī, Aḥmad b. Dāwūd, *al-Akhbār al-ṭiwāl*, ed. 'Abd al-Mun'im 'Āmir and Jamāl al-Dīn Shayyāl (Cairo: Wizārat al-Thaqāfa wa-l-Irshād al-Qawmī al-Iqlīm al-Janūbī, 1960).
Djait, Hichem, *al-Kūfa: Naissance de la ville islamique* (Paris: Maisonneuve et Larose, 1986).
Donner, Fred, "Modern Approaches to Early Islamic History," in *The New Cambridge History of Islam*, ed. Chase Robinson, 6 vols. (New York and Cambridge: Cambridge University Press, 2011), 1:625–47.
Narratives of Islamic Origins (Princeton: Darwin Press, 1998).
EI^2 = *Encyclopaedia of Islam, Second Edition*, ed. P. Bearman, T. Bianquis, C. E. Bosworth, E. van Donzel, and W. P. Heinrichs (Leiden: Brill, 1960–2007).
EI^3 = *Encyclopaedia of Islam, THREE*, ed. Kate Fleet, Gudrun Krämer, Denis Matringe, John Nawas, and Everett Rowson (Leiden: Brill, 2009–).

El-Hibri, Tayeb, *Parable and Politics in Early Islamic History* (New York: Columbia University Press, 2010).
Reinterpreting Islamic Historiography (Cambridge: Cambridge University Press, 1999).
Fishbein, Michael (trans.), *The Victory of the Marwanids*, vol. 21 of *The History of al-Ṭabarī* (Albany: SUNY Press, 2015).
Fornara, Charles, *The Nature of History in Ancient Greece and Rome* (Berkeley: University of California Press, 1983).
Gabba, Emilio, "True History and False History in Classical Antiquity," in *Greek and Roman Historiography*, ed. John Marincola (Oxford: Oxford University Press, 2011), 337–61.
Gehrke, Hans-Joachim, "Myth, History, and Politics – Ancient and Modern," in *Greek and Roman Historiography*, ed. John Marincola (Oxford: Oxford University Press, 2011), 40–71.
Görke, Andreas, "The Historical Tradition about al-Ḥudaybiya," in *The Biography of Muhammad*, ed. Harald Motzki (Leiden: Brill, 2000), 240–75.
"The Relationship between Maghāzī and Ḥadīth in Early Islamic Scholarship," *BSOAS* 74 (2011), 171–85.
Günther, Sebastian, "*Maqātil* Literature in Medieval Islam," *Journal of Arabic Literature* 25 (1994), 192–212.
Quellenuntersuchungen zu den "Maqātil aṭ-Ṭālibiyyīn" des Abū 'l-Farağ al-Iṣfahānī (gest. 356/967) (Hildesheim: Georg Olms, 1991).
Haider, Najam, "The Community Divided," *JAOS* 128 (2008), 459–76.
"The Contested Life of ʿĪsā b. Zayd (d. 166/783)," *JNES* 72 (2013), 169–78.
"The Geography of the *Isnād*," *Der Islam* 90 (2013), 306–46.
"On Lunatics and Loving Sons," *JRAS* 18 (2008), 109–39.
The Origins of the Shīʿa (Cambridge: Cambridge University Press, 2011).
Shīʿī Islam (Cambridge: Cambridge University Press, 2014).
"Yaḥyā b. ʿAbd Allāh," in *The I. B. Tauris Biographical Dictionary of Islamic Civilizations*, ed. Muhammad Abdel Haleem and Mustafa Shah (New York: I. B. Tauris, forthcoming).
"Zaydism," *Religion Compass* 4 (2010), 436–42.
Hawting, Gerald, "The Tawwabun, Atonement, and 'Ashura'," in *The Development of Islamic Ritual*, ed. Gerald Hawting (New York: Ashgate, 2006), 173–88.
Hayes, Edmund, "Alms and the Man," *JAIS* 17 (2017), 280–98.
Hinds, Martin, *Studies in Early Islamic History*, ed. Jere Bacharach, Lawrence Conrad, and Patricia Crone (Princeton: Darwin Press, 1996).
Hirschler, Konrad, *Medieval Arabic Historiography* (New York: Routledge, 2006).

The Written Word in the Medieval Arabic Lands (Edinburgh: Edinburgh University Press, 2012).
Hodgson, Marshall, "Two Pre-Modern Muslim Historians," in *Towards World Community*, ed. John Nef (The Hague: W. Junk, 1968), 53–68.
Hoyland, Robert, *In God's Path* (New York: Oxford University Press, 2015).
Seeing Islam as Others Saw It (Princeton: Darwin Press, 1997).
Humphreys, Stephen, *Islamic History: A Framework for Inquiry*, rev. ed. (Princeton: Princeton University Press, 1991).
Ibn A'tham, Aḥmad al-Kūfī, *al-Futūḥ*, ed. Suhayl Zakkār, 3 vols. (Beirut: Dār al-Fikr, 1992).
Ibn al-Athīr, 'Izz al-Dīn 'Alī b. Muḥammad, *al-Kāmil fī al-tārīkh*, ed. Carl Johan Tornberg, 13 vols. (Beirut: Dār Ṣādir, 1965).
Ibn Bābawayh, Muḥammad b. 'Alī, *Amālī*, ed. Muḥammad Mahdī al-Sayyid Ḥasan al-Mūsawī al-Kharsān (Najaf: al-Maṭba'a al-Ḥaydariyya, 1970).
'Uyūn akhbār al-Riḍā, ed. Muḥammad Mahdī al-Sayyid Ḥasan al-Mūsawī al-Kharsān, 2 vols. (Najaf: al-Maṭba'a al-Ḥaydariyya, 1970).
Ibn al-Jawzī, 'Abd al-Raḥmān b. 'Alī, *al-Muntaẓam*, ed. Muḥammad 'Abd al-Qādir 'Aṭā and Muṣṭafā 'Abd al-Qādir 'Aṭā, 19 vols. (Beirut: Dār al-Kutub al-'Ilmiyya, 2012).
Ibn Kathīr, Ismā'īl b. 'Umar, *al-Bidāya wa-l-nihāya*, 14 vols. ([Cairo]: Maṭba'at al-Sa'āda, 1932–9).
al-Bidāya wa-l-nihāya, ed. 'Abd Allāh b. 'Abd al-Muḥsin al-Turkī, 20 vols. (Giza: Hajr, 1997).
Ibn Khallikān, Aḥmad b. Muḥammad, *Wafayāt al-a'yān*, ed. Iḥsān 'Abbās, 8 vols. (Beirut: Dār Ṣādir, 1977).
Ibn Miftāḥ, 'Abd Allāh b. Abī Qāsim, *Sharḥ al-Azhār*, 10 vols. (Sanaa: Maktab al-Turāth al-Islāmī, 2003).
Ibn al-Murtaḍā, Ibrāhīm b. al-Qāsim, *Ṭabaqāt al-Zaydiyya* (MS Yemen).
Ibn Qudāma, 'Abd Allāh b. Aḥmad, *al-Mughnī*, ed. Muḥammad 'Abd al-Qādir 'Aṭā, 8 vols. (Beirut: Dār al-Kutub al-'Ilmiyya, 2008).
Ibn Sa'd, Muḥammad, *al-Ṭabaqāt al-kubrā*, ed. Muḥammad 'Abd al-Qādir 'Aṭā, 9 vols. (Beirut: Dār al-Kutub al-'Ilmiyya, 1990).
al-Irbilī, 'Alī b. 'Īsā, *Kashf al-ghumma*, ed. Ibrāhīm Mīyānjī, 3 vols. (Tabrīz: Kitābjī-i Ḥaqīqat, 1962).
al-Iṣbahānī, 'Alī b. al-Ḥusayn Abū al-Faraj, *Maqātil al-Ṭālibiyyīn*, ed. Sayyid Aḥmad Ṣaqr (Beirut: Mu'assasat al-A'lamī li-l-Maṭbū'āt, 1998).
Jaques, R. Kevin, *Authority, Conflict, and the Transmission of Diversity in Medieval Islamic Law* (Boston: Brill, 2006).
Jarrar, Maher, "Some Aspects of Imāmī Influence on Early Zaydite Theology," in *Islamstudien ohne Ende*, ed. Rainer Brunner (Würzburg: Deutsche Morgenländische Gesellschaft, 2002), 201–23.

Khalidi, Tarif, *Arabic Historical Thought in the Classical Period* (Cambridge: Cambridge University Press, 1994).
al-Khaṭīb al-Baghdādī, Aḥmad b. ʿAlī, *Tārīkh Baghdād*, ed. Muṣṭafā ʿAbd al-Qādir ʿAṭā, 24 vols. (Beirut: Dār al-Kutub al-ʿIlmiyya, 2004).
al-Kulaynī, Muḥammad b. Yaʿqūb, *al-Uṣūl min al-Kāfī*, ed. ʿAlī Akbar al-Ghaffārī, 8 vols. (Tehran: Dār al-Kutub al-Islāmiyya, 1983).
Lane, Edward, *Arabic–English Lexicon*, 8 vols. (London: Williams & Norgate, 1863).
Lecker, Michael, "The Death of the Prophet Muhammad's Father," *ZDMG* 145 (1995), 9–27.
Leder, Stefan, "Conventions of Fictional Narration in Learned Literature," in *Story-Telling in the Framework of Non-Fictional Arabic Literature*, ed. Stefan Leder (Wiesbaden: Harrassowitz, 1998), 34–60.
"Features of the Novel in Early Historiography," *Oriens* 32 (1990), 72–96.
Lindstedt, Ilkka, "al-Madāʾinī's *Kitāb al-Dawla* and the Death of Ibrāhīm al-Imām," in *Case Studies in Translation*, ed. Ilkka Lindstedt (Münster: Ugarit-Verlag, 2014), 103–30.
Madelung, Wilferd, "A Treatise of the Sharīf al-Murtaḍā on the Legality of Working for the Government," *BSOAS* 43 (1980), 18–31.
al-Masʿūdī, ʿAlī b. al-Ḥusayn, *Murūj al-dhahab*, ed. Charles Pellat, 7 vols. (Beirut: Manshūrāt al-Jāmiʿa al-Lubnāniyya, 1973).
Murūj al-dhahab, 6 vols. (Cairo: Sharikat al-Quds li-l-Taṣdīr, 2009).
Meisami, Julie, "History as Literature," *Iranian Studies* 33 (2000), 15–30.
"Masʿūdī and the Reign of al-Amīn," in *On Fiction and* Adab *in Medieval Arabic Literature*, ed. Philip Kennedy (Wiesbaden: Harrassowitz, 2005), 149–76.
Persian Historiography (Edinburgh: Edinburgh University Press, 1999).
Melvin-Koushki, Matthew, "Powers of One," *Intellectual History of the Islamicate World* 5 (2017), 127–99.
"The Quest for a Universal Science" (PhD dissertation, Yale University, 2012).
al-Mizzī, Yūsuf b. al-Zakī ʿAbd al-Raḥmān, *Tahdhīb al-kamāl*, ed. Bashshār ʿAwwād Maʿrūf, 35 vols. (Beirut: Muʾassasat al-Risāla, 1980–92).
Modarressi, Hossein, *Crisis and Consolidation in the Formative Period of Shīʿite Islam* (Princeton: Darwin Press, 1993).
Tradition and Survival (Oxford: Oneworld, 2003).
Motzki, Harald (ed.), *The Biography of Muḥammad* (Leiden: Brill, 2000).
The Origins of Islamic Jurisprudence, trans. Marion Katz (Leiden: Brill, 2002).

"Whither *Ḥadīth* Studies," in *Analyzing Muslim Traditions*, by Harald Motzki, Nicolet Boekhoff-van der Voort, and Sean Anthony (Leiden: Brill, 2010), 47–124.

al-Mufīd, Muḥammad b. Muḥammad al-Shaykh, *al-Ikhtiṣāṣ*, ed. Muḥammad Mahdī al-Sayyid Ḥasan al-Kharsān (Najaf: al-Maṭba'a al-Ḥaydariyya, 1971).

al-Irshād (Beirut: Mu'assasat al-A'lamī li-l-Maṭbū'āt, 1979).

Munt, Harry, *The Holy City of Medina* (New York: Cambridge University Press, 2014).

al-Najāshī, Aḥmad b. 'Alī, *Rijāl al-Najāshī*, ed. Muḥammad Jawād al-Nā'īnī, 2 vols. (Beirut: Dār al-Aḍwā', 1988).

al-Nāṭiq, Yaḥyā b. al-Ḥusayn, *al-Ifāda fī tārīkh a'immat al-Zaydiyya*, ed. Muḥammad Yaḥyā Sālim 'Azzān (Sanaa: Dār al-Ḥikma al-Yamāniyya, 1996).

al-Nawbakhtī, Ḥasan b. Mūsā, *Kitāb firaq al-Shī'a*, ed. 'Abd al-Mun'im al-Ḥifnī (Cairo: Dār al-Rashād, 1992).

Neuwirth, Angelika, *Scripture, Poetry, and the Making of a Community* (Oxford: Oxford University Press, 2014).

The New Cambridge History of Islam, ed. Chase Robinson, 6 vols. (Cambridge: Cambridge University Press, 2010).

Noth, Albrecht, "Fiktion als historische Quelle," in *Story-Telling in the Framework of Non-Fictional Arabic Literature*, ed. Stefan Leder (Wiesbaden: Harrassowitz, 1998), 472–87.

Noth, Albrecht, and Lawrence Conrad, *The Early Arabic Historical Tradition* (Princeton: Darwin Press, 1994).

al-Nuwayrī, Shihāb al-Dīn Aḥmad b. 'Abd al-Wahhāb, *Nihāyat al-arab fī funūn al-adab*, ed. 'Abd al-Majīd Turḥīnī, 34 vols. (Beirut: Dār al-Kutub al-'Ilmiyya, 2004).

Partner, Nancy, "The New Cornificius: Medieval History and the Artifice of Words," in *Classical Rhetoric and Medieval Historiography*, ed. Ernst Breisach (Kalamazoo: Medieval Institute Publications, 1985), 5–59.

Pierce, Matthew, *Twelve Infallible Men* (Cambridge, MA: Harvard University Press, 2016).

(Pseudo-) Ibn Qutayba, 'Abd Allāh b. Muslim, *al-Imāma wa-l-siyāsa*, ed. 'Alī Shīrī, 2 vols. (Beirut: Dār al-Aḍwā', 1990).

(Pseudo-) al-Nāshi' al-Akbar, 'Abd Allāh b. Muḥammad, *Masā'il al-imāma*, in *Frühe mu'tazilitsche Häresiographie*, ed. Josef van Ess (Wiesbaden: F. Steiner, 1971).

al-Qāḍī, Wadād, *al-Kaysāniyya fī al-tārīkh wa-l-adab* (Beirut: Dār al-Thaqāfa, 1974).

al-Qummī, Sa'd b. 'Abd Allāh, *Kitāb al-maqālāt wa-l-firaq*, ed. Muḥammad Jawād Mashkūr (Tehran: Markaz Intishārāt 'Ilmī wa Farhangī, 1982–3).

al-Rāzī, Aḥmad b. Sahl, *Akhbār Fakhkh*, ed. Māhir Jarrār (Tunis: Dār al-Gharb al-Islāmī, 2011).
Rao, Velcheru N., David Schulman, and Sanjay Subrahmanyam, *Textures of Time* (New York: Other Press, 2003).
Robinson, Chase, *'Abd al-Malik* (Oxford: Oneworld, 2005).
Islamic Historiography (Cambridge: Cambridge University Press, 2003).
Rubenstein, Jeffrey, *Talmudic Stories: Narrative Art, Composition, and Culture* (Baltimore: Johns Hopkins University Press, 1999).
Sadeghi, Behnam, "The Traveling Tradition Test," *Der Islam* 85 (2008), 203–42.
Sahlins, Marshall, *Islands of History* (Chicago: University of Chicago Press, 1985).
Schoeler, Gregor, *The Biography of Muḥammad*, trans. Uwe Vagelpohl and ed. James Montgomery (New York: Routledge, 2011).
The Genesis of Literature in Islam, trans. Shawkat Toorawa (Edinburgh: Edinburgh University Press, 2009).
al-Shahrastānī, Muḥammad b. 'Abd al-Karīm, *al-Milal wa-l-niḥal*, ed. Aḥmad Fahmī Muḥammad, 3 vols. (Cairo: Maktabat al-Ḥusayn al-Tijāriyya, 1948).
Sharon, Moshe, *Black Banners from the East* (Leiden: Brill, 1983).
Shoshan, Boaz, *Poetics of Islamic Historiography* (Leiden: Brill, 2004).
Stearns, Justin, *Infectious Ideas* (Baltimore: Johns Hopkins University Press, 2011).
"New Directions in the Study of Religious Responses to the Black Death," *History Compass* 7 (2009), 1363–75.
al-Ṭabarī, Muḥammad b. al-Jarīr, *Tārīkh al-Ṭabarī*, 5 vols. (Beirut: Dār al-Kutub al-'Ilmiyya, 1988).
al-Ṭūsī, Muḥammad b. al-Ḥasan, *Kitāb al-khilāf*, ed. Sayyid 'Alī al-Khurasānī, Sayyid Jawād al-Shahrastānī, and Muḥammad Mahdī Najaf, 6 vols. (Qumm: Mu'assasat al-Nashr al-Islāmī, 1995).
Mabsūṭ fī fiqh al-Imāmiyya, ed. Muḥammad Taqī al-Kashfī, 8 vols. (Beirut: Dār al-Kutub al-Islāmī, 1992).
al-Tustarī, Muḥammad Taqī, *Qāmūs al-rijāl*, 12 vols. (Qumm: Mu'assasat al-Nashr al-Islāmī, 2003).
Vacca, Alison, *Non-Muslim Provinces under Early Islam* (New York: Cambridge University Press, 2017).
Van Nuffelen, Peter, *Orosius and the Rhetoric of History* (Oxford: Oxford University Press, 2012).
Waldman, Marilyn, *Toward a Theory of Historical Narrative* (Columbus: Ohio State University Press, 1980).
Wansbrough, John, *Quranic Studies* (Oxford: Oxford University Press, 1977).

Wheeldon, M. J., "True Stories: The Reception of Historiography in Antiquity," in *History as Text*, ed. Averil Cameron (London: Duckworth, 1989), 33–63.

White, Hayden, *Metahistory: The Historical Imagination in Nineteenth-Century Europe* (Baltimore: Johns Hopkins University Press, 1975).

Wilcox, Donald, "The Sense of Time in Western Historical Narratives from Eusebius to Machiavelli," in *Classical Rhetoric and Medieval Historiography*, ed. Ernst Breisach (Kalamazoo: Medieval Institute Publications, 1985), 167–235.

Wiseman, T. P., "Lying Historians: Seven Types of Mendacity," in *Greek and Roman Historiography*, ed. John Marincola (Oxford: Oxford University Press, 2011), 314–46.

al-Ya'qūbī, Aḥmad b. Abī Ya'qūb, *Tārīkh al-Ya'qūbī*, ed. 'Abd al-Amīr Muhannā, 2 vols. (Beirut: Mu'assasat al-A'lamī li-l-Maṭbū'āt, 1993).

Yāqūt b. 'Abd Allāh al-Ḥamawī, *Mu'jam al-buldān*, ed. Farīd 'Abd al-'Azīz al-Jundī, 7 vols. (Beirut: Dār al-Kutub al-'Ilmiyya, 2011).

Zaman, Muhammad Qasim, "*Maghāzī* and the *Muḥaddithūn*," *IJMES* 28 (1996), 1–18.

al-Ziriklī, Khayr al-Dīn, *al-A'lām*, 8 vols. (Beirut: Dār al-'Ilm li-l-Malāyīn, 2007).

Index

'Abbād b. al-Ḥuṣayn, 97, 274
'Abbās b. Muḥammad, 127, 198
'Abbās b. Sahl, 36, 68, 87, 264, 274
'Abbāsids, 59–60
'Abd Allāh b. 'Abbās (Ibn 'Abbās), 28, 55, 56, 57–8, 106, 270
'Abd Allāh b. 'Abbās b. Ḥasan b. 'Ubayd Allāh b. 'Abbās b. 'Alī, 200
'Abd Allāh b. Ja'da b. Hubayra b. Abī Wahb al-Makhzūmī, 43, 67, 277
'Abd Allāh b. Ja'far al-Afṭaḥ (brother of al-Kāẓim), 116, 144, 179
'Abd Allāh b. Kāmil al-Shākirī, 54, 63, 70, 267
'Abd Allāh b. Mālik al-Khuzā'ī, 123
'Abd Allāh b. Muṣ'ab al-Zubayrī
  in *Akhbār Fakhkh*, 221
  in *al-Ifāda*, 233
  in *Maqātil al-Ṭālibiyyīn*, 229
  in "Zubayrid encounter" narrative, 199–201
'Abd Allāh b. Muṭī' (Ibn Muṭī'), 266
  in general, 29, 268, 269
  in *Ansāb al-ashrāf*, 63, 64
  in *al-Imāma wa-l-siyāsa*, 74
  in *Kitāb al-futūḥ*, 38, 41–2
  in *Murūj al-dhahab*, 105
  in *al-Ṭabaqāt al-kubrā*, 54
  in *Tārīkh* (al-Ṭabarī), 89–90, 91–2
  in *Tārīkh* (al-Ya'qūbī), 77
'Abd Allāh b. Ṣakhr, 236
'Abd Allāh b. Sharīk, 95
'Abd Allāh b. 'Umar (Ibn 'Umar)
'Abd Allāh b. Yazīd al-Khaṭmī, 37–8, 62, 89, 266
'Abd al-Malik b. Marwān, Umayyad caliph
  in *al-Akhbār al-ṭiwāl*, 82
  in *Ansāb al-ashrāf*, 69
  in *al-Imāma wa-l-siyāsa*, 74, 75
  in *Tārīkh* (al-Ṭabarī), 93
'Abd al-Raḥmān b. Mikhnaf al-Azdī, 46, 70, 94
'Abd al-Raḥmān b. Sa'īd b. Qays al-Hamdānī, 45, 77
'Abd al-Raḥmān b. Shurayḥ al-Shibāmī, 63
'Abd al-Ṣamad b. 'Alī, 198
'Abīda b. 'Amr al-Baddī, 62, 265
Abraham (biblical figure), 2
Abū Bakhtarī Wahb b. Wahb
  in general, 202, 214, 241, 243
  in *Akhbār Fakhkh*, 219, 222, 223
  in *al-Ifāda*, 232, 233
  in *al-Kāmil fī al-tārīkh*, 210
  in *Maqātil al-Ṭālibiyyīn*, 229, 230
  in *al-Maṣābīḥ*, 236
  in *Tārīkh* (al-Ṭabarī), 209
Abū Baṣīr, 167–8
Abū Ḥanīfa, 214
Abū Kanūd 'Abd al-Raḥmān b. 'Ubayd al-Azdī, 47–8, 276
Abū Khālid al-Zubālī, 144–5
Abū Mūsā al-Ash'arī, 41, 269
Abū Ṭālib, 20, 106, 154
Abū al-Ṭufayl 'Āmir b. Wāthila, 56
Abū 'Uthmān 'Abd al-Raḥmān b. Mall al-Nahdī, 39
Abū Yūsuf
  in general, 202
  in *Kashf al-ghumma*, 178
  mention of, 214
  in *Tārīkh Baghdād*, 216
  in *'Uyūn akhbār al-Riḍā*, 153, 167